1997

Managing Risk in International Business

Managing Risk in International Business

Techniques and applications

Ephraim Clark

Department of Finance
CERAM School of Management
Nice, France

and

Bernard Marois

Department of Finance
HEC School of Management
Jouy-en-Josas, France

INTERNATIONAL THOMSON BUSINESS PRESS
I ⓣ P An International Thomson Publishing Company

London • Bonn • Boston • Johannesburg • Madrid • Melbourne • Mexico City • New York • Paris
Singapore • Tokyo • Toronto • Albany, NY • Belmont, CA • Cincinnati, OH • Detroit, MI

Managing Risk in International Business

First published 1996 by International Thomson Business Press

 A division of International Thomson Publishing Inc.
The ITP logo is a trademark under licence

British Library Cataloguing-in-Publication Data
A catalogue record for this book is available from the British Library

First edition 1996

Typeset in 10/12½ Times by Words & Graphics Ltd., Anstey, Leicester
Printed in the UK by Clays Ltd, St Ives plc

ISBN 0–412–59720–9

International Thomson Business Press
Berkshire House
168–173 High Holborn
London WC1V 7AA
UK

International Thomson Business Press
20 Park Plaza
14th Floor
Boston MA 02116
USA

http://www.thomson.com/itbp.html

CONTENTS

PREFACE

The growing internationalization of economic activity throughout the world has generated an unprecedented increase in worldwide trade and cross border capital flows. Between 1964 and 1993, for example, world exports increased from $157 billion to $3774 billion. In 1994, foreign direct investment (FDI) reached $204 billion of which over $80 billion was earmarked for developing countries. Although flows to the developing world were somewhat concentrated, with 80% going to just 10 countries and China alone taking over $30 billion, private capital flows to Third World countries overall more than quadrupled between 1990 and 1993. This accelerating trend towards a truly international economy is making its mark on how companies do business. It is rare to find a company with no foreign links at all and many of the world's largest companies depend on foreign markets for over 50% of their turnover with production facilities spread worldwide.

The international phenomenon is not limited to the commerial realm. Pure financial flows are also involved. New Eurobond issues, for instance, are close to $400 billion per year and growing, volume on the world's stock markets was over $32 000 billion in 1994 and the derivative markets had a turnover of over $50 000 billion. A relatively new twist to all this activity is the growing importance of what has come to be called the 'emerging markets'. Volume for their debt on the secondary market alone was over $2000 billion in 1994, their share of world trade is over 30% and their stock markets are among the fastest growing in the world.

The upshot of all this is that most of the major economic agents in most countries, from the exporters, importers and global producers to the banks and investors seeking new opportunities for profit and higher returns as well as individual governments whose economies are ultimately affected by this activity, have a vested interest in understanding and mastering the opportunities and risks involved in international business transactions. The focus of this book is on the risk side of the equation and more specifically on the techniques and the practical applications showing how the risks that are inherent in international business transactions can be identified, assessed and managed.

Part One analyses the international business environment and the particular risks that it engenders. Having presented the international business environment and the associated risks, Part Two of the book develops the concepts and techniques involved in identifying and assessing these risks. Part Three deals with how international business risk can be managed once it has been identified and measured.

The book is intended for business and financial professionals and its aim is to serve as a fundamental reference for practical applications. However, MBA and upper level undergraduate students will also find it useful as an advanced complement to standard texts in corporate and international finance. Its method is first to present the concepts and techniques and then to illustrate them with case studies and detailed examples. Nevertheless, many of the concepts and techniques presented are on the cutting edge of the state of the art and are often based on sophisticated applications of modern economic and financial theory that require a minimum under-standing. In the text, these concepts and theories are presented with a focus on their practical relevance rather than on their mathematical formulation. The more theoretical issues and mathematical formulations are taken up in the appendices at the end of the chapters.

The help offered by reviewers of the book proposal and numerous drafts has been extremely important in improving the final product. We would especially like to thank John Calverly, Steve Cumby, Patrick Foley, Richard O'Brien and Terry Watsham. Thanks are also extended to the Chapman & Hall editorial staff and especially Sarah Henderson who most professionally handled the coordination of reviews and numerous other editorial jobs and was an inspiration from beginning to end.

Ephraim A. Clark
Bernard Marois

August 15, 1995

PART ONE

The Firm and the International Economy

1. THE INTERNATIONAL BUSINESS ENVIRONMENT

THE ORGANIZATION OF THE INTERNATIONAL ECONOMIC AND FINANCIAL SYSTEM

Today's economic and financial system is organized around the concept of the nation state and national sovereignty. Current international law recognizes the right of individual national governments to organize and administer the economic and financial framework within the geographic boundaries that they control. This means that they have the power to make and enforce the laws that determine how and where goods and services will be produced, who will own them, and how they will be exchanged. The degree of government involvement can vary considerably from country to country, but it usually falls somewhere between the pure *laissez-faire* capitalism of the 19th century and the discredited comprehensive central planning of 20th century communism. Most of the world's rich industrial countries, for example, have established systems based on markets and individual choice. Within this basic philosophy, however, there are many different models ranging from American rugged individualism to French state capitalism, Japanese oligopoly and Swedish socialism, among other forms.

Jurisdiction of individual national systems effectively ends at each country's border. There is no real supranational authority with the power to impose its will on the rest of the world – this is especially true since the collapse of the Soviet empire and the dissolution of the Eastern bloc. Relations between countries have to be negotiated. Negotiations can be undertaken on a narrow country-to-country basis, or they can be more comprehensive and include several countries. The tendency since the Second World War has been to multilateral agreements, and many international organizations have been created to facilitate the multilateral format. The International Monetary Fund (IMF), for example, oversees international payments and exchange rates, the World Bank (International Bank for

Reconstruction and Development) promotes economic development, and the World Trade Organization, formerly the General Agreement on Tariffs and Trade (GATT), is the format for negotiating international trade. The Bank for International Settlements (BIS), which was created after the First World War to manage German reparation payments and facilitate the transfer of funds among European countries whose currencies were not then convertible, now serves as a kind of central bank to the industrial countries' central banks, as well as a forum for monetary authorities from different countries to meet and exchange ideas. Other organizations, such as the Organization for Economic Cooperation and Development (OECD), which groups the world's 24 industrial economies, the European Union (EU, formerly the European Community) and the Organization of Petroleum Exporting Countries (OPEC) were founded to further the economic interests of particular groups of countries. Many other international organizations, too numerous to mention and covering a wide range of fields, also exist. Although all the foregoing organizations have little or no explicit supranational enforcement power, many have acquired institutional strength that enables them to exert considerable influence over the behaviour of individual countries.

Today's international economic and financial environment can thus be described as being composed of a number of sovereign nation states with distinct internal organizational structures competing against one another according to a set of guidelines determined by multilateral negotiation and monitored by the moral authority of the international organizations created for that purpose. The competition – or cooperation, for that matter – can involve governments as well as resident firms and individuals of the different countries. The outcome is reflected in each country's national accounts, balance of payments and exchange rate. In fact, the balance of payments and the exchange rate determine the economic and financial limits of domestic policy. They are also particularly sensitive to monetary phenomena. Since most countries associate monetary policy with national sovereignty and, consequently, issue and manage their own separate currencies, the balance of payments and the exchange rate play a prominent role in how the system works.

The balance of payments is the record of the economic and financial flows that take place over a specified period between residents and non-residents of a given country. Because transactions between different national jurisdictions fall outside the scope of the individual national authorities, and the supranational organizations generally lack effective enforcement power, on the international level resource allocation and income distribution across countries depend to a large extent on competitive forces. The outcome is recorded in the balance of payments and reflects the relative success of the different national economic policies in the international marketplace. In this sense it can be said that the balance of payments enforces accounting discipline on a national economy.

The resolution of the multitude of economic and financial forces competing under the constraint of balance of payments accounting discipline is reflected in the exchange rate. For residents, the exchange rate determines the domestic currency price of transactions undertaken with non-residents. For non-residents, it determines the foreign currency price of transactions undertaken with residents. In a free market, the exchange rate represents the point where the supply and demand of domestic currency for foreign currency are equal and experience has shown that the exchange rate can and does fluctuate depending on the evolution of supply and demand. Because of well-known and unwanted effects associated with currency fluctuations (which we will take up in Chapter 4), the monetary authority often uses its international reserves to influence the supply and demand for its currency in the foreign exchange market as a means of eliminating or reducing exchange rate fluctuations. The specific role that the monetary authority decides to play in the supply and demand for foreign currency gives rise to the various systems of exchange rate determination.

SYSTEMS OF EXCHANGE RATE DETERMINATION

The foregoing section has outlined the general framework and basic relationships governing today's international economic environment. How the system actually works, however, depends to a large extent on the organization of the **international monetary system**. We define the international monetary system as the framework within which countries borrow, lend, buy, sell, and make payments across political frontiers. The framework determines how balance of payments disequilibrium is resolved and the consequences that the adjustment process will have on the countries involved. Numerous frameworks are possible and most have been tried in one form or another.[1] Today's system is a combination of several different frameworks.

Systems of fixed exchange rates

Under systems of fixed exchange rates governments are committed to maintaining a target exchange rate. In other words, they intervene in the foreign exchange markets. The gold standard and the gold exchange standard are the two fixed rate systems that have been adopted internationally in the recent past.

The gold standard

Under the gold standard each country pegs its money to gold. For example, if the Bank of France fixes the price of gold at 100F per ounce of gold, it effectively stands ready to buy and sell gold at this rate. The same goes for the United States if the US Federal Reserve (the Fed) fixes the price of gold at $20 per ounce. The exchange rate, then, is simply the ratio of the two prices: 100FF/$20 means an exchange rate of 5FF for $1, or $20/100FF an exchange rate of $0.20 for 1FF. Under the gold standard, external disequilibrium is corrected through a process known as **price-specie flow**, whereby the domestic money supply contracts or expands as a result of central bank sales or purchases of gold.

The gold exchange standard

The depression of 1929–33 eventually ended the gold standard. It was replaced by the gold exchange standard in the Bretton Woods agreement of 1944. The gold exchange standard involved the United States pegging the dollar to gold, and the other countries pegging their currencies to the dollar. In this agreement the price of gold was fixed at $35 per ounce, at which price the United States promised to exchange dollars for gold. Other countries promised to exchange their currencies for dollars at an official, fixed exchange rate. The countries that pegged their exchange rates to the dollar were obliged to keep the market rate within 1% of the official parity rate. Maintaining the market rate within plus or minus 1% of official parity required the central banks to intervene in the foreign exchange markets by buying and selling domestic currency for dollars whenever market forces started to push the rate outside the permitted range.

Adjustment mechanisms in fixed rate systems

In a pure fixed rate system such as the gold standard, adjustment to changing conditions is automatic through corresponding changes in the money supply. In less than pure fixed rate systems such as the gold exchange standard, adjustment-induced changes in the money supply can be offset by the monetary authority. In this case, the normal adjustment process is frustrated. If nothing is done to correct the cause of disequilibrium, the monetary authority will eventually run out of foreign reserves and have to change the official parity rate. Figure 1.1 shows how the graph of a fixed rate might look. The solid line is the established official parity value. The

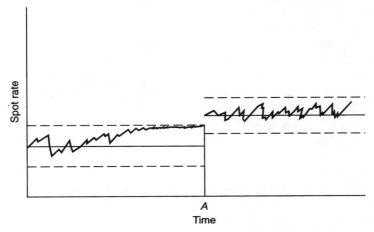

Figure 1.1 Fixed exchange rate.

dotted lines are the upper and lower limits around parity. In this case, as time goes on, the market rate is consistently in the vicinity of its upper limit. Finally, at point *A*, the central bank is unable to continue its intervention and devalues its currency by fixing a new parity value.

Floating and other exchange rate systems

Fixed exchange rate systems rely on the automatic adjustment process set off by changes in the money supply to function effectively. In a floating rate system, exchange rates are allowed to adjust freely to the supply and demand of one currency for another. Figure 1.2 shows how the graph of a floating rate might look. The basic argument for floating exchange rates is that they would allow a high degree of autonomy in the application of domestic economic policy, while automatically guaranteeing balance of payments equilibrium. In fact, this is incorrect. A change in the exchange rate causes relative price changes, income redistribution, reallocation of resources, and changes in the level and composition of output and consumption. Furthermore, floating exchange rates increase uncertainty and expose the economy to cyclical pressures and overshooting phenomena. Consequently, even in a generalized system of flexible exchange rates, the monetary authority usually cannot resist the temptation to intervene in the exchange markets in pursuit of its policy objectives. When it does, the outcome is somewhere between fixed and floating.

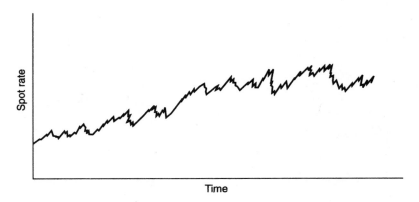

Figure 1.2 Floating exchange rate.

Managed float

The managed float, sometimes called a 'dirty float', is employed by governments to preserve an orderly pattern of exchange rate changes and is designed to eliminate excess volatility. Rather than resist the underlying market forces, the authorities occasionally intervene by buying or selling domestic currency to smooth the transition from one rate to another. At other times they intervene to moderate or counteract self-correcting cyclical or seasonal market forces.

Crawling peg

The crawling peg is an automatic system for revising the exchange rate. It involves establishing a par value around which the rate can vary within a given margin. The par value is revised regularly according to a formula determined by the authorities. Once the par value is set, the central bank intervenes whenever the market value approaches a limit point. Suppose, for example, that the par value of the Brazilian cruzeiro is 1000 cruzeiros for one dollar and can vary by plus or minus 2% around this rate, between 1020 cruzeiros and 980 cruzeiros. If the dollar approaches the rate of 1020 cruzeiros the central bank intervenes by buying cruzeiros and selling dollars. If the dollar approaches 980 cruzeiros, the central bank intervenes by selling cruzeiros and buying dollars. If it hovers around a limit point too long causing frequent central bank intervention, a new par value closer to this point is established. Figure 1.3 shows how the graph of a crawling peg rate might look. The heavy line is the par value and the dotted lines are the upper and lower limits around the par value. As time goes on, the market rate is

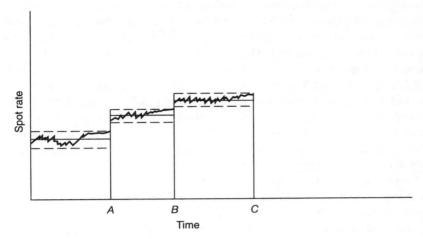

Figure 1.3 Crawling peg exchange rate.

consistently in the vicinity of its upper limit. Finally at points *A*, *B*, and *C*, the central bank readjusts the par value upwards.

Fixed rates with wider bands

Fixed rates with wider bands increase the intervention limits around official parity. They are supposed to reduce the magnitude and frequency of government intervention by discouraging speculation and allowing the exchange rate fluctuations themselves to accomplish some of the necessary adjustments. When the Bretton Woods gold exchange standard was breaking down in the early 1970s, for example, the members of the International Monetary Fund decided on a new set of parity rates and the conditions for maintaining them at a meeting in December 1971 at the Smithsonian Institute in Washington, DC. It was agreed that currencies were to be allowed to fluctuate within a band of plus or minus 2.25% around parity, rather than the previous limits of plus or minus 1%. In the monetary turmoil of late 1993, some countries participating in the European Monetary System took a similar tack and substantially increased the permitted bands of fluctuation around parity from plus or minus 2.25% to plus or minus 15%.

Fixed rate system with controls

Many governments attempt to achieve exchange rate stability by imposing exchange controls. Exchange controls short-circuit the allocation function of the foreign exchange market. One widespread practice is to impose restrictions on imports through tariffs and other barriers such as anti-dumping regulations, subsidies, technical standards, health regulations, quotas, and taxes. Another has been to prohibit residents from holding bank accounts in foreign currency. This, in effect, means that all foreign exchange must be turned over to the monetary authorities who, in turn, decide how the foreign exchange will be allocated, usually on the basis of government priorities. Two-tiered exchange rates are another popular measure. In this system different exchange rates are applied to different transactions. For example, the official fixed rate, which is usually overvalued, is applied to transactions associated with the current account while the market rate is applied to capital transactions.

Governments have been particularly creative in inventing foreign exchange controls, as can be seen in Table 1.1, which lists some of the most frequently used measures. Exchange controls distort prices and resource allocation and are a major source of risk for corporations and

Table 1.1 Examples of some common exchange controls

1. Import controls
2. Prohibition on holding bank accounts in foreign currency
3. Multiple exchange rates
4. Limits on direct investments abroad
5. Restrictions on certain types of remittances such as dividends, royalties, etc.
6. Restrictions on portfolio investment and bank lending
7. Prohibition or restriction of prepayments for imports
8. Government export monopolies
9. Export taxes
10. Interest-free deposits for a specified period tied to certain transactions such as imports, dividends, etc.
11. Minimum amounts of currency to be exchanged at the official rate by incoming travellers
12. Maximum amounts of currency to be exchanged by outgoing residents
13. Taxes on foreign-owned bank accounts
14. Limits on incoming direct investment
15. Limits on incoming portfolio investment or bank borrowing

individuals doing business in countries where they already exist or might be imposed.

THE CURRENT INTERNATIONAL FINANCIAL SYSTEM

The current international monetary system has its roots in a series of decisions that were taken by the authorities of the Allied Powers towards the end of the Second World War and in its immediate aftermath. Table 1.2 outlines some of the most important decisions and how they were followed up.

Table 1.2 Important dates in the international monetary system

1944 The conference at Bretton Woods establishes the gold exchange standard and creates the International Monetary Fund (IMF) and the International Bank for Reconstruction and Development (IRBD), better known as the World Bank.

1948 The bill appropriating funds for the reconstruction of Europe, the Marshall Plan, is signed. The Organization for European Economic Cooperation (OEEC) is set up to supervise the distribution of funds.

1949 Devaluation of the currencies of the major European and many other countries.

1950 European Payments Union (EPU) is created by recipients of the Marshall Plan.

1958 The European Economic Community (EEC) is established. The EPU is eliminated. Most European countries restore convertibility of their currencies into dollars and gold for non-residents.

1960 A run on gold causes the creation of the London gold pool by the major central banks in order to hold down the price of gold.

1961 Revaluation of the German mark and Dutch guilder. The Organization for Economic Cooperation and Development (OECD) comes into existence. The original member countries were: Austria, Belgium, Canada, Denmark, France, the Federal Republic of Germany, Greece, Iceland, Ireland, Italy, Luxembourg, the Netherlands, Norway, Portugal, Spain, Sweden, Switzerland, Turkey, the United Kingdom and the United States. The following countries became members subsequently: Japan (April 28, 1964), Finland (January 28, 1969), Australia (June 7, 1971) and New Zealand (May 29, 1973).

1962 France begins to sell dollars for gold.

1963 United States levies the interest equalization tax on non-resident borrowers.

1965 United States imposes 'voluntary' controls on foreign investment by US residents.

1967 A world monetary crisis follows the devaluation of the British pound.

1968 Voluntary controls on foreign investment became mandatory. A new run on gold forces governments to abandon the London gold pool and adopt a two-tiered gold market where central banks trade at the official price and private transactions take place at the market price.

1969 The French franc devalues. The German mark revalues after a short float.

1970 Special Drawing Rights are created.

1971 The United States runs its first trade deficit this century and a massive balance of payments deficit on a liquidity basis. The US gold stock falls below $10 billion. On August 15, convertibility of the dollar is suspended and the dollar is allowed to float. On December 17, the Smithsonian Agreement devalues the dollar against gold and fixes new parities with wider bands (plus or minus 2.25% instead of 1%). Dollar convertibility into gold is not reinstated.

1972 The EC countries, Denmark and Great Britain create the European Monetary Union whereby their currencies maintain a narrow band of 1.125% among themselves while maintaining the band of 2.25% with the dollar. Britain and Denmark leave the EMU.

1973 The dollar is devalued. Many currencies are allowed to float. The oil-producing countries establish an embargo.

1974 United States eliminates restrictions on capital outflows. France withdraws from the joint float. The IMF redefines the value of the SDR. Instead of reflecting the value of the dollar, it reflects a basket of 16 currencies.

1975 In November at Rambouillet, France, the leaders of the major countries acknowledge the need for a flexible exchange rate system.

1976 A new international monetary system of floating exchange rates is agreed on in Jamaica. Gold is demonetized.

1978 The IMF's articles of agreement are amended.

1979 On March 13, the European Monetary System (EMS) starts. On October 10, the Fed announces a new anti-inflation monetary policy that will focus on the money supply rather than interest rates.

1980 The IMF simplifies the value of the SDR. Instead of 16 currencies it will be based on a basket of the five currencies with the largest exports of goods and services between 1975 and 1979: the US dollar, German mark, French franc, Japanese yen and British pound.

1981 Adjustments are made in the par values of EMS to relieve downward pressure on the French franc.

1982 In February there is a new realignment of the EMS currencies. In August Mexico closes its foreign exchange markets and is unable to meet payments on its foreign debt.

1983 The IMF raises its quotas from SDR61.03 billion to SDR90 billion.

1985 The Group of Five announce policies to push down the value of the dollar.

1987 The Single European Act is established that will eliminate all remaining barriers on goods, labour and capital within the EC by 1992.

1990 The first step of the European Monetary Union called for in The Maastricht Treaty starts on July 1.

1994 The second step of the European Monetary Union begins with the creation of the European Monetary Institute, which is the precursor of the European Central Bank.

Where is the international financial system today? The answer to this question revolves around four facts.

1. The dollar is still the principal currency used in international transactions, but its unchallenged dominance is no longer taken for granted.
2. Japan is a confirmed economic and financial force.
3. The European Union is gaining importance as an economic and financial force.
4. Bretton Woods is dead but its child, the International Monetary Fund, has evolved with the times and is more important than ever as watchdog and arbiter of balance of payments disequilibrium.

The International Monetary Fund

One of the most important players in the current international financial system is the International Monetary Fund. The IMF was originally created to administer a code of fair exchange practices and provide compensatory financial assistance to member countries with balance of payments difficulties. As times have changed, the Fund has evolved with the perceived problems of the times. In 1963 it introduced the compensating financing facility to help countries with temporarily inadequate foreign exchange reserves resulting from events such as crop failure. In 1974 it set up the oil facility to help oil-importing developing countries. It also set up the extended fund facility for countries with structural difficulties. It created the Trust Fund of 1976 to allow the sale of gold for the development of third world countries. In the 1980s it negotiated special standby facilities for countries with foreign debt problems.

The Fund has also become active in guaranteeing the stability of the international financial system. In the 1980s and 90s it has played a high-profile role in settling the debt crisis by insisting on stabilization programmes and economic reform before granting access to Fund credits. Acceptance of IMF conditions are generally a *sine qua non* for countries seeking to negotiate agreements with their commercial bank creditors. In the Mexican peso crisis of 1995, for example, the IMF collaborated with the US and other OECD governments to put together a $50 billion rescue package to enable Mexico to avoid defaulting on its foreign debt obligations.

The European Union and the European Monetary System

The European Union

The European Union (EU) has become a major economic and financial force. It ranks with the United States and Japan as a giant of world trade. Excluding trade within the EU, by 1990 the 12 member countries accounted for about 20% of world exports, while the US accounted for only 15%. Their combined GDPs were also roughly as large as that of the United States. EU stockmarkets and bourses are among the most sophisticated and fastest-growing in the world and EU banks are among the largest and most active in international financial markets.

The EU has a shaky history and a modest beginning. It grew from the postwar recognition of the necessity of European economic cooperation, if further catastrophes were to be avoided. The first step on the road to cooperation came with the creation in 1948 of the Organization for European Economic Cooperation (OEEC) to àdminister the Marshall Plan. The next step was the establishment by Belgium, France, Italy, Luxembourg, the Netherlands and West Germany in 1952 of the European Coal and Steel Community (ECSC) to create a common market in steel and coal. The first big step on the road to today's economic integration was the Treaty of Rome, signed on March 25, 1957 by the same six countries, that created the European Economic Community (EEC), later shortened to the European Community and now known as the European Union.

The Treaty of Rome made it possible to organize the six signatories into a customs union and a common market. A customs union involves the erection of a common external tariff and the abolition of all restrictions on trade among members. A common market permits the free movement of capital and labour as well as all goods and services. By July 1968 all internal import duties had been abolished and the common external tariff established. By 1969 common market workers could move freely from one country to another in response to employment opportunities. By 1989 most capital controls had been abolished.

Over the years, the EU has grown from the original six member countries to the current 12. Great Britain, Ireland and Denmark joined the EU in 1973, Greece joined in 1981 and Spain and Portugal joined in 1986. It looks set to grow further with Turkey, the former Eastern bloc countries, and most of the European Free Trade Association (EFTA) countries clamouring to get in.[2]

The **Single European Act** (SEA) of 1987 affirmed the EU's intention to make the transition from a common market to a full economic union by January 1, 1993. An economic union involves the free movement of capital, labour, all goods and services as well as the harmonization and unification of social, fiscal and monetary policies. Full economic union implies the transfer of economic and financial sovereignty to the EU's supranational institutions. It means that tax systems must be harmonized by reducing the existing rate differentials across countries and that non-tariff barriers to trade, such as national technical standards, must be eliminated. It also means that sensitive services such as banking, insurance, and telecommunications must be liberalized.

Considerable progress has been made. An EU directive in 1988, effective since July 1990 except for Greece, Spain, Portugal and Ireland, requires the elimination of all remaining restrictions on capital movements within the EU. The principle of **mutual recognition**, which holds that certification provisions in one country must be recognized as equivalent to the provisions in force in another country, will make it possible for banks to operate EU-wide without prior harmonization of banking regulations across countries. The ·principle will be extended to many other sectors. Some of the most important progress has been made in the domain of harmonization of economic and monetary policy, on which the success of the endeavour ultimately hinges.

The European Monetary System

After the collapse of the Bretton Woods system in 1971, the EC countries, together with the United Kingdom and Denmark, which were to join the EC in 1973, agreed to maintain their currencies within a narrower band (2.25%) than the 4.5% permitted by the Smithsonian Agreement. This arrangement was referred to as the 'snake in the tunnel' because the EC currencies floated as a group against outside currencies such as the dollar or yen. The turmoil of the 1970s reduced the snake from eight to four participants (Germany, the Netherlands, Belgium, and Denmark) and it was decided in 1978 that a new effort to achieve monetary cooperation was necessary.

Led by Germany and France, the European Monetary System, regrouping all EC members, was launched in 1979. The goal of the EMS is to create a zone of monetary stability in Europe. Its major features are:

1. a system of bilateral exchange rates defining par values and limiting variations to a band of 2.25% around the par value (the band has since been widened to 15% as a result of the monetary turmoil in 1993);[3]
2. the creation of the **European Currency Unit (ECU)**, which is a weighted average of each of the EMS currencies, as the special unit of account that is used in all intrasystem balance of payments settlements;
3. establishment of the **European Monetary Cooperation Fund** (EMCF),

which allocates ECUs to members' central banks in exchange for 20% of those central banks' gold and dollar holdings;
4.   the provision of credit facilities for compensatory financing of balance of payments deficits.

A central feature of the EMS system of fixed exchange rates is that the central banks of both of the currencies involved in the rate are obliged to intervene if the market rate approaches a limit point. Suppose, for example, that the French franc is approaching its lower limit on the the **parity grid**. (The parity grid is a square matrix showing the par value as well as the upper and lower limits of each pair of currencies.) The French authorities are required to buy French francs and the German authorities are required to sell German marks. The difference between this system and the gold exchange standard is that in the gold exchange standard the required intervention was only on one side. If, for example, the French franc was approaching its lower limit with the dollar, the French authorities were required to intervene by buying francs. There was no requirement on the part of the US authorities to cooperate by selling dollars.

The advantages of bilateral intervention are obvious. The adjustment process is spread across both countries. When the French central bank buys francs, the money supply falls and sets the adjustment process of lower prices, investment and output in motion. When the German central bank sells marks, the money supply increases and sets in motion the adjustment process of higher prices, investment and output. Since both countries are participating simultaneously, the adjustment should be swifter and less painful than if one of the two had intervened alone.

The EMS does allow for realignments of the par values. Where realignments are concerned, it is important to be able to single out the country or countries responsible for the realignment. In our example, for instance, is the franc too low or is the mark too high? This question can be answered by using the ECU.

Besides bilateral exchange rates, each currency has limit points with respect to its value *vis-à-vis* the ECU. The country at fault when a limit point with another currency is reached will also be near the same limit point with the ECU. If the French franc is near its lower limit point with the German mark because of its overly expansive monetary policy, it will also be near its lower limit with the other EMS currencies and thus with the ECU. For the same reason, if the German mark is near its upper limit with the French franc because of an overly restrictive monetary policy, it will also be near its upper limit with the ECU. Since realignments are discouraged, the 'guilty' country is expected to take corrective action or explain to the other members why it cannot.

The success of the EMS has been mixed. Up to 1988 there had been 11 realignments, in spite of some heavy intervention. The values of the German mark and the Dutch guilder have risen spectacularly while the French franc and the Italian lira have flopped. It is said that defending the franc in 1983 cost the Socialist French government over $5 billion in two weeks. Since then, France has reined in its monetary policy and fallen in behind Germany. It is now generally recognized that success of the Single European Act requires a common monetary policy, and progress has been made towards the creation of a European central bank with the ultimate goal of a common European currency. The monetary turmoil of late 1993, however, all but destroyed the EMS and set back the schedule of the projected European Monetary Union.

Current system of exchange rates and reserves

Composition of international reserves
It is interesting to note that the composition of international reserves has evolved over the years. International reserves are composed of gold, foreign currency, SDRs and the net position with the IMF. Figure 1.4 shows the composition of total world reserves between 1977 and 1993. The relative importance of foreign exchange has increased considerably over the period, going from 75% of reserves in 1977 to 90% in 1993. Much of this increase has come at the expense of gold, whose relative importance has fallen from close to 15% in 1977 to less than 5% in 1993.

Current system of exchange rate agreements
With this in mind we can now resume the current situation of exchange rate arrangements. The basic system is one of flexible exchange rates. We know that since 1985 the dollar, the most important reserve currency, has been in the throes of a managed float against the other major currencies. Within this system many countries have decided to peg their currencies to another currency or a basket of currencies. In Table 1.3 we can see that as of December 31, 1994, 23 currencies were pegged to the US dollar, four were pegged to the SDR, 14 were pegged to the French franc, and 21 currencies were pegged to various baskets of currencies other than the SDR. Nine small countries – Bhutan, Eritrea, Estonia, Kiribati, Lesotho, Namibia, San Marino, Swaziland and Tajikistan – had their currencies pegged to the currency of their major trading partner and, given the organization of the

EMS, it could be said that the 10 EMS countries had their currencies pegged to the ECU. Since the French franc is part of the EMS, the 14 currencies in the franc zone are effectively pegged to the ECU as well. The gulf countries of Bahrain, Qatar, Saudi Arabia and the United Arab Emirates had their currencies targeted to the dollar, but allowed a certain amount of flexibility.

It is clear that there is recognition on the part of many countries of the need for some kind of exchange rate stability. The overall trend, however, is

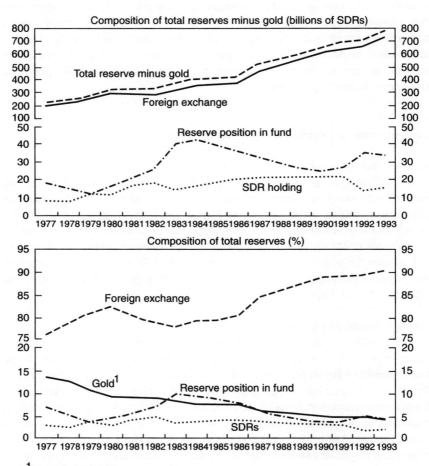

[1] Valued at SDR 35 per ounce

Figure 1.4 International reserves.
(Source: *International Financial Statistics,* April 1995, p. 3.)

towards more flexible exchange rate arrangements, insofar as 59 countries, 11 from the OECD, were floating independently, 31 were on a managed float and three were on a crawling peg.

INTERNATIONAL BANKING AND THE EUROCURRENCY MARKET

International institutions and agreements have evolved over the years in response to the growth in cross-border trade and capital flows as well as the revolution in communications and information processing. The same forces have been at work in the evolution of the private component of the international financial system, international banking. The traditional system of correspondent banking where banks maintain deposits, subject to local regulations, in the domestic currency of the country where they are located has been overtaken by today's system of banks taking and holding deposits in any currency, regardless of banks' location. Deposits of this type are outside the jurisdiction of the monetary authorities where the currencies are legal tender. They can be bought and sold, borrowed and loaned, with little or no interference from politicians and regulators. Any interference in one location only has the effect of chasing business to another where none exists. Furthermore, the development of communications networks and data processing has increased the speed and efficiency of transfer and settlement to the point where geographic location is almost irrelevant.

For the international financial system the consequences have been revolutionary. International liquidity, interest rates, and the magnitude and direction of capital flows have all undergone profound changes. Even domestic banking systems have been influenced, since they are crosslinked through the offshore operations in their currencies.

The characteristics of the Eurocurrency market

The Eurocurrency market refers to the offshore international banking system. We can define a **Eurocurrency** as any freely convertible currency, such as a dollar or a mark, deposited in a bank outside its country of origin. Thus, a mark held on deposit with a bank in Paris is a Euromark, and a dollar held on deposit with a bank in London is a Eurodollar. It is the residency of a bank and not its nationality that determines the 'Euro' nature of the deposit, so the Euromark could be held with a Paris branch of a German bank and the Eurodollar could be held with a London branch of an

Table 1.3 Exchange rate arrangements

(As of December 31, 1994)[1]

Currency pegged to					Flexibility limited in terms of a single currency or group of currencies		Adjusted according to a set of indicators	More flexible	
US dollar	French franc	Other currency	SDR	Other composite[2]	Single currency	Cooperative arrangements		Other managed floating	Independently floating
Antigua & Barbuda	Benin	Bhutan (Indian rupee)	Libya	Bangladesh	Bahrain	Austria	Chile	Algeria	Afghanistan, Islamic State of
Argentina	Burkina Faso	Eritrea (Ethiopian birr)	Myanmar	Botswana	Qatar	Belgium	Ecuador	Angola	Albania
Bahamas, The	Cameroon	Estonia (deutsche mark)	Rwanda	Burundi	Saudi Arabia	Denmark	Nicaragua	Belarus	Armenia
Barbados	C. African Rep.	Kiribati (Australian dollar)	Seychelles	Cape Verdi	United Arab Emirates	France		Brazil	Australia
Belize	Chad	Lesotho (South African rand)		Cyprus		Germany		Cambodia	Azerbaijan
Djibouti	Comoros	Namibia (South African rand)		Czech Republic		Ireland		China, P.R.	Bolivia
Dominica	Congo	San Marino (Italian lira)		Fiji		Luxembourg		Colombia	Bulgaria
Grenada	Côte d'Ivoire	Swaziland (South African rand)		Hungary		Netherlands		Croatia	Canada
Iraq	Equatorial Guinea	Tajikistan, Rep. of (Russian ruble)		Iceland		Portugal		Dominican Rep.	Costa Rica
Liberia	Gabon			Jordan		Spain		Egypt	El Salvador
Lithuania	Mali			Kuwait				Georgia	Ethiopia
Marshall Islands	Niger			Malta				Greece	Finland
Micronesia, Fed. States of	Senegal			Mauritania				Guinea-Bissau	Gambia, The
Nigeria	Togo			Morocco				Honduras	Ghana
Oman				Nepal				Indonesia	Guatemala
Panama				Slovak Republic				Israel	Guinea
St. Kitts & Nevis				Solomon Islands				Korea	Guyana
St. Lucia				Thailand				Lao P.D. Rep	Haiti
St. Vincent and the Grenadines				Tonga				Malaysia	India
Syrian Arab Rep.				Vanuatu				Maldives	Iran, I.R. of
Turkmenistan				Western Samoa				Mauritius	Italy
Venezuela								Pakistan	Jamaica
Yemen, Republic of								Poland	Japan
								Singapore	Kazakhstan
								Slovenia	Kenya
								Sri Lanka	Kyrgyz Rep.
								Sudan	Latvia
								Tunisia	Lebanon
								Turkey	Macedonia, FYR
								Uruguay	Madagascar
								Viet Nam	Malawi
									Mexico
									Moldova
									Mongolia
									Mozambique

(As of December 31, 1994)[1]

Currency pegged to					Flexibility limited in terms of a single currency or group of currencies		More flexible		
US dollar	French franc	Other currency	SDR	Other composite[2]	Single currency	Cooperative arrangements	Adjusted according to a set of indicators	Other managed floating	Independently floating
									New Zealand
									Norway
									Papua New Guinea
									Paraguay
									Peru
									Philippines
									Romania
									Russia
									Sao Tome & Principe
									Sierra Leone
									Somalia
									South Africa
									Suriname
									Sweden
									Switzerland
									Tanzania
									Trinidad and Tobago
									Uganda
									Ukraine
									United Kingdom
									United States
									Zaire
									Zambia
									Zimbabwe

[1] For members with dual or multiple exchange markets, the arrangement shown is that in the major market.
[2] Comprises currencies which are pegged to various 'baskets' of currencies of the members' own choice, as distinct from the SDR basket.
[3] Exchange rates of all currencies have shown limited flexibility in terms of the U.S. dollar.
[4] Refers to the cooperative arrangement maintained under the European Monetary System.
[5] Includes exchange arrangements under which the exchange rate is adjusted at relatively frequent intervals, on the basis of indicators determined by the respective member countries.
[6] Starting May 24, 1994, the Azerbaijan authorities ceased to peg the manat to the Russian ruble and the exchange arrangement was reclassified to 'Independently floating'.
[7] Excluding Uzbekistan, which as of end-December 1994 has not notified the Fund of its exchange rate arrangement.
(Source: *International Financial Statistics*, April 1995, p. 8)

American bank. The term Eurocurrency also refers to this type of deposit held in non-European financial centres, although the term **offshore currency** is sometimes used in its place.

Eurocurrency deposits are typically conventional term deposits of one day to one year's duration. Conventional term deposits are non-negotiable bank deposits with a fixed term where the interest rate is fixed for the duration of the deposit. In Eurocurrency transactions, the currency that is used is always a foreign currency to at least one of the two parties, and one of the two parties is always a bank. The other party can be another bank, a central bank, a government or a large corporate entity. In fact, transactions between banks and other financial institutions constitute the core of the Eurocurrency market. This interbank Eurocurrency market is organized as an international over-the-counter market whose members are linked by telephone and telex. Access to this market is reserved to institutions of top quality. The sums involved are huge, with one million dollars the usual minimum transaction. Eurocurrency markets are outside the jurisdiction of any single regulatory authority and the interest rates are determined by pure supply and demand.

As we can see in Table 1.4, the Eurocurrency market has grown by leaps and bounds. Its nature is such that some cost savings are inherent. As a wholesale market dealing in large quantities, economies of scale can be achieved, which lower costs. Since the participants are also all professionals,

Table 1.4 Size of the Eurocurrency market

Year	Bank liabilities in foreign currencies (billions of US dollars)
1968	33.71
1976	310.65
1985	1980.60
1986	2526.90
1987	3230.60
1988	3505.20
1989	4186.30
1990	4936.70

(Source: Bank for International Settlements: Annual Reports (February 1988 and August 1991).)

costly regulatory oversight and consumer protection such as deposit insurance are unnecessary. Furthermore, Eurocurrency transactions are simply more convenient in today's global economy. The development of cross-border commercial transactions has generated multiple currency cash flows that corporate treasurers are obliged to manage. It is impractical to deal with a different bank in a different country for each separate currency. Alternatively, dealing with one bank would also be costly and inefficient if it meant systematically converting all foreign currency cash flows into domestic currency when they arrive, only to reconvert into foreign currency when payments must be made. The Eurocurrency market makes it possible to deal with an easily accessible, well-known bank that can handle all currency needs.

Thus, the factors of cost and convenience are behind the emergence and growth of all the Eurocurrencies. Depositers want to receive the highest yield and borrowers want to pay the lowest cost. The nature of the Euromarket and the absence of restrictions make it possible to fulfil these requirements.

Eurocurrency interest rates

Eurocurrency rates are closely related to the rates in the currency's home market but, because of lower costs, spreads are lower. Large differentials, however, can exist. Since the cost of shifting funds from one market to another is negligible, substantial interest rate differentials between the domestic market and the Euromarket suggest the presence of differences in perceived risk or effective controls. For many years Euro French franc rates were considerably higher than domestic rates, due to French restrictions on loaning abroad combined with domestic credit controls. With the supply limited, credit-starved French borrowers dodging the domestic controls maintained the differential by borrowing Eurofrancs whenever the interest rate began to fall. On the other side of the coin, Euromark and Euro Swiss franc rates have seen periods when they were considerably lower than domestic rates, because of measures seeking to discourage capital inflows. One such measure was minimum reserves on certain types of non-resident deposits. The minimum reserve requirement raised the cost of funds for domestic banks borrowing abroad. This caused them to lower the rate they were willing to pay for foreign funds to bring their total cost into line with the cost of domestic funds. In both cases controls caused considerable interest rate differentials between the two markets. Controls designed to restrict capital outflows will tend to push the Euro-rate above the domestic rate while controls designed to restrict capital inflows will tend to push the Euro-rate below the domestic rate.

Anticipating controls that do not yet exist can also cause an interest rate differential. If there is a possibility that at some future date funds will be unable to cross the border, investors will require a premium for holding assets in the domestic market. In this case the interest rate differential is due to higher perceived risk on assets held in the domestic market.

The Eurocurrency market and balance of payments adjustment

In the Eurocurrency system, bank intermediation plays a key role in the international adjustment of balance of payments disequilibrium by taking deposits from surplus countries and lending to deficit countries. One of the best, or worst, examples of this role came in the wake of the first oil shock in 1973–4. The oil-exporting countries were unable to transform all their oil revenues into purchases of goods and services. They therefore had a tremendous trade surplus. The oil-importing countries had a corresponding trade deficit. The surplus countries were unwilling to lend directly to many of the deficit countries, and much of the proceeds of their surplus was held as foreign exchange reserves in the Eurocurrency market. To the Eurobanks' ever-lasting regret, they performed their role of intermediation with extreme efficiency. They channelled hundreds of billions of what were called 'petrodollars' from the oil-exporting countries to the oil-importing countries, many of which were among the poorest and most economically inefficient in the world. Unfortunately, the banks failed to appreciate the risks they were taking by indiscriminately recycling the oil-exporting countries' balance of trade surplus; this came back to haunt them in the 1980s in the form of the 'debt crisis'.

THE FOREIGN EXCHANGE MARKET

Most international financial transactions sooner or later involve an exchange of one currency for another. This is why the exchange rate and exchange rate determination play such an important role in international financial theory. How theory comes out in reality, however, depends on the systems and procedures that are effectively used for executing the exchange. Costs and delays in execution can be the determining factors in whether or not certain operations can be profitably undertaken. Hence, the efficiency of the international financial system and its degree of integration with the individual national financial systems depends to a large extent on how cheaply and quickly foreign exchange transactions can be effected.

The interbank market

Foreign exchange transactions involve buying and selling one currency for another. In reality, notes and coins rarely change hands – what is involved is the exchange of a demand deposit denominated in one currency for a demand deposit denominated in another currency. The transactions can be made for immediate delivery on the spot market, or for future delivery on the forward market. The core of the foreign exchange market is the interbank market, which is closely linked to the Eurocurrency interbank market. It is an informal, over-the-counter, around-the-clock market that includes the major commercial banks and some specialized brokers located in the principal financial centres throughout the world. They are linked by telephone and telex, and most use a special satellite communications network called SWIFT (Society for Worldwide International Financial Telecommunications).

The interbank market is composed of **traders** and **brokers**. The roles of the trader and the broker are essentially different. The trader usually operates out of the foreign exchange trading room of a major bank. He is essentially a **market maker** and stands ready to buy and sell foreign currencies on a more or less continuous basis. He takes positions on buying and selling based on his feeling for the market and on orders from his clients.

Actual trading is accomplished through an informal, straightforward procedure. A trader is contacted for a quote by another trader, who does not reveal the amount of the transaction he has in mind or whether he wants to buy or sell. The trader who has been called will then give the caller two prices, the price at which he will buy the currency in question and the price at which he will sell it. This is the same system as in the Eurocurrency market; the difference between the two prices is the spread. These prices refer to minimum quantities of $1 million or its foreign exchange equivalent, but standard transactions are up to about $3 million in the interbank market. Once the caller has the trader's quote, he only has about a minute in which to decide what he wants to do. After that, convention has it that the trader has the right to change his quote. If the caller decides to act, the trader is bound to honour his quote and the caller will tell the trader whether he wants to buy or sell and the amount of the transaction. Written confirmation of the trade follows the oral agreement, so it is important that traders establish a reputation for honesty and reliability.

Bank traders cannot always find a counterparty to the trades they want to make and sometimes find it necessary or convenient to call on the services of a broker. When a trader calls a broker, he does not have to hide his position. He can tell the broker whether he wants to buy or sell, the amount involved, and the rate he is willing to pay. The broker thus has knowledge of what is available in the market and this he communicates to other traders until he matches a buy and a sell. Once the match is made, the trade takes place. The broker keeps the names of his customers secret so until the deal is made neither of the counterparties knows who they are dealing with. Once it is finalized the broker supplies the names of the counterparties and collects a fee from both sides. This makes going through a broker more expensive than direct dealing, but has the advantage of dealing at the desired price and keeping the trader's identity secret until the trade is made.

Thus, the broker serves three important purposes. First of all, he is a precious source of information for the traders in a high-stakes game where one or two basis points can mean a difference of thousands of dollars on a contract. Secondly, he brings buyers and sellers together and contributes to market efficiency. Thirdly, he makes it possible for traders to remain anonymous when knowing their identity would put them at a disadvantage. Suppose, for example, that a trader has a comfortable long position in sterling and sterling is on the rise. He feels that the rise is almost over and would like to undo his position. However, the other traders recognize him as the current 'specialist' in sterling and are watching his quotes and whether he buys or sells. If he enters the market directly as a seller, he might reverse the rising trend of sterling and cause himself some heavy losses in the process. In this case he might find it advantageous to contact a broker and quote some buy and sell prices for sterling, without divulging whether he wants to buy or sell but making the prices more likely to attract a buyer than a seller. His anonymity protected by the broker, he can undo his position without tipping off the market.

The foreign exchange market and the Eurocurrency market

There is a close relationship between the foreign exchange market and the Eurocurrency market. The theoretical relationship is derived from the interest rate parity hypothesis that links the spot and forward exchange rates to the interest rates of the two currencies. In practice the relationship is closest in the interbank markets, where regulation is minimal and transactions costs are low. The participants in both markets are the same and quotes for foreign exchange and Eurocurrency interest rates are carried on the same communications network. The Eurocurrency markets are also a ready source of funds for financing foreign currency purchases and a convenient depository for placing the proceeds of foreign currency sales. In fact, the two markets are so thoroughly integrated that forward cross rates are often calculated from the interest rate differential.

ORGANIZATION OF THE INTERNATIONAL BANKING SYSTEM

The transactions described in the foregoing paragraphs imply the existence of a well-developed communications network and an organized system of financial cooperation. This, in fact, is the case. Banks are linked by telephone and telex, and most use the SWIFT satellite communications network. Based in Belgium, SWIFT connects over 1800 banks, brokerage firms and non-banking financial institutions worldwide and makes it possible to transmit financial messages in a standardized format that reduces errors that might crop up due to different languages and banking customs. It has grown so rapidly that it has virtually replaced the mail and telex as the standard method of communication. Financial cooperation is achieved through informal arrangements called **correspondent banking**, or the more formal formats of representative offices, agencies, and foreign branches and subsidiaries.

Correspondent banking

A correspondent bank is a bank located in another city, state or country that provides a service for another bank. Correspondent banking originally developed to facilitate long-distance payments, both domestic and foreign. In return for this service, client banks kept relatively large, interest-free balances with the correspondent bank. The term 'correspondent' refers to the days before telecommunications, when the mail and the telex were used for settling accounts. Today, as we mentioned, these have largely been replaced by SWIFT and computerized international clearing houses such as CHIPS (Clearing House Interbank Payments System) in the US and CHAPS (Clearing House Automated Payments System) in the UK.

International correspondent banking has evolved over the years as it has become more competitive. Cross-border funds transfers are still the largest single area of international correspondent banking, although services can extend to granting loans, setting up business contacts and giving advice. While interest-free demand balances remain the glue that ties the banks together and represents the main way that banks pay for correspondent services, fees have assumed a certain importance. Banks can now opt to pay by fee, or a combination of fees and interest-free balances. When balances represent payment, they are now more rigorously enforced than they were in the past.

Most smaller banks have correspondents in countries where they do business and large banks have correspondent arrangements in most countries where they have no office of their own. Correspondent banking has the advantage of offering a range of international banking services, while making it possible to scale costs to the amount of service required in a given area. The disadvantage is that correspondents are not likely to give top priority to another bank's clients.

Representative offices

Representative offices are a way to establish a formal presence in foreign markets. They are not authorized to perform banking services such as effecting transfers and taking deposits. The purpose of these offices is to provide information on local business practices and markets, supply financial contacts with host country institutions and commercial contacts for the bank's home customers, as well as to offer them assistance with local rules and regulations. They are also useful in expediting the services of the local correspondent bank. Although they have the advantage of on-the-spot supervision, they are relatively costly and difficult to staff with competent people because of their lowly status in the banking hierarchy.

Foreign branches and subsidiaries

Foreign branches are banks, just like local banks, and can offer the same types of services. They are subject to the same rules and regulations as local banks but many countries also impose other restrictions on deposit-taking and local expansion.

Foreign branching has grown dramatically with the growth of international banking in general. In the 1950s only seven US banks had overseas branches. By 1980 this figure had grown to over 130. The EU has also seen a proliferation of cross-border branches of other community members, as well as the growth of community member branches in the United States and Asia. Japan's banks have followed its commercial successes and established branches in most of the major financial centres. Most countries have at least one or two banks with a network of branches in the major financial centres.

Foreign branching has grown for many reasons. First of all, commerce has become intrinsically international in nature. It is rare for a medium-sized company to be isolated from foreign suppliers and customers, and many of the larger companies do more business abroad than in their home markets. Establishing a foreign branch was a way of keeping clients that might otherwise have been lost. Secondly, a foreign branch affords access to foreign money markets. This access is indispensable to the larger banks that have funding needs in many currencies. It also offers them investment opportunities that might be unavailable in the domestic market. Finally, foreign branching is a way to diversify cash flows. Economic expansion and contraction vary across countries. A downturn in Japan might accompany an expansion in the EU or the US. Since banking activity is closely tied to economic activity, a diversified geographical presence should give a diversified range of cash flows.

While foreign branching has occurred on a widespread level, its growth has been curtailed because most countries restrict branch banks' activities in order to protect local banks from aggressive competition. This was true in many EU countries, where local banks grew bloated and inefficient. The UK, of course, has been pretty liberal in allowing foreign banks to operate and owes its position as a major financial centre partly to that. Banking restrictions for EU member banks were due to come down in 1992 and this caused a flurry of merger activity as local banks positioned themselves for a competitive onslaught. The International Banking Act of 1978 provides for the regulation and supervision of foreign banks in the US. They may be granted a license in states where this is allowed but are restricted to that one state. They have access to the Federal Reserve services and must respect reserve requirements and provide deposit insurance.

Rather than establish branches, some banks decide to create a subsidiary. A subsidiary differs from a branch insofar as the branch is part of a company that is incorporated elsewhere, whereas the subsidiary is incorporated locally and owned either completely or partially by a foreign parent. Generally speaking, a subsidiary is indistinguishable from a locally owned bank. Most major countries provide some scope for foreign branch banking.

Branches and subsidiaries have the advantage of expanding a bank's presence and offering a wider range of international services to its home clients as well as the possibility of cultivating local clients. On the other hand, branches and subsidiaries are costly to start up and run. They need to generate a considerable amount of business to make them worthwhile and it may take years before they establish a presence. For this reason many banks try to enter a local market through a merger or acquisition.

Mergers and acquisitions make it possible to hit the ground running. An existing bank is a going concern. It has an ongoing deposit base, a functioning management team knowledgeable in the customs and culture of the home country, and a network of contacts and clients. For these same reasons, mergers and acquisitions are expensive. Furthermore, they don't always work. In fact, they often fail and failures are costly both monetarily and in terms of reputation.

An overview of the system

The international banking system has its roots in the domestic monetary systems of each individual country. Banks in the domestic monetary systems include foreign branches and subsidiaries and are supervised by the domestic monetary authorities. They are linked by the domestic communications system of telephone, telex, fax and mail. Domestic transactions are cleared by the domestic clearing system.

Besides transactions with domestic financial institutions, banks also deal with foreign financial institutions. For these transactions a foreign intermediary is necessary. The most common relationship is a correspondent agreement, whereby domestic banks undertake transfers on behalf of the clients of foreign banks. Transfers between the correspondent bank and the foreign bank's client are cleared on the domestic clearing system. Transfers between the foreign bank and its correspondent are cleared either bank to bank, or through the domestic system of the currency that is being transferred. Communications between correspondent and foreign bank are carried out by telephone, telex, fax, mail and more commonly through the specialized SWIFT network.

Banks that require a higher level of service maintain representative offices or agencies in foreign countries. An even higher level of service can be achieved by establishing a branch or a full fledged subsidiary. Communications between branch or subsidiary and parent are closer than correspondent-foreign bank communications but they are basically carried out on the same systems.

International banks have developed offshore networks of transactions that are outside the jurisdiction of any single regulatory authority. These transactions routinely use both domestic and international communications systems and clearing facilities. Operations are conducted from financial centres with a developed domestic financial system such as London, Paris or New York. They are also conducted from centres with relatively small domestic financial systems specializing in international transactions, such as the Cayman Islands, Singapore, and the Channel Islands of Jersey and Guernsey.

Communications and information processing have evolved to the point that geographical distance has almost become irrelevant. The well-developed network of correspondent arrangements and physical presence in the form of representatives, agencies, branches, and subsidiaries ensures that the communications possibilities are exploited intensely and in increasingly inventive ways. The result is a highly integrated system in which it is often difficult to discern where one market begins and the other ends.

NOTES

[1] For a detailed presentation of the effects of an exchange rate variation on a national economy, see: Clark, E., Levasseur, M. and Rousseau, P. (1993) *International Finance*, Chapman & Hall, London. Chapter 2.

[2] Sweden, Finland and Austria were admitted as of 1995.

[3] Except for the Netherlands, which kept to the previous band of plus or minus 2.25%, and Greece, Italy and the UK, whose currencies were allowed to float freely.

[4] We will take up the international parity relations in Chapter 2.

2 THE CHARACTERISTICS OF INTERNATIONAL BUSINESS RISK

Business transactions between residents of different countries are subject to risks that would not otherwise be present. Besides cultural differences in institutions, legal and financial traditions, information sources and the like, there can be other serious constraints such as legal barriers, transactions costs and discriminatory taxation that can affect the outcome of a cross-border business transaction. Each country has its own distinct set of economic and financial conditions reflecting its human and natural resources and the way these resources are managed. Since international economic and financial activity is organized around the concept of national sovereignty, where each country has its own economic, financial, political and legal organization which determines resource allocation and income distribution within the geographic area it controls, events or anticipated events at the national level can have serious effects on the business climate in the country where they occur. For example, a looser monetary policy by the German Bundesbank will tend to lower interest rates and increase investment and consumption expenditure.

This is not the whole story, however. Events or anticipated events at the national level will also affect the relative performance of resident economic and financial agents *vis-à-vis* the rest of the world. Other things being equal, the looser German monetary policy that lowers interest rates and increases investment and consumption expenditure will also tend to lower the value of the mark relative to other currencies.

The analysis can be further extended to include political, social, geographic, and strategic considerations likely to affect the outcome of business transactions between resident and non-resident economic agents. Expropriations, revolutions, natural catastrophes and wars are some of the most obvious examples that come to mind.

As a concept, then, international or cross-border business risk is vast and complex. It refers to the volatility of returns on international business transactions caused by events associated with a particular country, as opposed to events associated with a particular economic or financial agent. In this chapter we will develop the concept of risk in general and then discuss the different types of risk associated with the business environment in a particular country.

THE NATURE OF RISK

Before we get into the specifics of risk associated with international business transactions, it is important to develop a precise definition of what exactly is meant by the word 'risk'. Risk can have different meanings in different contexts. Consider, for example, the ongoing controversy between academics and practitioners about the effect of stock index arbitrage on stock market risk. Practitioners argue passionately that stock index arbitrage has made stock market prices more volatile or riskier. No academic researcher takes this charge seriously, since the overwhelming evidence of studies on equity rates of return shows that volatility in the years since index futures and options contracts were introduced has not been notably high by past historical standards. While volatility, a statistical term that measures dispersion around the mean, has not increased as a result of stock index arbitrage, what has increased is the 'velocity' of price changes. In the open outcry system of the futures market, prices can adjust more rapidly to new information than they can in the cash market where market makers are obliged to walk prices up and down one-eighth of a point at a time. This creates arbitrage opportunities. Market makers as well as practitioners who enter limit orders on their books get hurt by the rapid price changes set in motion by arbitrage operations. Market makers and limit orders get 'hit' an eighth of a point at a time as the cash price moves up or down to a new level.[1] Thus, both practitioners and academics are essentially correct in their arguments and the disagreement between them is one of semantics. To avoid problems of this sort in the discussion of international business risk, we need a clear idea of exactly what we mean by risk and how it can be measured.

Expected return and standard deviation

Risk can generally be defined as the probability of unfavourable outcomes. In finance, for example, interest centres on the effects of risk on the valuation of assets and liabilities. Thus, one measure of risk might be the probability that the return on an investment will fall below a certain level. We might say, for example, that there is a 30% probability that the return on an investment in Newmont Mining shares will fall below 15%. As a risk measure, it is better than nothing but still is not very informative. It would be better if we knew by how much it was likely to be below 15%. Our perception of the riskiness of the investment would certainly be different if the return could fall as low as -20% instead of + 10%. A more complete way to look at risk would be to associate a probability to each possible outcome. This **probability distribution** would make it possible to calculate the most likely outcome, as well as by how much the real outcome is likely to diverge from the most likely outcome.

Suppose that the return on an investment depends on economic conditions. If economic conditions are good, the investment will show a return of 16%. If economic conditions are average, it will show a return of 10%. If economic conditions are bad, it will only show a return of 4%. Research reveals that there is an equally likely probability (one-third) of any one of the three economic situations actually happening. In these conditions, what is the return that the investor should expect? In fact, expected return means the arithmetic average. Expected return is calculated by multiplying each possible outcome by the probability that the outcome will occur, and summing. The expected return can thus be calculated as:

$$\left(\frac{1}{3} \times 16\%\right) + \left(\frac{1}{3} \times 10\%\right) + \left(\frac{1}{3} \times 4\%\right) = 10\%.$$

The investor now knows what to expect from his investment. How risky it is depends on how much it is likely to diverge from its expected value. The **standard deviation** is the most commonly used statistical measure of how much a variable is likely to diverge from its expected value. It is sometimes referred to as **volatility** and in finance it is often used to indicate the riskiness of an asset, a portfolio of assets, or a market. The standard deviation is the square root of the variance.

The variance of a variable is the arithmetic average of the squares of the deviations around the variable's arithmetic average. The variance of the return on the foregoing investment can be calculated by taking the difference between each possible outcome and the average outcome, squaring it, multiplying the squared difference by the probability of the outcome occuring, and summing:

$$(16\% - 10\%)^2 \times \frac{1}{3} + (10\% - 10\%)^2 \times \frac{1}{3} + (4\% - 10\%)^2 \times \frac{1}{3} = 24.$$

The variance of the returns on the investment is 24. Variance is converted into the original units of percentages by taking the square root. The square root of 24 is about 4.9, so the standard deviation is 4.9%. It measures how much actual returns are likely to diverge from the expected return. In the present case, it is plus or minus 4.9%. Consequently most actual returns should fall between 5.1% and 14.9%. The Greek letter sigma (σ) is often used to denote standard deviation.

Mean-variance analysis

To resume, then, we can say that standard deviation is an estimate of the probable divergence of an actual return from an expected return. It measures the degree of uncertainty. Expected return and standard deviation or variance as parameters for economic and financial decision making are often referred to as the mean-variance criterion. Combined with two entirely plausible assumptions about investor preferences, mean variance analysis is a powerful tool in modern economic and financial theory. The first assumption is that investors prefer more return to less return. The second assumption is that they prefer less risk to more risk. In other words, they are risk averse. The implication is that there is a trade-off between risk and return, such that riskier securities require higher returns than less risky ones. Thus, if another investment offered an expected return of 10% but had a standard deviation of 4%, this investment would be preferred to the investment described above. If it offered an expected return of 11% but had the same standard deviation, it would also be preferred. If it had a higher standard deviation and a higher expected return, the two investments could be compared by dividing the standard deviation of each investment by its expected return to calculate the **coefficient of variation**. The investment with the lowest coefficient of variation would be preferred.

Diversification and risk

Diversification is another important factor in measuring risk. Diversification means reducing risk by not putting all your eggs in one basket. In business and finance it means reducing risk by not putting all your wealth into one asset, client, or transaction. In modern portfolio theory it can be shown that by spreading wealth over a variety of assets selected on the basis of their expected returns and the correlations between the individual expected returns, portfolio risk can be reduced for a given level of expected return or, conversely, expected portfolio return can be increased for a given level of risk. The principle of diversification, then, extends the criterion of mean-variance analysis to include the concepts of **correlation** and **covariance**.

The covariance between two variables is the arithmetic average of the products of deviations around each variable's arithmetic average. The covariance between two random variables is related to the correlation between them. In fact, covariance is equal to the **correlation coefficient** multiplied by the standard deviation of each of the two variables. The correlation coefficient can take values between + 1.0 and -1.0. A correlation coefficient of + 1.0 means that the two variables are perfectly synchronized in their movements, while a correlation coefficient of -1.0 means that the variables move in opposite directions. The correlation coefficient can be calculated by dividing the covariance by the product of the standard deviations of each variable. Generally speaking, as more and more uncorrelated assets are added to a portfolio, the portfolio coefficient of variation, the ratio of portfolio risk to portfolio return, should fall. Given the importance of the diversification principle in modern financial theory and practice, it is a good idea to see exactly how it works.

Take a portfolio of n assets. The expected return on a portfolio of n assets is equal to the sum of the expected returns of each asset weighted by the percent of the portfolio invested in the asset:

$$E(R_p) = \sum_1^n x_i E(R_i) \tag{2.1}$$

where
x_i = percent of funds invested in asset i
R_{ij} = jth return on asset i
R_p = return on the portfolio
E = expectation operator
σ_i^2 = variance of returns on asset i
σ_{ik} = covariance of returns between assets i and k.

The variance of the portfolio can be calculated as follows:

$$
\begin{aligned}
\sigma_p^2 &= E[R_p - E(R_p)]^2 \\
&= E[x_1 R_{1j} + x_2 R_{2j} + \ldots + x_n R_{nj} - x_1 E(R_1) - x_2 E(R_2) - \ldots - x_n E(R_n)]^2 \\
&= \sum_1^n x_i^2 \sigma_i^2 + \sum_{\substack{i=1 \\ i \neq k}}^n \sum_{k=1}^n x_i x_k \sigma_{i,k}
\end{aligned}
\tag{2.2}
$$

Equation 2.2 shows that the variance of a portfolio can be divided into two parts. The first part is the sum of the variances of the individual assets weighted by the square of the weight of each asset in the portfolio. The second part is the sum of the covariances of all the pairs of assets weighted by the product of the weights of both assets in the portfolio.

Suppose that the same amount is invested in each asset. Since there are n assets, $1/n$ will be invested in each one so that equation 2.2 becomes:

$$\sigma_p^2 = \sum_{1}^{n} \frac{1}{n^2} \sigma_i^2 + \sum_{\substack{i=1 \\ i \neq k}}^{n} \sum_{k=1}^{n} \frac{1}{n^2} \sigma_{i,k} \tag{2.3}$$

The single summation has n terms and the double summation has $n(n\text{-}1)$ terms. If we factor $1/n$ from the single summation and $(n\text{-}1)/n$ from the double summation, what remain in the summations are averages. The single summation is the average of the variance terms of all the individual assets and the double summation is the average of all the covariance terms:

$$\sigma_p^2 = \frac{1}{n}\sum_{1}^{n} \frac{1}{n} \sigma_i^2 + \frac{n-1}{n} \sum_{\substack{i=1 \\ i \neq k}}^{n} \sum_{k=1}^{n} \frac{1}{n(n-1)} \sigma_{i,k} \tag{2.4}$$

Hence, as n tends to infinity (as more and more assets are added to the portfolio), $1/n$ tends to zero and the contribution of the variance of the individual assets to the variance of the portfolio tends to zero. In other words, this type of risk can be eliminated through diversification and is referred to as **diversifiable** or **unsystematic** risk. Since it can be diversified away, unsystematic risk is not priced in the market. However, as n tends to infinity, $(n\text{-}1)/n$ tends to one and the variance of the portfolio tends to the average of the covariance terms. This type of risk, referred to as **undiversifiable** or **systematic** risk, cannot be eliminated by diversification and is therefore priced by the market. The lower the covariance terms, the lower the variance of the portfolio. This means that in the context of a portfolio, the riskiness of the individual assets is less important than the correlation of its returns with the returns of the other assets. Individually risky assets with low correlation may be better additions to a portfolio than less risky assets with higher correlation.

The Markowitz optimization of the diversification principle suggests that the risk averse investor can diversify over a security universe by selecting those securities which provide portfolios with maximum expected return for a given level of risk, or minimum risk for a given level of expected return.[2] The family of portfolios having the greatest expected return for a given level of risk forms the curve of the **efficient frontier**. Depending on his risk/return trade-off, the investor can select his desired portfolio from this group. The shaded portion of Figure 2.1 represents all the feasible portfolios of risky assets and the concave envelope represents the efficient frontier. Portfolios M and A, for example, have the same risk measured at σ_1 on the x-axis. However, portfolio M, which is on the efficient frontier, has a higher return measured at R_M on the y-axis than portfolio A, whose return is only R_A.

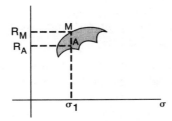

Figure 2.1 The efficient frontier.

The capital asset pricing model

Equilibrium pricing of individual assets draws on the diversification principle and mean-variance Markowitz optimization presented above to develop the capital asset pricing model (CAPM). The CAPM is one of the most important developments in modern finance over the last 50 years and is widely used by both practitioners and academics in the pursuit of effective risk management. In this book we will make extensive use of the CAPM and, therefore, it is useful to review it briefly in order to have a clear idea of the issues involved. The treatment here, of course, is limited to a refresher review of the model's major elements. Anyone interested in a more rigorous derivation of the model and the issues involved can consult any standard financial textbook.

The capital asset pricing model is the first well-known and widely used model of market equilibrium. Its objective is to project a simplified view of the world that captures all the most important aspects of reality. The simplification is necessary because the real world is too complex to analyse down to its last detail. The complexities of the real world are simplified in the CAPM by making certain restrictive assumptions. These assumptions can be summarized as follows:

- Investors are concerned only with risk and return. They prefer higher expected returns and lower risk.
- Every investor has the same information which he analyses and processes in the same way, which means that everyone agrees about future prospects for securities.
- An individual investor cannot affect the price of a stock by his buying and selling.
- All assets, including human capital, are marketable.
- There are no transactions costs or taxes.
- There exists a riskless rate of interest and investors can borrow or lend any amount of funds at this rate.

The introduction of a 'riskless' asset into the family of portfolio possibilities greatly simplifies the problem of optimal portfolio selection. By definition, the portfolio composed only of the riskless asset has a standard deviation of zero. In Figure 2.2 we represent the return on the riskless asset by R_F on the y-axis. Line R_FMZ represents all the combinations of the riskless asset with portfolio M, the portfolio attained where the line R_FZ is tangent to the efficient frontier. This line is called the **capital market line** and portfolio M is called the **market portfolio**. Any portfolio of risky assets other than M would yield lower returns for a given level of risk than portfolios on the capital market line. For example, portfolio C on the efficient frontier has the same risk as portfolio B on the capital market line, but its return is lower. Therefore, all investors who believed they faced the efficient frontier and the riskless lending and

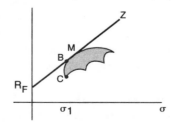

Figure 2.2 The capital market line.

borrowing rate shown in Figure 2.2 would hold the same portfolio of risky assets, portfolio M. The more risk averse would combine the riskless asset with portfolio M and find themselves somewhere between R_F and M on the capital market line. The less risk averse would borrow and invest the funds in M and find themselves between M and Z on the capital market line. The ability to determine the optimum portfolio without having to know anything about the investor except that he is risk averse is known as the **separation theorem**. From here it is just a short step to equilibrium pricing of individual securities.

The expected return on the market portfolio can be written as:

$$E(R_M) = R_F + [E(R_M) - R_F] \tag{2.5}$$

where $[E(R_M) - R_F]$ is the market premium for risk. It can be shown that in equilibrium the required rate of return on a given asset is a linear function of the market premium for risk:[3]

$$E(R_i) = R_F + \beta_i[E(R_M) - R_F] \tag{2.6}$$

where β is the covariance of the returns on asset i with the returns on the market portfolio divided by the variance of the returns on the market portfolio:

$$\beta_i = \frac{\sigma_{iM}}{\sigma_M^2}$$

Equation 2.6 is called the **security market line** (SML). β measures the risk that each asset or portfolio of assets contributes to the market as a whole. This is the systematic risk that cannot be eliminated through diversification. The implications of the CAPM for returns on individual securities or portfolios of securities is illustrated in Figure 2.3. The figure shows expected return on the y-axis and the degree of systematic risk, β, on the x-axis. The security market line maps the expected rate of return that is required for taking different amounts of systematic risk. For example, a security with no systematic risk ($\beta = 0$) will only offer the riskless rate of return. A security with the same systematic risk as the market portfolio has a beta of one and offers the same return as the market portfolio. A security with an expected return above the security market line, like security A, will be recognized by investors as a bargain. Demand for security A will rise, causing its price to rise and its expected return to fall until it reaches equilibrium on the SML. A

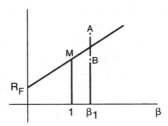

Figure 2.3 The security market line.

security with an expected return below the security market line, like *B*, will be recognized by investors as a loser. Investors will sell the security, causing its price to fall and its expected return to rise until it reaches equilibrium on the SML.

The conclusions of the CAPM are that in equilibrium all investors should hold the same portfolio of risky assets and that each individual asset or portfolio of assets will offer an expected rate of return equal to the risk-free interest rate plus a risk premium that is linearly related to the risk that the asset or portfolio of assets contributes to the market as a whole.

Although there are some well-known problems with the CAPM, it can be a valuable tool when assessing the risks associated with international transactions. In Chapter 5 we take up the CAPM in more detail, discuss some of the problems that it poses generally and at the international level in particular, and show how it can be applied to the assessment of country-specific risk. In Chapter 9 we relate the CAPM to options pricing theory and show how the two can be combined to estimate appropriate discount rates for cross-border direct investment projects.

Further comments on risk

The discussion of risk does not necessarily end with mean-variance. For example, other measures of dispersion could be used instead of variance and standard deviation. Some of the most common are the **range**, the **semi-interquartile range**, the **mean deviation** and **semi-variance**. The range is the difference between the largest and smallest values of a distribution. The semi-interquartile range is one half of the difference between the value of the outcome greater than 75% of the observations and the value of the outcome greater than 25% of the observations. The mean deviation is the average of the absolute value of the difference between each observation and the mean, the mode or the median. Semi-variance measures the average of the squares of the deviations of unfavourable outcomes.

The problem with these measures of dispersion is that they are either imprecise or unsuited to algebraic calculations. The range, for example, considers only the extreme values of the sample and has nothing to say about the other values. The semi-interquartile range considers only the two values that cut off the upper and lower 25% of the sample. The mean deviation does not have the imprecision drawback but, since it deals with absolute values, it is inconvenient for algebraic calculation. Semi-variance does not have the imprecision drawback either. It is also particularly interesting because it measures the average of the squares of deviations of unfavourable outcomes only. This fits well with the general definition of risk, but it is difficult to handle in the context of a portfolio. Furthermore, the empirical evidence shows that most distributions in economics and finance are fairly symmetrical, thereby making semi-variance proportional to variance. Consequently, most of the economics and finance literature uses variance or standard deviation as the measure of dispersion.

When a distribution is not symmetric about a maximum, but instead has one of its 'tails' longer than the other, measures describing this assymetry are called coefficients of **skewness**. **Kurtosis**, on the other hand, measures the degree of peakedness of a distribution. Because of the importance of the normal distribution in financial theory, a sample's skewness and kurtosis, which can be measured as the third and fourth central moments of a distribution, are often calculated to determine whether the distribution actually is normal. There is an ongoing debate about whether or not most economic and financial variables are normally distributed and, if they are not, what the consequences are for the current state of the art in financial theory and practice. Of course, this is not a problem that we will take up in this book. In fact, most of our analysis relies heavily on the mainstream of accepted financial theory using mean-variance and the normal or log-normal distributions. When possible, we do, however, make some interesting applications that do not rely on these assumptions and that can be extremely useful for successful risk management.

COUNTRY-SPECIFIC RISK: ECONOMIC, FINANCIAL AND CURRENCY

Country-specific risk refers to the volatility of returns on international business transactions caused by events associated with a particular country, as opposed to events associated with a particular economic or financial agent. The definition is clear and broad enough to include most of the other terms that have been used at one time or another to designate one facet or another of international risk-taking. The concept of **country risk**, for example, evolved in the 1960s and 1970s in response to the banking sector's efforts to define and measure its exposure to loss in cross-border lending. As a term, it has been shrouded in conceptual confusion from the beginning, often referring indiscriminately to transfer risk, sovereign risk, political risk, economic risk, financial risk, or any other type of risk that could conceivably affect the ability or willingness of an economy or government to honour its financial obligations. In fact, the confusion existed because it was unclear what exactly was supposed to be measured.

At one time, before the advent of widespread international lending, country risk was synonymous with **transfer risk**, the risk that a government might impose restrictions on debt service payments abroad. When governments themselves became major bank borrowers, the concept of **sovereign risk** appeared on the scene. Sovereign risk is broader than transfer risk, insofar as it includes the idea that even if the government is willing to honour its external obligations, it might not be able to do so if the overall economy cannot generate the necessary foreign exchange. Taking a page from the multinational corporations, which had a long history of direct cross-border investment, some analysts began referring to sovereign risk as political risk. This is a term used by industrial firms to describe adverse events outside their particular market sector. The events can be traced to macroeconomic, social, political or strategic factors.

The death knell for the heyday of 'country risk analysis' sounded with Mexico's financial default in 1982 followed by the other 'crisis countries' that left the banks' balance sheets in a shambles. The fact that the analysts had failed so generally and so completely for so long in their mission was certainly a contributing factor to the demise of the traditional country risk analysis. A more important factor, however, was the globalization of financial markets and the growth of portfolio investment that brought in its wake the widespread application of the powerful tools of modern portfolio theory. It became clear that much of what the country risk analysts had concentrated on was unsystematic risk that could be diversified away, and much of the rest was unsuitable in its content or presentation for portfolio building. Emphasis shifted to diversification and hedging techniques, including formal model building and increasingly sophisticated statistical analysis.

With this in mind, we will use the term country-specific risk and present it in a framework that makes analysis compatible with portfolio-building, hedging operations, and sophisticated statistical treatment. This involves breaking it down into four major components: **economic risk, financial risk, currency risk** and **political risk.** The economic, financial and currency components are market-based and correspond to well-known concepts in modern economic and financial theory. Political risk is broader and refers to the possibility or probability that decisions that are unfavourable to the firm's interests will be taken at the political level. Besides the methods of traditional political and country risk analysis, risk of this type lends itself to analysis with the tools borrowed from the new theory of the firm where agency costs, signalling, and stakeholding, rather than market forces, play the major roles. Although we distinguish between four types of risk, it is important to keep in mind that they are interactive. Political decisions will have consequences for the economic, currency and financial situation, just as the economic, currency and financial situation will have consequences on the political climate as well as on each other.

Country economic risk

Country economic risk measured as the volatility of real GDP or GNP
Country economic risk is analogous to business or operating risk in corporate finance. It refers to the volatility of macroeconomic performance, which is often measured by real gross national product (GNP) or real gross domestic product (GDP). It is an important element in international business risk because a country's macroeconomic environment plays a fundamental role in determining the outcome of individual business transactions undertaken within its borders. Generally speaking, a volatile macroeconomic environment is likely to generate volatility in the profits of resident firms and financial institutions, thereby increasing their riskiness. In Figure 2.4 the heavy line shows the long-term trend of real GDP. It represents the path that real GDP would take if all the factors of production were fully employed. Full employment real GDP depends on the economy's infrastructure and natural and human resources, its capital stock and financial system. The evolution of these elements determines the full employment path.

The thin line represents cyclical variations around the long-term trend

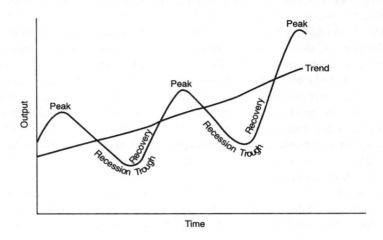

Figure 2.4 Long-term trend of real GDP.

and is called the **business** or **trade cycle**. This more or less regular pattern of
expansion and contraction of real GDP reflects one measure of country
economic risk. Generally speaking, the business cycle is associated with
forces set in motion by the normal process of investment and disinvestment.[4] It can also be aggravated by monetary phenomena.[5] For a particular
country, it depends on the economy's structure and management as well as
on the range and volume of its output that is competitive internationally.
The range and volume of internationally competitive output is especially
important. Because of the diversification principle, other things being equal,
an economy with a wide range of internationally competitive products will
be less volatile than an economy with a narrow range.

Postwar Argentina is a good example of the major issues involved in
country-specific economic risk. Argentina is a developing country with
many characteristics of a developed country. It has no really developed pre-
capitalistic subsistence sector and illiteracy is low. It is well-endowed with
fertile land and natural resources, has a qualified labour force and its
economic infrastructure is relatively well-developed. At one time Argentina
even had the fifth highest per capita income in the world. However, since the
end of the Second World War, Argentina has stumbled from one economic
crisis to another and is now solidly entrenched as a less developed country
(LDC). Argentina's problem, as numerous studies have pointed out, is the

'structural conflict' that faces wage earners, the industrial sector and the agricultural sector.[6] In this scenario, only the agricultural sector produces competitively at the international level. However, investment and technical innovation in this sector are discouraged by the economy's internal organization, which is maintained by tariffs, subsidies, taxes, rationed bank credit, and other controls. Consequently, output stagnates or lags far behind what could potentially be achieved. The industrial sector, built and maintained on the principle of import substitution, is non-competitive and most of its output is sold domestically. Because of the incoherent tariff structure, most of what it does export costs more foreign exchange value to produce than it is worth. Thus Argentina's long-term growth trend has been disappointing.

But whereas Argentina's long-term growth trend has been relatively flat, its business cycle has been characterized by sharp fluctuations. Besides the aforementioned structural conflict and big-time economic mismanagement, a major reason for this is the relatively undiversified nature of its internationally competitive output. Furthermore, one of its principal internationally competitive products, beef, has an inherently volatile cycle of investment and disinvestment.

The principal input in beef production is the animal itself. Hence, an increase in beef output requires an investment in larger herds. The result is a tendency toward a super cobweb effect called the **beef cycle**. When prices are favourable, producers invest by holding back output and increasing their herds. This causes prices to rise further. After a couple of years when herds have been increased, producers bring their cattle to market. The increased supply causes prices to fall. When prices have fallen under a certain level, production is no longer profitable. Producers begin to disinvest by liquidating their herds and converting their land to crops. This causes prices to fall further. When herds have been reduced, output falls, prices begin to rise, and a new cycle begins.

The final contributor to Argentina's economic volatility has been its monetary policy. A lax monetary policy, used as a means to cushion or offset the painful effects of current cyclical swings, ended up by intensifying the amplitude of later ones through galloping inflation and currency depreciation.

The upshot of all this is that economic agents operating within the country have experienced wide swings in income and profitability in domestic currency. For foreign investors the situation has been aggravated by the sharp loss in the value of the Argentine currency on the foreign exchange market.

Country economic risk measured as the volatility of the macroeconomic rate of return

The volatility of real GDP is a pretty crude tool for measuring country economic risk. First of all, GDP (and GNP) are composed entirely of flow data gross of costs. Flow data gross of costs are incomplete as measures of economic performance because they give no information on the economy's overall outstanding assets and liabilities or the contribution of the flow data to the evolution of assets and liabilities. Basing an analysis on such limited information is roughly equivalent to assessing the economic and financial health of a firm based only on the firm's turnover, without regard to operating costs or how the turnover is financed. A balance sheet linking the macroeconomic flows net of costs over time is necessary to complete the analysis. This implies a system of accounting discipline where consequences on the various categories of assets and liabilities are explicit. It also implies that concepts such as profits and costs be defined appropriately. Profits reported in the national accounts are generally useless where cross-border risk is concerned because they only reflect the criteria for income distribution as defined within the geographic area of the country itself. The international criteria for income distribution may be far different. Relative price discrepancies between countries can further mask international economic reality.

A more relevant measure of country economic risk, and one that corresponds to business risk in the financial literature, is the volatility of macroeconomic profits before interest and dividends paid abroad, with macroeconomic profits defined in terms of international criteria for income distribution and estimated in foreign exchange value.[7] The causes for country economic risk defined this way are the same as those that cause variations in real GDP or GNP, that is, the process of investment and disinvestment, monetary phenomena, the economy's structure and management as well as the range and volume of internationally competitive output. The difference is that when estimating macroeconomic profits in foreign exchange value based on international criteria for income distribution, investment and disinvestment do not have the same definition. In the real GDP-GNP format, investment and disinvestment do not include capital gains and losses. In the macroeconomic profit format, they do. The methodology for calculating these capital gains and losses will be the subject of Chapter 5.

Country financial risk

Country financial risk is analogous to financial risk in corporate finance. In corporate finance, financial risk refers to the firm's ability to meet its financial obligations of interest and principal. Interest payments are determined by the extent to which the assets of the firm are financed with debt, while principal payments depend on the debt's amortization schedule. Country financial risk refers to the ability of the national economy to generate enough foreign exchange to meet payments of interest and principal on its foreign debt. As in the corporate case, the ability to meet payments of interest and principal on foreign debt depends on the extent to which the country's assets are financed with foreign loans, and the amortization schedules of foreign loans.

The link between macroeconomic financial risk and GNP is explicit. No country possesses the range of consumer goods, investment goods, raw materials, and technological know-how necessary to attain economic self-sufficiency. Some level of imports is required to assure acceptable levels of output and consumption. Imports can only be obtained by exporting or by foreign borrowing. Foreign borrowing, however, is nothing more than a temporary solution since what is borrowed must eventually be paid back with interest. Therefore, in the long run, exports are the only means of acquiring the necessary imports. They must also be large enough to pay interest and principal on the outstanding foreign debt. If they are not, the foreign exchange will not be available to meet payments on the debt service. Even profitable companies in domestic currency will be unable to honour their foreign obligations if the required foreign exchange is unavailable. The more volatile the country's economic performance, that is, the higher its economic risk, the more likely it is that in any given year the economy will be unable to generate the foreign exchange necessary to meet foreign interest and principal payments.

Macroeconomic financial risk is usually identified with cross-border bank lending. During the 1970s, banks monopolized the field of macroeconomic financial risk analysis as a sub-category of their more general but unfocused pursuit of overall country risk analysis. Through a series of specific ratios such as debt service/exports, total external debt/GDP, etc., interest centred on countrys' long-term solvency and short-term liquidity, and default risk became the key to assessing countrys' creditworthiness. Since then, however, it has become clear that macroeconomic financial risk affects more than just cross-border bank loans. In fact, it is relevant to any non-resident holding claims or doing business in a country. Without the required foreign exchange, all types of foreign claims are in danger of being paid late or not at all.

The debt crisis of the developing countries in the 1980s is a vivid example of the consequences of macroeconomic financial risk. Because of over-borrowing and unproductive use of the resources that were borrowed, the crisis countries were unable to generate the exports necessary to service their foreign debt and maintain the levels of imports required for GNP growth. Consequently, GNP stagnated or declined. The lack of foreign exchange made it impossible for even the government and profitable companies to meet their foreign liabilities. The resulting defaults and reschedulings devastated the lending banks' balance sheets.

To summarize, then, we can say that country financial risk depends on three parameters: the total amount of a country's external debt, its maturity structure, and the country's economic risk. The amount of debt determines the size of the interest payments. The maturity structure determines the size and timing of principal payments and a country's economic risk determines the probability of default due to fluctuations in the country's overall economic performance.

Currency risk

Currency risk is the most ubiquitous and best-known type of country-specific risk. It can be defined as the volatility of the exchange rate. As we will see in Chapter 4, the exchange rate has major consequences on a country's level and composition of output and consumption, as well as on its overall economic well-being. It also has major consequences for non-residents investing in the country or doing business with it. Apparently profitable transactions can suddenly turn sour if the exchange rate moves in the wrong direction. The current system of floating exchange rates that replaced the Bretton Woods fixed rate system has made currency risk an important component of international business risk.

The effect of currency variations on international transactions is straightforward. Consider a sterling-based investor who pays £1 million for 225 million yen worth of Japanese government bonds sold at par and paying 5%. At the end of the year, the investor collects his interest of 11.25 million yen and sells the bonds, whose price is unchanged, for 225 million yen. He now has 236.25 million yen and his return in yen is 5% (11.25/225). If the yen/£ exchange rate has not changed over the period, his return is 5% in sterling as well. However, if, over the year, the value of the pound has fallen from 225 yen for one pound to 200 yen for one pound, the situation is different. When he converts his yen into pounds he will have £1 181 250. This represents a gain in sterling of over 18% (£1 181 250/£1 000 000−1).

Market risk and currency risk

Currency risk goes hand in hand with market risk. Market risk refers to variations in the returns on an investment in host country currency and is especially relevant to portfolio investment. In fact, returns on portfolio investment are often measured in two steps. The first step is an economic analysis of the host country economy and an assessment of the reaction of individual securities or types of securities in host country currency to the economic forecast. The second step involves analysing the behaviour of the exchange rate to determine the return on the investment in the investor's base currency.

Consider, for example, a sterling-based investor who wants to invest £1 in the US stockmarket. He first purchases dollars at the spot rate, which will leave him with

$$\frac{1}{S_0(\pounds/\$)}\$$$

where $S_0(\pounds/\$)$ is the spot exchange rate expressed as the value in pounds sterling of $1 at time 0.

He then uses these dollars to make his investment. The expected dollar value of the investment at the end of the period depends to a certain extent, as we have said, on the economy's overall performance, as well as on the stock's reaction to the economic environment. It will be equal to the initial dollar value of the investment increased by the expected dollar return on the investment over the period. This can be written as

$$\frac{1}{S_0(\pounds/\$)}\$(1 + R_\$^*)$$

where the asterisk denotes expectation and $R_\$^*$ is the expected dollar rate of return on the investment.

Assuming that the investor converts the entire amount into pounds at the end of the period, the expected value of the investment in sterling will be equal to the expected dollar value of the investment at the end of the period multiplied by the expected spot exchange rate at the end of the period:

$$(1 + R_\pounds^*) = \frac{S_1^*(\pounds/\$)}{S_0(\pounds/\$)}(1 + R_\$^*) \tag{2.7}$$

$\frac{S_1^*(\pounds/\$)}{S_0(\pounds/\$)}$ can be written as $(1+\Delta S^*)$ where ΔS^* represents the expected percentage change in the exchange rate. Thus, the expected value of the investment in sterling can be separated into two parts. The first part, $1+\Delta S^*$, depends on the expected evolution of the relative values of the two currencies, and the second part, $1 + R_\$^*$, depends on the expected performance of the investment in dollars:

$$(1 + R_\pounds^*) = (1 + \Delta S^*)(1 + R_\$^*) \tag{2.8}$$

The expected return in the investor's base currency is often presented as the linear approximation of equation 2.8, obtained by ignoring the cross product on the right-hand side $(\Delta S^* \times R_\$^*)$ and subtracting 1 from both sides:

$$R_\pounds^* = \Delta S^* + R_\$^* \tag{2.9}$$

Expressed in this way, base currency returns are clearly divided into their currency and foreign market components. This makes it possible to separate the risk associated with base currency returns into currency risk and market risk. The variance of base currency returns is:

$$E(R_\pounds - R_\pounds^*)^2 = E[(\Delta S - \Delta S^*) + (R_\$ - R_\$^*)]^2 = \sigma_\pounds^2$$
$$= \sigma_{\Delta S}^2 + \sigma_{R_\$}^2 + 2\rho\sigma_{\Delta S}\sigma_{R_\$} \tag{2.10}$$

where ρ is the correlation coefficient between the exchange rate and the return on the dollar investment and E is the expectation operator.

Equation 2.10 shows that the variance of sterling returns on a dollar investment can be divided into currency risk, the variance of the sterling–dollar exchange rate, market risk, the variance of the return on the dollar investment, and the covariance between the exchange rate and the return on the dollar investment. Since ρ, the correlation coefficient, is less than 1, the standard deviation of the return in sterling will be less than the sum of the standard deviations of currency risk and market risk. To illustrate this, we can take an example using the following data:

$$\sigma_S = 0.2$$
$$\sigma_\$ = 0.3$$
$$\rho = 0.5$$

Using equation 2.10 we have:

$$\sigma_£^2 = (0.2)^2 + (0.3)^2 + 2(0.5)(0.2)(0.3) = 0.16$$

and

$$\sigma_£ < \sigma_S + \sigma_\$$$

since

$$\sqrt{0.16} = 0.4 < 0.2 + 0.3$$

Currency risk and country-specific economic risk
The relationship between currency risk and country-specific economic risk is clear from the foregoing example. The return on the investment in dollars, the local currency, depends to a large extent on US macroeconomic performance over the period. However, insofar as the exchange rate is also a function of US macroeconomic performance over the period, the effect of currency fluctuations on the investment outcome in base currency depends on the correlation between domestic currency investment outcomes and currency movements. Understanding the underlying forces that determine exchange rates and why they are likely to vary is a fundamental and indispensable requirement for judicious international financial decision making that we will discuss in Chapter 4.

POLITICAL RISK

The concept of political risk has been widely analysed. In 1971, S. Robock was one of the first to address it[8] By 1979, the eve of the debt crisis, the literature was extensive.[9] More recently, in light of the debt crisis, T. Brewer has explored new directions for research, while D. Roddock has undertaken an investigation at the corporate level.[10] In spite of the widespread coverage of the subject, however, political risk has not received a clear-cut definition. For Robock and Simmonds, for instance, 'political risk in international investment exists when discontinuities occur in the business environment, when they are difficult to anticipate, and when they result from political change'.[11] F. Root makes a distinction between transfer risks (potential restrictions on transfer of funds, products, technology and people), operational risks (uncertainty about policies, regulations, governmental administrative procedures which would hinder results and management of operations in the foreign country) and, finally, risks on control of capital (discrimination against foreign firms, expropriation, forced local shareholding, etc.).[12] In fact, as we mentioned above, there is no general agreement on exactly what political risk assessment is supposed to measure.

To throw some light on the problem, it is interesting to look at some of the distinctions that are made. A first distinction is usually made between global political risk, which is related to a firm with several foreign subsidiaries, and specific political risk, which is inherent to one particular investment in a given country. A second distinction opposes macro-risk to micro-risk. Macro-risk is sometimes called country risk and includes all events or measures likely to affect foreign investment in general. These are often divided into 'soft' and 'hard' measures. For instance, blacklisting, ecologist protest movements, strikes in a particular industry or the incorporation of a competing firm by the public authorities can be considered as soft political risk. On the other hand, expropriations or nationalizations would be considered hard political risk. Micro-risk concerns a particular firm in a given country. It depends on factors such as the nationality of the foreign firm, its previous history in the country, its sector of activity, etc. Some authors make a further distinction between political risk and country risk, where country risk refers to loans made by commercial banks to developing countries and political risk refers to direct foreign investments.

Although the foregoing distinctions are often useful for analysing a particular problem, they can confuse the subject when a more general discussion is in order. Consequently, in this book, we adopt the definition of political risk as 'the probability of politically motivated change that affects the outcome of foreign-based transactions'. In this sense, some effects will be direct and explicit, such as expropriations, nationalizations, and strikes. Others, such as taxes and monetary policy, will be indirect, manifesting themselves in macroeconomic performance, foreign debt levels and currency fluctuations.

Sources of political risk

From the foregoing definition, it is clear that political risk covers a wide field. Some authors like to distinguish between political events such as war, revolution, riots, strikes, etc., and political decisions in the form of laws or decrees. Political events can be sudden and unpredictable and, therefore, difficult to forecast, whereas political decisions that alter the business environment are often more gradual and easier to assess. Two kinds of definition can be given to political decisions of this type. The first reduces them to measures taken by the public authorities. The second broadens the definition to include the activities of various groups such as pressure groups, political parties, lobbies and revolutionaries.[13]

The motivating factors behind political risk are also diverse. Ideology, for example, is a major motivation. It generated the Soviet expropriation of foreign investors, to turn Russia and its captive countries into planned economies and was a major source of world conflict during the years of the Cold War. Another series of nationalizations came from sociological causes as newly independent countries sought to assert their sovereignty over local resources by expropriating foreign investors. Similarly, sociological considerations are behind the ethnic and religious strife that deteriorate the overall economic atmosphere and can culminate in the destruction of human and material assets. Rwanda, Bosnia, South Africa and Northern Ireland are some of the most prominent examples in the news today. The psychology of political leaders is another major factor in risk-generating political decisions. Saddam Hussein's invasion of Kuwait and Ayatollah Khomeini's xenophobic economic policy are two notorious recent examples. Finally, economic constraints can explain many of the political strains on foreign firms. Lack of hard currencies will cause restrictions on remittances abroad; recession can lead to conservative policies concerning transfer of

Table 2.1 Classification of factors generating political risk (by decreasing order of importance)

1. Political instability
2. Nationalistic ideology of political leaders
3. Low level of economic development
4. The investment sector
5. Social unrest
6. Nationality of the parent company

(Source: Marois, B. (1982) *French firms and political risk abroad*, HEC Working Paper no. 197.)

funds, recruitment of foreigners, production standards, taxation and price controls.

Table 2.1 lists the six major factors causing political risk as perceived by French firms in 1982. They range from general political stability to the particular nationality of the parent company and illustrate just how broad the concept of political risk really is.

The effects of political risk: direct investment

To summarize the foregoing discussion, we can put the measures and events affecting foreign operations into three general categories: **hard political risk, administrative** or **soft political risk and social risk**. As we mentioned, the first group includes expropriation, confiscation, nationalization, forced local shareholding etc., the second group covers decisions such as control of prices, foreign exchange, remittances etc. and, finally, social risk encompasses strikes, lack of an experienced labour force, war, ethnic strife, etc. Using the distinction between social risk and hard and soft political risk, we can rate the risk according to two factors: the degree of visibility and the degree of violence. In Figure 2.5 the degree of visibility is plotted on the Y-axis and the degree of violence is on the X-axis. The worst events in terms of visibility and violence are associated with social risk and lead to the loss of the assets, kidnapping, etc. The least onerous events are associated with soft measures that focus on hindering the normal functioning of the foreign agent.

The usual effects of soft measures are to reduce profitability. For example, taxes and price controls reduce net income; capital controls delay cash flows, thereby reducing the project's internal rate of return; indigenization of management increases training costs and often reduces efficiency. The effects of hard measures can often include the partial or total loss of the foreign operation. The post-Second World War years were particularly noted for this. In Iran in the 1950s, Mossadegh nationalized the multinational petroleum companies. The North African and Middle Eastern countries followed suit in the 1960s and early 70s. Chile's Allende carried out numerous expropriations in 1972. Between 1956 and 1972, foreign investments were nationalized or expropriated by at least 40 LDC governments to the tune of 25% of the outstanding stock of foreign-owned capital invested in LDCs at the end of 1972.[14] As we can see in Table 2.2, radical change does, however, seem to be taking place. Between 1970 and 1975, 336 acts of expropriation have been identified, versus 87 between 1976 and 1979, 15 from 1980 to 1985, and only one between 1986 and 1992.[15] As for geographic trends, Africa was the area with the highest number of nationalizations in the 1960s and 1970s,

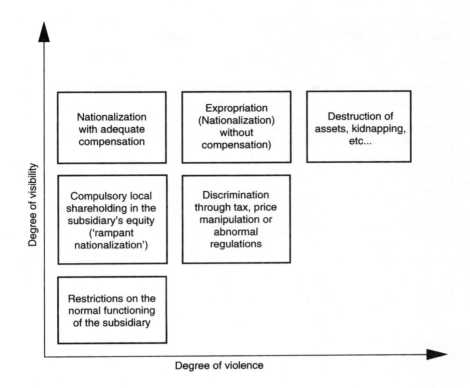

Figure 2.5 The effects of political risk.

whereas Latin America and Asia were more active in the 1980s. The most popular sectors for expropriation were agriculture and the oil industry. According to Kobrin, the main reasons for the decline in mass nationalizations seem to have been the growing capacity of new independent states to manage their economy, the highly desirable investment flows at a time of reduced supply of bank credit, the attractiveness of privatizations, and the initiatives of the international organizations such as the IMF and the World Bank to protect private investors.

In a study of French firms in the early 1980s, it was noted that the average value of the subsidiary nationalized was approximately 46 million francs, representing an average of 8% of the consolidated balance sheet of the firms in question but varying between 1% and 60%.[16] The average time of the nationalization was about 10 months, varying between one month in the Algerian expropriations and 36 months in the rampant nationalizations in Morocco. The financial arrangements in the nationalizations also varied a

Table 2.2 Expropriation acts by year

Year	Number of acts	Percentage of total	Number of countries expropriating
1960	6	1.0	5
1961	8	1.4	5
1962	8	1.4	5
1963	11	1.9	7
1964	22	3.8	10
1965	14	2.4	11
1968	5	0.9	3
1967	25	4.3	8
1968	13	2.3	8
1969	24	4.2	14
1970	48	8.3	18
1971	51	8.9	20
1972	56	9.7	30
1973	30	5.2	20
1974	68	11.8	29
1975	83	14.4	28
1976	40	6.9	14
1977	15	2.6	13
1978	15	2.6	8
1979	17	2.9	13
1980	5	0.9	5
1981	4	0.7	2
1982	1	0.2	1
1983	3	0.5	3
1984	1	0.2	1
1985	1	0.2	1
1986	1	0.2	1
1987	0	0.0	0
1988	0	0.0	0
1989	0	0.0	0
1990	0	0.0	0
1991	0	0.0	0
1992	0	0.0	0
	575*	99.8**	

* date is missing for four acts
** error due to rounding

Source: Minor, M. (1994) The Demise of Expropriation as an Instrument of LDC Policy, 1980–1992, *Journal of International Business Studies*, **25**(1), 180.)

Table 2.3 Main factors constituting a political risk, according to French firms (by decreasing order of importance)

Ranking	Items
1	Destruction of assets following a war, revolution
2	Expropriation or confiscation
3	Nationalization
4	Breaking of agreement made by local government
5	Requisition
6	Boycott by a group of states (e.g. Arab countries' blacklist)
7	Forced sale
8	Restriction on remittances
9	Forced local shareholding
10	Tax discrimination
11	Discrimination on public procurement
12	Strikes
13	Competition from a state-owned enterprise
14	Loss of profits through abusive price controls
15	Policies pertaining to workforce (visa constraints)
16	Internal boycott (e.g. on food products)
17	Discriminatory manufacturing standards

(Source: Marois, B. (1982) *French Firms and Political Risk Abroad,* HEC Working Paper no. 197.)

great deal. In some cases (Libya and the Central African Republic) the expropriated firms were not fully compensated. In other cases (Morocco), nationalized firms received rapid compensation. The companies nationalized in Algeria had to wait eight years before receiving the balance of indemnities due them by the Algerian government. Table 2.3 gives a rundown on the major effects of political risk as perceived by the French firms in the study.

Besides the consequences on ownership and profits, political risk can also affect the security of physical assets, intellectual property and personnel. In fact, these issues are becoming more important in the assessment of foreign investment risk. Physical and intellectual assets must be protected or insured against damage and destruction. Factories, offices, and cars can be burned, bombed, battered or damaged in many ways. Intellectual property is especially vulnerable to damage and loss. Patent and licence abuses, pirated merchandise, imitations and fakes, not to mention industrial espionage and computer viruses, are some of the most obvious examples that come to mind. Personnel security is perhaps the most difficult problem of all. Kidnapping is a major problem in some countries. Blackmail and extortion are not far behind. Civil disorder, natural disasters and epidemics can also put personnel at risk. Events such as these are difficult, probably impossible, to forecast and their consequences are difficult to estimate in price terms. Nevertheless, when they do happen, their effects are often disastrous for the investment.

Political risk can also have a positive connotation when it relates to incentives to invest. Germany, for instance, has set up some interesting programmes for firms wishing to invest in the Eastern part of the country, where the authorities have sought to attract foreign enterprises in order to make the transition to the market economy easier for the former East Germany *Länder*. Direct subsidies from the federal government can reach 12% of the total investment and financial incentives from the state authorities 23% more, for a total discount of 35%. Air Liquide, the world leader in the gas industry, bought 40% of the existing equipment in this sector in what was formerly East Germany. Besides the direct subsidies of 35% offered by the central government and the state authorities it also took advantage of an income tax deferral and a first year depreciation rate of 50%. As a result, the market share of Air Liquide in reunified Germany rose from 6% to 12% on an annual turnover of 300 million marks in 1991.

Political risk: cross-border loans

As we mentioned above, many analysts make a distinction between political risk and country risk, where political risk is associated with direct investment and country risk is used by bankers to distinguish between foreign and domestic loan risk. Both foreign and domestic loans can suffer default by the borrower, but only the foreign loan can incur a risk of transfer, due either to economic constraints or to political expediency. Following this line of reasoning, country risk is often defined as the probability that economic, political, or social factors within a country will create a situation in which borrowers in that country will be unable to service or repay their debts to foreign lenders in a timely manner. This definition, however, makes it clear that the distinction between political and country risk based on whether direct investments or bank loans are at stake is artificial and confuses the issue. In fact, a more appropriate distinction is the one we have adopted in this book between what we have defined as economic, financial and currency risk. Political risk is common to both types

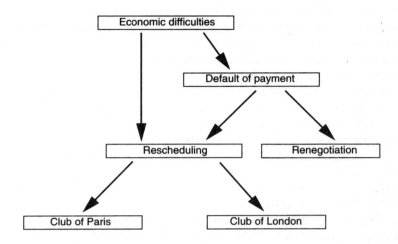

Figure 2.6 The rescheduling process.

of investment. In this context, bank loans are primarily affected by a
country's financial risk represented by the economy's capacity to generate
enough foreign exchange to maintain the required level of imports and
service the external debt, whereas direct investments are affected by
economic and currency risk as well as financial risk. Although the specific
decisions and events affecting each one may differ, both direct investments
and cross-border loans are vulnerable to political considerations.[17]

If a country does default, loans are either rescheduled or renegotiated.
Figure 2.6 outlines this situation. Loans by public authorities or state
agencies are renegotiated in the framework of the Club of Paris where the
borrowing government meets its lenders and tries to arrange for a
rescheduling of its debt. Loans by commercial banks take a different
route. The banks set up a steering committee in charge of negotiating the
rescheduling which takes place in the framework of the Club of London.

Political risk: portfolio investment

Besides the economic, financial, and currency risk associated with cross-border portfolio investment, political risk is also a major consideration. The political authorities typically monitor and regulate the financial markets in their geographical jurisdiction. Thus, they have a major say in who participates in the markets; the types of instruments available to investors; the transactions, settlement and delivery procedures; the brokerage fees, stamp duties and other costs for a foreign investor; and in the taxation and other regulations affecting the foreign investor. Their response to different situations can have a major effect on the outcome of an investment.

Taxes, commissions, and transaction costs are the most obvious example. After the performance of the security itself, tax effects are probably the single most important factor in determining the investor's ultimate rate of return. Commissions and other transaction costs can also significantly affect an investment's rate of return. Politically motivated changes in the tax, commission or transaction cost structure will consequently affect the outcome of a foreign portfolio investment.

Another consideration arises from the structure of share ownership. Share ownership across different categories of investors differs widely from country to country. In Korea, for example, 68% of shares are held by private individuals while in Australia they hold only 4%. Institutional investors dominate the US and Japanese markets, holding 46% and 47% respectively. In the Netherlands 50% of equity is held by foreigners.

Different patterns of shareholdings lead to different political responses to changing market conditions. The recent fall in the Korean market caused widespread protests by individual investors and sparked government attempts to prop up prices. It is said that complicity between the Japanese Ministry of Finance and the financial institutions that own 42% of Japanese equity buoyed stock prices there in the massacre of October 1987. This sort of collusion would be impossible in the US because commercial banks are prohibited by law from participating in their clients' equity. On the other hand, the holding of equity by Japanese banks is a double-edged sword when prices continue to fall in spite of efforts to prop them up. In the early 1990s Japanese banks were finding it difficult to meet minimum BIS capital requirements in the face of a falling stockmarket, thereby causing them to restrain lending to their clients, which further exacerbated the falling stock prices.

At the least, these considerations can have a significant short-term effect on share prices and represent another source of risk that the foreign investor should consider before undertaking an investment. In fact, the structure of the stockmarket may make it more or less susceptible to political manipulation. Other things being equal, the public stockmarkets of France, Belgium, Spain, Italy, Greece and some Latin American countries are more highly regulated and susceptible to political control than the private stock exchanges found in the US, Japan, Canada, Australia, South Africa, and the UK, or the Germanic bankers' exchanges found in Germany, Austria, Switzerland, Scandinavia and the Netherlands. Although subject to some government regulation, the private exchanges are probably the most independent of the three types. Bankers' bourses have the disadvantages associated with the concentration of power in the hands of a narrow interest group.

Government regulations on foreign participation in domestic financial markets can also have an important effect on the cost and returns from cross-border portfolio investment. Many emerging markets, for example, restrict foreign participation in their equity markets to officially approved funds. Consequently, the approved funds often trade at a premium to the value of the securities they own. A change in the regulations can have dramatic effects on the price of the fund. If, for example, the government decides to expand foreign participation by accrediting more funds, the price of existing funds is likely to fall.

Switzerland is the classic case of government restrictions on foreign equity holdings causing substantial price changes. Until 1988, the Swiss equity market was divided into three categories: bearer shares, registered shares and participation certificates. Registered shares, which carried voting and certain other rights, were restricted to Swiss nationals and traded at a considerable discount to the bearer shares available to foreign investors. Since Nestlé's decision in November 1988 to make its registered shares available to foreigners, the distinction between registered and bearer shares has changed considerably and caused a sharp reduction in the price differential between the two types of security.

NOTES

[1] Miller, M.H. (1990) Index arbitrage and volatility, *Financial Analysts Journal*, July–August, 6–7.

[2] Markowitz, H. (1959) *Portfolio Selection: Efficient Diversification of Investments*, John Wiley & Sons, New York.

[3] See, for example, Elton, E.J. and Gruber, M.J. (1984) *Modern Portfolio Theory and Investment Analysis*, 2nd edn, John Wiley & Sons, New York, or any other standard textbook on finance.

[4] See Hayek, F. (1941) *The Pure Theory of Capital*, Routledge and Kegan Paul, London, Hayek, F. (1933) *Monetary Theory and the Trade Cycle* (trans. N. Kaldor and H.M. Croome), Jonathan Cape, London, Hicks, J. (1987) *Capital and Time: A Neo-Austrian Theory*, Clarendon Press, Oxford and Hicks, J. (1950) *A*

Contribution to the Theory of the Trade Cycle, Clarendon Press, Oxford.

5   Hayek, F. (1975) *Prix et Production* (trans. Tradecom), Calmann-Levy, Vienna.

6   Diaz Alejandro, C.F. (1970) *Essays on the Economic History of the Argentine Republic*, Yale University Press, New Haven and London; Leisserson, A. (1966) *Notes on the process of industrialization in Argentina, Chile and Peru*, Institute of International Studies, University of California, Berkeley; Eshag, E. and Thorp, R. (1965) Economic and social consequences of orthodox economic policies in Argentina in the post war years, *Bulletin of the Oxford University Institute of Economics and Statistics*, **27** (1), 44; Smithies, A. (1965) Argentina and Australia 1930–1960, *American Economic Review*, **55** 31; Kelly, R. (1965) Foreign trade of Argentina and Australia 1930–1960, *Economic Bulletin for Latin America*, **X** (2), 188–203; Hayn, R. (1962) Inflacion, formacion de capital, y balance de pagos de la Argentina 1940–1958, *Revista de Economica y Estadistica*, **VI** (2), 21–49.

7   See Clark, E. (1991) *Cross Border Investment Risk: Applications of Modern Portfolio Theory*, Euromoney Publications, London.

8   Robock, S. (1971) Political Risk: Identification and Assessment, *Colombia Journal of World Business*, **6** (4).

9   For an exhaustive review of the subject, see S. Kobrin, S. (1979) Political Risk: A Review and Reconsideration, *Journal of International Business Studies*, **X** (1).

10 Brewer, T. (1986) *Political Risk in International Business: New Directions for Research, Management, and Public Policy*, New York; Roddock, D. (1986) *Assessing Corporate Political Risk*, Rowman and Littlefield Publishers, Totowa, N.Y.

11 Robock, S. and Simmonds, K. (1973) *International Business and Multinational Enterprise*, R. Irwin, Homewood.

12 Root, F. (1973) Analysing Political Risks in International Business, in *Multinational Enterprise in Transition* (eds Kapoor and Grub), Darwin Press, Princeton.

13 For instance, D.W. Zinc describes it this way: 'the State as the main channel through which an enterprise is put under pressure'. See Zinc, D.W. (1973) *The Political Risks for Multinational Enterprise in Developing Countries*, Praeger. Robock and Simmonds (1973), *op. cit.* n. 11 above, adopt the broader definition.

14 Williams, M. (1975) The Extent and Significance of the Nationalization of Foreign Owned Assets in Developing Countries, *Oxford Economic Papers*, **27**, 260.

15 Kobrin, S. (1984) Expropriations as an Attempt to Control Foreign Affiliates, 1960–1979, *International Studies Quarterly*, *3* (September), 329–48; Minor, M. (1994) The Demise of Expropriation as an Instrument of LDC Policy, 1980–1992, *Journal of International Business Studies*, **25** (1), 177–88.

16 Marois, B. (1982) French Firms and Political Risk Abroad, Working Paper n°. 197, Groupe HEC.

17 The evolution of country risk analysis is reflected in the literature. In the 1970s the long-term debt service capacity of a borrower was the main variable in the evaluation process. See, for example: Frank, C. and Cline, W. (1971) Measurement of Debt Servicing Capacity: An Application of Discriminant Analysis, *Journal of International Economics*, (1) 327–44; Feder, G. and Just, R.

(1976) A Study of Debt Service Capacity Applying Logit Analysis, *Journal of Development Economics*, **4**, 25–39. In the 1980s scholars tried to distinguish between solvency, liquidity and default risks. See: Eaton, J., Gersovitz, M. and Stiglitz, J. (1986) The Pure Theory of Country Risk, *European Economic Review*, **30**, 481–513 and Krugman, P. (1985) Internal Debt Strategies in an Uncertain World, in *International Debt and the Developing World*, (eds G. Smith and J. Cuddington), World Bank, Washington, who show that debt default can result from a debtor's cost-benefit analysis. Finally, in the recent past, some authors have tried to introduce political risk in the analysis of country creditworthiness. See: Brewer, T. and Rivoli, P. (1990) Politics and Perceived Country Creditworthiness in International Banking, *Journal of Money, Credit and Banking*, **22** (3), 357–69 and Cosset, J.C. and Roy, J. (1991) The Determinants of Country Risk Rankings, *Journal of International Business Studies*, **22** (1) 135–42.

PART TWO

Assessing International Business Risk

3 POLITICAL RISK ANALYSIS

Political risk has a long history as an important aspect of international business decisions. Nevertheless, as we have already mentioned, there is no real consensus on the exact definition of political risk. In general, most would agree that it concerns the effects of non-economic variables on business transactions that are undertaken abroad. Just exactly what political risk analysis can achieve is also open to question. In contrast to the hard data of economic and financial analysis, the political world is a vast quagmire of nebulous, subjective terrain. This perception has been reinforced by the inability of political risk analysts, ranging from individual consultants to large consulting firms, to deliver on the promises they make when promoting their services. The impression is often given that with the right methodological framework, or the key, well-placed contact, political risk in a given country can be accurately forecast. It can't! The reality is just too complex. What can be achieved, however, is a guide for reducing some of the uncertainty surrounding the foreign political and social developments that can affect foreign business transactions. In this chapter, we address the issue of how and to what extent political risk can be assessed.

METHODS AND TECHNIQUES

Comparative techniques

The aim of the comparative techniques in political risk analysis is to compare all countries, or some subset of them, such as the LDCs, according to an analytical grid based on a set of relevant parameters. Because of the nature and scope of political risk, the set of what is deemed to be the relevant parameters is wide-ranging and often includes elements that are difficult to measure with any precision. The comparison itself can be achieved either through an ordinal rating system or a mapping exercise on a two-axis space.

Rating systems

Quite a few specialized think tanks such as the Business Environment Risk Index (BERI), Business International, and the Economist Intelligence Unit have adopted the rating approach, which proceeds in two stages. First, each country is graded on the parameters selected as judgemental criteria. Second, the resulting data are weighted into a global rating which makes it possible to compare all the countries on the same scale. The success of the operation depends, of course, on the relevance of the judgemental parameters and the weights assigned to each as well as on the accuracy of the grading exercise.

To illustrate this presentation we can describe the method adopted by one of these forecasting firms, Credit Risk International, whose system is summarized in Table 3.1. This system designates four parameters to assess the degree of a country's riskiness:

1. market prospects and flexibility in coping with changes;
2. financial risks;
3. political instability;
4. the business environment.

Various criteria and sub-criteria are selected in determining the score for each parameter. For example, parameter number 4, the business environment, is based on three criteria:

1. the economic management of the country, which counts for 40% of the parameter's value;
2. the foreign investment climate, which counts for 40% of the parameter's value;
3. working conditions, which counts for 20% of the parameter's value.

The foreign investment climate, criterion 11 in Table 3.1, is divided into 11 sub-criteria:

1. market share of foreign direct investment in the local economy (7%);
2. legal restrictions to foreign control of local firms (5%);
3. legal restrictions to capital flows (remittances of dividends) (3%);
4. stability of business law (3%);
5. frequency of intervention of local government in business life (3%);
6. availability and cost of local financing (4%);
7. cost of labour (4%);
8. cost of local transportation (3%);
9. cost of energy (3%);
10. price level of local real estate (3%);

11. degree of modernism of distribution channels (2%).

In all, there are 100 sub-criteria.

Table 3.1 Credit Risk International's rating system

---

*Parameter 1: market prospects and flexibility in coping with changes
 criterion 1: economic size (weight: 30%)
 criterion 2: level of economic development (40%)
 criterion 3: standard of living (30%)

*Parameter 2: financial risks
 criterion 4: financial vulnerability (30%)
 criterion 5: external debt (30%)
 criterion 6: financial rating (40%)

*Parameter 3: political instability
 criterion 7: homogeneity of social fabric (30%)
 criterion 8: government political regime stability (50%)
 criterion 9: foreign relationships (20%)

*Parameter 4: business environment
 criterion 10: management of the economy (40%)
 criterion 11: foreign investments (40%)
 criterion 12: working conditions (20%)

To assess each criterion, Credit Risk International follows the 'Delphi technique'. This methodology involves submitting a series of identical questions to a group of experts. The experts, who remain anonymous to each other, receive continual feedback on the responses of the other members of the group. The goal of the exercise is to reach a group position on a particular issue. In the Credit Risk International process, a group of experts on each country gives its feeling on each sub-criterion, which is then translated into a grade between 1 (worst) and 7 (best). Once each sub-criterion has been assessed, the overall, weighted rating is computed with a maximum of 700 and a minimum of 100. In the 1994–5 ratings, Singapore, for instance, was rated number 1 with a score of 628 points, Morocco 29th with 415 points, and Zaire last with 168 points.

This global rating can be adjusted according to whether the risk is associated with an export transaction, a direct investment, or a loan. Morocco, for example, gets 396 points and the 29th rank from the exporter's point of view, 456 points and the 27th rank when direct foreign investment is considered, and 394 points and the 29th rank as a borrower. Furthermore, these ratings can be translated into risk classes, from class 7 (no risk) to class 1 (danger). Based on this rating, Credit Risk International derives its decision-making rules. For a country belonging to class 3 (high risk), for instance, Credit Risk International suggests a risk premium of 75% of the risk-free rate of interest.[1]

Many other types of rating system are in use which include economic and financial indicators, along with estimates of political risk. For instance, *Euromoney* publishes annual credit ratings assigning a 25% weight to economic data, 25% to political risk, 10% to financial data based on ratio analysis, 10% to default performance, 10% to credit ratings and 5% each to access to bank financing, access to short-term finance, access to capital markets and access to forfaiting.[2] The economic score is compiled from a survey of 35 economists from leading banks, financial and economic institutions. The political risk score is compiled from a poll of risk analysts, risk insurance brokers, and bank credit officers. The financial ratios are taken from the World Bank World Debt Tables and include the debt service to export ratio, the current account balance to GNP ratio and the external debt to GNP ratio. The default performance is measured by the amount of debt rescheduled or in default over the preceding three years. Credit ratings are obtained as the average of sovereign ratings from Moody's and Standard and Poor's. Unrated countries receive a score of zero and countries with only a short-term rating receive a score based on a rating of BBB. Access to bank finance is calculated from disbursements of long-term private non-guaranteed debt as a percentage of GNP. Access to short-term financing is calculated according to which OECD consensus group the country belongs to. Access to capital markets is based on an analysis by *Euromoney* of the international bond and syndicated loan issues since 1989, plus a judgement of current accessibility. Access to forfaiting is scored from a combination of maximum tenor (up to seven years) and the forfaiting spread over the riskless countries.

Institutional Investor also publishes regular country credit ratings based on a semi-annual survey among the major international banks. Bankers are asked to grade a country's creditworthiness from 0 to 100, where 0 represents the lowest level. Other institutions, such as Frost and Sullivan, Inc. and Business Risk Service, also supply some type of country rating.

Institutions such as Moody's and Standard and Poor's produce country ratings but, in contrast to *Euromoney* and the other institutions, their weighting system is not transparent. They tend to rate specific financing instruments like Eurobonds or Euro-commercial paper using a scale going from AAA to C, according to increasing solvency risk.

Insofar as rating systems go, it can be helpful to consider their evolution across time. In Table 3.2 we show *Institutional Investor's* rating for 29 countries between 1979 and 1991. It is interesting to note that only three of the countries had a better credit rating in 1991 than they did in 1979. It is also interesting to note that in 1979 Mexico, the country that introduced us to the debt crisis, had the second best credit rating after Venezuela. Argentina and Brazil, the two countries that defaulted on Mexico's heels were also among the best-rated countries. This indicates how fast ratings and financial positions can change. To capture this effect, we also show the average rating and standard deviation. This procedure adds a new dimension to the use of rating systems by casting the problem in mean-variance space. A high rating with a high standard deviation indicates that the rating is unstable and subject to wide fluctuations. On the other hand, more confidence could be placed in a high rating with a low standard deviation that indicates stability over time.

Other types of indirect ratings also exist. Interest rate risk premiums on Eurobond issues by government agencies calculated as the number of basis points over the benchmark (T-bonds for the dollar, Bunds for the mark) are one of these. The use of this method is relatively limited, however, because only high-quality borrowers can tap the Eurobond market and the basis point premiums on the benchmark are often distorted by the issuing process whereby syndicate managers trade basis points for higher fees. Nevertheless, some market sentiment should still be reflected in this premium.

Mapping systems

The mapping approach is similar to the rating approach insofar as it uses a set of relevant parameters in the process of risk estimation. However, rather than an ordinal ranking of the countries under consideration, the analytical results are mapped on a two-dimensional graph divided into four quadrants separated by two axes. Each axis represents a distinct parameter of risk. For example, one axis might reflect political risk while the other reflects the economic risk. In this case, the first quadrant will contain the countries with

Table 3.2 Mean and standard deviation (in parentheses) of credit ratings published by Institutional Investor, 1979 to 1991[a]

	1979–1991	1979	1986	1991
Global Average	42.73 (5.70)	55.7	40.5	37.9
Countries included in the Study				
1. Algeria	48.99 (8.71)	58.6	50.4	34.2
2. Argentina	32.67 (17.26)	62.4	24.9	20.2
3. Bolivia	13.78 (7.49)	31.6	8.0	15.0
4. Brazil	37.92 (12.54)	64.9	35.2	26.5
5. Cameroon	33.55 (5.04)[b]	35.0[c]	38.4	23.1
6. Chile	37.64 (12.16)	54.9	25.1	41.1
7. Colombia	45.50 (9.93)	60.7	39.2	36.6
8. Costa Rica	22.05 (10.44)	44.7	17.0	22.5
9. Ecuador	31.10 (13.50)	53.2	26.7	19.6
10. Egypt	30.03 (5.92)	33.9	29.5	23.4
11. Greece	52.66 (6.26)	62.6	47.6	47.2
12. India	47.66 (3.60)	54.2	50.7	38.4
13. Indonesia	50.05 (4.57)	53.2	47.6	50.4
14. Ivory Coast	30.98 (9.99)	48.2	27.5	17.2
15. Korea	61.55 (5.52)	71.2	58.4	68.1
16. Malaysia	64.60 (6.76)	70.3	59.9	62.0
17. Mexico	43.89 (17.08)	71.8	30.8	38.7
18. Morocco	29.57 (7.32)	45.5	23.1	28.3
19. Nigeria	32.42 (15.17)	54.1	22.8	19.5
20. Peru	22.86 (11.99)	30.7	14.9	12.2
21. Philippines	30.63 (11.08)	53.7	21.4	24.5
22. Portugal	55.19 (5.04)	52.0	51.8	63.3
23. Sudan	8.43 (3.81)	18.5	7.3	6.1
24. Thailand	55.05 (3.96)	54.7	53.3	62.5
25. Tunisia	42.02 (5.72)	50.0	39.7	37.5
26. Turkey	30.78 (11.43)	14.8	38.6	42.7
27. Uruguay	32.78 (5.64)	41.0	27.8	31.2
28. Venezuela	45.99 (15.07)	72.4	38.1	37.2
29. Yugoslavia	34.87 (10.68)	57.5	31.4	24.5

[a] The range of credit ratings is from 0 to 100, where 100 represents the most creditworthy country
[b] Credit rating for Cameroon starts in year 1982.
[c] The number represents credit rating for year 1982.

(Source: Lee, S.H. (1993) Relative importance of political instability and economic variables on perceived country creditworthiness, *Journal of International Business Studies*, **24**(4), 803.)

both high political and economic risk, while quadrant 3 will contain the countries with both low political and economic risk. Quadrants 2 and 4 will contain the countries with high risk in one category and low risk in the other. In the early analysis done by Business International, the two axes identified risk and market prospects.

The weakness of comparative systems is obvious. First of all, there is no objective theoretical basis for the inclusion or exclusion of the numerous parameters employed in the different rating systems. Secondly, the process for attributing the respective weights given to the various parameters has no indisputable foundation. Different weights might give different results. Third, the same grid is applied to all countries, whatever their regional location or specific characteristics. Moreover, 'extreme' situations (e.g. the Iranian revolution or the Gulf War) cannot be anticipated from comparative approaches. Nevertheless, comparative methods can be useful as a screening process designed to eliminate the countries that are completely unacceptable. It seems that American firms are keener on accepting the comparative techniques than are their European and Japanese counterparts.

Analytical techniques

Whereas comparative approaches encompass all the countries at the same time, the analytical techniques focus on one country at a time. Among these, we have the 'special report' approach, the 'probabilistic' approach, the 'sociological' approach based on dynamic segmentation, and finally the 'expert systems' approach.

Special report approach
The special report approach to political risk analysis is the most descriptive of the analytical approaches. It involves one or several experts that examine the key variables that are supposed to describe a given country's main characteristics and who communicate their findings in the form of a special report. Thus, for each country under study, the report usually contains an analysis of the political, social, and economic outlook that explicitly takes into account the specifics of the local environment. As an example, before the end of apartheid, a French company that specialized in political and economic risk assessment acknowledged eight special features pertaining to the South African Republic, namely:

- the production and export of gold;
- the impact of embargo and its consequences;
- the 'borderline' with Namibia, Angola, etc.;
- the evolution of apartheid, the institutional framework;
- the policies of white minorities;
- the policies of black parties;
- the Zulu factor.

The special reports themselves usually sum up a country's overall strengths and weaknesses and focus on such aspects as the country's political life, the major characteristics of the current regime, the degree of stability of the domestic currency, the tax system, regulations pertaining to foreign investment, the social structure and climate and the country's economic prospects.

The advantages of the special report are its ability to focus on the particularities of each country, its low cost and its immediacy. Its main drawbacks are its subjectivity, lack of scientific analysis and relative partiality. In fact, the quality of any special report basically depends on the capabilities and intuitions of the analyst.

The probabilistic approach

Using the decision tree process, the probabilistic approach is based on computing various alternative outcomes, each one being allocated a certain probability of occurrence and implying specific measures with regard to foreign investment. For example, the outcome of an important election in an

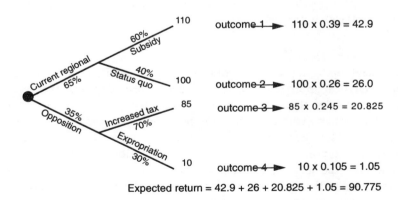

Figure 3.1 The probalistic approach.

African country might be depicted by two scenarios: the current government remains in power or the opposition takes over. Each scenario might have a different probability, such as 65% for the current regime and 35% for the opposition, but the probabilities must sum to 100%. Once the government is

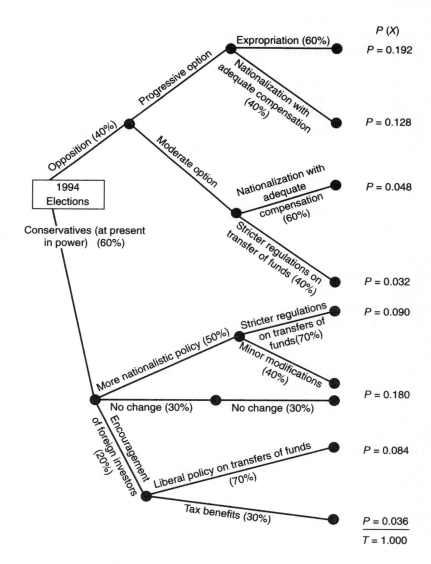

Figure 3.2 The probalistic approach.

elected, it will be faced with several choices. Probabilities are then assigned to the possibility of each choice occurring. For example, if the current government remains in power, its choices might be a subsidy for foreign investment, with a 60% probability, or the status quo, with a 40% probability. If the opposition wins, its choices might be an increased tax on the foreign operation, with a 70% probability, or expropriation, with a 30% probability. The effects of each choice are then calculated. The subsidy might make the investment worth $110, the status quo $100, the increased tax $85 and expropriation $10. All this information is summarized in Figure 3.1, where we can find the value of the investment by multiplying the joint probability by the value of each outcome and summing. In this case investment is worth $90.775.

The same methodology can be applied to more complicated situations, as in Figure 3.2. The obvious difficulty is calculating the different probabilities and estimating the effect that the different measures will have on the outcome of the investment.

The sociological approach
In its most general form, the sociological approach to political risk analysis seeks to identify a set of variables that can be specific to each country as a means of defining the country's 'degree of stability'. The variables can range from the realities of state hegemony and political terrorism, to such concepts as a democratic tradition and the capacity to live in peace. Each country gives rise to a new set of variables and a distinct methodology. The advantage of this approach is its tailor-made nature that makes it possible to individualize the analysis. The disadvantage is that it lacks scientific rigour and is difficult to apply in a comparative context.

One of the oldest and most respected ·techniques of the sociological approach is the 'dynamic segmentation' methodology, known as the ALLY method, which seeks to analyse the fundamental trends of a country that are likely to influence the relationship between the investing company and the political powers.

Dynamic segmentation divides a society into various behaviour-homogeneous groups, called segments. A segment can be socio-economic or ethnic. Power in the society is based on the coalition of a number of these segments, while the segments outside the coalition form the opposition. Over a long period, new segments may appear and others disappear, but most of them continue to exist no matter what coalitions come to power. It is recognized that demographic, economic and social developments in a given country can, in the space of a few years, substantially modify the relative importance of the individual segments. However, certain segments occupy a pivotal position, thereby guaranteeing them a place in all possible power coalitions. It is, therefore, essential to focus information-gathering on the medium-term developments and short-term fluctuations of these pivotal segments.

Some segments have natural or historic ties which make it possible to identify the coalitions of segments that are likely to wield power. From these, the coalition of maximum homogeneity and importance is selected and its future evolution is assessed by answering such questions as whether it will stay in power, or when it will be replaced by another coalition. Based on these forecasts, the investing foreign corporation will attempt to take advantage of the situation by modifying its policy.

As an illustration of the dynamic segmentation methodology we can take the case of Morocco. In step one, a group of qualified experts designates what it feels are the 10 fundamental segments in Moroccan society:

- the palace (the King, his family and his officers);
- the technocracy (trained mostly in Europe);
- the traditional bourgeoisie (the *fassi*), who originate generally from the city of Fez;
- the new bourgeoisie (the *soussis*), which traces its origins to the berber elements of the Souss region in the South;
- the rural 'notables', who are a dispersed elite exercising political leadership over the peasant population;
- the intelligentsia, a small group;
- the urban proletariat, a growing segment due to the country's industrialization;
- the peasants, who, so far, display great fidelity to the throne;
- the army;
- the 'Muslim Brothers', a fundamentalist minority.

In step two, the various segments are mapped as circles of varying sizes on two axes, where the *y*-axis represents political power and the *x*-axis economic power. The size of each circle is proportional to the importance of the given segment. The distance between the circles is determined by indices of affinity between the segments taken two by two. The experts then estimate the affinity indices by analysing how each segment behaves *vis-à-vis* the others. Closer affinity means closer proximity on the graph. From the mapping, different coalitions are ascertained and their strengths and weaknesses are analysed. Figure 3.3, for example, shows three possible outcomes forecast for the year 2000. Coalition 1 is composed of all the segments except the intelligentsia, the proletariat and the Muslim Brothers. It represents a kind of status quo. Coalition 2 includes only the technocrats,

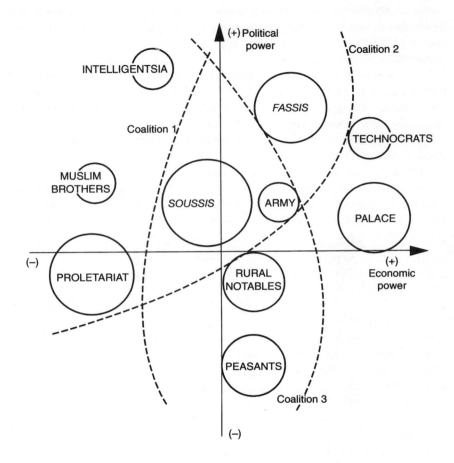

Figure 3.3 Application of dynamic segmentation to the case of Morocco.

the palace, the rural notables, and the peasants. Thus it is more unstable due to the fact that the army and the bourgeoisie are either neutral or in opposition. Coalition 3 includes the palace, the technocrats and the bourgeoisie, the army again remaining neutral. It is clear that Coalition 1 is the most favourable to foreign investors as far as the political stability of Morocco is concerned because it is the broadest and includes the army. The two other coalitions are narrower and imply a possibly destabilizing reinforcement of the fundamentalist influence. Once the different coalitions have been identified, the last step involves estimating the probability of each coalition occurring, and analysing the implications.

The expert systems approach

The expert systems approach is adapted to analyses in conditions of uncertainty. It essentially requires a data base and an inference paradigm. The data base includes quantitative information such as population, economic growth, current account balance, etc., as well as symbolic information that ranges from management definitions and rules to the description of international institutions (IMF, World Bank, etc.), national institutions (the government, the central bank, armed forces, etc.) and private agents (multinational firms, domestic firms, etc.). The inference paradigm replicates the thinking of an expert through chains of causality, such as event x causes effect y which causes effect z. For example, the Institut Français de Polémologie has set up a system to examine the potential consequences of a blockage of the Strait of Hormuz on the economic situation in certain European countries. Chains of causality are drawn from the effects of this blockage on the world oil supply and prices to the effects on the energy equilibrium of each European country and from this to the effects on inflation, economic growth and employment. In a parallel exercise, experts are interviewed to explain their vision of possible military events in the wake of a blockage of the Strait of Hormuz. Thus, the Institut's expert system enables potential users to ponder real consequences of a political event (the blockade) on a series of different actors.

Another organization, COFACE, the official French insurer of cross-border transactions, has developed three expert systems, one to estimate country-specific economic risk, another to estimate country-specific political risk and the third associated with the legal aspects of cross-border commercial transactions.

Econometric techniques

Econometric techniques for political risk estimation have concentrated on debt default and rescheduling. In contrast to the techniques discussed above, the econometric approach is completely objective. It starts from the assumption that certain economic indicators, such as growth rates, debt ratios, current account balance, etc., have predictive value. During the late 1970s and early 1980s many banks began to develop their own econometric models. The World Bank and several central banks, including the Bank of England, also experimented with them. Although the shortcomings of econometric forecasting are well known, it is widely accepted that econometric analysis can be a powerful complement to the comparative and analytical techniques described above. The two most popular econometric techniques have been discriminant analysis and logit models.

Discriminant analysis

Discriminant analysis is a statistical technique that makes it possible to classify an observation into one of several *a priori* groupings. In the case of political risk analysis, the idea is to classify countries according to whether they are likely to default or not. Basically, three steps are involved.

1. Establish mutually exclusive group classifications. Each group is distinguished by a probability distribution of the characteristics.
2. Collect data for each of the groups.
3. Derive the linear combinations of the characteristics that best discriminate between the groups. 'Best' in this sense means discrimination that minimizes the probability of misclassification.

Consider, for example, the case where two variables, x_1 and x_2, are used to discriminate between two types of countries – defaulters, and non-defaulters. Let x_1 stand for the country's growth rate and x_2 for the ratio of debt to exports. Let

$$Z = a_1 x_1 + a_2 x_2 \tag{3.1}$$

be a linear combination of x_1 and x_2. The problem is to establish a criterion and use past data in order to determine the values of a_1 and a_2 that will make Z useful for discriminating between members of the two groups. The idea, then, is to minimize the number of misclassifications. In a perfect model, there would be no misclassifications. In order to minimize the number of misclassifications, we maximize the function

$$G = \frac{(\overline{Z}_1 - \overline{Z}_2)^2}{\sum_{i=1}^{2} \sum_{j=1}^{n_i} (Z_{ij} - \overline{Z}_i)^2} \tag{3.2}$$

where the numerator represents the separation of the two groups and the denominator is a measure of the variation of Z within the groups. Z_{ij} is the Z value for the jth country in the ith group ($i = 1, 2$). n_i is the number of countries in group i and $\overline{Z}_i$ is the mean of the Z values in group i. The values

a_1 and a_2 can be found by partial differentiation.

Once the values of a_1 and a_2 have been found, the Z values for each country can be calculated and compared in order to determine the cut-off value. A cut-off value is necessary because there will usually be a 'zone of ignorance' where some defaulting countries will have higher Z values than some non-defaulting ones. Suppose, for example, that the zone of ignorance lies between Z values of 1.81 and 2.67. The point of minimum misclassification might lie at 2.05. Thus, $Z > 2.05$ classifies a country as non-defaulting and $Z < 2.05$ classifies a country as defaulting.

As an example of how discriminant analysis can be used, suppose that a large commercial bank is contemplating a sizeable loan to the Philippine government. To see if the Philippine government is statistically likely to default or reschedule over the life of the loan, the analyst assigned to the Philippines uses the bank's in-house model to compute the country's Z value. He finds that the Z value is substantially lower than the cut-off point, and that the Philippines is classified as a country that is likely to default. With this classification in mind, he then proceeds with his own in-depth analysis of the country's economic, financial, social, and political outlook, which shows that the Philippines is effectively relatively risky compared with other countries in the region. This conclusion, combined with the country's default classification derived from the discriminant analysis, leads the analyst to recommend that the loan be refused.

Frank and Cline published the first systematic empirical study of debt rescheduling.[3] Their fundamental unit of analysis was a country year. They examined data from 26 countries over a period of nine years but, because of holes in the data, they only had 145 country years, with 13 reschedulings in their sample. Their original analysis included eight macroeconomic variables and they found that three of these, the lagged ratio of debt to export trend, the ratio of imports to international reserves, and the reciprocal of the maturity of the country's foreign debt, had significant explanatory power to discriminate between cases of rescheduling and cases of normal payment. Since the Frank and Cline study, many other models have been developed and the list of relevant explanatory variables has grown with them.

Logit analysis
The logit model is similar to discriminant analysis insofar as it describes an either-or proposition. Either the country defaults or it doesn't. The dependent variable y_i can be defined as

$$y_i = \begin{cases} 1 & \text{if default occurs} \\ 0 & \text{if it does not occur} \end{cases}$$

Let x_i be a $k \times 1$ vector of independent variables and a a $k \times 1$ vector of coefficients. The logit model assumes that the conditional probability that y_i equals 1 is

$$\frac{1}{(1 + e^{-x_i'a})}$$

The a coefficients can be calculated using iterative techniques such as maximum likelihood methods. One drawback of the logit model is that its power to discriminate is most sensitive near the midpoint when the probability is equal to 0.5. As the probability moves away from 0.5, changes in the independent variables have less and less impact on the probability that y_i equals 1.

One way of using logit analysis in cross-border lending decisions is to assign a maximum default probability above which no loans will be granted. As we mentioned, however, it is more common to use the data from logit analysis as a complement to other analytical techniques.

Feder and Just were the first to use a logit model for studying debt rescheduling.[4] Like Frank and Cline, their analytical unit was the country year. Their sample spanned 41 countries and eight years but, because of incomplete data, it only included 238 country years, with 21 cases of rescheduling. In fact, they experienced some difficulties in determining just when an episode of rescheduling had occurred. They ended up finding six macroeconomic variables that were statistically significant in explaining a country's likelihood of rescheduling debt:

- per capita income;
- the rate of growth of exports;
- the ratio of imports to foreign exchange reserves;
- the ratio of debt service payments to total exports;
- the ratio of capital inflows to debt service payments;
- the ratio of amortization to the outstanding stock of total foreign debt.

APPLICATIONS

Measuring exposure in direct investments

Three factors determine the extent of the foreign investor's exposure to political risk:

- the strategic dimension of the investment;
- the bargaining power of the foreign firm;
- the foreign firm's relation with the host country.

The strategic dimension of the investment is related to the size of the subsidiary and the industrial sector it belongs to. Several studies have shown that size is synonymous with high visibility and hence with political risk.[5] The larger the investment, the more critical the risk becomes. Some industries are also more vulnerable to political risk than others. Table 3.3 shows that between 1960 and 1974, banks and insurance companies were especially vulnerable to nationalization.

Table 3.3 Nationalizations between 1960 and 1974 by sector.

Sector	*Percentage*
Banks and insurance companies	30%
Manufacturing industries	16%
Oil industry, including refineries	16%
Agriculture	15%
Mines	7%
Public services (infrastructure, etc.)	6%
Trade	4%
Miscellaneous	7%

(Source: United Nations, Document E 5425/1975.)

The bargaining power of the foreign firm depends on two variables. First there is the degree of complexity of the foreign subsidiary. This complexity can result either from the sophistication of the technical process embedded

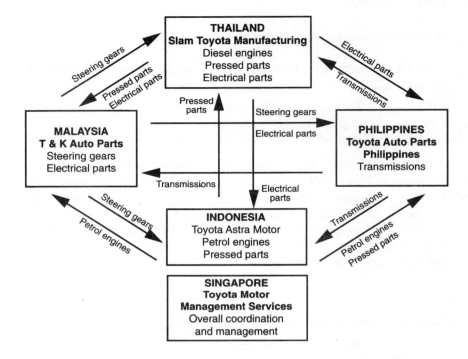

Figure 3.4 Toyota's international division of production in ASEAN countries.
(Source: Sakura Institute of Research, Tokyo, 1993.)

in the factory, or from the manufacturing process and the international division of production in which each subsidiary is linked to other subsidiaries of the same multinational in various countries, buying from them and selling to them components and parts of the final products. Figure 3.4 shows an example of this in Toyota's organization of its Asian operations. The five subsidiaries of the Japanese automotive firm in Thailand, Malaysia, Philippines, Indonesia, and Singapore are closely linked by cross-purchases and sales of different components. A more complex, interdependent system reduces exposure. In fact, firms that integrate their production at a world or region-wide level make any form of nationalization useless. A similar approach would consist of making foreign subsidiaries dependent on the parent company's technology. A recent study, however, shows, that in order to effectively reduce exposure, it is important that the host country understands to what extent the local investment is dependent on parent technology or integrated production, in order to avoid self-damaging expropriations.[6]

The second determinant in the bargaining power of the foreign firm with the host country is the net added value it brings to the economy. If the foreign investor brings hard currencies, new jobs, regional development, transfers of technology and executive training, it increases its bargaining power and reduces its exposure.

The firm's relationship with the local authorities is more ambiguous. The behaviour of the host country's authorities will probably differ, depending on whether the foreign investor is a new entrant or has been active in the host country for a long time. Long-time investors might hope to get better treatment than newcomers except, of course, if they have been too involved with local political parties. Since political power can and does change hands, it is probably better to stay out of local politics as much as possible, although many companies have ignored this cautious view. ITT in Chile and United Fruit in Guatemala, for example, who were identified with reactionary governments, suffered a backlash from the new governments when the former regimes were toppled.

The behaviour of the host country's authorities will also probably differ, depending on the nationality of the investor. For example, American companies in Cuba were all expropriated when Fidel Castro took over, while Swedish firms fared much better. Usually, the current attitude of the local government relates to its past experience with regard to the foreign investor as well as to the foreign investor's country.

The first task, then, of a company going abroad is to identify its potential exposure to political risk by determining what the main threats to its project are and how to improve security. First, the political risk relating to the project's environment must be assessed. This involves an application of one or more of the techniques described above. As a first step, for example, the rating approach could be used to screen countries on a comparative basis to create a shortlist of potential host countries. The special report method could then be used to contribute to the final decision on the country or countries that are selected. Before a final decision can be made, however, the political risk associated with the investment itself must be assessed and exposure estimated. The exposure estimation involves an appreciation of the strategic positioning and bargaining power mentioned above. It also involves an appreciation of the political risks at the local level, which can be very different from those of the central authority. The capacity for interference by local authorities must be appraised and the reliability of local partners assessed. In this context, the quality and reliability of local

Table 3.4 Political risk assistance services: the Control Risks Group

Established in 1975, the Control Risks Group provides political risk assessment, crisis management and security forecast services to over 2000 clients, from corporations and financial institutions to governments, in over 100 countries. Its services include:

• Security forecasts
Through analysis of political events or situations, its experts assess the implications of these events for business operations and commercial design-making. For each of the 80 countries covered in depth, there is a risk rating for the month ahead with a brief view on the outlook for six months. The 'travel security guide' estimates the risks to travellers from forthcoming political events, crime and terrorism. An aviation section focuses on threats to international airlines.

• Security advice, training and support
Control Risks provides on-site training for executives, employees and families. An appropriate survey examines the various risks at home and in the workplace. Staff receive straightforward security guidelines for everyday life and in the event of an emergency.

• Crisis management, planning and solving
Threats to a company take many forms: kidnapping, extortion, detention, etc. Since 1975, Control Risks has advised on more than 500 business crises around the world. It helps companies prepare contingency plans to respond rapidly to changing circumstances and reduce the exposure of personnel and assets if security deteriorates. It also offers protection to a company's intellectual property and computer systems. Finally, it conducts investigations worldwide to provide evidence in connection with theft, fraud, counterfeiting, industrial espionage, information leaks, bribery, corruption, conflicts of interest, breach of confidence, and contract and insurance claims.

banks, suppliers, and clients is particularly important. Once the investment has been completed, ongoing analysis is necessary to monitor events and ensure the protection of physical and nonphysical assets, as well as the individual security of personnel. The initial and ongoing political risk analysis can be conducted in house or with the aid of specialized institutions such as the Control Risks Group (Table 3.4), which offers a wide range of services from security forecasts, training and support to crisis management, planning and problem-solving.

Measuring political risk

If they are to have any practical use, the political risk assessments presented in the foregoing paragraphs must be integrated into the capital budgeting process. The orthodox theory of capital budgeting and investment under uncertainty taught in most business schools and economics departments revolves around the net present value (NPV) rule. The theoretical superiority of the NPV rule to the other approaches such as the payback period, the accounting rate of return or the internal rate of return explain its widespread acceptance in practice.[7] According to this rule, expected flows of income and expenditure are estimated for each period and discounted at the appropriate rate. The present values for expenditure are then subtracted from the present values of income to find the NPV. Positive NPV indicates that the investment should be accepted, negative NPV that it should be rejected. In Chapter 9 we will go into the more advanced capital budgeting techniques and how they can be applied to cross-border investing. For the moment we can take a look at how political risk estimates can be integrated into the traditional NPV capital budgeting process.

Adjusting the discount rate
One way to include political risk in NPV analysis is to adjust the discount rate to reflect the incremental political risk. Let

W = a risk factor that depends exclusively on the country in which the investment is to be located. It can be interpreted as the premium required to compensate the investor for the political risk

CF_t = the net cash flow for period t

r = the project's required rate of return per period in the absence of the country specific political risk.

In the absence of country-specific political risk, the risk-adjusted discount factor is equal to $(1 + r)$. With country-specific political risk, the discount factor is adjusted to $(1 + r + W)$. The project's NPV adjusted for political risk can thus be expressed as:

$$\text{NPV} = \sum_{t=0}^{n} CF_t(1 + r + W)^{-t} \qquad (3.3)$$

The NPV will be smaller because the discount factor is larger.

Besides the difficulty in estimating the value of W, this procedure also has a strong theoretical drawback. It treats all political risk as non-diversifiable and thus it does not distinguish between systematic risk which, according to portfolio theory, should be priced, and unsystematic risk which should not.

Adjusting the expected cash flows
A more theoretically sound method of accounting for political risk involves adjusting the cash flows to reflect the country specific political risk. Let

U_t = a risk factor for year t that depends exclusively on the country where the investment is to be located with $0 < U < 1$. It can be interpreted as the probability that something bad will **not** happen.

In the absence of country specific political risk, the expected net cash flow for year t is CF_t. With country-specific risk, the expected cash flow is reduced by $(1 - U_t)CF_t$ and the expected cash flow will be $U_t CF_t$. The project's NPV adjusted for political risk can thus be expressed as:

$$\text{NPV} = \sum_{t=0}^{n} U_t CF_t(1 + r)^{-t} \qquad (3.4)$$

The difficulty with this method is how the U coefficients can be determined. However, its advantage lies in associating a specific coefficient to each period. This makes it possible for the analysis to reflect the specific time profile of the country's political, social and economic cycles. For example, the U's in election years or renegotiation years for union contracts might be adjusted downwards, while years when international agreements take effect might be adjusted upwards.

Monte Carlo simulations
Monte Carlo simulations are another well-known and widely used approach to capital budgeting under uncertainty. Basically, they use a table of random

numbers to generate the possible probabilities. The whole process involves three steps.

1. The first and most important step in the simulation process is to give the computer a precise model of the project under consideration. This requires identifying the relevant variables and their interdependencies across time. The complete model would include a set of equations for each variable describing their evolution over time. The more complete the model, the more complex the system of equations.
2. The probabilities for forecast errors must then be drawn up for each variable.
3. The computer samples from the distribution of forecast errors, calculates the resulting cash flows for each period and records them. After a large number of simulations, accurate estimates of the probability distributions of the project's cash flows are obtained.

In a Monte Carlo simulation, the effects of political risk are estimated directly and the role of the political risk analyst is to identify the relevant variables and the probabilities for forecast errors. The Hertz method is particularly well adapted to this task.[8] Under the Hertz method the decision-maker is not required to assign specific probabilities to the individual variables. He is only required to choose:

1. the pertinent variables;
2. the expected value of each variable;
3. the upper estimate of each variable.
4. the lower estimate of each variable.

Thus, this system only requires what a good political risk analyst is likely to know or be able to estimate with some accuracy. The Monte Carlo simulation is then used to generate the required probability distributions.

The Monte Carlo method also permits assignment of values that reflect differing degrees of dependence between some events and other subsequent events. For example, the project's expected sales and prices might be determined by the intensity of competition in conjunction with the total size of market demand and the country's growth rate. A further advantage of the Hertz technique is that by separating the individual factors that determine profitability, the separate effects of each factor can be estimated and the sensitivity of profitability to each factor can be determined. If the effects of a particular factor on the final results are negligible, it is not necessary for management to spend time on analysing that factor. Thus, certain aspects of the myriad possible sources of political risk can be ruled out at the beginning, thereby simplifying the analysis.

Despite some serious drawbacks such as cost, complexity and difficulty in estimating the interrelationships between variables and their underlying probability distributions, the Monte Carlo method can be a valuable tool for assessing a project's riskiness and determining its NPV.

An example of political risk analysis: the case of NPC

NPC is one of the major utility companies in Western Europe, with a turnover of about $35 billion and a profit of $550 million in 1993. It exports about 15% of the 420 billion kWh of energy it produces. Until recently, it enjoyed a national monopoly on its own territory. In the wake of European deregulation of the European energy market, however, NPC is trying to invest abroad as a means of offsetting its diminishing home market share. This process can take four different forms:

1. *As a consultant* Under this label, NPC is only a seller of services, namely feasibility studies for new power plants. Political risk in this activity is limited to credit risk.
2. *As manager of a plant* As plant manager, the main risks lie in pricing policy (and possible government intervention), foreign exchange controls and the solvency of clients.
3. *As a concessionaire* In this case NPC has complete control of the company, only paying concession fees to the host government. Besides the risks associated with plant management, political risks also encompass possible internal or external conflicts that could cause asset destruction.
4. *As a shareholder* In this role, political risks are greatest since in addition to the risks associated with the status of concessionaire, expropriation and nationalization are also possible. In the case of a joint venture, risks related to local partners must also be considered.

In addition to the foregoing risks, two sector-specific risks can also arise:

1. environmental risk, in particular with regard to nuclear energy, concerning strict safety rules and lobbies from ecology groups;
2. changes in the regulatory framework, such as intervention by the host government on tariff rates, privatization of distribution networks or tax changes.

In response to the process of internationalization and the problems that it poses, NPC has set up a number of procedures designed to deal with political risk. First of all, an International Committee, consisting of members belonging to the various operational divisions and staff 'departments, is in charge of the general assessment of a potential host country's political situation. A checklist (see Table 3.5) has been established identifying five indicators of political risk, namely:

1. political instability;
2. local interference;
3. regulatory risk;
4. tariff fluctuations;
5. counterparty risk.

For each item, a risk level, a probability of occurrence and an estimate of potential losses is determined. The risk level and probability of occurrence are rated on an increasing scale of 1 to 10 while the actual figure is used for the loss estimate. This procedure is used as a first screening for a foreign investment project, with emphasis assigned to the various criteria depending on the nature of the project. If it is a consultancy project, for example, the item 'counterparty risk' will be privileged.

When the project has passed the screening, the Finance Department examines it, using the traditional NPV method. First, total net cash flows associated with the project are calculated for each year. Each cash flow is then discounted back to the present. This procedure involves determining the discount rate by adding a risk premium to the project's required rate of return. To derive the risk premium NPC subscribes to a rating service. It uses the rating supplied by the service to express the risk premium as a percentage of the project's required rate of return. For instance, if the required rate of return is 10% and Chile's rating puts it in the 15% risk bracket, Chile's risk premium will be 1.5% and the total discount rate will be 11.5%. If the net present value of all the discounted cash flows is greater than or equal to zero, the project is accepted.

Once a project has been undertaken, the International Division monitors it in terms of political risk. In general, the various risks related to each project are examined on a regular basis. In case of emergency, the International Division activates a 'crisis management planning and solving' scheme. Contingency plans are devised to respond rapidly to changing host country circumstances by reducing exposure of assets and personnel. Implementation is managed by the International Division.

NPC's methodology breaks down risk into three categories:

1. project-specific;
2. sector-specific;
3. country-specific.

Table 3.5 NPC checklist of political risks

Political risk indicators	Risk level (0 to 10)	Probability of occurrence (0 to 10)	Potential losses (amount)	Comments (e.g. hedging alternatives)
1. Political instability				
2. Local interference				
3. Regulatory risk				
4. Tariff fluctuations				
5. Counterparty risk				

Each item encompasses several sub-items, weighted according to their importance.

Political instability:
- at the regional level
- at the national level
- at the local level

Local interference:
- from state administrations (government, agencies, civil servants, etc.)
- from 'informal groups' (lobbies, local competitors, associations of users)

Regulatory risk:
- environmental constraints
- manufacturing standards
- legal framework (property rights, technology transfers)

Tariff fluctuation:
- price controls and indexation
- taxation

Counterparty risks:
- private versus state companies
- conflicts of interest (between shareholders, in joint ventures, for instance)
- solvency of the main partners.

Project-specific and sector-specific risks are taken into consideration at the level of cash flow estimation when the probability and amount of potential losses are calculated. Country-specific risk is accounted for by adding a risk premium to the project's required rate of return to determine the discount factor for the net present value calculation. Rather than employing in-house analysts to determine the risk premium, NPC subscribes to a rating service to express the risk premium as a percentage of the project's required rate of return. It is clear that NPC's methodology uses a combination of analytical procedures described above.

An example of political risk analysis: a direct investment project in Mexico

An international corporation headquartered in Europe, Eurobell ranks as one of the leading communications systems suppliers[9]. It designs, manufactures, sells and services equipment both for its home markets and for customers around the world. Its business activities span network systems, radio communications, space and defence, power and telecommunications cable, business systems, professional electronics, network engineering and installation. Eurobell's origins go back to the previous century when some of its companies were founded to supply Europe's first telephone equipment. In 1991 it had sales and marketing operations serving clients in more than 110 countries around the world, manufacturing facilities in 25 countries and research centres in 12 countries.

In December 1991, Eurobell was considering entering the Mexican market and setting up a subsidiary to manufacture and sell communications systems, in particular advanced switching and line transmission systems. The factory to be built would produce 500 000 lines per year, implying an initial investment of $800 million, a workforce of 650 people and a yearly turnover of $600 million. Sales would be aimed at both the local and American markets.

To assess this project thoroughly, an investigation of the political and economic situation of the prospective host country was conducted by an in-house task force. The first report on the main political features read as follows:

- Relative stability of the Mexican government due to the prominence of Partido Revolucionario Institucional (PRI) since 1930. In the last polls (August 1991), 321 seats out of a possible 500 were won by PRI, the rest split between PAN on the right and PRD on the left.
- The current president, Carlos Salinas, leader of PRI, will end his mandate

in 1994. His programme focuses on private initiative, internationalization of the Mexican economy, and privatization.

- However, discrepancies between rich and poor are quickly rising. Improvement in social conditions appears to be slow, particularly in rural areas.
- Public opinion believes that most elections in Mexico are tarnished by frauds and embezzlements. Despite its recent success, PRI seems to have a bad reputation as far as transparency and fairness go.
- The economic situation can be summed up in the following table:

	1989	1990	1991	1992 (forecast)
GNP growth %	3.1	3.9	4.5	4.5
Investment %	5.9	13.4	10	10.5
Inflation %	19.7	29.9	20	18
Currency % change	-	-12.5	-	-
Budget deficit/GNP	5.5	3.5	2	2.5
Trade balance $bn.	-0.65	-3	-9	-4
Bal. of Pay. $bn.	-0.2	0.2	7.5	6
Reserves $bn.	6.8	10.2	16.7	15
Foreign debt/GNP	60	51	42	33
Capital flight	-	-	15	10

- Considering the administrative environment, these points can be listed:

  - Privatization is very active. The public sector consisted of 1200 enterprises in 1982. Eight years later it had fallen to 285 firms. In the Directive of May 1989, total privatization of the telecommunications sector is provided for.
  - Various fiscal incentives are linked to setting up in the Northern part of the country, close to the US border (law on 'maquilladoras').
  - Labour regulations are considered to be strict.

- Another factor has to be taken into account: the coming participation of Mexico in the North American Free Trade Association (NAFTA), set up by the United States and Canada. The removal of customs duties and other trade barriers would be quite positive for Mexican exports to the States, which are currently close to $30 billion.
- As for the Mexican government, its position is strongly favourable to the Eurobell project for the following reasons: the future factory will create

jobs, transfer technology to Mexico, bring hard currencies from exports, favour economic development in a less industrialized area, and enhance business for sub-contractors.

Thus, the report to the CEO of Eurobell stressed the various features bound to make the project promising:

- low political risk on a short to medium-term basis;
- an improving economic situation (fall of foreign debt/GNP ratio, high level of investment, limitation of budget and trade deficit, currency stability, no capital flight);
- continued privatization and openness to foreign investment;
- Mexico poised to join NAFTA, which would enable Eurobell to export to the United States on favourable terms;
- presence of private domestic investors likely to participate in the equity of the local subsidiary, if necessary.

The report advised the adoption of a risk premium equal to 10% of the required rate of return on a similar European project. When the risk-adjusted discount rate was applied to the project's expected cash flows, NPV was positive and so Eurobell decided to proceed with construction of the plant as soon as possible.

An example of political risk analysis: a bank loan to Indonesia

AMB[9], a large European bank, was considering a loan to Indonesia in early 1992. AMB's assessment methods include the following approaches that are managed together.

1. *The country profile* Two-page country profiles are prepared and regularly updated on 140 countries. They include the main relevant data such as balance of payments, GNP, exports, imports, inflation rate, external debt, official reserves, etc. This short symposis can be used by anyone travelling abroad for meetings with potential borrowers or dealing with exporters wanting to obtain buyer credits.
2. *An in-house rating system* Some 110 countries are rated on a scale of 1 to 10 from the less to the more risky. The final score reflects some elementary grades given to 17 criteria such as the ratio of debt service to exports, the ratio of total external debt to GDP, number of months of exports covered by reserves, the export/import ratio etc.
3. *A ceiling per country* Each year the Credit Committee, in collaboration with the Department of Economic Research, sets a borrowing limit for

each country that the bank works with. This session usually takes place in October after the annual meetings of the IMF and the World Bank. Limits are updated twice a year.

4. *An econometric model*   The parameters of the econometric model based on discriminant analysis are updated at least once a year. Classification as defaulting or non-defaulting plays an important role in determining the individual country debt ceilings. It is also used as a decision variable for managing past loans such as which credits will be transferred to other banks, sold on the secondary market, securitized or transformed in a swap.

The decision-making process proceeds as follows. Once the ceiling has been set for a country, this figure becomes the reference for the 'line' people and new loans are made in accordance with it. However, an 'emergency procedure' can be adopted in the case of a strategic operation. The in-house rating system and the updated country profiles are used in determining the risk premium associated with each country.

Although Indonesia had not yet reached its debt ceiling with AMB and its in-house rating was a relatively strong 3, the updated country profile raised some troubling questions. First of all, Indonesia was close to the upper limit of what AMB considered a reasonable external debt/GDP ratio. Secondly, it was facing international scrutiny over its treatment of East Timor. In light of this, the Credit Committee asked the analysts responsible for Indonesia to look at the situation in more detail. The resulting report concluded that although the situation merited increased monitoring, there was no cause to modify Indonesia's medium-term credit outlook. Based on this conclusion the Credit Committee decided to go ahead with the loan.

NOTES

[1] See Chapter 2 for a definition of the risk-free rate of interest.
[2] See *Euromoney*, September 1993 pp. 363–8.
[3] See: Frank, C.R. and Cline, W.R. (1971) Measurement of Debt Servicing Capacity: An Application of Discriminant Analysis, *Journal of International Economics*, 1, 327–44.
[4] See: Feder, G. and Just, R.E. (1976) A Study of Debt Servicing Capacity Applying Logit Analysis, *Journal of Development Economics*, 4, 25–39.
[5] See, for example: Poynter, J. (1980) Government Intervention in Less Developed Countries: the Experience of Multinational Companies, Working Paper no 238, University of Ontario, March.
[6] See: Raff, H. (1992) A Model of Expropriation with Asymmetric Information,

Journal of International Economics, **33**, 245–65.

7   See, for example, Copeland, T.E. and Weston, J.F. (1988) *Financial Theory and Corporate Policy*, Addison-Wesley Publishing Company, Reading, Mass., pp. 17–76.

8   See: Hertz, D.B. (1976) Uncertainty and Investment Selection in *The Treasurer's Handbook* (eds J.F. Weston and M.B. Goudzwaard), Dow Jones-Irwin, Homewood, III., Chapter 18, pp. 376–420.

9   Names have been changed to preserve confidentiality.

4 THE ECONOMICS OF COUNTRY-SPECIFIC RISK ASSESSMENT

The macroeconomic performance of individual countries is intimately related to their international economic and financial environment. Although individual countries have the right to regulate transactions within the geographic area they control and are responsible for organizing domestic resource allocation and income distribution, transactions between different national jurisdictions are a different matter. As we pointed out in Chapter 1, the jurisdiction of the individual national systems effectively ends at each country's border. Consequently, at the international level, resource allocation and income distribution across countries depend to a large extent on competitive forces. The outcome reflects the relative success of the different national economic policies in the international marketplace and is measured by the economic and financial flows between countries, presented in the balance of payments. The economics of cross-border risk assessment involves understanding the relationships between these flows, economic activity, and the exchange rate.

In this chapter we present the relationships between a national economy and the international economic and financial system that form the basis for country-specific economic, financial and currency risk assessment. The fundamental nature of the relationships and their analytical applications make them indispensible for a book of this sort. Thus, for the uninitiated, this chapter should be read in its entirety. However, most readers will already be acquainted with many of the areas treated in the chapter. Consequently, it is structured so that it can be read piecemeal or used as a reference to be referred to when needed. Readers well versed in international economics and traditional cross-border risk analysis can go on to the more advanced techniques in the next chapter with no loss of continuity.

THE BALANCE OF PAYMENTS AND THE ECONOMY

In the balance of payments accounting system, a credit entry gives rise to an increase in external purchasing power. This could also be described as a demand for local currency. Conversely, a debit which gives rise to a use of external purchasing power could be described as a supply of local currency. The purpose of approaching the balance of payments in terms of supply and demand of local currency for foreign currency is to bring out the relationship between the balance of payments and the exchange rate. We have already seen that variations in the exchange rate constitute an important risk in international business transactions. They also affect economic and financial variables like output, employment, price levels and interest rates. Consequently, a thorough understanding of how exchange rates are determined and what effects they have on other economic and financial variables is crucial for the assessment of international business risk. The first step is to see that the exchange rate results from the supply and demand of local currency for foreign currency and to understand that supply and demand are reflected in the balance of payments.

The monetary authorities and the exchange rate

The exchange rate is the price of foreign currency in units of local currency or, conversely, the price of local currency in units of foreign currency. For convertible currencies, the price depends on the supply and demand of one for the other. Just as in any market, prices will adjust to equate supply with demand. If the *ex ante* supply and demand for local currency is not in balance, the exchange rate will change to restore equilibrium. This effectively means that certain transactions that were projected *ex ante* will not be realized *ex post* and others that were not projected *ex ante* will be realized *ex post*.

If we look at the balance of payments accounts in Table 4.1, we see that we can draw a line under the account 'counterpart items'. Everything above the line represents the combined supply and demand of local currency for foreign currency generated by autonomous transactions. Below the line, the account 'change in reserves' represents the supply and demand of local currency for foreign currency generated by the monetary authorities. If there is a disequilibrium above the line, the monetary authorities have two choices. They can either intervene through the account 'change in reserves' to make up the difference, or they can do nothing. Intervention has the effect of preventing the exchange rate from changing. Non-intervention means that the exchange rate will move to equate supply with demand.

The limits to intervention are obvious. Intervention to prevent a depreciation of the local currency by purchasing local currency and selling foreign currency can only last as long as reserves hold out. The limits to

Table 4.1 Standard components of the balance of payments

Current account

	Exports f.o.b.
−	Imports f.o.b.
=	Trade Balance
+	Exports of Non-Financial Services
−	Imports of Non-Financial Services
+	Investment Income (Credit)
−	Investment Income (Debit)
+(−)	Private Unrequited Transfers
+(−)	Official Unrequited Transfers
=	Current Account Balance

Capital account

+(−)	Direct Investment
+(−)	Portfolio Investment
+(−)	Other Long-term Capital
+(−)	Other Short-Term Capital
+(−)	Net Errors and Omissions
+(−)	Counterpart Items
+(−)	Total Change in Reserves
=	Capital Account Balance

intervention designed to prevent currency appreciation are also obvious. They are determined by the willingness of the monetary authorities to accumulate foreign assets. Furthermore, both policies, intervention and non-intervention, are fraught with consequences for the overall economy. As we will see later on in this chapter, a change in the exchange rate tends to change the quantities and types of merchandise that are produced and consumed in the economy, while intervention affects the economy through changes in the money supply.

Macroeconomic accounting discipline

Besides a direct link to the exchange rate, the balance of payments also plays a prominent role in an economy's overall performance. In its most general sense, this role is one of macroeconomic accounting discipline. By this, we mean that an economy's consumption and investment of resources cannot be greater than the resources that it produces plus the resources that it borrows. We can appreciate how this accounting discipline is achieved if we examine how the external sector, reflected in the balance of payments, fits into the schema of overall economic performance.

Most economists refer to **gross domestic product** (GDP) or **gross national product** (GNP) as a measure of economic performance. GDP measures an economy's output defined as the total flow of goods and services produced by an economy over a specified time period. It is obtained by valuing the outputs of both final and investment goods and services at the market prices of the country in question and then aggregating. Intermediate goods are netted out but are implicitly included in the prices of the final goods.[1] GDP is usually broken down as follows:

+ *Exports*
− *Imports*
+ *Private Consumption*
+ *Government consumption*
+ *Gross fixed capital formation*
+ *Variation in stocks*
= GROSS DOMESTIC PRODUCT

GNP measures an economy's total income. It is equal to GDP plus the income from abroad accruing to domestic residents minus income generated in the domestic market accruing to non-residents.

$$GNP = GDP + (-) \text{ net factor payments (from) abroad}$$

Hence, GDP shows what can be produced with factors located within the country's geographic bounds while GNP shows what can be earned with factors located domestically or abroad but owned by domestic residents.

Let's start with GDP. Using the symbols in Table 4.2, we can define GDP by the accounting identity:[2]

$$GDP = X - M + C + \Delta stk + I \qquad (4.1)$$

By the same token, the balance of payments accounting identity can be written:

$$BP = X - M + FS + F \qquad (4.2)$$

Note that BP refers to the account 'change in reserves', where the change refers to an *increase* in reserves. In other words, if reserves increase, BP is positive and if reserves decrease, BP is negative.

Table 4.2 Definition of variables

$X =$ merchandise exports plus exports of all non-financial services plus unrequited transfers and other non-financial income (credit)
$M =$ merchandise imports plus imports of all non-financial services plus unrequited transfers and other non-financial income (debit)
$FS =$ net investment income (investment income (credit) minus investment income (debit))
$F =$ net foreign capital not counting the change in reserves (capital account balance minus the change in reserves)
$BP =$ the increase in reserves
$C =$ private consumption plus government consumption
$I =$ gross fixed capital formation
$\Delta stk =$ increase in stocks

If we compare equations 4.1 and 4.2, it is clear that the role of the balance of payments is explicit in the overall economy. GDP is constrained by

$$X - M = BP - FS - F.$$

Practically speaking, what this means is that an economy can only use more resources than it produces ($X < M$) to the extent of its foreign reserves ($\sum BP$), its investment income (FS), or the willingness of the rest of the world to extend credit (F). This fact can be appreciated if we look at the balance of payments in terms of saving and investment.

GNP represents an economy's total income:

$$GNP = GDP + FS \qquad (4.3)$$

Then saving is equal to income minus consumption:

$$Saving = GDP + FS - C = X - M + FS + \Delta stk + I \qquad (4.4)$$

We recognize ($X - M + FS$) as the current account balance and ($\Delta stk + I$) as gross investment. Then, bringing gross investment to the left-hand side:

$$Saving - Gross\ investment = Current\ account\ balance$$

The difference between saving and gross investment is equal to the current account balance. Remember that the current account balance is equal to the variation in official reserves less net foreign investment. Thus:

$$Saving - Gross\ investment = Current\ account\ balance = BP - F$$

This is a basic relation between the external sector and the overall economy. Any excess in the current account balance is matched by an excess in domestic saving over domestic investment and this will be reflected in the capital account balance by an increase in reserves and net foreign lending. On the other hand, any deficit in the current account balance is matched by an excess in domestic investment over domestic saving and this will be reflected in the capital account balance by net foreign borrowing and a decrease in reserves.

The exchange rate and economic adjustment

Although transactions with the external sector ultimately end in a zero sum accounting equation, the various paths leading to this result have their own consequences on current and future economic performance. The consequences are not always desirable.

The problem is often presented in terms of conflict between domestic and external equilibrium. Domestic equilibrium refers to full employment and a certain standard of living. External equilibrium refers to the *ex ante* equality between the supply and demand of domestic currency on the foreign exchange markets. Since balance of payments discipline ensures that the *ex post* supply and demand of domestic currency will always be equal, any incompatibility between domestic and external equilibrium suggests that it will be domestic equilibrium that suffers. At the time of the gold standard or even fixed exchange rates, this meant a painful deflation, where levels of output and consumption were reduced to the point where *ex ante* external equilibrium was restored. This can still be the case when the disequilibrium is minor or temporary. Since the advent of active nationalistic monetary policies, however, and especially since the last link between currencies and gold was cut in 1971 by the US, solutions to major fundamental external disequilibrium have usually revolved around a change in the exchange rate. On the surface, a change in the exchange rate seems to involve nothing more than a change in the price of one currency for another. In fact, the effects, with varying time lags, magnitudes and intensities, penetrate to the core of the economy and ultimately generate a new set of economic conditions, with resulting consequences for the balance of payments, the supply and demand for foreign currency and the exchange rate. Understanding the forces and relationships involved is therefore indispensible for judicious international financial analysis.

Exchange rate depreciation: relative price effects
The elasticities approach to exchange rate depreciation (devaluation) considers the problem of devaluation and balance of payments adjustment in terms of the supply and demand of exports and imports. Exports are assumed to account for the only supply of foreign exchange and imports the only demand for foreign exchange. In other words, there are no capital flows between countries. The only way that foreign exchange can be obtained is by exporting and the only need for foreign exchange is to pay for imports. Figure 4.1 shows how this could look for the French economy if the pound sterling is the unit of account used to measure foreign exchange value. The x-axis represents the amount of foreign exchange and the y-axis represents the price of one unit of foreign currency in French francs. At the spot exchange rate, S_0, the supply of foreign exchange is A. Since exports are assumed to account for the only supply of foreign exchange, A is calculated by multiplying the number of export units by the price per unit in foreign currency. At the same exchange rate, the demand for foreign currency is B,

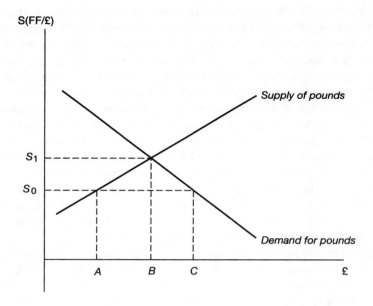

Figure 4.1 Supply and demand for foreign currency.

calculated by multiplying the number of import units by the price per unit in foreign currency. The current account balance is thus in disequilibrium by the amount $B - A$ and a devaluation is in order.

The goal of the devaluation is to bring the supply and demand of foreign exchange into equilibrium. In Figure 4.1, the supply of foreign exchange is equal to the demand at C when the exchange rate is at S_1. According to the elasticities approach, the key to the success of the devaluation depends on the **price elasticities of demand** for exports and imports, which can be defined as the percentage change in the quantity demanded divided by the percentage change in price. The price elasticity of demand can be written algebraically as:

$$\text{Demand elasticity} = -\frac{dQ/Q}{dP/P} \qquad (4.5)$$

where Q is quantity and P is price. There is a minus sign before the price elasticity because for normal demand curves there is a negative relation between price and demand so that when price goes up the quantity demanded goes down, and vice versa. A devaluation implies a fall in the price of exports in foreign currency and a rise in the price of imports in domestic currency. Thus, the higher the absolute value of demand elasticities, the more exports should rise and the more imports should fall.

This brings up the question of **supply elasticities**. Supply elasticities are similar to demand elasticities, except that there is normally a positive relation between prices and the quantity supplied. In a devaluation the role of the supply elasticities is to determine the effects of the devaluation on the **terms of trade**. The terms of trade refer to the number of units of imports that one unit of exports will buy (or vice versa) and can be calculated by dividing the price of exports by the price of imports. If, for example, the price of one unit of exports in foreign currency is £3 and the price of one unit of imports is £1, the terms of trade are £3/£1 = 3. In other words, one unit of exports will buy three units of imports.

Suppose that supplies of exports can be increased without increasing costs in domestic currency and supplies of imports can be reduced without causing a fall in their foreign currency price. Then the price of exports in domestic currency will remain constant and their price in foreign currency will fall by the full amount of the devaluation while the foreign currency price of imports remains constant. In this case the terms of trade will deteriorate by the full amount of the devaluation. Hence, the deterioration of the terms of trade due to a devaluation· is maximum when supply elasticities are infinite, that is, when the exports and imports of the devaluing country are supplied at constant cost. It is minimum when the supply elasticities are zero, that is, when costs rise proportionately in the devaluing country or fall proportionately in the rest of the world.

The elasticity of the supply of foreign exchange
The elasticity of the supply of foreign exchange depends on two things: the elasticity of foreign demand for domestic exports and the elasticity of the supply of domestic exports. If foreign demand is sensitive to price changes, a decline in export prices resulting from the devaluation will increase the quantities of goods that are exported. The actual decline in export prices depends on the supply elasticity of exports. Thus, the supply of foreign exchange will tend to increase because of the increase in export volume and decrease because of the fall in the foreign exchange price at which this volume can be sold.

Demand is considered elastic when the elasticity is greater than one, and inelastic when the elasticity is less than one. In practice, whether or not exports are elastic depends on many things, such as the type of product and the market share of the exporter, the affluence of the importer and trade restrictions. Consumer durables like automobiles sold in the United States, for example, are probably more demand elastic than rice exports to Bangladesh. In any case, trade restrictions, including tariffs, quotas, oligopolies and cartels restrict competition and reduce the demand elasticities by reducing the role of price in buying decisions.

It is also difficult to generalize about export supply elasticities, which also depend on many factors such as the type of product, its production function, stocks of intermediate and raw materials, available qualified labour, etc. It is probably safe to say that in the short run context of a devaluation, supply elasticities depend to a large extent on the domestic economy's position in the trade cycle. In a downturn, increments in products available for export at little extra cost are more likely to be forthcoming than in the later stages of an expansion when stocks are low and factors of production are being used at close to full capacity.

The elasticity of the demand for foreign exchange
The elasticity of the demand for foreign exchange depends on the elasticity of supply and demand for imports. Other things being equal, a devaluation raises the price of imports in domestic currency. If domestic demand is sensitive to price changes, an increase in domestic import prices resulting from the devaluation will decrease the quantities of goods that are imported. The actual rise in domestic import prices depends on the supply elasticity of imports. Thus, the demand for foreign exchange will tend to decrease because of the decrease in import volume. This decrease will be offset to the extent that supply elasticities are not infinite and the price of imports in foreign exchange tends to fall with the fall in demand.

Like export demand elasticities, import demand elasticities depend on the type of product and the affluence of the domestic market. Probably more important, however, is the supply of **import substitutes** produced by the domestic economy. When domestic products compete with imports, the higher prices of imported products should cause a switch from imports to domestic substitutes, thereby raising the import demand elasticity.

Where import supply elasticities are concerned, most countries are in the position of a **price taker**. In other words, they are too small to have much effect on world prices. In this case supply elasticities, if not infinite, are likely to be very high. However, in the case of large, affluent countries like the United States that account for an important share of world trade in many products, the price-taking assumption is less likely to be valid.

Elasticities and the balance of payments

To summarize, then, the elasticities approach underlines the price effects of exchange rate changes on the balance of payments. A devaluation makes imports more expensive in the domestic market and, depending on the demand elasticity, this should cause imports to fall. The devaluation should also make exports cheaper on foreign markets and, again depending on the demand elasticity, this should make exports rise. The extent to which the domestic price of imports rises and the foreign price of exports falls depends on the supply elasticities of the two types of products. The combined effects of the price elasticities will determine whether the devaluation will be successful in restoring external equilibrium.[3] The empirical question of actually measuring these elasticities has never progressed very far because of the variations in the prices, quantities and types of products that are exported and imported.[4]

In spite of its empirical shortcomings, the elasticities approach is a theoretically sound short-term explanation of the reaction of the balance on current account to exchange rate changes. To the extent that these reactions do tend to occur, it has considerable analytical value. However, there is some confusion and inconsistency arising from the use of two units of account – national currency and foreign exchange – in the measurement of the relevant variables. Furthermore, it neglects devaluation-induced effects on income and expenditure. The absence of time lags and capital movements also limits its scope.

Exchange rate depreciation: income effects

The shortcomings of the elasticities approach to devaluation analysis led to the development of what is called the **absorption approach**.[5] The absorption approach abandons the partial elasticities of the preceeding section, that is, the effects of price variations on the quantities supplied and demanded when the other relevant variables remain unchanged, in favour of what it calls the total elasticities. Total elasticities refer to the effects of price variations on the quantities supplied and demanded when the other relevant variables have been allowed to change. In other words, the absorption approach takes into consideration the variations in income and consumption caused by the devaluation.

The income effects

There are three major devaluation-induced effects on income or GNP. The first effect we have already considered. It concerns the terms of trade and depends on how much the supply elasticities cause the terms of trade to deteriorate. A deterioration in the terms of trade tends to reduce domestic income. The second effect depends on the demand- elasticities and on whether or not the economy is working at full capacity. If the economy has excess capacity, the increased demand for exports and import substitutes should increase output and employment in industries producing these products. If the economy is working near full capacity, however, supply elasticities are likely to be low and the increased demand will translate into price increases. The third effect concerns resource allocation. Income should increase if the relative price changes induced by the devaluation improve resource allocation by transferring factors of production to sectors where they are more productive. For long-term external equilibrium, this is a key consideration.

Absorption effects
Absorption refers to the economy's total consumption of resources. It is equal to private and government consumption plus total gross investment $(C + \Delta stk + I)$. The first and most important effect on absorption is the result of an **income redistribution** that takes place within the domestic economy. Producers of **importables** and **exportables** should experience an increase in income due to the elasticity effects discussed above. On the other hand, consumers of importables and exportables should experience a reduction in real income due to the higher prices of these products. Importables and exportables refer to products actually imported and exported, as well as their close substitutes produced domestically. A second effect on absorption is caused by the desire of investors to maintain their real cash balances. The rise in prices following the devaluation causes real cash balances to decline. This causes investors to sell stocks and bonds in an effort to maintain them. A fall in bond prices means a rise in the rate of interest. The resulting rise in the interest rate causes a reduction in investment and consumption. Finally, there may be other diverse effects from devaluation such as anticipated price rises inciting immediate consumption or a high import content in investment goods causing a reduction in investment because of the higher cost of imports.

The combined effects of income and absorption
In this context the devaluation will improve the external balance on current account if the increase in income caused by the devaluation is greater than the devaluation-induced increase in absorption. The new exchange rate is the key to success.

The new exchange rate determines the volume of exports and the division of absorption between imports and domestic importables. In this way the exchange rate fixes the relative price of exports on foreign markets and the relative price of imports on domestic markets. Income and absorption, then, are two distinct functions of the exchange rate, the long-term success of the devaluation depending on the ability of these functions to maintain income greater than, or at least equal to, the level of absorption. Let's examine some of the characteristics of these functions.

Relative price effects on income and absorption
The initial effects of a devaluation should increase the domestic price of importables and exportables relative to **non-tradables**. Non-tradables are goods and services produced and consumed domestically that are not close substitutes of exportables and importables. The actual amount of the price increases depends partly on the supply elasticities and partly on the demand elasticities. For exportables, a lower supply elasticity and a higher foreign demand elasticity will cause a larger increase in the domestic price. This is because the lower the supply elasticity, the greater the reduction in the supply of exportables to the domestic market as exports increase in response to the increased foreign demand. A lower supply in the face of an unchanged demand will cause prices to rise. For importables the domestic price increase will be greater the higher the supply and the lower the demand elasticities. Higher prices and increased demand for exportables should stimulate output. Higher prices and the substitution of domestic importables for imports should stimulate output in this sector as well. Therefore, there should be a switch in absorption from foreign to domestic importables and the increase in exports should increase domestic income. The ultimate increase will depend on the foreign trade income multiplier.[6]

Non-tradable goods
Since, by definition, the demand for non-tradables is strictly domestic, their price is not directly affected by a devaluation. However, their cost is determined by the international markets directly, if imported intermediate products, investment goods and raw materials are direct inputs, and indirectly, if importable and exportable goods are consumed by the labour force. Higher prices for importables and exportables make direct inputs more expensive. They also reduce labour's real income and lead to demands for higher wages that raise costs.

The income redistribution resulting from the devaluation affects the demand for non-tradables. The winners in the redistribution are the producers of importables and exportables. If they are consumers of non-tradables, some of their incremental income will be spent on non-tradables. This will raise the demand for non-tradables. The losers in the redistribution are the consumers of importables and exportables. If they are also consumers of non-tradables their loss of real income should reduce the demand for non-tradables. The net effect determines whether overall demand for non-tradables will increase or decrease. In fact, an overall decrease is the usual outcome. Thus, it is the reaction of the non-tradable sector during the period between devaluation and the response of the balance on current account that explains the apparent paradox of a devaluation causing a recession.[7]

The wealth effect

For countries exporting raw materials, income can be influenced by the wealth effect. When the supply of exports is inelastic in the long term (limited by land, mineral deposits, etc.) or in the short term (limited by mines, wells, herds, etc.), a devaluation increases the wealth of the owners of these resources even if output does not increase. Resource allocation can be disturbed if the owners of the inputs count on the effects of relative price movements to increase their wealth, rather than increasing it through investments that will increase output. This phenomenon occurred at the international level when oil-producing countries limited their output but increased their wealth through higher prices that increased income and the value of their reserves underground.

The wealth effect can have serious consequences if the exportable products are also wage goods, such as in Argentina where beef and wheat, besides being major export products, are also consumed in large quantities by the general population. The devaluation-induced income redistribution depresses real income and standards of living while the wealth effect tends to perpetuate or prolong the situation.

Strategic imports

Strategic imports are intermediate goods that are necessary to maintain current levels of output, or investment goods necessary to maintain future output. If imports of intermediate goods for current output are reduced, current income will fall by several times the value of the reduction in imports. A reduction in imports of investment goods will reduce the economy's potential productive capacity and future output will be limited.

Time lags and the composition of exports

Although world supply elasticities may be considered as infinite or very high for a price-taking country, the supply elasticities of the country itself cannot usually be considered in the same way. Most products require a time lag before they can respond to demand signals. A prime example is agricultural products. The season has to be right and the plants take time to grow. Even industrial output requires an interval between the moment that increased demand manifests itself and production can be increased and distributed to meet this demand. Thus, in the short term, exports can only increase at the expense of domestic consumption of exportable goods. This will be the case if the domestic prices of exportable goods rise faster than the incomes of those that consume them, thereby exacerbating the income transfer from consumers to producers of exportables.

Structural change
We have seen that the exchange rate plays an important part in how resources are allocated. It determines the economy's external terms of trade, that is, the relative prices of exports to imports. It also determines the economy's internal terms of trade, the relative prices of tradable goods to non-tradable goods. These relative prices then determine the economy's structure of production and the composition of output and consumption. Thus, a variation in the exchange rate implies a change in the economy's structure of production as the modified relative price structure induces a reallocation of the economy's resources. Resource reallocations can take many forms. A temporary, more or less intensive use of labour and capital in the same basic processes such as production cutbacks or overtime are the forms likely to manifest themselves in the early phases of the devaluation. The later stages are likely to see resource shifts between sectors and the appearance of entirely new processes and technologies, as well as the elimination of the production of certain products and the creation of processes for products not formerly produced. The reorganization process will have long- and short-term consequences on levels of output and growth. In the case of idle resources and excess capacity, the beneficial effects should be felt relatively quickly. However, as is more likely to be the case, when it is necessary to make investments in order to create the required resources and incremental capacity, the beneficial effects will be longer in coming, while the negative effects will be felt immediately. Furthermore, capital losses will appear in industries losing out in the devaluation. Many operations will become unprofitable and have to shut down.

Thus, there will be powerful forces working against the structural change. Losers in the income redistribution will fight to restore their standard of living, while industries benefiting from tariffs, subsidies and controls will strive to maintain their privileges. If the income redistribution is allowed to progress and privileges are effectively eliminated, many producers will be forced out of business. The resulting lay-offs and reduced output will create political and social pressures that cannot be resisted indefinitely. The time element, then, is crucial to the outcome. How long it takes for the beneficial effects of the resource reallocation to begin to offset the negative effects often determines whether the devaluation will be successful in establishing the conditions for the long-term equilibrium of the external sector.

The J-curve

How the balance on current account eventually reacts to the elasticities, income and absorption forces of the preceeding sections depends on the time it takes for each one to make itself felt. Price elasticities may be smaller in the short run than in the long run. Income and absorption effects may take several years to work themselves through the economy. Structural adjustment may take much longer. Consequently, the time path of the current account balance can take different forms. One of the forms frequently observed is an initial worsening of the current account balance, followed by a gradual improvement.[8] A graph of the time path shows it to look like a J, as in Figure 4.2; hence, it has become known as the J-curve effect.

The J-curve effect is usually explained as the result of flexible prices and sticky quantities.[9] In other words, the external terms of trade deteriorate

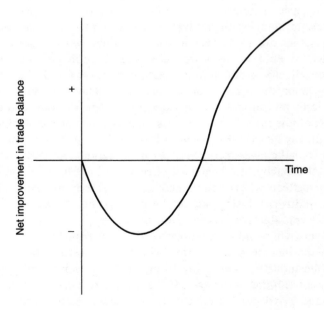

Figure 4.2 The J-curve.

faster than quantities of exports and imports can adjust to them. It is not 'entirely clear exactly why this should be the case. However, an interesting explanation of this phenomenon holds that immediately following a devaluation, the anticipation of higher prices for tradables causes a strong intertemporal substitution effect between tradables and non-tradables. Anticipating price rises in tradables as a result of the devaluation, economic agents rush to make purchases before the price rises occur, thereby causing a temporary reduction in exports and an increase in imports.[10]

There are many combinations of short- and long-term supply and demand elasticities that can produce the J-curve effect. The important point to remember is that it depends on different time lags in the adjustment process set off by the devaluation. When it appears, it tends to increase the disequilibrium between the supply and demand for foreign currency.

THE BALANCE OF PAYMENTS, THE EXCHANGE RATE AND THE MONEY SUPPLY

Intervention in the exchange markets

Many governments would like to avoid the adjustment process outlined above and the economic, social and political consequences it implies. As we pointed out above, this can be done by using foreign reserves to make up the difference between the supply and demand of domestic currency on the foreign exchange markets. By intervening, the monetary authorities keep the exchange rate from changing and avoid the consequences of the adjustment process. Intervention, however, is not without its economic and financial consequences. A *ceteris paribus* sale of foreign currency to prevent a depreciation of the local currency causes a reduction in the money base and, through the operation of the money supply multiplier, a proportional reduction in the overall money supply. A *ceteris paribus* purchase of foreign currency to prevent an appreciation of the local currency causes an increase in the money base and, through the operation of the money supply multiplier, a proportional increase in the money supply. Hence, the economic effects of intervention are introduced through the monetary system and depend on how the quantity of money and changes in the quantity of money affect economic performance.

Consider intervention aimed at preventing currency appreciation. Table 4.3 shows a representative national monetary system. When the central bank purchases foreign currency, account 1, foreign assets, increases (*BP* is positive). The central bank pays for the foreign currency with a claim or

Table 4.3 A national monetary system

Central Bank Monetary Authorities	
1. Foreign assets	3. Money base
2. Claims on the economy	4. Foreign liabilities
Deposit Money Banks	
5. Reserves	8. Demand deposits
6. Foreign assets	9. Time deposits
7. Claims on the economy	10. Foreign liabilities

cheque drawn on itself, which causes account 3, the money base, to increase. The money base is composed of currency and coins held outside the banking system plus liabilities to the deposit money banks. The money base increase causes a corresponding increase in account 5, deposit money bank reserves, and either account 8, deposit money bank demand liabilities, or account 10, deposit money bank foreign liabilities. Since the deposit bank is required to hold reserves equal to only a fraction of its short-term liabilities (the reserve ratio), through successive loans and deposits, the increase in reserves enables the banking system as a whole to increase its balance sheet by a multiple of the increase in reserves. On the one hand, account 7, claims on the economy, increases, while on the other hand, accounts 8 and 9, demand and time deposits, which constitute the bulk of the money supply in a modern economy, also increase. According to the **quantity theory of money**, an increase in the money supply will cause prices to rise. The higher prices worsen the trade balance by attracting imports and diverting exportables from foreign markets to the domestic market.

At the same time, the increase in credit to the economy increases spending on investment and, through the investment income multiplier, causes an increase in overall income and expenditure. The ultimate magnitude of the increase depends on the investment income multiplier.[11] Some of the incremental expenditure will be on imports and exportables, further worsening the trade balance. Furthermore, if the incremental money supply exceeds the demand for cash balances necessary to assure the increased economic activity, the excess will be used to purchase financial assets, both domestic and foreign. An increase in the purchase of foreign assets worsens the capital account. Increased demand for domestic assets raises their price and lowers the domestic interest rate. A lower domestic interest rate stimulates investment, expenditure and the demand for imports and exportables. It also makes domestic assets less attractive relative to foreign assets and tends to further worsen the capital account. The ultimate outcome of all this depends on the economy's production possibility curve, its demand function for money, the marginal propensity to save and the marginal propensity to import. If, for example, the economy is operating at full capacity in all sectors, the increase in expenditure will fall disproportionately on imports and foreign assets. Any increase in expenditure on non-tradables will translate into price increases. If only one or two sectors are operating at full capacity, increased expenditure on their output will also raise their prices. In any case the effects of intervention will tend to bring the supply and demand for foreign currency into equilibrium and the adjustment process will affect income distribution, the level and composition of output, resource allocation, and the price level.

Now consider intervention aimed at preventing a depreciation of the currency. Account 1, foreign assets, decreases (*BP* is negative) and account 3, the money base, also decreases. Through the same process as before, a decrease in the money base should lead to a reduction in credit to the economy and a corresponding decrease in the money supply. According to the quantity theory of money, a decrease in the money supply reduces demand and causes prices to fall. Lower demand and prices reduce imports and divert exportables from the domestic market to foreign markets.

The reduction in credit to the economy reduces investment and causes a reduction in overall income and expenditure. The ultimate magnitude of the reduction depends on the investment income multiplier. Since some of the reduction in expenditure will fall on imports and exportables, the trade balance should improve. Furthermore, if the reduction in the money supply exceeds the reduction in demand for cash balances due to the reduced level of transactions, domestic residents will rebuild them by selling financial assets both domestic and foreign. A decrease in the purchase of foreign assets improves the capital account. Reduced demand for domestic assets lowers their price and raises the domestic interest rate. A higher domestic interest rate discourages investment, expenditure and the demand for imports and exportables. It also makes domestic assets more attractive relative to foreign assets and tends to improve the capital account. The overall price level as well as relative prices will be affected. As before, the ultimate outcome of all this depends on the economy's production possibility curve, its demand function for money, the marginal propensity to save and the marginal propensity to import. In any case the effects of intervention will tend to bring the supply and demand for foreign currency into equilibrium and the adjustment process will affect income distribution, the level and composition of output, resource allocation and the price level.

Offsetting the monetary effects of intervention

It turns out that the adjustment process set off by changes in the money supply is just as traumatic as the adjustment process set off by the devaluation. Unfortunately, it is easy for governments to offset the effects of intervention and thereby postpone the adjustment process. For example, the sale of foreign currency by the monetary authorities can be offset by the purchase of domestic securities (account 1 decreases and account 2 increases by an equal amount, thereby leaving account 3, the money base, unchanged). On the other hand, the purchase of foreign currency can be offset by the sale of domestic securities (account 1 increases and account 2 decreases by an equal amount, thereby leaving account 3, the money base, unchanged). When the external disequilibrium is seasonal or temporary, no harm is done and some may even be avoided.

Seasonal disequilibrium occurs when the production and consumption of a nation's exports and imports vary seasonally and when the seasonal variation is not the same for both. Seasonal disequilibrium is usually short-lived and offsetting. France, for example, virtually closes down its industry for the month of August, when most of its workforce goes on vacation. This causes a seasonal reduction in the demand for imports. On the other hand, as a major tourist attraction, French service exports are likely to increase, leading to a disequilibrium in the current account. The surge in economic activity and the reduction in tourism at the *rentrée* in September, however, offsets the August disequilibrium as service exports decrease and industrial imports increase.

Other, irregular or random disturbances may cause temporary external disequilibrium. Crop failure can reduce exports or make it necessary to increase imports of foodstuffs. Labour strikes and natural disasters such as floods and earthquakes can also upset the balance of payments. When these disturbances are such that they are self-correcting or one-off affairs and have no lasting effect on the economy, central bank intervention in the exchange markets and a compensating monetary policy can be justified as a means of avoiding the needless adjustment process that will be set in motion by a change in the exchange rate. However, when the external disequilibrium is caused by relative price distortions or structural shortcomings, the adjustment is necessary and this type of policy only puts off the inevitable and makes the adjustment that much more painful.

The monetary approach to the balance of payments

The preceding section established the link between the domestic monetary situation and the external sector. We saw that changes in the domestic monetary situation induced by disequilibrium in the external sector set in motion a self-correcting process as prices and cash balances adjust to the new situation. The monetary approach concentrates on the relationship between the money supply, prices, and real cash balances to explain balance of payments equilibrium.[12]

Remember that the total supply elasticities of the traditional approach to balance of payments discipline and devaluation theory recognize the importance of price differentials or relative rates of inflation between the devaluing country and the rest of the world. The traditional approach also recognizes the importance of real cash balances in determining balance of payments equilibrium. In these respects it resembles the monetary approach. Unfortunately, it concentrates on flow adjustments such as exports, imports, income and absorption and fails to consider stock adjustments. The monetary approach recognizes money as a stock concept and its importance for balance of payments equilibrium. Therefore, its analysis is conducted in terms of stock adjustments in the supply and demand for money. For example, a deficit in the balance of trade can be considered as a reduction in the level of cash balances in favour of goods and services beyond the domestic economy's productive capacity. A deficit on capital account can be considered as a reduction of cash balances in favour of other types of financial assets or as a level of outstanding credit in excess of the economy's capacity to save.

The monetary approach assumes a stable functional demand for money and considers the world economy as a closed system where optimal prices are those determined in the international marketplace. Relative prices that deviate from those in the international marketplace due to tariffs, subsidies and controls are viewed as sources of sub-optimal resource allocation and impediments to balance of payments equilibrium. Balance of payments equilibrium is achieved through equilibrium in the supply and demand for money. When monetary equilibrium is not respected, the consequences will fall on the price level because, according to the quantity theory of money on which the monetary approach is based, a nominal money supply that exceeds or falls short of the real cash balances demanded by domestic economic agents will affect the price level. An excess supply of money raises the price level and a shortage lowers it. By focusing on the money supply, the monetary approach underlines the importance of the domestic price level for external equilibrium. In the following section on international parity relations, we will take a long look at how prices or, more precisely, the price level, affects external equilibrium and the exchange rate.

The monetary approach to the balance of payments is a powerful tool for international financial analysis. Where the traditional approach relies on knowledge of complicated micro- and macroeconomic relationships as well as generally unmeasurable supply and demand elasticities, the monetary approach concentrates on one observable variable, the money supply and the prospective performance of the economy's external sector can be judged by domestic monetary policy represented by domestic credit. Some caution is in order, however. First of all, except in the most unsophisticated financial systems, there is some confusion surrounding the financial aggregates corresponding to the definition of 'money'.[13] Secondly, the velocity of money is probably not a constant but rather a stable function of certain variables such as prices, interest rates and wealth.[14] In Appendix 4.1 we present a mathematical model of the monetary approach to the balance of payments.

The portfolio balance approach

Another explanation of exchange rate determination adds demand functions and equilbrium conditions for bond markets to the traditional monetary approach. This approach, called the portfolio balance approach, assumes that investors desire diversified portfolios and, hence, will hold both domestic and foreign assets. Whereas the monetary approach assumes that bond markets always clear, the portfolio balance approach, through supply and demand functions for bonds and equilibrium conditions setting bond supply equal to demand, shows how bond markets clear. With this modification the effects of changing bond supplies and demands can have consequences on interest rates and the exchange rate that differ in the short run from what is forecast in the monetary approach.

Suppose, for example, that the central bank buys domestic bonds on the market. From the preceding section we know that this will increase the money base and, through the reserve ratio multiplier, cause an increase in the domestic money supply. Other things being equal, the primitive formulations of the monetary approach predict that the exchange rate will depreciate by the percentage increase in the money supply. The portfolio approach argues that by reducing the supply of bonds in circulation, the central bank has created an excess demand that will raise bond prices and lower interest rates. Lower interest rates have well-known consequences on investment, output and prices that will affect the exchange rate. In Appendix 4.2 we present a mathematical model of the portfolio balance approach to the balance of payments.

THE INTERNATIONAL PARITY RELATIONS

The international parity relations, embodied in the writings of J. Keynes, G. Cassel, and I. Fisher, form the basis of most analysis of exchange rate behaviour. They are an elegant set of simple equilibrium relationships between the prices of goods and services, interest rates, and the spot and forward exchange rates. Although they are highly stylized and depend on some demonstrably unrealistic assumptions, they constitute a powerful theoretical framework for understanding and explaining the international financial environment.

Purchasing power parity

Of all the factors that influence exchange rate movements and long-term external equilibrium, price increases or inflation stand out as particularly important. The theory linking inflation and exchange rate movements is known as purchasing power parity (PPP). The theory of purchasing power parity has its source in the mercantilist literature of the 17th century, but it came into prominence through the writings of Gustav Cassel in the early 1900s.[15] Since then it has come to occupy an important place in international economic and financial analysis. PPP, for example, is often the long-run equilibrium condition for the exchange rate in dynamic exchange rate models. In systems of fixed exchange rates it has been widely used by monetary authorities for establishing new par values when the existing ones were clearly out of line. Money managers also commonly use PPP for forecasting exchange rates or for determining the currency composition of their portfolios.

The theory of PPP is based on the **law of one price**. This states that identitical commodities or goods must have the same price in all markets. If this were not the case, arbitrage would take place whereby profit-seeking entrepreneurs could exploit the situation by buying in the market with the lower price and selling in the market with the higher price. The increased demand in the market with the lower price would tend to raise the price in that market while the increased supply in the higher priced market would tend to lower its price. This activity would continue until the prices in both markets equalized, thereby eliminating the potential for profit.

Even without arbitrage, the law of one price should hold for internationally traded goods because outside buyers would only buy in the market with the lowest price. In practice, of course, it costs money and takes time to ship goods from one place to another and there are often restrictions of various forms on international trade. In this sense prices might differ somewhat. For example, a banana should cost more in Holland than in Honduras where it is produced because of the cost of shipping the banana from Honduras to Holland.

PPP describes the relation between average price levels in each country and the equilibrium exchange rate. In its absolute form it states that the exchange rate should be equal to the ratio of the average price levels of the two currencies. This relation is very restrictive and can only be valid if goods and financial markets are perfect and the same commodities appear in the same proportions in each country's market basket. This is an unrealistic proposition, insofar as it ignores the effects of market imperfections, transactions costs, product differentiation, and restrictions on international trade such as quotas and tariffs.

The **relative form** of PPP, more commonly used today, is less restrictive than the absolute form. It states that in comparison to a period when exchange rates were in equilibrium, changes in the ratio of domestic to foreign prices indicate the appropriate adjustment in the exchange rate. Let $S_t(G/\$)$ represent the spot number of guilders for one dollar at time t and i_n and $i_\$$ the rate of inflation in the Netherlands and the United States respectively. Then the relative form of PPP can be expressed as:

$$\frac{S_t(G/\$)}{S_0(G/\$)} = \frac{1 + i_n}{1 + i_\$} \tag{4.6}$$

Relative PPP can also be presented as the percentage change in the exchange rate over the period by subtracting 1 from both sides of equation 4.6:

$$\frac{S_t(G/\$) - S_0(G/\$)}{S_0(G/\$)} = \frac{i_n - i_\$}{1 + i_\$} \tag{4.7}$$

This is the most usual presentation of relative PPP. When inflation rates are low, equation 4.7 can be approximated as the difference between the two countries' rates of inflation.

To take an example of the relative form of PPP, suppose that on December 31, 1993 the guilder/dollar exchange rate is 2 guilders = $1, that the US consumer price index goes from 100 to 110 from December 31, 1993 to December 31, 1994 and the Dutch consumer price index goes from 200 to 250 over the same period. The rate of inflation in the US is thus 10% and in the Netherlands it is 25%. Using equation 4.6, we can calculate the exchange rate on December 31, 1994:

$$\frac{S_t(G/\$)}{2} = \frac{1.25}{1.1}$$

and

$$S_t(G/\$) = 2.2727.$$

Whether or not PPP holds is an ongoing controversy. The reasons why it might not hold are numerous. The strictest form of PPP requires that:

1. financial markets are perfect, with no controls, taxes, transactions costs, etc.;
2. goods markets are perfect, with international shipment of goods able to take place freely, instantaneously and without cost;
3. there is a single consumption good common to everyone; **or**
4. the same commodities appear in the same proportions in each country's consumption basket.

These assumptions are clearly unrealistic. Goods and financial markets are not perfect. Goods cannot be shipped instantaneously, transport costs are high, and import restrictions of various forms are widespread. Taxes, transactions costs and controls are present in the financial markets. There are also many types of consumption goods, and economic agents throughout the world have different tastes and preferences, so that a common basket of consumption goods does not exist. Furthermore, the PPP hypothesis designates relative inflation differentials as the only source of exchange rate variations. This is clearly false, since, at least in the short run, other non-monetary phenomena such as changes in relative prices as well as changes in the level and composition of output and consumption influence the supply and demand for foreign currency and thus the exchange rate.

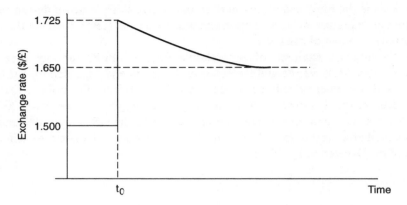

Figure 4.3 Exchange rate overshooting.

Another popular explanation for significant short-term deviations from PPP is the theory of overshooting. This theory marries the concepts of PPP, sticky prices and the asset market approach. Suppose that PPP holds in the long run but the prices of non-traded goods are sticky and adjust slowly to their new equilibrium level after a disturbance such as a unilateral increase in the domestic money supply. Eventually prices will rise in proportion to the increase in the money supply, and the nominal exchange rate, driven by changes in PPP, will depreciate in proportion to the change in prices. In the short term, however, the price level increases less than the money supply due to the sticky prices for non-traded goods. The resulting excess supply of money will be spent at least partially on bonds, thereby causing bond prices to rise and interest rates to fall. Because investors have rational expectations and anticipate the eventual depreciation of the currency, they require higher interest rates to offset the depreciation. This is because total expected returns include interest plus or minus the expected appreciation or depreciation of the currency. But current interest rates are lower than before. Thus, in order for investors to buy domestic assets the currency must overshoot or depreciate to a point below its long-term PPP equilibrium level, from where it is then expected to appreciate. In this way its anticipated appreciation will compensate for the lower interest rates. An example of exchange rate overshooting is shown in Figure 4.3 where a disturbance requires a depreciation of 10% in the dollars's long-term PPP value, from $1.50 per pound to $1.65 per pound. In order for financial markets to return to equilibrium, however, the dollar depreciates by 15%, to $1.725. This is because prices in the goods markets take time to change, so that much of the short-term adjustment must come from the financial markets. Gradually over time the prices in the goods markets adjust and the exchange rate appreciates to its long-term equilibrium level.

With all these qualifications, the question is, then, to what extent purchasing power parity exists as a real world phenomenon. Some studies find little support for the PPP hypothesis. Studies by J.D. Richardson, P. Isard, and I.B. Kravis and R.E. Lipsey found substantial deviations from the law of one price in the commodities markets.[16] If the law of one price does not hold, then PPP is not likely to hold either. However, another series of studies has found that PPP does hold, but with a considerable time lag.[17] H. Galliot tested PPP between the United States and Canada, Great Britain, France, West Germany, Italy, Japan, and Switzerland from 1900 to 1967.[18] H. Edison tested the dollar/pound exchange rate between 1890 and 1978.[19] Both authors found that PPP is often violated in the short run but holds up well in the long run. Abuaf and Jorion, analysing annual data over the period 1900–72 found that deviations from PPP, although substantial in the short term, take about three years to be reduced by half.[20] Despite disagreements over some specific points, the consensus emerging from the vast literature on the subject is that PPP in its relative form is generally valid, at least in the long run.[21]

The evidence is also growing that PPP is more than a long-run phenomenon. R. Rogalski and J. Vinso, studying a period of floating exchanges in the early 1920s and middle 1950s, found that freely floating markets react immediately or almost immediately to changes in relative inflation rates and noted that their finding was consistent with both PPP and the efficient markets theory.[22] The efficient market hypothesis holds that all relevant information is fully and immediately reflected in a security's market price.[23] R. Roll applied the efficient markets hypothesis to PPP by assuming that the current spot rate reflects anticipated exchange-adjusted inflation differentials, rather than a slow adjustment to past inflation differentials.[24] His results on 252 pairs of countries over the period 1957–76 strongly supported this hypothesis and suggested that for most countries, and for all the largest trading nations, the adjustment duration is less than one month.

In summary, then, in spite of the evidence of significant short-term departures from PPP, it is clear that there is a strong correspondence between relative rates of inflation and changes in the exchange rate. However, because PPP is not a complete theory of exchange rate determination, the correspondence is not perfect and there is no theoretical imperative to associate departures from PPP with market disequilibrium.

Interest rate parity

Interest rate parity is the cornerstone to most if not all of today's international financial transactions. As a theory it was first developed by J.M. Keynes in 1930.[25] The interest parity relation states that on perfect money markets the forward discount or premium on the foreign exchange market is equal to the relative difference between the two nominal interest rates. It can be expressed as:

$$\frac{F_1(G/\$)}{S_0(G/\$)} = \frac{1 + r_n}{1 + r_\$} \tag{4.8}$$

where $F_1(G/\$)$ represents the forward exchange rate for time 1 and r_n and $r_\$$ represent the nominal interest rates on the guilder and the dollar over the period.

Subtracting 1 from both sides gives the forward discount or premium:

$$\frac{F_1(G/\$) - S_0(G/\$)}{S_0(G/\$)} = \frac{r_n - r_\$}{1 + r_\$} \tag{4.9}$$

When $r_\$$ is low, the forward discount or premium can be approximated as the difference between the two interest rates.

If the spot guilder/dollar exchange rate is 2 guilders for \$1 and the nominal interest rates on guilders and dollars are 6% and 12% respectively, we can use equation 4.8 to find the forward exchange rate compatible with interest rate parity:

$$\frac{F_1(G/\$)}{2G/\$_1} = \frac{1.06}{1.12}$$

and

$$F_1(G/\$) = 1.8929.$$

The forward rate should be 1.8929 guilders for each dollar. Otherwise, riskless arbitrage opportunities would exist.

The evidence for the validity of interest rate parity in the Eurocurrency markets is convincing. Three studies, one by R. Aliber, one by R. Marston and another by R. Roll and B. Solnik, found that it holds almost perfectly in the Eurocurrency markets.[26] This not surprising, because the Eurocurrency markets come close to the condition of perfect financial markets, they have very low transactions costs and they are devoid of taxes and controls. When transactions costs are considered, the conclusion is much the same. They do not contribute substantially to departures from interest rate parity. The literature on the subject is extensive, but it is generally recognized that uncovered or one-way interest arbitrage is the reason for this. One-way interest arbitrage, as opposed to covered interest arbitrage, is just another way of saying that people will borrow where they get the lowest rate and lend where they get the highest rate.[27] When controls exist, however, the conclusion is different. Otani and Tiwari found that Japanese capital controls caused the interest rate parity relation to break down in the Tokyo market.[28]

The general consensus is that interest rate parity holds nicely in the integrated and unregulated Eurocurrency markets. In markets where there seem to be substantial departures from interest parity, these departures can be attributed to transactions costs, taxes and other types of controls.

The international Fisher relation

The interest rates used in day-to-day financial transactions are **nominal rates**. Nominal rates express the rate of exchange between current money and future money. For example the interest rates that we quoted in the example for interest rate parity were nominal rates. They indicate that a one guilder deposit today will be worth 1.06 guilders one year in the future or that a one dollar deposit today will be worth $1.12 one year in the future. However, the nominal rates do not indicate how many more goods and services might be purchased with the 1.06 guilders or the $1.12. This is because price changes or inflation (deflation) may change the value of money over the course of time. In fact, a changing value of money over time is the rule rather than the exception.

Irving Fisher suggested that because investors are concerned with the real interest rate, the nominal interest rate should be composed of two elements: the real interest rate that we can call the real required rate of return (ρ) and the expected rate of inflation (i^*).[29]

Stated formally, this relation is known as the **Fisher relation** and can be written:

$$1 + r = (1 + \rho)(1 + i^*) \qquad (4.10)$$

Where more than one currency is involved, the Fisher relation can be generalized. Take the dollar and the guilder, for example, and apply equation 4.10:

$$\frac{1 + r_n}{1 + r_{n\$}} = \frac{(1 + \rho_n)(1 + i_n^*)}{(1 + \rho_\$)(1 + i_\$^*)} \tag{4.11}$$

where the asterisks refer to expected values. This is called the international Fisher relation or the **Fisher open condition**, where 'open' refers to an open economy. It gives the ratio of nominal investment values in terms of relative real rates of interest and expected rates of inflation. It should not be forgotten that this relation is not a market arbitrage condition like PPP and interest rate parity. It is a general equilibrium condition derived from first-order optimality conditions from individuals' utility optimization.

Arbitrage conditions can be applied, however, to generate other forms of the international Fisher relation. It is often argued that if expected real returns on identical assets were higher in one country than another, arbitrage would cause capital to flow from the country with the lower real return to the country with the higher real return. Assuming perfect markets, this arbitrage would continue until real returns became equal. In this case, equation 4.11 would become:

$$\frac{1 + r_n}{1 + r_\$} = \frac{(1 + i_n^*)}{(1 + i_\$^*)} \tag{4.12}$$

The right-hand side of equation 4.12 corresponds to the efficient markets formulation of PPP, found by writing equation 4.6 in terms of expected values of inflation and the exchange rate, so that equation 4.12 could be written:

$$\frac{S_t^*(G/\$)}{S_0(G/\$)} = \frac{1 + r_n}{1 + r_\$} \tag{4.13}$$

The historical evidence is consistent with the Fisher relation. It seems that most if not all the variation in nominal interest rates can be attributed to changing inflationary expectations. Most countries show a strong correlation between inflation and nominal interest rates. Whether or not real interest rates are stable and equal across countries is a more difficult proposition. E. Kane and L. Rosenthal studied the Eurocurrency market for six major currencies over the period 1974–9 and found support for this argument.[30] F. Mishkin, on the other hand, found evidence that real interest rates are somewhat variable over time and differ across countries.[31] The problem, of course, is that verification requires a measure of expected inflation. Since expected inflation cannot be observed directly, the validity of the conclusions depends to a large extent on how well the estimated expected inflation approximates the actual figure. In any case it is hard to believe that real interest rate differentials could last for very long in fully integrated international financial markets. Most economists agree that the increasingly integrated nature of today's financial markets and the vast supply of liquid capital that nourishes them are causing real interest rates to converge in most of the major economies.

Some caution is in order. The limit to this type of convergence depends on the risk characteristics of the different countries. A country with an economy that is inherently riskier than another will incite foreign investors to demand a higher real rate of return to compensate for the incremental economic risk. E. Clark has recently shown that there are wide discrepencies in risk levels even between the major industrialized countries.[32]

The relation between the exchange rate and nominal interest rate differentials (equation 4.13) also seems to have some weak support. The first observable fact is that currencies with high rates of inflation and high nominal interest rates have a tendency to depreciate. In Mexico, for example, between 1982 and 1988 the treasury bill rate averaged over 67%. Over the same period the exchange rate went from 96.5 pesos per dollar to 2,281 pesos per dollar, a loss of over 95% of its value. The same phenomenon can be observed in all the high inflation countries like Argentina, Brazil, Israel, etc. In an interesting empirical study, however, R. Cumby and M. Obstfeld reject a predictable relationship between the nominal interest rate differential and the exchange rate.[33] On the other hand, other empirical studies indicate that interest differentials correctly anticipate exchange rate changes, which implies that currencies with relatively high nominal rates can be expected to depreciate *vis-à-vis* currencies with relatively low nominal rates.[34]

Here again some caution is in order. Nominal interest rates are composed of the real interest rate and expected inflation. If expected inflation is the cause of the nominal interest rate differential, the exchange rate can effectively be expected to depreciate. However, if the nominal interest rate differential is caused by a change in the real interest rate, the opposite will occur. Suppose, for example, that the differential widens because the real interest rate increases relative to other countries. The exchange rate will then appreciate as investors buy the currency in order to take advantage of the higher real interest rate. The Dornbusch theory of overshooting, for example, relies on the mechanism of temporary shifts in the real interest rate to explain seemingly excessive fluctuations in the exchange rate.

In summary, then, although there is substantial evidence for a relationship between changes in the nominal interest rate differential and movements in the exchange rate, the evidence that the relationship is stable and predictable is not conclusive.

Forward rate parity

The **forward rate parity hypothesis** states that the forward exchange rate quoted at time 0 for delivery at time 1 is equal to what the spot rate is expected to be at time 1. This hypothesis is based on the important role that expectations play in financial decision-making and the close link between the forward and spot rates through interest rate parity. It is usually written:

$$F_1(G/\$) = S_1^*(G/\$) \tag{4.14}$$

where the asterisk denotes expectation.

If the future spot rate were known with certainty this relation would have to hold. Otherwise there would be an opportunity for riskless arbitrage. It is a well-known fact, of course, that the future spot rate is not known with certainty. It is often argued, however, that forward parity will still hold in the presence of uncertainty because the forward rate is an unbiased predictor of the future spot rate. Others argue that the forward rate is a biased predictor of the future spot rate because risk averse investors will demand a risk premium for bearing foreign exchange risk and therefore equation 4.14 will not hold.[35] A risk premium of this type is a common feature of modern portfolio investment theory. It is well known from modern portfolio theory, however, that only risk that cannot be eliminated through diversification is rewarded with a premium. A major argument against the existence of a risk premium in the forward exchange market is that currency risk can be diversified away. If this is true, a risk premium on the foreign exchange market is unnecessary and the forward exchange rate will indeed be an unbiased predictor of the expected future spot exchange rate. Ultimately, the forward rate parity hypothesis boils down to an empirical issue rather than a theoretical one.

The literature on the relation between forward and future spot rates is extensive. First of all, it seems that since the inception of floating exchange rates in 1973 the forward exchange rate has had a very inefficient predictive performance. One recent study comparing the US dollar to the British pound, the Japanese yen, and the German mark from April 1975 to June 1985 has found that losses from a forward transaction averaged 5% per year and that from early 1980 to February 1985 annual losses averaged 15%. Furthermore, regressions linking the one-month percentage change in the spot dollar price of these foreign currencies to the corresponding one-month forward premium from the previous month had less than 3% explanatory power (R^2) and tended on average to mispredict the direction in which the dollar exchange rate would move during the subsequent month.[36]

Other tests have been performed to determine whether the forward exchange rate is an unbiased and efficient predictor of the future spot rate. One approach has been to calculate the average error of the difference between $F_1(.)$ and $S_1(.)$.[37] These results found that the mean forecast error is not statistically different from zero, thereby suggesting a zero risk premium. However, when the sample was divided in half so that the risk premium could take two values over the whole observation period, evidence of a non-zero risk premium was present.

Another approach has been to search for serial correlation in the prediction error. There is evidence that the exchange rate forecast errors are serially correlated, which implies that there is a risk premium that fluctuates between positive and negative values.[38]

The upshot of most studies that seem to confirm the presence of a risk premium is that the risk premium, if it exists, seems to change signs. Sometimes it is positive, sometimes it is negative and it usually averages close to zero. Many studies fail to find evidence for the existence of any risk premium at all. Therefore, in the absence of a more precise econometric model, it seems perfectly acceptable to adopt the forward parity hypothesis and treat the forward rate as an unbiased estimator of the future spot rate.

ASSESSING THE RISK

Variables and ratios for economic risk assessment

Economic risk analysis involves an assessment of the country's ongoing and prospective economic situation, as well as an estimate of the accuracy of the assessment itself. Based on the discussion in the preceding paragraphs, we can designate the economic variables pertinent to assessing cross-border economic risk. They can be divided into variables associated with the domestic economy and variables associated with the balance of payments.

The principal domestic economic variables are:

- GNP or GDP broken down by sector (agriculture, manufacturing, construction, services);
- gross domestic investment;
- gross domestic fixed investment;
- private and public consumption;
- gross domestic savings (remember that gross domestic savings are equal to GNP minus total domestic consumption);
- the resource gap, defined as the difference between gross domestic savings and gross domestic investment (remember that this is equal to the current account balance);
- the money supply;
- the government budget deficit (a government budget deficit implies dissaving, thereby lowering gross domestic saving and increasing the resource gap);
- the GNP deflator (a Paasche index);[39]
- the consumer price index (a Laspeyre index).[40]

The principal variables associated with the balance of payments are:

- exports of goods and services in dollars or SDRs (X) broken down by product or product class (primary products, manufacturers);
- imports of goods and services in dollars or SDRs (M) broken down by product or product class (energy, intermediate goods, investment goods, consumption goods);
- the trade balance;
- the current account balance;
- the export price index in dollars or SDRs;
- the import price index in dollars or SDRs;
- the exchange rate;
- foreign reserves (RES).

Standard economic risk assessment consists of combining these two sets of variables to generate a structured qualitative report based on economic analysis and a number of ratios considered as significant indicators of the ongoing and prospective economic situation. One set of ratios aims at assessing the prospects for long-term growth in GDP or GNP. It includes:

- gross domestic fixed investment/GDP (or GNP);
- gross domestic savings/GDP (or GNP);
- marginal capital/output (the number of dollars of increase in investment necessary to increase output by one dollar);

- net capital imports/gross domestic fixed investment;
- gross domestic savings/gross domestic fixed investment.

The ratio of gross domestic fixed investment/GDP measures the economy's propensity to invest. It is usually assumed that a higher rate of investment will lead to increased output and higher rates of growth of GDP. The extent to which this is true depends on exactly what type of projects the investment represents. Poor investment decisions will yield poor returns. One way of measuring the quality of gross fixed investment is through the marginal capital/output ratio. This ratio is supposed to measure the marginal productivity of capital. It is usually calculated by dividing gross fixed domestic investment in one period by the increase in GDP one or two periods later. A lower ratio signifies a higher productivity of capital, and the higher the productivity of capital, the better the outlook for GDP growth. The net capital imports/gross domestic fixed investment ratio indicates the extent to which GDP growth is dependent on goods produced abroad. The higher the ratio the more dependent the economy. Combined with the gross domestic savings/gross domestic fixed investment ratio, it indicates how dependent the economy is on foreign resources. The lower domestic savings to domestic investment, the more dependent the economy. Dependence on foreign resources is usually interpreted as a negative factor, insofar as economic risk assessment is concerned. Whether or not this is true is another question. For example, the resource gap can be large due to profitable investment opportunities and the willingness of foreigners to lend. It is hard to see why this should be a negative. On the other hand, in the absence of profitable investment opportunities, the resource gap can also be large due to a high propensity to consume. This, of course, is a negative because it signals that current consumption is being financed with foreign borrowing and that the rate of return on domestic investment is lower than the cost of the foreign resources.

Another set of ratios are used as indicators of price stability:

- government budget deficit/GDP (or GNP);
- percentage increase in the money supply.

Since price instability is considered undesirable, the outlook for price stability and economic performance should be more favourable when both the government budget deficit and the growth in the money supply are reduced.

The principal ratios for assessing the evolution of the balance of payments are:

- percentage change in exports/percentage change in world GDP (or the

GDP of the main customer countries). This represents the income elasticity of the demand for exports;

- percentage change in imports/percentage change in GDP. This represents the income elasticity of demand for imports;
- imports/GDP;
- commodity exports/total exports;
- official reserves/imports.

A high income elasticity of the demand for exports and a low income elasticity of the demand for imports is usually considered favourable for the balance of payments. On the other hand, a high ratio of imports to GDP is considered unfavourable. Because of the well-known volatility of commodity prices, a high ratio of commodity exports to total exports is also considered unfavourable, while a high ratio of reserves to imports is favourable.

Variables and ratios for financial risk assessment

Financial risk analysis involves an assessment of the country's foreign obligations compared to its ongoing and prospective economic situation. The variables pertinent to assessing cross-border financial risk include those presented above that are commonly used for domestic macroeconomic analysis. They also include information on the country's foreign debt and interest.[41]

- Total external debt (EDT) which can be broken down into:

  - long-term public and publicly guaranteed outstanding and disbursed (DOD);
  - long-term private non-guaranteed;
  - short-term;
  - use of IMF credit.

- Total debt service (TDS) which can be broken down into:

  - interest payments (INT);
  - principal payments.

Long-term external debt refers to debt that has an original or extended maturity of more than one year and which is owed to non-residents and is repayable in foreign currency, goods, or services.[42] It has three components: public debt, publicly guaranteed debt, and private, non-guaranteed external debt.

- Public debt is an external obligation of a public debtor, including the national government, a political subdivision or agency of either, and autonomous public bodies.
- Publicly guaranteed debt is an external obligation of a private debtor that is guaranteed for repayment by a public entity.
- Private non-guaranteed external debt is an external obligation of a private debtor that is not guaranteed by a public entity.

Short-term external debt refers to debt that has a maturity of one year or less and includes no distinctions between public and private non-guaranteed short-term debt.

Use of IMF credit refers to repurchase obligations to the IMF with respect to all uses of IMF resources, excluding those resulting from drawings in the reserve or first credit tranche.

Total debt service is the sum of (1) principal repayments and interest payments on long-term debt, (2) repurchases and charges on use of IMF resources, (3) principal and interest payments on short-term debt.

Information on a country's external debt can be combined with the economic and balance of payments variables to generate a number of ratios considered as significant indicators of the ongoing and prospective financial situation. Some of the most common financial ratios are:

- total external debt / exports (EDT / X);
- total external debt / GNP (EDT / GNP);
- official reserves / total external debt (RES / EDT);
- official reserves / imports (RES /M);
- long-term public and publicly guaranteed outstanding and disbursed / exports (DOD / X);
- long-term public and publicly guaranteed outstanding and disbursed / GNP (DOD / GNP);
- total debt service / exports (TDS / X);
- total debt service / GNP (TDS / GNP);
- interest payments / exports (INT / X);
- interest payments / GNP (INT / GNP);
- official reserves / long-term public and publicly guaranteed outstanding and disbursed (RES / DOD).

In corporate finance, **financial leverage** plays a major role in determining financial risk. Financial leverage is measured by the extent to which the assets of the firm are financed with debt. It shows up as interest expense, causing variability in net income over and above the variability in operating income caused by operating risk. Where macroeconomic financial risk is concerned, the same type of effect is present. Financial leverage again shows up as interest expense, causing variability in GDP or GNP over and above the variability caused by economic risk. However, in the absence of a macroeconomic balance sheet, GNP and exports are used as proxies for determining financial leverage. Thus, ratios such as EDT / X, EDT / GNP, DOD / X, and DOD / GNP can be interpreted as measures of the economy's financial leverage. The lower these ratios, the better the economy's financial position. How reliable these ratios are in signalling an economy's financial position depends on how accurately the variables X and GNP reflect the state of the economy's balance sheet. In the next chapter we will see that GDP and the traditional presentation of its component parts can be very misleading regarding the state of an economy's health. Consequently, these ratios should be used with caution.

Other types of leverage ratios used in corporate finance, such as times interest earned and cash flow coverage, seek to determine the extent to which current obligations are covered by current income. The times interest earned ratio relates earnings before interest and taxes to current interest charges, while the cash flow coverage ratio relates earnings before interest and taxes to total current financial obligations including payments for interest and principal. Thus, INT / X and INT / GNP resemble a times interest earned ratio and TDS / X and TDS / GNP resemble a cash flow coverage ratio. Lower ratios indicate a better financial position.

These latter leverage ratios are probably more reliable than the former proxy balance sheet ratios for determining a country's financial health. Nevertheless, they are conceptually different from the corresponding ratios in corporate finance, whose starting point is earnings net of operating costs. The country ratios use exports and GNP which are gross of costs and do not reflect the net flows such as earnings or net exports $(X - M)$ that the economy can generate and make available to honour its external financial obligations.

The ratio RES / M complements the leverage ratios and resembles a **liquidity ratio** in corporate finance. Liquidity ratios measure the firm's ability to meet its maturing short-term obligations. The RES / M ratio measures a country's ability to maintain import levels with current cash in hand.

Forecasting the exchange rate

The simplest technique for forecasting exchange rate movements is to trust the market and use the forward rate as a forecast of the future spot rate. We have seen that the forward rate is just as likely to overestimate as to underestimate the future spot rate and, consequently, is an unbiased estimator of the future spot rate. However, we have also seen that it explains only a very small percentage of actual exchange rate movements. Furthermore, the percentage that it does explain tends to diminish as the forecasting period is lengthened. Nevertheless, currencies selling at a forward discount do tend to depreciate, while those selling at a premium tend to appreciate.

Since widespread forward rates only exist on maturities of up to a year, longer-term forward rates have to be deduced from the interest rate differential. This can be done by extending the single-period interest rate parity relation presented in equation 4.8 to include several periods. Let $r_{\$, n}$ and $r_{\pounds, n}$ be the annual interest rate on a zero coupon loan lasting n years. Because of compounding over n periods, at the end of n years the loans will be worth $[1 + r_{\$, n}]^n$ and $[1 + r_{\pounds, n}]^n$ respectively. The same arbitrage argument holds in the multiperiod case as in the single-period case. It should not be possible for an investor to make a profit by borrowing in one currency, selling the currency spot for another currency, lending the second currency and buying the first currency back in a forward transaction. Thus, the multi-period forward rate implied by interest rate parity can be written:

$$\frac{F_n(\$/\pounds)}{S_0(\$/\pounds)} = \frac{(1 + r_{\$,n})^n}{(1 + r_{\pounds,n})^n} \tag{4.15}$$

Suppose the $/£ spot rate is $2 = £1$, $n = 5$ years, $r_{\$, 5} = 10\%$ and $r_{\pounds, 5} = 15\%$, then applying this information in equation 4.15, gives:

$$\frac{F_n(\$/\pounds)}{\$2/\pounds1} = \frac{(1.10)^5}{(1.15)^5}$$

$$F_n(\$/\pounds) = \$2\frac{1.6105}{2.0114} = \$1.6014.$$

The five-year forward exchange rate implied by the interest rate differential is $1.6014 for £1.

Although the forward rate seems to indicate trends in exchange rates, its short-term inaccuracy makes it a poor predictor of future spot rates. **Fundamental analysis** is an alternative approach to the market-based forward rate for exchange rate forecasting. Fundamental analysis involves examining the macroeconomic variables and policies that are likely to influence a currency's performance. We have seen that the relevant variables are numerous and the functional relationships among them are complex so that one of the problems facing the forecaster is to develop a model complex enough to mirror reality but simple enough that it can be understood. The basic variables relevant to fundamental analysis are those found in the international parity relations: spot and forward exchange rates and relative interest rates and rates of inflation. Interpreting these variables depends on the analyst's model of exchange rate determination.

The literature on exchange rate determination is vast but the theories currently being used can generally be broken down into two categories: a balance of payments flow adjustment model and an asset market stock adjustment model.

The balance of payments flow adjustment model

The balance of payments flow adjustment model focuses on macroeconomic flows and their impact on the balance of payments. Through macro-economic analysis based on the elasticities-absorption approach to balance of payments theory outlined above, the forecaster attempts to determine the imbalances that will occur in the various sub-accounts in the balance of payments identity. In this way he can estimate the overall supply and demand for foreign currency as well as the exchange rate where supply just equals demand. Remember that in the elasticities-absorption approach the relationships between macroeconomic flows, interest rates and prices are complex and depend on such things as supply and demand elasticities, marginal rates of saving and investment, interest rate differentials and the economy's structural organization. Using these tools for exchange rate forecasting involves determining the relevant relationships and then estimating the direction and magnitude of their effects on the supply and demand for foreign currency.

The asset market stock adjustment model

The asset market stock adjustment model rejects the view that the exchange rate is determined in flow markets. The asset market approach considers exchange rates as asset prices traded in an efficient market. Like other asset prices, today's price depends on expectations about the future. When expectations change, investors rebalance their portfolios, which causes a change in the prices of the stock of outstanding assets. Thus, a change in the exchange rate represents a change in the value of an economy's stock of assets. Using the asset market stock adjustment model to forecast exchange rates involves macroeconomic analysis aimed at estimating the values of variables such as profits, real interest rates and rates of inflation, which are likely to influence asset prices.

Purchasing power parity

We have seen that the monetary approach to balance of payments theory concentrates on one type of asset, money, in exchange rate determination. It assumes that all the other asset markets clear and that monetary phenomena are the only source of price disturbances.[43] Combined with the efficient markets form of purchasing power parity, the monetary approach to exchange rate determination supplies the forecaster with a policy variable, domestic credit, that can be used to predict exchange rates by estimating the future rate of inflation.

This use of the efficient markets form of PPP contrasts with the traditional form of PPP forecasting that assumes that a lag exists between price level changes and exchange rate changes. If, for example, it takes three months for an increase in prices to work its way through to the exchange rate, PPP will be useful in predicting the future exchange rate. It should be remembered, however, that there is an inherent conflict between the efficient markets concept and the predictive power of any lagged variable.

Forecasting models

Forecasting models can be subjective, econometric or a combination of the two. The goal of some models is to discover divergence between actual market rates and a set of theoretical exchange rates derived from fundamental analysis on the assumption that the divergence will be quickly corrected by market forces. Other models in the efficient markets tradition assume that currencies are correctly priced and attempt to forecast the variables that are likely to affect their values in the future.

Different approaches to exchange rate determination can lead to different conclusions about a currency's future value. The balance of payments flow adjustment approach, for example, often concludes that economic growth will cause a balance of trade deficit by increasing imports and decreasing exports and therefore lead to currency depreciation. On the other hand, the asset market approach often concludes that economic growth will lead to currency appreciation caused by foreign capital inflows attracted by expected higher returns.[44] The issues involved were discussed above, where we presented the major cause-effect relationships linking economic activity, monetary policy, balance of payments discipline and exchange rate determination. The relationships are complex, often differing in magnitude and direction, and with varying time lags. The outcome depends on a process of stock adjustments to economic and financial flows as well as flow adjustments to changes in economic and financial stocks. An example of a change in a financial flow could be an increase in GDP. One of the stock adjustments that this might cause could be a reduction in money holdings in favour of increased equity holdings. The effects on the balance of payments of an increase in GDP might be a decrease in exports and an increase in imports, thereby putting downward pressure on the exchange rate. On the other hand, the rise in equity prices that the stock adjustment implies might attract foreign capital, thereby putting upward pressure on the exchange rate.

Most models of fundamental analysis incorporate one or both sides of this adjustment process. Understanding these relationships and using them to forecast exchange rates is a difficult proposition. Subjective fundamental analysis risks lacking objectivity and often suffers from the limits on the complexity it can attain. Econometric models, even when they are theoretically sound, suffer from the fact that their accuracy depends on forecasts of key exogenous variables such as the central bank's monetary policy or the government's fiscal policy. These exogenous variables are no easier to forecast than the model's endogenous variables. Furthermore, structural relationships can and do change over time, thereby making it necessary to re-estimate the model. However, since models are estimated with historical data, it might take a while before the new structural relationships become statistically significant enough to appear in the coefficients.

Technical analysis
Another popular method of exchange rate forecasting is based on technical analysis, so named because it makes no use of the economic and financial fundamentals deemed relevant to exchange rate determination. It focuses on prices and seeks to detect repetitions of past price patterns. The two primary methods for detecting these patterns are **chartism** and **trend analysis**. Chartism relies on the study of charts to find recurring price patterns. Trend analysis uses mathematical calculations or computer-based models such as moving averages, filters, or momentum to identify turning points or trends. If it is effective at all, technical analysis is only useful for very short-term forecasting (from several days to several weeks). This is because it is designed to detect trends, which, due to the competitive nature of the markets, tend to disappear rapidly.

The effectiveness of foreign exchange forecasting
Foreign exchange forecasting services are many and varied, covering market models, subjective and econometric models based on fundamental analysis

as well as numerous methodologies based on chartism and trend analysis.[45] Just how effective any of these services are at forecasting future spot rates is very doubtful. First of all, reliable statistics are hard to come by. Secondly, it is not clear how the performance of these forecasts can be judged. Should the forecasting model be compared in magnitude to the forward rate, should it be judged on the percentage of the number of times that the forecast rate is on the correct side of the forward rate, or should some type of rate of return on an investment strategy based on the forecast be calculated? *Euromoney* began running an annual survey on the performance of foreign exchange forecasting in August 1978.[46] This shows that over the years the performance of the advisory services has been irregular. In 1983, for example, no single service was able to beat the treasury bill rate and their percentage of correct signals was only 44.9%.[47] In other years some services had outstanding results while others were big losers. No services had consistently outstanding results over all years. *Euromoney* concluded that it is difficult to judge whether or not on the whole the advisory services bring any value added to the problem of exchange rate determination, because not all the services participated in the survey each year, most had changed forecasting methods over the years, and because the figures used in the survey were provided by the forecasters themselves, very few of them being audited.[48]

APPENDIX 4.1 A MATHEMATICAL PRESENTATION OF THE MONETARY APPROACH TO THE BALANCE OF PAYMENTS

In this appendix we present a formal mathematical model of the monetary approach to the balance of payments. Let:

M_{1d} = quantity of nominal money balances demanded;
M_{1s} = country's money supply;
M_o = $(D+F)$ = country's money base;
D = domestic component of the country's money base;
F = foreign component of the country's money base;
P = domestic price level;
Y = real output;
r = interest rate;
a = price elasticity of demand for money;
b = income elasticity of demand for money;
c = interest elasticity of demand for money;
m = money multiplier;
g_i = growth rate of variable i;
ε = error term.

Remember that PY = GNP. Then start with the traditional assumption that the complete demand function for money has the following form:

$$M_{1d} = \frac{P^a Y^b \varepsilon}{r^c} \qquad (4A.1.1)$$

The demand for money is positively related to GNP and inversely related to the interest rate.

As we saw in the section on the effects of exchange rate intervention on the money supply, the money supply is a multiple of the country's money base:

$$M_{1s} = m(D + F) \qquad (4A.1.2)$$

In equilibrium, money supply equals money demand:

$$M_{1d} = M_{1s}$$

or

$$\frac{P^a Y^b \varepsilon}{r^c} = m(D + F) \qquad (4A.1.3$$

To get this equation into testable form, take the natural logarithm of both sides:

$$a\ln P + b\ln Y + \ln \varepsilon - c\ln r = \ln m + \ln(D + F) \qquad (4A.1.4)$$

Differentiate equation 4A1.4 with respect to time:

$$a\frac{1}{P}\frac{dP}{dt} + b\frac{1}{Y}\frac{dY}{dt} + \frac{1}{\varepsilon}\frac{d\varepsilon}{dt} - c\frac{1}{r}\frac{dr}{dt} = \frac{1}{m}\frac{dm}{dt} + \frac{D}{D+F}\frac{1}{D}\frac{dD}{dt} + \frac{F}{D+F}\frac{1}{F}\frac{dF}{dt}$$
$$(4A.1.5)$$

Remember that $(D + F) = M_0$, let $\frac{1}{P}\frac{dP}{dt} = g_p$, $\frac{1}{Y}\frac{dY}{dt} = g_y$, etc., and rearrange:

$$\frac{F}{M_0}g_F = ag_p + bg_Y + g_\varepsilon - cg_r - g_m - \frac{D}{M_0}g_D \qquad (4A.1.6)$$

Equation 4A.1.6 is the general form of the equation usually used in empirical tests of the balance of payments. It says that the weighted growth rate of the country's international reserves, $\frac{F}{M_0}g_F$, is a function of the growth rates and elasticities of the different variables. It is interesting to note that the weighted growth rate of the country's reserves is negatively related to the weighted growth rate of the domestic component of the country's money base. In other words, other things being equal, a change in the central bank's credit to the economy, D, will produce an automatic equal and opposite change in F. Thus, under fixed exchange rates, a country can only determine the composition of the money base. It cannot control the size of the money base itself and, consequently, it has no control over its monetary policy.

APPENDIX 4.2 A MATHEMATICAL PRESENTATION OF THE PORTFOLIO BALANCE APPROACH TO THE BALANCE OF PAYMENTS

Let:

W	= country's wealth;
B	= demand for domestic bonds;
SB^*	= demand for foreign bonds in domestic currency;
S	= the exchange rate (number of units of domestic currency for one unit of foreign currency);
r	= domestic interest rate;
r^*	= foreign interest rate;
$h, i,$ and j	= the percent of wealth held in each type of asset with $h + i + j = 1$.

The model can be summarized in four equations:

$$M_{1d} = h(r, r^*)W \tag{4A.2.1}$$

$$B = i(r, r^*)W \tag{4A.2.2}$$

$$SB^* = j(r, r^*)W \tag{4A.2.3}$$

$$W = M_{1d} + B + SB^* \tag{4A.2.4}$$

The first three equations postulate that the proportions of wealth held as money, domestic bonds, and foreign bonds are functions of the domestic and the foreign interest rates. M is inversely related to both the domestic and foreign interest rates. B is directly related to the domestic interest rate and inversely to the foreign interest rate. SB^* is directly related to the foreign interest rate and inversely to the domestic interest rate.

According to the portfolio balance approach equilibrium occurs when the quantity demanded of each financial asset equals the quantity supplied. Assuming that each financial market is in equilibrium, we can solve for SB^*:

$$SB^* = W - M_{1d} - B = W - i(r, r^*)W - h(r, r^*)W$$
$$SB^* = W[1 - i(r, r*) - h(r, r^*)] \tag{4A.2.5}$$

and

$$S = \frac{W}{B^*}[1 - i(r, r^*) - h(r, r^*)] \tag{4A.2.6}$$

From equation 4A.2.6 we can postulate that the exchange rate is directly related to W and r^* and inversely related to B^* and r. An increase in wealth resulting from an increase in savings increases the demand for all three financial assets. As the country exchanges domestic currency for foreign currency to purchase the foreign bonds, the domestic currency will depreciate. The same goes for a rise in the foreign interest rate. As the country exchanges domestic currency for foreign currency to purchase the foreign bonds, the domestic currency will depreciate. On the other hand, an increase in the supply of the foreign bond will lower its price and reduce the wealth of domestic residents, which causes them to reduce their holdings of all financial assets. As they sell the foreign bonds and exchange foreign currency for domestic currency, the value of the domestic currency appreciates. The same thing happens if the domestic interest rate rises.

NOTES

[1] The main international standard for a comprehensive and systematic framework
    for collecting and presenting the economic statistics of a nation is: United
    Nations (1968) *A System of National Accounts, Studies in Methods*, Series no. 2,
    Rev. 3, New York.

[2] For economies that are net borrowers, GDP is usually retained as the measure of
    economic performance. Here we define GDP to include unrequited transfers in
    exports and imports. The principles applied in compiling the balance of payments
    are generally the same as those governing the construction of the external segment
    of the national accounts. The major differences are outlined in IMF (1977) *The
    Balance of Payments Manual, op. cit.*, pp. 177–80, Washington D.C.

[3] The Marshall-Lerner condition is a more precise statement of the requirements
    for stable equilibrium in the foreign exchange market. Assuming infinite supply
    elasticities for imports and exports, it states that devaluation will always improve
    the trade balance if the *sum* of the demand elasticities for imports and exports is
    greater than one.

[4] The IMF estimates demand elasticities for its world trade model. See: Deppler,
    M.C. and Ripley, D. (1978) The World Trade Model: Merchandise Trade Flows,
    Staff Papers, March, 147–206.

[5] See: Alexander, S.S. (1952) Effects of a Devaluation on a Trade Balance, *Staff
    Papers*, II (2), 263–78.

[6] Let S represent saving; then the foreign trade income multiplier is equal to

$$\frac{1}{\frac{dS}{dGNP} + \frac{dM}{dGNP}}$$

where $\frac{dS}{dGNP}$ is the marginal propensity to save and $\frac{dM}{dGNP}$ is the marginal propensity
to import. This can be shown as follows. Remember that saving is equal to the
current account balance plus gross investment:

$$S = B_c + I_g$$

where B_c represents the current account balance and I_g represents gross
investment.
Let financial services be included in exports and imports so that $B_c = X - M$.
Then:

$$S + M = X + Ig$$

A change in exports is a change in income equal to dX that will induce a change in
savings and imports. Assume that I_g is unaffected. Then

$$dX = dS + dM$$

and dividing both sides into *dGNP* gives

$$\frac{dGNP}{dX} = \frac{1}{\frac{dS}{dGNP} + \frac{dM}{dGNP}}$$

[7] See: Pearce, I.F. (1961) The Problem of the Balance of Payments, *International Economic Review*, **II** (1), 1–28; Gerakis, A.S. (1964) Recession in the Initial Phase of a Stabilisation Program: The Experience of Finland, *Staff Papers*, **XI** (1), 434–45.

[8] Considerable attention was paid to this phenomenon when the massive depreciation of the dollar between 1985 and 1988 was accompanied by a worsening of the US trade deficit.

[9] See: Baldwin, R. and Krugman, P. (1987) The Persistence of the U.S. Trade Deficit, *Brookings Papers on Economic Activity*, (1), 1–43 and Dornbusch, R. and Krugman, P. (1976) Flexible Exchange Rates in the Short Term, *Brookings Papers on Economic Activity*, (3), 537–75.

[10] See: Gelach, S. (1989) Intertemporal Speculation, Devaluation and the J-Curve, *Journal of International Economics*, **27**, 335–45.

[11] The investment income multiplier is the same as the foreign trade income multiplier but is generated by an autonomous increase in investment instead of exports.

[12] See: International Monetary Fund (1977) *The Monetary Approach to the Balance of Payments*, IMF, Washington D.C.

[13] See: Belongia, M.T. and Chalfant, J.A. (1989) The Changing Empirical Definition of Money: Some Estimates from a Model for Money Substitutes, *Journal of Political Economy*, **97** (2), 387–97; Barnett, W.A. (1983) New Indices of Money Supply and the Flexible Laurent Demand System, *Journal of Business and Economic Statistics*, **1** (January), 7–23.

[14] See: Friedman, M. (1956) The Quantity Theory of Money, A Restatement, in *Studies in the Quantity Theory of Money*, (ed. M. Friedman), The University of Chicago Press.

[15] Cassel, G. (1916) The Present Situation in the Foreign Exchanges, *Economic Journal*, 62–5; Cassel, G. (1918) Abnomal Deviations in International Exchanges, *Economic Journal*, 413–15.

[16] Richardson, J.D. (1978) Some Empirical Evidence on Commodity Arbitrage and the Law of One Price, *Journal of International Economics*, May, 342–51; Isard, P. (1977) How Far Can We Push the Law of One Price?, *American Economic Review*, December, 942–8; Kravis M.B. and Lipsey, R.E. (1978) Price Behaviour in the Light of Balance Of Payments Theory, *Journal of International Economics*, May, 193–246.

[17] Hodgson, J. and Phelps, P. (1975) The Distributed Impact of Price Level Variation on Floating Exchange Rates, *Review of Economics and Statistics*,

February, 58–64 find that differential inflation rates precede the change in exchange rates by up to 18 months. In an attempt to forecast exchange rates W.R. Folks, Jr. and S.R. Stansell ((1975) The Use of Discriminant Analysis in Forecasting Exchange Rate Movements, *Journal of International Business Studies*, Spring, 71–81) find that exchange rates only adjust differential rates of inflation after a long lag.

[18] Galliot, H.J. (1971) Purchasing Power Parity as an Explanation of Long Term Changes in Exchange Rates, *Journal of Money, Credit and Banking*, August, 348–57.

[19] Edison, H.J. (1987) Purchasing Power Parity in the Long Run: A Test of the Dollar/Pound Exchange Rate (1890–1978), *Journal of Money, Credit, and Banking*, August, 376–87.

[20] Abuaf, N. and Philippe Jorion, P. (1990) Purchasing Power Parity in the Long Run, *Journal of Finance*, March, 157–74.

[21] For extensive coverage of the PPP issues and literature, see: Adler, M. and Dumas, B. (1983) International Portfolio Choice and Corporation Finance: A Synthesis, *Journal of Finance*, June, 925–84; Shapiro, A.C. (1983) What Does Purchasing Power Parity Mean?, *Journal of International Money and Finance*, 295–318; Solnik, B. (1988) *International Investments*, Addison-Wesley Publishing Co.

[22] Rogalski, R.J. and Vinso, J.D. (1977) Price Variations as Predictors of Exchange Rates, *Journal of International Business Studies*, Spring-Summer, 71–83.

[23] The efficient market hypothesis is usually divided into the strong form, where the information set includes all currently known information, the semi-strong form, where the information set includes all publicly available information, and the weak form, where the information set includes the previous prices of securities. See: Fama, E. (1970) Efficient Capital Markets: A Review of Theory and Empirical Work, *Journal of Finance*, May.

[24] Roll, R. (1979) Violations of Purchasing Power Parity and Their Implications for Efficient Commodity Markets, in *International Finance and Trade* (eds M. Sarnat and G. Szego) Ballinger, Cambridge, Mass.

[25] Keynes, J.M. (1930) *A Treatise on Money*, Macmillan, London.

[26] Aliber, R. (1973) The Interest Rate Parity Theorem: A Reinterpretation, *Journal of Political Economy*, 1451–9; Marston, R. C. (1976) Interest Arbitrage in the Eurocurrency Markets, *European Economic Review*; Roll, R. and Solnik, B. (1977) A Pure Foreign Exchange Asset Pricing Model, *Journal of International Economics*.

[27] See, for example: Frenkel, J. and Levich, R. (1977) Transactions Costs and Interest Arbitrage: Tranquil versus Turbulent Periods, *Journal of Political Economy*, 1209–26; Oskooee, M.B. and Das, S.P. (1985) Transactions Costs and the Interest Parity Theorem, *Journal of Political Economy*, August, 793–9; Callier, P. (1981) One Way Arbitrage, Foreign Exchange, and Securities Markets: A Note, *Journal of Finance*, December, 1177–86; Clinton, K. (1988) Transactions Costs and Covered Interest Arbitrage: Theory and Evidence, *Journal of Political Economy*, April, 358–70; Deardorff, A.V. (1979) One Way Arbitrage and Its Implications for the Foreign Exchange Markets, *Journal of Political Economy*, April, 351–64.

[28] Otani, I. and Tiwari, S. (1981) Capital Controls and Interest Rate Parity: The Japanese Experience 1978–81, *IMF Staff Papers*, 793–815.

[29] Fisher, I. (1930) *The Theory of Interest*, Macmillan, New York.

[30] Kane, E. and Rosenthal, L. (1982) International Interest Rates and Inflationary Expectations, *Journal of International Money and Finance*, April.

[31] Mishkin, F.S. (1984) Are Real Interest Rates Equal Across Countries? – An Empirical Investigation of International Parity Relations, *Journal of Finance*, December.

[32] Clark, E. (1991) *Cross Border Investment Risk: Applications of Modern Portfolio Theory*, Euromoney Publications, London.

[33] Cumby, R. and Obstfeld, M. (1981) A Note on Exchange Rate Expectations and Nominal Interest Differentials: A Test of the Fisher Hypothesis, *Journal of Finance*, 697–703.

[34] See, for example: Aliber, R.A. and Stickney, C.P. (1975) Accounting Measures of Foreign Exchange Exposure: The Long and the Short of It, *The Accounting Review*, January, 44–57; Giddy, I.H. and Dufey, G. (1975) The Random Behaviour of Flexible Exchange Rates, *Journal of International Business Studies*, Spring, 1–32.

[35] See, for example: Solnik, B. (1974) An Equilibrium Model of the International Capital Market, *Journal of Economic Theory*, August; Roll, R. and Solnik, B. (1977) A Pure Foreign Exchange Asset Pricing Model, *Journal of International Economics*, May; Adler, M. and Dumas, B. (1983) International Portfolio Choice and Corporation Finance: A Synthesis, *Journal of Finance*, June.

[36] Kaminsky, G. and Peruga, R. (1990) Can a Time Varying Risk Premium Explain Excess Returns in the Forward Market for Foreign Exchange? *Journal of International Economics*.

[37] Stockman, A.C. (1978) Risk, Information, and Forward Exchange Rates, in *The Economics of Exchange Rates* (eds J.A. Frenkel and H.G. Johnson) Addison-Wesley, Reading, Mass.; Frenkel, J.A. (1980) Test of Rational Expectations in the Forward Exchange Market, *Southern Journal of Economics*, 1083–101.

[38] Geweke, J. and Feige, E. (1979) Some Joint Tests of the Efficiency of Markets for Forward Exchange, *Review of Economics and Statistics*, 334–41; Cumby, R. and Obstfeld, M. (1981) A Note on Exchange Rate Expectations and Nominal Interest Differentials: A Test of the Fisher Hypothesis, *Journal of Finance*, 697–704; Hansen, L.P. and Hodrick, R.J. (1983) Risk Averse Speculation in the Forward Exchange Market: An Econometric Analysis of Linear Models, in *Exchange Rates and International Macroeconomics*, (ed. J.A. Frenkel) University of Chicago Press.

[39] A Paasche price index is weighted by current consumption patterns. Thus, if p stands for price per unit and q for the number of units, with superscripts referring to the individual goods and subscripts referring to time, a Paasche price index can be expressed as follows:

$$\frac{\sum_j p_t^j q_t^j}{\sum_j p_0^j q_t^j}$$

Most introductory statistics textbooks deal with the different types of index numbers. See, for example, Grais, B. (1982) *Statistique Descriptive*, Dunod, Paris.

40 A Laspeyre index is weighted by consumption patterns of the base year. Using the same notation as in n.39, a Laspeyre price index can be expressed as follows:

$$\frac{\sum_j p_t^j q_0^j}{\sum_j p_0^j q_0^j}.$$

41 In its *World Debt Tables*, the World Bank publishes detailed statistics on the foreign debt of over 110 developing countries. The information includes undisbursed debt, commitments, disbursements, principal repayments, net flows, interest payments, net transfers, debt service, average terms of new commitments, debt restructurings and debt service projections. The information is broken down by type of creditor and type of loan.

42 These definitions are those used by the World Bank. See: the World Bank (1989) *World Debt Tables 1989–1990*, vol. 2, the World Bank, Washington D.C., pp. xii–xvi.

43 John Hicks has shown that even in conditions of monetary equilibrium and full employment, real economic phenomena can cause price disturbances. See Hicks, J. (1987) *Time and Capital*, Clarendon Press, Oxford.

44 Care must be taken when associating financial qualities with economic growth. A recent study by R. Barro and X. Sala i Martin (*World Real Interest Rates*, NBER Working Paper 3317), for example, finds that economic growth tends to reduce the real interest rate by increasing saving while expected increases in profitability increase the demand for capital and raise the real rate of interest.

45 The types of foreign exchange forecasting services available range from fundamental subjective analysis to econometric models to technical analysis. See: 'An A to Z Guide of the Services', *Euromoney*, August 1987, 127–30.

46 Because of difficulties in determining a common set of evaluation criteria, the rating was suspended in 1986, restarted in 1987 in a less rigorous format, and abandoned again on a pessimistic note in 1988.

47 *Euromoney*, August 1984.

48 See: *Euromoney*, August 1986, 198–201; August 1987, 121–4; August 1988, 99–104.

5 ADVANCED TECHNIQUES FOR MACROECONOMIC RISK ASSESSMENT

Modern financial theory has made major strides in improving our understanding of economic and financial risk and how it can be measured and managed. These same methods have been applied to the problem of country-specific risk and have made it possible to give a much more accurate and precise picture of what is involved. This, in turn, has enhanced the importance of traditional political risk analysis, which enters the framework as a valuable input in the process of parameter estimation. In this chapter, we discuss the shortcomings of traditional international risk analysis. We then develop the new analytical framework that makes it possible to apply the tools of modern financial theory to the assessment of country-specific risk. Finally, we show how the new framework can be applied to assess the economic and financial health of a national economy.

THE SHORTCOMINGS OF TRADITIONAL INTERNATIONAL RISK ANALYSIS

The conventional cross-border economic and financial risk analysis presented in Chapter 4 suffers from a number of shortcomings in the analytical framework, that make systematic comparisons across countries conceptually inappropriate.[1] First of all, the data are unadapted to the task at hand. Looking back at the variables and ratios, is is clear that most of the relevant economic data come from the national accounts – GDP, GNP, exports, imports, savings, investment, etc. Flow data gross of costs, such as GDP and its derivatives, are incomplete as measures of economic performance because they give no information on the economy's overall outstanding assets and liabilities or the contribution of the flow data to the evolution of assets and liabilities. Secondly, through tariffs, taxes, subsidies, and controls, the data reflect domestic criteria for income distribution, rather than international criteria. Thirdly, insofar as the authorities are free to create unlimited amounts of money, there is no explicit mechanism for imposing accounting discipline. Basing an analysis on such questionable information is roughly equivalent to assessing the economic and financial health of a firm using only an income statement prepared at prices decreed by the firm without regard to what its output could actually be sold for, what its inputs actually cost, or how the turnover is financed.

The problem has long been recognized. We saw that the monetary approach to the balance of payments underlines the importance of stock adjustments in economic analysis and one of its major tenets is that international prices and not domestic prices are relevant for international economic analysis. Little and Mirrlees and UNIDO address the problem on the microeconomic level.[2] On the macroeconomic level, however, little has been done and, as we saw in Chapter 4, the problem is generally handled by means of price indices or the exchange rate. The World Bank, for example, converts domestic economic data into dollars. Other analysts deflate domestic economic data using various price indices. The analysis then concentrates on the growth of GDP or GNP and the factors that are likely to affect it. While this framework is useful in many respects, flow data in dollars or deflated by a price index are still only flow data and still reflect domestic criteria for income distribution between profits and wages, rather than international criteria. As such they can be misleading, where cross-border risk analysis is concerned.

Consider, for example, an economy with GDP of $100 composed in the following way:

Exports	$10
Imports	$10
Private and public consumption	$70
Change in stocks	$0
Gross fixed capital formation	$30
GDP	**$100**
Depreciation	$30
Employee compensation	$50
Corporate profits and net interest	$20
NDP	**$70**

Suppose that every $10 of GDP requires $1 of imported inputs. In the absence of foreign lending, GDP could then only grow as fast as exports. When foreign resources are available, however, growth can occur independently of exports. If a local resident such as the government takes out a $1 loan for one year at 10% from a foreign bank and uses it to increase imported inputs, thereby making it possible to increase output by $10, all of which accrues to consumption, the national accounts will look like this:

Exports	$10
Imports	$11
Private and public consumption	$81
Change in stocks	$0
Gross fixed capital formation	$30
GDP	**$110**
Depreciation	$30
Employee compensation	$57
Corporate profits and net interest	$23
NDP	**$80**

The economic performance seems impressive. GDP has grown by 10%, consumption has risen by 15.7%, and profits have risen by 15%. From the perspective of the foreign lender, however, nothing could be further from the truth. Income distribution between profits, interest and employee compensation reflects domestic priorities and relative prices, and tells nothing about the economy's ability to pay off the foreign loan. In fact, it is clear in this simple example that the new level of economic activity cannot be maintained without supplementary foreign resources. Furthermore, the economy now has a debt of $1.10 and, although this only represents 1% of GDP and 11% of exports, paying it off requires either a reduction in imports, which implies a sharp reduction in GDP, or an increase in exports, which implies a reduction in domestic consumption and overall welfare. Clearly, GDP, NDP, gross investment and profits as defined in the national accounts have serious shortcomings as the raw materials of cross-border risk assessment.

The difficulty stems from the fact that national accounts are prepared and presented in the context of traditional macroeconomic analysis whose perspective is the domestic authority seeking to maximize internal levels of output, employment, and consumption. The international investor, however, has a different perspective. He can buy and sell, borrow and lend elsewhere than the particular country in question. His interest in internal levels of output, employment and consumption concerns the extent to which they affect the risk and return on his investment in terms of his base currency. In this context, the crucial element is the economy's ability to generate the net foreign exchange value necessary to meet current and future foreign interest, dividend and principal obligations. This change of perspective substantially alters the context surrounding macroeconomic analysis and the discussion of cross-border risk. It implies that the analysis should be effected in the investor's base currency or, more precisely, a fully convertible foreign currency, that it should include a balance sheet and that profits should be defined to reflect international criteria for income distribution.

THE NEW ANALYTICAL FRAMEWORK

The analytical framework developed in this section uses the discounted cash flow model to establish the relationship between macroeconomic cash flows from period to period and the macroeconomic balance sheet. Cash flows are measured in foreign exchange (dollars, in our examples) and defined so that they reflect the perspective of the international investor whose concern is the economy's ability to generate the net foreign exchange value necessary to meet foreign interest, dividend, principal and depreciation payments.

A presentation of the model

When macroeconomic performance is measured in foreign currency, accounting discipline is imposed through the transactions involving the external sector. The reason is straightforward. While the economic and financial authorities of a sovereign nation are potentially free from accounting discipline in their own currency through unlimited access to central bank credit, the same cannot be said for their position in foreign currency. Foreign currency must either be earned with exports or borrowed. This is known as balance of payments discipline or the foreign exchange constraint, which we presented in equation 4.2. In this chapter, we want to concentrate on the role of interest and dividend payments abroad. Therefore, we simplify the notation by including BP in F. Thus, equation 4.2 becomes:

$$X_t - M_t + FS_t + F_t = 0 \tag{5.1}$$

where
X = merchandise exports plus exports of all services except investment income plus unrequited transfers and other income (credit);
M = merchandise imports plus imports of all services except investment income plus unrequited transfers and other income (debit);
FS = net investment income (investment income (credit) minus investment income (debit));
F = net inflow (outflow) of foreign capital including operations by the monetary authority.

The next step is to determine the macroeconomic cash flows relevant to the international investor. Let b_t represent the foreign exchange value of income from the sale of the economy's output of final goods and services for period t and a_t the foreign exchange value of the economy's expenditure on final goods and services for period t. From the standpoint of the international economic agent, exports, whether raw materials or investment goods, represent final output because they leave the domestic economy. Thus, the b_ts are equal to the foreign exchange value of exports plus the foreign exchange value of internal sales of domestically produced final goods and services. The foreign exchange value of domestically produced final goods and services is equal to total consumption less imports of consumption goods. This can be written:

$$b_t = X_t + (C_t - M_{ct}) \tag{5.2}$$

where C is domestic consumption and M_c represents imports of consumption goods.

The a_ts comprise the foreign exchange value of the economy's expenditure on final goods and services and as such represent the cost of production of the economy's gross output, including consumption and investment goods. Thus, the a_ts are composed of the foreign exchange value of the final goods and services consumed by the sector producing consumption goods (the cost of production of consumption goods), the foreign exchange value of the final goods and services consumed by the sector producing replacement investment goods (cost of production of replacing worn out investment goods), and the foreign exchange value of the final goods and services consumed by the sector producing new net investment (cost of production of net investment). Imports, regardless of their nature, come from outside the economy and therefore represent a final expenditure for the economy. The a_ts, then, include the foreign exchange value of imports plus the foreign exchange value of internal expenditure for domestically produced final goods and services:

$$a_t = M_t + (C_t - M_{ct}) \tag{5.3}$$

Since the foreign exchange value of internal expenditure for domestically produced final goods and services is exactly equal to the foreign exchange value of internal sales of domestically produced final goods and services, $(b_t - a_t)$ will always be equal to $(X_t - M_t)$. From equation 5.1 we can see that this is an expression of balance of payments accounting discipline. It is clear from the balance of payments identity that net exports determine the ability of an economy to meet interest, dividend, principal and depreciation payments on its foreign borrowing. In the absence of foreign capital inflows, interest, dividend, principal and depreciation payments abroad are limited by the level of net exports. Foreign capital inflows will be forthcoming only if expected levels of net exports are deemed sufficient to meet the expected payments associated with foreign liabilities. Take a bank loan, for example. In the absence of new borrowing over the life of the loan, the economy's ability to meet interest and principal payments depends on its outstanding financial obligations and the level of net exports. If the level of net exports is deemed inadequate, the loan will only be granted if it is decided that foreign capital will be available to make up the shortfall. When that time comes, the same type of analysis will determine whether or not the required capital is forthcoming. Thus, at any point in time the net supply of foreign capital, F, depends on the expected future flows of net exports. Consequently, the supply and demand for foreign exchange is determined by current effects of past borrowing represented by financial service payments, the current flow of net exports and expected future flows of net exports. Any disequilibrium will be reflected in the exchange rate.

With this in mind we can use the cash flows of income and expenditure to measure the foreign exchange value of the economy at time T. Suppose that all transactions take place on the first day of each period and that the capital markets are in equilibrium so that the economy's cost of capital is equal to its internal rate of return, r. The foreign exchange value of the economy at time T is:

$$V_T = E\left[(b_T - a_T) + (b_{T+1} - a_{T+1})R^{-1} + \ldots + (b_n - a_n)R^{-(n-T)}\right] \tag{5.4}$$

where V_T represents the capital value of the economy at the beginning of period T, $R = 1 + r$, and E is the expectations operator.

It is important to see the relationship between equation 5.4 and the traditional national accounting equation. Taking the formula for V_{T+1} gives:

$$V_{T+1} = E\left[(b_{T+1} - a_{T+1}) + (b_{T+2} - a_{T+2})R^{-1} + \ldots + (b_n - a_n)R^{-(n-(T+1))}\right]$$

$$(5.5)$$

Substituting 5.5 into 5.4, multiplying by $1+r$ to obtain the value of the economy at the end of period T, rearranging, and remembering that b_T and a_T are known because they take place on the first day of the period, yields the national accounting equation for period T:

$$r(V_T + a_T - b_T) + a_T = b_T + (V_{T+1} - V_T) \qquad (5.6)$$

where $r(V_T + a_T - b_T)$ represents profits before interest and dividends paid abroad, a_T represents cost, b_T represents income and $(V_{T+1} - V_T)$ represents net investment. It can be more easily recognized if we substitute equations 5.2 and 5.3 into 5.6 and rearrange:

$$r(V_T + M_T - X_T) + C_T = X_T - M_T + C_T + (V_{T+1} - V_T) \qquad (5.7)$$

The right-hand side of equation 5.7 is immediately recognized as a derivative presentation of net domestic product. The difference between this presentation and the traditional format is that unrequited transfers and other non-financial income are included in exports and imports. The left-hand side of the equation shows the economy's earnings before interest and dividends paid abroad plus consumption. Consumption, then, appears directly as a cost. However, it does not represent the total cost. Total cost would include expenditure on imports of investment goods.

This presentation of the national accounts has several practical advantages. On the one hand, net national product is well known to economists and macroeconomic data is usually presented in this format. On the other hand, the left-hand side of the equation presents net national product in a new format that is pertinent to the international investor and more useful for financial analysis – earnings and consumption broken down to reflect international criteria for income distribution.

Applying the model

Generating the foreign currency values

The individual V_ts in the foregoing accounting format cannot be observed directly for two reasons. First of all, we are dealing with expected future flows and, secondly, a country's national accounts are presented in domestic currency rather than foreign currency. The market information does, however, exist so that they can be estimated. The estimation procedure involves using the exchange rate to link the V_ts to the domestic currency statistics presented in the national accounts.

The domestic currency equivalent of equation 5.4 is:

$$V'_T = E\left[(b'_T - a'_T) + (b'_{T+1} - a'_{T+1})R'^{-1} + \ldots + (b'_n - a'_n)R'^{-(n-T)}\right] \quad (5.8)$$

where the primes denote domestic currency values and $R' = 1 + r'$. r' is the economy's internal rate of return in domestic currency. Since $b - a$ equals $X - M$, equation 5.8 can be rewritten using the exchange rate. Let

$$X'_t = S_t X_t$$

and

$$M'_t = S_t M_t$$

where S_t is the spot exchange rate at time t expressed as the number of units of domestic currency for one unit of foreign currency. Then

$$V'_T = E\left[S_T(X_T - M_T) + S_{T+1}(X_{T+1} - M_{T+1})R'^{-1} \right.$$

$$\left. + \ldots + S_n(X_n - M_n)R'^{-(n-T)}\right] \quad (5.9)$$

Using the forward rate parity and interest rate parity hypotheses, in the appendix at the end of the chapter we show that:

$$V'_T = S_T V_T \quad (5.10)$$

so that:

$$V_T = \frac{V_T'}{S_T}$$ (5.11)

and at the end of the period

$$V_{T+1} = \frac{V_{T+1}'}{S_{T+1}}$$ (5.12)

V' can be estimated directly from readily available statistical data. The domestic currency value of net investment at market prices is a component of the traditional presentation of the national accounts or it can be estimated from gross fixed capital formation, which is also presented therein. The domestic currency value of what has been invested in the economy from time 0 to the end of $T-1$ is:

$$V_T' = \sum_{t=0}^{T-1} (V_{t+1}' - V_t')$$ (5.13)

and

$$V_{T+1}' = \sum_{t=0}^{T} (V_{t+1}' - V_t')$$ (5.14)

Thus, the right-hand side of equation 5.7 can be obtained by applying the spot exchange rate to X', M' and C' and using equations 5.11–5.14 to estimate V_T and V_{T+1}.

Generating new analytical parameters: the case of Korea

The estimation of V_T and V_{T+1} is straightforward. The necessary information is gross fixed capital formation in local currency, which can be found in numerous sources. We use the information supplied by the International Monetary Fund.

Column 1 of Table 5.1 shows Korea's gross fixed capital formation from 1977 to 1986. We then estimate capital depreciation for each year and subtract it from column 1 to get annual net investment in column 2. Column 3 is the sum of the preceeding year's net capital stock plus the net investment of the current year. Column 4 is the won/$ end-of-period exchange rate. Column 5, the dollar value of the country's capital stock, is found by dividing column 3 by column 4.

Table 5.1 Estimating V' and V for Korea, 1977–86

	Gross investment	Net investment	V'_t	Won/$ exchange rate	$V_t = 3 \div 4$
	1	2	3	4	5
	billion won	billion won	billion won	end of period	$ billion
1977			15 625.00	484.00	$32.28
1978	7464.00	6423.00	22 048.00	484.00	$45.55
1979	10 240.00	8750.00	30 798.00	484.00	$63.63
1980	11 836.00	9733.00	40 532.00	659.90	$61.42
1981	12 931.00	10 147.00	50 679.00	700.50	$72.35
1982	15 487.00	11 993.00	62 672.00	748.80	$83.70
1983	18 480.00	14 146.00	76 818.00	795.50	$96.57
1984	20 795.00	15 471.00	92 289.00	827.40	$111.54
1985	22 436.00	16 029.00	108 318.00	890.20	$121.68
1986	26 426.00	18 717.00	127 036.00	861.40	$147.48

(Source: IMF, *International Financial Statistics*, several issues

Calculating macroeconomic profits
Subtracting C_T from both sides of equation 5.7 gives a measure of the economy's annual profits based on international criteria for resource allocation and income distribution:

$$r(V_T + M_T - X_T) = X_T - M_T + (V_{T+1} - V_T) \qquad (5.15)$$

Table 5.2 shows how this figure can be estimated for the Korean economy for the years 1984, 1985, and 1986.
Columns 3 and 4 have been taken from Table 5.1. In order to calculate

Table 5.2 Estimation of macroeconomic profits for Korea, 1984–86

	Exports X $ billion	Imports M $ billion	Capital value end of period V_{T+1} $ billion	Capital value start of period V_T $ billion	Total profits $(1-2)+(3-4)$ $ billion
	1	2	3	4	5
1984	33.656	31.799	111.54	96.57	16.827
1985	33.118	30.822	121.68	111.54	12.436
1986	42.377	34.552	147.48	121.68	33.625

(Source: IMF (1992) Balance of Payments Statistics, *Yearbook*, part 1, pp. 394–5.)

columns 1 and 2, remember the definitions for exports and imports:

X = merchandise exports plus exports of all services except investment income plus unrequited transfers and other income (credit);
M = merchandise imports plus imports of all services except investment income plus unrequited transfers and other income (debit).

Investment income is not included in exports and imports. In this way profits reflect earnings on the country's entire stock of assets before considering whether the assets were financed by domestic or foreign capital. This corresponds to the concept of earnings before interest and taxes in corporate finance. Reliable balance of payments statistics in US dollars are available for most countries. The International Monetary Fund's Balance of Payments Statistics, for example, give dollar data broken down into 112 categories for close to 150 countries (depending on country births and deaths). Thus, X, column 1 of Table 5.2, can be calculated directly in dollars as the sum of total credit for goods, services and income (Code 1T.A4) plus total credit for unrequited transfers (Code 1L.A4) less credits for investment income (lines 11, 13, 15, 17, and 19). M, column 2, is equal to the total debit of goods, services, and income (Code 1T.B4) plus total debit for unrequited transfers (Code 1L.B4) less debits for investment income (lines 12, 14, 16, 18, and 20). According to equation 5.15, then, the economy's total profits are equal to column 1 minus column 2 plus column 3 minus column 4.

The macroeconomic balance sheet

Another important piece of information for judicious cross-border risk assessment is an appropriate macroeconomic balance sheet. One can easily be constructed from the preceding model. The first step in constructing a macroeconomic balance sheet involves presenting economic activity in the form of sources and uses. Let s equal the percent of profits before interest and dividends reinvested in the economy. Then $(1 - s)$ represents the percent of profits paid out to foreign investors and $(1 - s)r(V_T + M_T - X_T) = FS_T$ = interest and dividends paid abroad. Subtracting this from both sides of equation 5.15 gives:

$$sr(V_T + M_T - X_T) = X_T - M_T - (1 - s)r(V_T + M_T - X_T) + (V_{T+1} - V_T)$$
$$(5.16)$$

which is the expression for net macroeconomic profits after payments of interest and dividends to non-residents.

From equation 5.1 we know that when FS is negative,

$$-F_T = X_T - M_T - r(1 - s)(V_T + M_T - X_T)$$

and if we substitute this into equation 5.16 and rearrange, we have the net macroeconomic sources and uses for the period:

$$(V_{T+1} - V_T) = sr(V_T + M_T - X_T) + F_T \qquad (5.17)$$

where the sources on the right-hand side of the equation represent the economy's retained earnings plus net inflows of foreign capital and the uses on the left-hand side represent net investment. The balance sheet is the sum of these figures from 0 to T. Table 5.3 shows how it would look.

Return on investment (ROI)

A workable balance sheet is a valuable tool for assessing a country's economic and financial health. In its absence, traditional cross-border risk assessment has had to rely on proxy variables such as GDP or GNP. For example, the traditional measure of economic performance has been growth of GDP or GNP. We have seen above how misleading this can be. A more appropriate measure of economic performance from the perspective of the international investor would be the rate of growth of the country's capacity to generate net foreign exchange value. From an *ex post* point of view, this

Table 5.3 Macroeconomic balance sheet

assets	*liabilities*
	Net short-term foreign liabilities outstanding at the end of T
	Net medium and long-term foreign liabilities outstanding at the end of T
	Net portfolio and direct investment outstanding at the end of T
Sum of net investment from 0 to the end of T $\sum_{t=0}^{T}(V_{t+1} - V_t) = \$147.48$ billion at the end of 1986	Sum of $sr(V_t + M_t - X_t)$ from 0 to the end of T

involves calculating the rate of growth of the country's balance sheet from 0 to T. From an *ex ante* point of view, it involves estimating what the growth rate is likely to be. Classic discounted dividend models use return on investment (ROI) and the rate of reinvestment out of profits to estimate the growth rate. Following this approach, the country's ROI can be estimated from current profits and the balance sheet:[3]

$$\text{ROI} = \frac{X_T - M_T + (V_{T+1} - V_T)}{\sum_{t=0}^{T}(V_{t+1} - V_t)} \tag{5.18}$$

Table 5.4 shows Korea's ROI between 1977 and 1986. Column 1, macroeconomic profits, was calculated according to the procedure outlined in Table 5.2, and column 2, the economy's capital value, was taken from column 5 in Table 5.1. Column 3, the economy's ROI, was calculated by dividing the value in column 1 for year t by the value in column 2 for the year $t-1$.

One way to estimate the rate of growth is to take the geometric mean over the period and extrapolate. By this method, Korea's growth rate between 1978 and 1986 was:

$$\sqrt[8]{\frac{147.48}{45.55}} - 1 = 0.1582 \text{ or } 15.82\%.$$

Table 5.4 Return on investment for Korea, 1977–86

	Profits $X_T - M_T + (V_{T+1} - V_T)$	Capital value $\sum_{t=0}^{T}(V_{t+1} - V_t)$	ROI $\dfrac{X_T - M_T + (V_{T+1} - V_T)}{\sum_{t=0}^{T}(V_{t+1} - V_t)}$
	$ billion 1	$ billion 2	3
1977		32.28	
1978	11.49	45.55	35.6
1979	13.68	63.63	30.0
1980	-5.43	61.42	-8.5
1981	9.25	72.35	15.1
1982	11.83	83.70	16.4
1983	14.04	96.57	16.8
1984	16.827	111.54	17.4
1985	12.436	121.68	11.2
1986	33.625	147.48	27.6

Another way to estimate the rate of growth is to calculate s, the percent of profits reinvested in the economy, and multiplying this by the ROI. For Korea, total profits from 1978 to 1986 amounted to $117.76 billion. Total investment income (debit) over the period amounted to $28.074 billion, or 23.8% of total profits. Thus, s is equal to $100\% - 23.8\% = 76.2\%$. ROI averaged 17.96% over the period. Thus, g, the rate of growth of the economy's capital value is ROI $\times s$:

$$17.96\% \times 76.2\% = 13.69\%.$$

These figures might seem too optimistic a forecast: in fact, they are pretty close to the mark. Between 1986 and 1993 the dollar value of Korea's GDP grew by 17.25%. A word of caution is.in order, however. Extrapolating the past into the future is fraught with danger, and many a guru's bones mark this trail. The foregoing estimate of growth is meant as an example of how ROI and savings out of ROI can be used to get an estimate of growth. At the time the growth estimate was made, we saw no reason why the medium-term future should be any different from the medium-term past. If in-depth analysis had led to the conclusion that a change was in order, forecasting the growth rate would have involved applying the expected changes to ROI and savings out of ROI to get a new estimate of the growth rate.

Estimating financial leverage

As we have seen, s is determined by FS and depends on the amount of outstanding foreign liabilities and the rate of return required by foreign investors for investment in the economy. This brings up the question of the economy's financial structure, since the foreign investor's required rate of return is likely to depend on the proportion of the economy's assets financed by non-residents. The proportion of assets financed by non-residents is:

$$\text{Foreign liabilities / Assets} = \frac{\text{Foreign liabilities}}{\sum_{t=0}^{T}(V_{t+1} - V_t)} \qquad (5.19)$$

The capital structure can be broken down further, depending on the type of liability in question. Foreign debt is especially important since it concerns rigid payment schedules. In the absence of a workable balance sheet, traditional cross-border risk analysis has used proxy ratios such as total external debt/GNP or total external debt/exports as a measure of the economy's financial structure. With a balance sheet, however, it is possible to generate the more precise debt/assets ratio familiar to company financial analysts:

$$\text{Debt / Assets} = \frac{\text{Total external debt}}{\sum_{t=0}^{T}(V_{t+1} - V_t)} \qquad (5.20)$$

Using the capital values calculated in Table 5.1 and information on Korea's outstanding debt, in Table 5.5 we have estimated Korea's financial leverage for the years 1984, 1985, and 1986. Column 3, financial leverage, is calculated by dividing column 1 by column 2.

Table 5.5 Korea's financial leverage, 1984–86

	Total external debt $ billion	Capital value end of period V_{T+1} $ billion	Financial leverage $1 \div 2$ (percentage)
	1	*2*	*3*
1984	43.2	111.54	38.7
1985	47.6	121.68	39.1
1986	45.1	147.48	30.6

(Source: World Bank (1987–8) *World Bank Debt Tables*, vol. II, p. 206.)

Two other important leverage ratios are the financial service coverage ratio, sometimes called the times interest earned ratio, and the cash flow coverage ratio. For cross-border risk analysis, the financial service coverage ratio measures the extent to which earnings can decline without endangering the country's ability to meet its payments for interest and dividends. It also gives an idea of how much capital is available for new investment:[4]

$$\text{Foreign financial service coverage} = \frac{X_T - M_T + (V_{T+1} - V_T)}{FS_T} \quad (5.21)$$

The cash flow coverage ratio measures the extent to which the country's cash flows can decline without endangering its ability to meet payments abroad for dividends, interest and principal:

$$\text{Cash flow coverage} = \frac{X_T - M_T + (V_{T+1} - V_T) + \text{depreciation}}{FS_T + \text{principal payment}} \quad (5.22)$$

These two ratios have distinct advantages over the interest/exports and total debt service/exports ratios that are usually employed in traditional cross-border analysis. The traditional ratios present only one side of the coin, the export side. However, the ability to meet foreign obligations depends on net exports, that is, exports minus imports. Furthermore, the levels of exports and imports are intimately related to domestic economic activity. Taking exports out of context gives no indication of what net exports will be or of the economic cost of meeting foreign obligations if things go wrong. The foreign financial service coverage and cash flow coverage ratios do not have these shortcomings since they include net exports and incorporate the role of domestic economic activity in net investment.

Measuring the degree of financial leverage complements the foregoing ratios. The degree of financial leverage is defined as the percentage change in earnings available to country residents that is associated with a percentage change in earnings before interest and dividends paid abroad:[5]

$$\text{Degree of financial leverage } = \frac{X_T - M_T + (V_{T+1} - V_T)}{X_T - M_T + (V_{T+1} - V_T) - FS_T} \quad (5.23)$$

Where the interest and cash flow coverage ratios indicate the economy's ability to meet eternal obligations in the absence of external resources, the degree of financial leverage indicates the vulnerability of domestically financed investment to fluctuations in expected profits. It measures the percentage increase (decrease) in domestic net investment per percentage increase (decrease) in overall macroeconomic profits. A high degree of financial leverage means that small variations in profits will cause large variations in investment. Because of the well-known links between investment, output and employment, governments are likely to sacrifice foreign creditors if honouring commitments to them causes too much hardship at home. The likelihood of this happening increases with increased volatility in profits themselves.

The foregoing ratios are resumed in Table 5.6. Many other ratios could be generated from the framework developed above, depending on the statistical sophistication of the country in question. As with any ratio analysis, however, care must be taken when interpreting them.

APPLICATION

Case study: the international creditworthiness of Argentina, Brazil and Mexico, 1979–82

To get an idea of the analytical value of the foregoing information and how it can be used, we can go back to the debt crisis. In August of 1982, Mexico surprised the analysts and announced that it could not meet payments on its

Table 5.6 Foreign financial service coverage, cash flow coverage and degrees of financial leverage, Korea 1984-86

	Investment income (debit) FS	Principal payment	Profits $X_T - M_T + (V_{T+1} - V_T)$	Foreign financial service coverage $\dfrac{X_T - M_T + (V_{T+1} - V_T)}{FS_T}$	Cash flow coverage (without depreciation) $\dfrac{X_T - M_T + (V_{T+1} - V_T)}{FS_T + \text{principal payment}}$	Degree of financial leverage $\dfrac{X_T - M_T + (V_{T+1} - V_T)}{X_T - M_T + (V_{T+1} - V_T) - FS_T}$
	$ billions	*$ billions*	*$ billions*			
	1	*2*	*3*	*4*	*5*	*6*
1984	3.95	2.91	16.827	4.26	2.45	1.31
1985	3.98	4.24	12.436	3.12	1.51	1.47
1986	4.02	7.36	33.625	8.36	2.95	1.14

Table 5.7 Selected traditional parameters for country risk analysis: Argentina, Brazil and Mexico

	Argentina	*Brazil*	*Mexico*
Debt/exports	3.02	2.96	2.57
Debt/GNP	0.66	0.30	0.34
Growth of GNP (%)	2.3	9.2	27.6
Exports/interest + dividends	2.57	2.31	2.95

(Source: IMF (1987) Balance of Payments Statistics, *Yearbook*, vol. 38, part 1; International Financial Statistics, several issues; World Bank (1987–8) *World Bank Debt Tables*.)

foreign debt. Brazil and Argentina quickly followed suit and within the year 47 countries were negotiating with their creditors to reschedule their debt. Table 5.7 shows some of the major traditional analytical parameters for Mexico, Argentina, and Brazil at the end of 1981. From these data, Mexico looks marginally better off than the other two. Its debt/exports ratio is slightly lower, its exports/interest + dividend ratio is higher, and the dollar value of its GNP grew by over 27%. Argentina looks the worst off, with a debt/GNP ratio considerably higher than the other two countries and growth in the dollar value of its GNP of only 2.3%. Otherwise, the figures did not look bad and no one was forecasting the debt crisis.

Table 5.8 Selected parameters for Argentina, Brazil and Mexico at the end of 1981

	Argentina	*Brazil*	*Mexico*
Profits	-27.67	-8.77	29.13
V_T	28.40	89.70	174.20
Debt/assets ratio	1.26	0.89	0.45
Financial service coverage	–	–	2.83
Degree of financial leverage	–	–	1.58

(Source: IMF (1987) Balance of Payments Statistics, *Yearbook*, vol. 38, part 1; International Financial Statistics, several issues; World Bank (1987–8) *World Bank Debt Tables*.)

The information in Table 5.8, generated within the accounting framework developed above, shows a different picture. Argentina and Brazil are clearly in trouble. Both economies recorded substantial losses in 1981. This contrasts with the growth of the dollar value of their GNPs. Argentina's loss was particularly massive, wiping out almost half of the economy's total value. Their debt/assets ratios are also far too high: for Argentina the foreign debt is 26% higher than the total value of the economy. For Brazil the foreign debt is 89% of the economy's total value.

Measuring and using economic risk
Mexico looks better off than Argentina or Brazil. It recorded substantial profits in 1981 and profits cover foreign interest and dividend payments by 2.83 times. However, its debt/assets ratio is high at 45% and the degree of financial leverage is 1.58. A closer look at the past performance makes this information look even worse. Between 1970 and 1981 Mexico's ROI averaged 13.24%. In 1981 foreign borrowing cost Mexico on average 15.1%, almost two percentage points higher than the return the funds could be expected to generate. Furthermore, the standard deviation of ROI over the period was high at 13.24%, suggesting wide swings in year-to-year returns. The volatility of macroeconomic ROI is one measure of economic risk. One way of taking this volatility into consideration is to look at an average of profits over the recent past, rather than one year's figures. Between 1970 and 1981 Mexico's profits averaged $10.53 billion per year. In 1981 interest and dividends paid abroad amounted to $10.31 billion. Using average profits, the financial service coverage ratio falls to 1.02 and the degree of financial leverage rises to 44.8. These figures show the extreme precariousness of Mexico's financial situation. This precariousness is all the more glaring if we consider that the standard deviation of profits over the period under consideration was $12.88 billion, far larger than average profits of $10.53 billion. The volatility of macroeconomic profits is another measure of economic risk.

The approach outlined above also detects the financial fragility of the three economies years before the onset of the debt crisis. Table 5.9 shows average profits and the standard deviation of average profits over the periods 1970–9 and 1970–80. It also shows the financial service coverage ratio and the degree of financial leverage, using average profits, for the years 1979 and 1980. From this, Argentina, Brazil and Mexico can clearly be seen as having been in severe financial difficulty as far back as 1979. Brazil was the worst off. Its expected profits did not even half-cover interest and dividend expense and the standard deviation of profits was almost five times as large as expected profits. Argentina's standard deviation of profits was

Table 5.9 Selected analytical parameters for Argentina, Brazil and Mexico, 1979 and 1980

	Argentina		Brazil		Mexico	
	1979	*1980*	*1979*	*1980*	*1979*	*1980*
Average profits 1970–	1.98	3.83	2.87	2.92	6.53	8.88
Standard deviation	18.72	18.78	14.30	13.63	10.12	12.17
Financial service coverage	1.22	1.38	0.43	0.35	1.40	1.29
Degree of financial leverage	5.5	3.65	–	–	3.47	4.40

(Source: IMF (1987) Balance of Payments Statistics, *Yearbook*, vol. 38, part 1; International Financial Statistics, several issues; World Bank (1987–8) *World Bank Debt Tables*.)

over nine times as large as expected profits and expected profits only barely covered interest and dividend expense. Mexico's standard deviation of profits was also high and its financial service coverage ratio was low. All this translates into a precarious financial position for the three countries. The extremely high degree of financial leverage confirms the precarious nature of their financial positions. Small variations in their profits caused wide swings in domestically financed investment. In fact, the high standard deviation of profits indicates that variations in profits were very large in all three countries – much larger even than the level of expected profits. Thus, levels of domestic investment and, consequently, of output, consumption and employment were inherently unstable. In down years, ongoing foreign financial commitments could not be honoured without sizeable inflows of foreign capital. Since Brazil could not even cover its dividend and interest payments, it was far past the point where domestic resources played a major role in financing investment and where the degree of financial leverage had any meaning.

Estimating the systematic risk

In the foregoing case studies, the standard deviation of profits and rate of return was used to measure the countries' riskiness. This measure of risk is appropriate for a decision of whether or not a country is creditworthy. It is not, however, appropriate, for a decision of whether or not or to what extent a creditworthy country should be included in an investment portfolio. We know from Chapter 2 that systematic or undiversifiable risk, which depends on the covariance structure of asset returns, is the appropriate parameter for this type of question. We also know that beta in the CAPM is a measure of systematic risk widely used by both practitioners and academics. The framework developed in the beginning of the chapter can be applied to get estimates of country betas in order to estimate systematic country economic risk. In this section, we will first show how the country betas can be estimated. We will then discuss whether or not the techniques outlined in this section have any practical value.

Estimating country betas

Problems with the CAPM

The practical value of the capital asset pricing model as an effective tool for portfolio management suffers from the necessity to use proxy portfolios to represent the true market portfolio. Roll, for example, pointed out that the theory is untestable unless the exact composition of the true market portfolio, which must include all risky assets – stocks, bonds, commodities, real estate, and even human capital – is known and used in the tests.[6] In fact, most proxy portfolios· contain only a sample of common stocks. The implication of his paper is that the choice of the proxy portfolio determines the empirical content of the model. The point is important because, more recently, Fama and French have reported such a weak relation between beta and average returns that they call into question the CAPM itself.[7] Roll and Ross, however, show that the cross-sectional relation is very sensitive to the choice of a proxy index and that if the proxy index is not on the mean-variance efficient frontier, the Fama-French results can occur even when the CAPM holds.[8]

On the international level the problem is even more complicated. For equilibrium pricing of international assets to follow the CAPM, it is necessary for investors throughout the world to have identitical consumption baskets and for purchasing power parity (PPP) to hold exactly. In fact, deviations from PPP are a major source of exchange rate variation and consumption preferences also differ from country to country. Under these conditions, investors will want to hedge against real exchange rate risk so that in equilibrium each investor's optimal investment strategy will be a combination of two portfolios: a risky portfolio common to all investors and a portfolio specific to each investor used to hedge the real exchange risk as he perceives it. Furthermore, the common risky portfolio will not be the world market portfolio, because the world market portfolio contains assets correlated with the investor's consumption basket. Adler and Dumas showed that when there is no uncertainty about inflation rates in any country and when currency hedging is fully available, the common risky portfolio reduces to the world market portfolio.[9] Finding an adequate proxy for the world market portfolio is even more difficult than finding an adequate proxy for a national market portfolio.

The usual procedure is to adopt an index calculated in a base currency such as the US dollar with a representative mix of the major stocks from the world's stock markets. Bonds are sometimes included as well. However, Solnik points out that, judging from historical data, international market portfolios seem far from efficient, implying that there is much room for improvement.[10] However, in a forthcoming paper, Clark argues that a general international market index, which does, in fact, include all risky assets, can be generated by applying the model developed at the beginning of this chapter.[11]

Generating the index for calculating country betas
Equation 5.4 gives the capital value of an economy at the beginning of period T. As we show in the appendix, it can be estimated by applying equation 5.11. Thus, the world index at time t is simply the sum of the capital values in dollars of all the individual national economies from 1 to m:

$$I_t = \sum_{i=1}^{m} V_{it} \qquad (5.24)$$

where I is the world index.

Let R_{wt} represent the return on the world index for period t. Since, at the world level, total exports equal total imports, the return on the world index is:

$$R_{wt} = \frac{I_t}{I_{t-1}} - 1 \qquad (5.25)$$

The return on the world index corresponds to R_m in equation 2.6 in Chapter 2.

Estimating the country beta
To estimate the individual country betas we proceed with an ordinary least squares regression of the form:

$$(R_{it} - R_{ft}) = a + b_i(R_{wt} - R_{ft}) \tag{5.26}$$

where R_{it} is the return on country i for year t, and a and b are estimated coefficients. b represents the beta coefficient in the CAPM and in equilibrium a should be equal to zero. R_{ft} represents the riskless rate of return in the CAPM and for dollar-denominated assets is often represented by the rate of return on US T-bills.

The case of Korea
Suppose we want to estimate Korea's beta as it stood at the end of 1987. Looking at equation 5.26, we can see that we need to know R_w, R_f, and R_i for each year of the estimation period 1970–87. To calculate R_w, we use equation 5.25 and to calculate R_i, we use the procedure outlined in Table 5.4. For R_f, we use the average rate of return of the US T-bill for each year. This information is then used in the least squares regression on equation 5.26, where we find $b = 0.56$.

Thus, Korea's beta at the end of 1987 was 0.56. This is relatively low and indicates that Korea has relatively low systematic risk. By applying the CAPM, we can translate the systematic risk into interest rate basis points. Consider the following information:

$$E(R_w) = 9.72\%$$
$$R_F = 8.38\%$$

Applying this information in equation 2.6 (the security market line), gives:[12]
$$E(R_i) = 0.0838 + 0.56(0.0972\text{-}0.0838) = 0.0913$$
where the risk premium is:

$$0.56(0.0972 - 0.0838) = 0.0075$$

In other words, the risk premium associated with Korea's macroeconomic risk was equal to 75 basis points at the end of 1987.

Does the index work? Some proof from portfolio investment

The usefulness of the index developed above for estimating a country's systematic risk depends ultimately on how well it works. Some strong proof exists that it does.

Using the international market index to estimate betas for portfolio investment

The systematic risk of individual assets can be estimated using the macroeconomic market index developed above. In the Clark study mentioned below, betas were estimated for three asset classes: money market instruments, long-term government bonds and equity indexes. The method was straightforward. Returns for each country in each asset class were regressed against the index in an ordinary least squares regression of the form:

$$(R_{it} - R_{ft}) = a + b_i(R_{wt} - R_{ft})$$

where R_{it} is the return on the asset in country i for year t, R_{wt} is the return on the world index for year t, and a and b are estimated coefficients. b represents the beta coefficient in the CAPM and in equilibrium a should be equal to zero. R_{ft} represents the riskless rate of return in the CAPM. For the money market, the average rate of return on *US* T-bills for year t was used. For the long-term government bond and equities, the average rate of return on *US* T-bills for the whole estimation period was used. The reason for the difference is that different estimates of R_f produced better regression results. One explanation for this is that the money market has a shorter memory than the long-term government bond market and equities, which by definition have longer investment horizons.

In the article mentioned above, Clark constructed an index comprising 60 countries.[13] He then tested the index's ability to forecast the risk–return relationship over a 10-year period (1982–91) across a wide range of countries in three separate asset classes: money market instruments, long-term government bonds and equity indices. The procedure involves using the index to estimate the betas for each country in each asset class. He then uses the estimated betas and historical expected rates of return, variance and standard deviation as forecasts, to generate forward-looking portfolios for each year from 1982–91 using the Elton-Gruber-Padberg procedure to maximize the Sharpe index.[14] Forward-looking means that the portfolio for 1982 was generated with data available at the end of 1981, the portfolio for

1983 with data available at the end of 1982, and so on to the end of the period under consideration. Rather than the full covariance matrix, the Elton-Gruber-Padberg procedure uses betas in the optimization procedure.[15] Thus, if the betas estimated against the index capture the covariance structure of country returns, this should be reflected in the performance of the optimized portfolios.

The test consists in comparing the *ex post* performances of the individual optimized portfolios with the performances of portfolios generated by 'naive' diversification strategies. The 'naive' diversification strategies include portfolios of equal weights for all countries in the potential investment universe, weights based on relative gross domestic products (GDP), and an equally weighted portfolio comprising Germany, Japan, and Switzerland. The results are unambiguous. Clark finds that in every case the optimized portfolio outperforms all the others in terms of the arithmetic mean, the geometric mean, return per unit of risk, and excess return per unit of risk for all periods and sub-periods. Table 5.10 shows the results for the Sharpe index over the whole ten year period.

Table 5.10 Excess return to standard deviation (Sharpe index) for selected portfolios over the period 1982–91

	Optimized	*Equal weights*	*Jap.–Germ.–Switz.*
Money market	0.700	0.331	0.210
Long-term govt. bond	0.567	0.364	0.261
Equity index	0.484	0.409	0.375

(Source: Clark, E. (1995) A General International Market Index, *International Journal of Finance*, vol.3, 1288–1312.)

APPENDIX 5.1 DERIVATION OF MACROECONOMIC MARKET VALUE IN FOREIGN CURRENCY

Remembering that $b_t - a_t = X_t - M_t$, we can rewrite equation 5.4 as:

$$V_T = E\left[(X_T - M_T) + (X_{T+1} - M_{T+1})R^{-1} + \ldots + (X_n - M_n)R^{(-n-T)}\right]$$

$$(5A.1.1)$$

The corresponding expression for equation 5.5 is:

$$V_{T+1} = E\left[(X_{T+1} - M_{T+1}) + (X_{T+2} - M_{T+2})R^{-1} + \ldots (X_n - M_n)R^{-(n-(T+1))}\right]$$

$$(5A.1.2)$$

Remembering that $X_t' = S_t X_t$, and $M_t' = S_t M_t$, gives equation 5.9 in the text:

$$V_T' = E\left[S_T(X_T - M_T) + S_{T+1}(X_{T+1} - M_{T+1})R'^{-1}\right.$$

$$\left. + \ldots + S_n(X_n - M_n)R'^{-(n-T)]} \right] \qquad (5A.1.3)$$

Forward rate parity can be expressed as:

$$E[S_t] = F_t \qquad (5A.1.4)$$

Assuming linear independence and substituting 5A.1.4 into 5A.1.3 gives:

$$V_T' = S_T E(X_T - M_T) + F_{T+1} E(X_{T+1} - M_{T+1})R'^{-1}$$

$$+ F_{T+2} E(X_{T+2} - M_{T+2})R'^{-2} + \ldots + F_n E(X_n - M_n)R'^{-(n-T)}$$

$$(5A.1.5)$$

Interest rate parity can be expressed as:

$$F_{Tt} = S_T \frac{R'^t}{R^t} \qquad (5A.1.6)$$

Substituting 5A.1.6 into 5A.1.5 and simplifying gives:

$$V'_T = S_T E\left[(X_T - M_T) + (X_{T+1} - M_{T+1})R^{-1} + \ldots + (X_n - M_n)R^{-(n-T)}\right]$$

$$(5A.1.7)$$

Substituting 5A.1.1 into 5A.1.7 gives equation 5.11 in the text. Equation 5.12 can be derived in the same way.

NOTES

[1] For a discussion of this problem and the theoretical background for the new techniques of cross-border risk assessment, see: Clark, E.A. (1991) *Cross Border Investment Risk: Applications of Modern Portfolio Theory*, Euromoney Publications, London. This chapter deals with capital importing countries with low levels of foreign assets. Capital exporting countries or countries with substantial foreign assets require a slightly different presentation.

[2] Little, I. and Mirrlees, J. (1969) Manuel d'analyse des projets industriels dans les pays en voie de développement, in: *L'analyse coûts-avantages du point de vue de la collectivité*, vol. 2, OECD, Paris; UNIDO (1973) *Directives pour l'evaluation des projets*, United Nations, New York.

[3] If capital markets are in equilibrium, ROI will be equal to *r*.

[4] Some analysts might prefer these ratios net of dividends as they are presented in corporate finance.

[5] The earnings available to residents are total profits less interest payments:

$$\frac{\Delta(\text{profits} - D)/\text{profits} - D}{\Delta \text{profits}/\text{profits}}$$

Since D is fixed:

$$\Delta(\text{profits} - D) = \Delta \text{profits}$$

and

$$\frac{\Delta(\text{profits})/\text{profits} - D}{\Delta \text{profits}/\text{profits}} = \frac{\text{profits}}{\text{profits} - D}$$

Substituting the definition of profits from equation 5.15 gives the formula in the text.

[6] Roll, R. (1977) A Critique of the Asset Pricing Theory's Tests, *Journal of Financial Economics*, March, 349–57.

[7] Fama, E.F. and French, K.R. (1992) The Cross Section of Expected Stock Returns, *Journal of Finance*, **XLVII** (2), 427–65.

[8] Roll, R. and Ross, S.A. (1992) On the Cross Sectional Relation between Expected Returns and Betas, paper presented at the French Finance Association's International Conference in Finance, June 29.

[9] Adler, M. and Dumas, B. (1983) International Portfolio Choice and Corporation Finance: A Synthesis, *Journal of Finance*, (3), 925–84.

[10] Solnik, B. (1988) *International Investments*, Addison-Wesley Publishing Co. Inc.

[11] To see that this is true, go back to the beginning of the chapter and see how the cash flows, the *a*s and the *b*s, were defined. They include all income and

expenditure on final goods and services. Clark, E. (1995), A General International Market Index, *International Journal of Finance*, 1288–1312, vol. 3.

[12] For the reader's convenience, equation 2.6 is given as follows:

$$E(R_i) = R_F + \beta_i[E(R_M) - R_F] \tag{2.6}$$

[13] See: Clark, E. (1995) A General International Market Index, *International Journal of Finance*, 1288-1312, vol. 3. The 60 countries include: Argentina, Australia, Austria, Belgium, Bolivia, Brazil, Canada, Chile, Colombia, Costa Rica, Denmark, Dominican Republic, Ecuador, Egypt, El Salvador, Finland, France, Germany, Greece, Guatemala, Honduras, Iceland, India, Indonesia, Ireland, Israel, Italy, Japan, Jordan, Kenya, Morocco, Malaysia, Mexico, Netherlands, New Zealand, Nigeria, Norway, Pakistan, Panama, Paraguay, Peru, Philippines, Portugal, Singapore, South Africa, South Korea, Spain, Sri Lanka, Sweden, Switzerland, Taiwan, Thailand, Tunisia, Turkey, United Kingdom, United States, Uruguay, Venezuela, Zambia, Zimbabwe.

[14] The Sharpe index is:

$$y = \frac{E(R_p) - R_f}{\sigma_p}$$

where $E(R_p)$ is the expected return on the portfolio, and σ_p is the portfolio's standard deviation.

[15] For details on the optimization process see: Elton, E.J., Gruber, M.J. and Padberg, M.F. (1976) Simple Criteria for Optimal Portfolio Selection, *Journal of Finance*, **11** (5), 1341–57; Elton, E.J. Gruber, M.J. and Padberg, M.F. (1977) Simple Rules for Optimal Portfolio Selection: the Multi-Group Case, *Journal of Financial and Quantitative Analysis*, **12** (3), 329–45; Elton, E.J. Gruber, M.J. and Padberg, M.F. (1978) Simple Criteria for Optimal Portfolio Selection: Tracing Out the Efficient Frontier, *Journal of Finance*, **13** (1), 296–302; Elton, E.J., Gruber, M.J. and Padberg, M.F. (1978) Optimal Portfolios from Simple Ranking Devices, *Journal of Portfolio Management*, **4** (3), 15–19.

6 ADVANCED TECHNIQUES FOR ASSESSING INTERNATIONAL COUNTRY CREDITWORTHINESS

A country's ability to service foreign debt obligations depends to a large extent on its financial health. The methods and financial ratios developed in Chapters 3, 4, and 5 give a good indication of a country's financial health, but fall far short of the more precise formulations prevalent in more advanced areas of financial theory and practice. One of the most important recent developments in the field of finance has been in options pricing theory and its application to all sorts of financial contracts. The technique is regularly applied to analyse investments in stocks, bonds, currencies, commodities and real estate.

In this chapter we will show how options pricing theory can be applied to the problem of assessing a country's financial health and international creditworthiness.[1] First, we show how options pricing theory can be used to value corporate equity and debt. Particular emphasis is placed on two problems that are especially important in country-specific financial risk analysis, subordination of outstanding claims and agency conflict. We then go on to show how options pricing techniques can be applied to assessing country-specific financial risk. Procedures for generating all the relevent information and applying the model are presented in detail, and special attention is paid to estimating the financial risk premium and using it to distinguish between short-term liquidity problems and full-blown solvability crises. In this context, we bring out the role of the political risk analyst and show how his knowledge and skills can be effectively applied in the options pricing approach to generate estimates of maximum debt levels and future volatility. We conclude the chapter with some empirical evidence of the option pricing approach's actual performance.

USING OPTIONS TO VALUE SECURITIES

Using options pricing theory for debt valuation

Options pricing theory has become a standard tool in modern financial analysis and is employed extensively by both academics and practitioners to estimate the equilibrium market value of a wide range of corporate securities, including stocks, bonds, warrants and other types of debt instruments. It has recently been extended to the realm of project evaluation, a subject we will deal with in Chapter 9.[2]

In this chapter we will show how it can be employed to estimate country-specific financial risk. We start with an example of how option pricing theory can be used to evaluate corporate equity and debt. The basic information on options and the Black-Scholes pricing formula are given in the two following boxes.

Options: characteristics and definitions

An option gives its owner the right for a given period of time to buy or sell a given amount of a security or commodity at a fixed price, called the **exercise price** or the **strike price**. If the right can be exercised at any time during the life of the option it is called an **American option**. If the right can be exercised only at the option's expiration date, it is called a **European option**. The right to buy is called a **call**. The right to sell is called a **put**. The buyer of the option pays the seller, or the **writer**, a certain sum, called the **premium** or price, for the right to buy or sell at the prescribed price. In summary, the characteristic elements of an option contract are:

- the nature of the transaction: call or put;
- the underlying asset;
- the quotation asset;
- the amount of the underlying asset;
- the strike price;
- the expiration date;
- the premium or price of the option.

In this chapter we will be dealing essentially with European call options.

The Black-Scholes Option Pricing Formula

Black and Scholes were the first to provide a closed form solution for the valuation of European calls. They recognized that under certain stylized assumptions it is possible to form a risk-free hedge portfolio consisting of a long position in the underlying security and a short position in the European call written on that security. In the appendix at the end of the chapter, we show how to derive this formula, which is given as:

$$C_0 = V_0 N(d_1) - Ee^{-rt} N(d_2) \qquad (6.1)$$

where C_0 is the present value of the call, V_0 is the present value of the underlying security, E is the exercise price, and $N(d)$ is the value of the standardized normal cumulative distribution evaluated at d.

d_1 and d_2 are given by:

$$d_1 = \frac{\ln(V_0/E) + (r + \sigma^2/2)t}{\sigma\sqrt{t}} \qquad (6.2)$$

$$d_2 = \frac{\ln(V_0/E) + (r - \sigma^2/2)t}{\sigma\sqrt{t}} \qquad (6.3)$$

where r is the continuously compounded riskless rate of interest, σ is the standard deviation of the underlying security's continuously compounded annual rate of return, and t is the time to maturity or the duration of the call.

Equations 6.1, 6.2, and 6.3 express the exact pricing formula for a call option developed by Black and Scholes. The derivation of the formula is based on the creation of a perfectly hedged portfolio by buying the underlying security and selling the number of calls so that the value of the portfolio will be unchanged by a change in the value of the underlying security. Such a portfolio should yield the riskless rate of interest.[3]

In the example given by Black and Scholes, suppose that the stock price is $15, that the value of a call option on this stock is $5, and that if the stock price changes by $1, the value of the option changes by $0.50. The hedged position is then created by buying one share of stock and selling two options. One share of stock costs $15 and the sale of two options brings in $10, so that the net investment (equity position) comes out to $5. If the value of the share goes to $16 the value of the option goes to $5.50 and the net investment is still $5:

$$\$16 - (2 \times \$5.50) = \$5$$

If the share price falls to $14, the value of the option goes to $4.50 and the net investment is still $5:

$$\$14 - (2 \times \$4.50) = \$5$$

Thus, this portfolio is riskless. Since it is riskless, it should earn the riskless rate.

In their original article Black and Scholes showed how options pricing theory can be applied to the equilibrium market pricing of corporate equity and debt. Corporate debt can be considered as a sale of the company's assets to creditors, with shareholders owning an option to buy the assets back. On the exercise date, if the value of the assets is higher than the nominal value of the debt, the shareholders will exercise their option and buy back the assets by paying off the debt. In the opposite case, the company defaults and the creditors take possession of the assets. An example will make this clear.

Take Company A that has all its assets invested in company B.[4] Company A owns 1000 shares of company B with a total value of $150 000 ($150 per share). Thus, since all company A's assets are invested in company B, the total value of company A is $150 000. Company A has two classes of securities outstanding: 1000 shares of its own common stock and 140 **zero coupon bonds**, each of which will pay $1000 at maturity in 365 days. A zero coupon bond is a bond which pays no interest premiums but which is issued at a discount to its face value. Thus, at maturity the total amount due on the bonds will be $140 000. Company B pays no dividends and, consequently, company A will make or receive no cash payments until the maturity date.

On the maturity date, company A plans to pay off the old debt with a new debt issue. However, if company B is worth less than $140 per share on the maturity date, it will be unable to do so because no one will pay $140 000 for a partial claim on assets worth less than $140 000. In this case, ownership of the stock of company B will pass into the hands of the bondholders. In other words, company A's shareholders have an option on the company's assets with an exercise price of $140 000 and a maturity of one year.

What we want to know is the present market value and financial risk premium on company A's debt. Suppose that research shows that the value of company B's stock follows a continuous process with a constant standard deviation of 0.4 and that the rate on a one-year treasury bill, the riskless rate, is 10%. With this information the options pricing formula can be applied to determine the correct current value and risk premium on the bonds issued by company A. Three steps are involved:

1. the market value of company A's common stock is estimated in the options pricing formula;
2. the market value of the debt is determined by subtracting the market value of the common stock from the total value of company;[5]
3. by comparing the value of the debt given by this formula with the value it would have if there were no default risk, the financial risk premium is determined.

Applying this information on companies A and B in equations 6.2 and

6.3, we have

$$d_1 = [\ln(150\,000/140\,000) + (0.1 + 0.16/2)]/0.4 = 0.6225$$
$$d_2 = d_1 - 0.4 = 0.2225.$$

By looking up these values in the cumulative normal curve tables, we find:

$$N(d_1) = 0.7332$$
$$N(d_2) = 0.5881$$

and substituting this information into equation 6.1 gives:

$$C_0 = \$150\,000(0.7332) - \$140\,000(0.5881)e^{-0.1} = \$35\,481.$$

Hence, the value of company A's equity is equal to $35 481. Since the total value of the company is equal to $150 000, the value of the zero coupon bonds can be found by subtracting the equity value from the total value of the company. The market value of the bonds is thus equal to

$$\$150\,000 - \$35\,481 = \$114\,519.$$

The risk-adjusted interest rate can be found by taking the natural logarithm of the face value of the bonds divided by their current market value:

$$\ln(\$140\,000/\$114\,519) = 0.2009 = 20.0\%.$$

The financial risk premium is equal to the risk-adjusted interest rate less the riskless interest rate:

$$0.2009 - 0.1 = 0.1009 \text{ or } 10.09\%.$$

Hence, the financial risk premium depends on three parameters:

1. the company's capital structure represented by the reciprocal of the debt/total assets ratio (V/E);
2. the firm's operating risk represented by the standard deviation (σ) or variance of the percentage change in firm's total market value;

3. the maturity of the debt (t).

It is important to note that the firm's financial risk always increases as its operating risk ˙and debt/market value ratio increase. As we will see below, this fact gives rise to agency problems between the different categories of securities holders. However, the maturity of the debt has no such straightforward effect. For low and medium debt ratios an increase in the debt's maturity will increase the financial risk premium, while for high debt ratios it will decrease the financial risk premium. It is said that this is because the probability of default increases with time for low debt ratios, while it decreases with time for high debt ratios.

Pricing subordinated debt

The possibility of subordinating one class of debt to other types of claims is a major consideration for country-specific financial risk assessment. This is because of the relative autonomy that national governments have in determining when, how, and if foreign creditors will be paid. The link between subordination and risk can be illustrated by an example.

Suppose that Company A, in addition to its 140 zero coupon bonds, has also issued 30 subordinated zero coupon bonds, each of which promises to pay $1000 in 365 days.[6] These subordinated bonds will be paid off only after the 140 senior bonds have been paid in full. If Company A is worth less than $140 000 on the maturity date, all the assets will go to the senior bondholders. If Company A is worth between $140 000 and $170 000, the senior bondholders will be paid in full and the subordinated bondholders will receive the difference. If the company is worth more than $170 000, all the bondholders will be paid in full and the shareholders will receive the difference.

The senior bondholders' situation has not changed from the previous example but the shareholders' situation has. Each share of stock now represents a call option on the company's assets, with a strike price of $170 instead of $140. The subordinated bondholders are in the position of someone who owns a call option with a strike price of $140 and who has sold another call option with the same maturity date and a strike price of $170. The value of the subordinated bonds can be found by evaluating both types of options and subtracting the value of the option with the strike price of $170 from the value of the option with the strike price of $140 and multiplying by 1000, the number of shares.

Using the options pricing formula we find:

- value of the option ($140 strike price) = $35 481;
- value of the option ($170 strike price) = $22 217;
- value of subordinated debt = ($35.481-$22 217) × 1000 = $13 264.

The yield to maturity is:

$$\ln(\$30\,000/\$13\,264) = 0.8161 = 81.61\%.$$

and the risk premium is:

$$81.61\% - 10\% = 71.61\%.$$

The agency problem

An agency problem exists when principals and agents have a conflict of interest. In the absence of protective covenants, for example, the owners of Company A could benefit at the expense of both types of bondholders by taking actions that change the firm's volatility or its debt/asset ratio. Suppose that the owners sell the shares of Company B whose volatility is 0.4 and purchase $150 000 of a firm whose volatility is 0.6. Table 6.1 compares the outcomes for the different classes of security holders with the outcomes of the preceding case. Owners gain $11 727 at the expense of senior bondholders, who lose $10 048, and junior bondholders, who lose $1679. Owners clearly have an interest in increasing the firm's volatility whereas the bondholders clearly have an interest in preventing them from doing so.

Table 6.1 Volatility-induced wealth transfers according to type of claimholder

	Former case: volatility of underlying assets = 0.4	Case 2: volatility of underlying assets = 0.6	Difference
Senior bondholders	$114 519	$104 471	-$10 048
Junior bondholders	$13 264	$11 585	-$1 679
Owners	$22 217	$33 944	+$11 727

Table 6.2 Leverage-induced wealth transfers according to type of claimholder

	Original position	Position after issue of $5 000 in debt and dividend distribution	Difference
Bond value	$114 519	$117 095	$ + 2 576
Equity value	$35 481	$32 905	$-2 576
Dividend	$0	$4 038	$ + 4 038
Value of original bondholder claims	$114 519	$113 057	$-1 462

To see the effect of increased financial leverage on the bondholders' position, we can go back to the original scenario, where Company A owns $150 000 worth of Company B and has only two classes of securities outstanding: 1000 shares of its own common stock and 140 zero coupon bonds. Suppose that the firm issues zero coupon senior debt with a face value of $5000, the proceeds of which it will distribute to shareholders as a dividend. Total face value of outstanding debt goes up to $145 000, which means that the new exercise price of the shareholders' option goes up to $145 000 as well. The new bondholders will pay what the bonds are worth under the new debt/ assets structure. The market value of the total $145 000 debt is worth $117 095 and their share is 5/145. Thus, they pay $4038, which is distributed to the shareholders as a dividend. Table 6.2 summarizes the outcome. The new bondholders pay the fair market price for their investment. The shareholders lose $2576 in equity value but receive the dividend worth $4038. Their net gain is $1462, which comes at the expense of the original bondholders, whose claims fall from a value of $114 519 to $113 057.

Agency conflicts and the effects of subordination are particularly pertinent for cross-border lending. Through legislation and other incentives and controls, national governments have the power to influence domestic resource allocation and to control investment policy. As major international borrowers they can influence the country's capital structure. Under the guise of national sovereignty, they also have wide scope for issuing unilateral decrees that have the effect of creating subordinating clauses where formerly there were none. Macroeconomic policy influences resource allocation, economic performance and its volatility. Capital flight financed with foreign loans is the equivalent of a debt-financed stock buy-back. Debt moratoriums or decrees to the effect that external obligations will be honoured only up to a certain percentage of export income have the effect of subordinating foreign claims to the claims of residents. Judicious country-specific financial risk assessment requires awareness of these realities, as well as the specific means of measuring their consequences

Estimating the maturity of non-zero coupon debt

Before moving on to practical applications of option pricing theory to the assessment of country-specific financial risk, one last problem must be addressed. In the preceding example, Company A's debt was composed entirely of one-year zero coupon bonds. Therefore, it was equal to the bond's maturity. In reality, a company's or a country's debt is more likely to be composed of many different maturities and cash flow profiles. One possible solution to this problem is to evaluate each cash flow separately. However, the practical obstacles to such a procedure are prodigious. Another more promising route involves estimating the debt's average maturity (t).

Consider a bond with a nominal value of $100 000 that will be repaid in full at the end of five years and that makes annual interest payments of $20 000. To calculate the average time to maturity we can consider each payment as a zero coupon bond, the first payment with a maturity of one year, the second with a maturity of two years, and so on. The last payment of $120 000 ($20 000 of interest and $100 000 of principal) will have a maturity of five years. The overall bond issue will then be a portfolio of zero coupon bonds with the following payment profile:

- $20 000 one-year maturity;
- $20 000 two-year maturity;
- $20 000 three-year maturity;
- $20 000 four-year maturity;
- $120 000 five-year maturity.

What we need to know in equation 6.1 is the present value of the nominal debt discounted at the riskless rate (Ee^{-rt}). The nominal debt, E, is equal to the total liabilities arising from the loan, that is, the sum of the five payments:

$$\$20\,000 + \$20\,000 + \$20\,000 + \$20\,000 + \$120\,000 = \$200\,000.$$

Suppose that the riskless rate is 10%. We can find t by setting Ee^{-rt} equal to the sum of the present values of the individual payments (CF) and solving for t:

$$Ee^{-rt} = \sum_{T=1}^{5} CF_T e^{-rt} \tag{6.4}$$

$$\$200\,000e^{-0.1t} = \$20\,000e^{-0.1} + \$20\,000e^{-0.2} + \$20\,000e^{-0.3}$$
$$+ \$20\,000e^{-0.4} + \$20\,000e^{-0.5}$$

$$t = \frac{\ln\left(\frac{\$200\,000}{\$135\,478}\right)}{0.1} = 3.895 \text{ years}$$

It is important to note that although the nominal value of the bond is $100\,000, the total amount of debt outstanding is $200\,000 because the interest payments for each year also constitute a claim on the company and must be included.

USING OPTION PRICING THEORY IN COUNTRY-SPECIFIC FINANCIAL RISK ASSESSMENT: THE CASE OF BRAZIL

Before going on to discuss how the Black-Scholes options pricing formula can be applied to country-specific financial risk assessment, we should say something about some of the potential problems. The Black-Scholes option pricing formula depends on at least 10 unrealistic assumptions:

1. the stock's volatility is known and does not change over the life of the option;
2. the stock price changes smoothly, insofar as it never makes large changes in a short period of time;
3. the riskless rate never changes;
4. anyone can borrow or lend as much as he wants at a single rate;
5. a short seller will have the use of all the proceeds of the sale and receive all returns from investing these proceeds;
6. there are no trading costs for either the stock or the option;
7. there are no tax consequences;
8. the stock pays no dividends;
9. exercise of the option can occur only at expiration;

10. there are no takeovers or other events that can end the option's life early.

Although these assumptions are false and, consequently, the formula is wrong, no other formula has been developed that gives better results in a wide range of circumstances. In fact, after more than 20 years, the formula has proved its reliability and is more popular than ever with practitioners. When pricing longer-term securities, such as corporate bonds and cross-border debt, however, the assumptions concerning constant volatility and interest rates are particularly unrealistic. Fisher Black and Cox and Rubenstein[7] discuss the loss of precision that these shortcomings entail, as well as ways of deriving the parameters so as to minimize the problem. Other formulas have been derived to specifically overcome them.[8] In the following presentation, then, we are aware that the level of precision probably falls short of what can be achieved with traditional short-term European options pricing. Nevertheless, we present strong evidence that, compared to the results of traditional techniques (logit and discriminant analysis, for example), the level of precision is surprisingly high.

Estimating the parameters

To evaluate the financial situation of a national economy the procedure is the same as for a corporation. However, where corporate market values, rates of return, and volatility can normally be determined directly from published sources, the framework developed in Chapter 5 must be applied to generate the relevant data for the economy of a sovereign nation. Once the economy's market value, rate of return, and standard deviation have been calculated, the remaining information concerning riskless interest rates and the nominal value of outstanding debt is available in numerous publications.[9] This is all the necessary data for using the options pricing formula to assess macroeconomic financial risk. It is worthwhile to work through an example to see how this can be done.

Going through the steps outlined in Chapter 5 for Brazil from 1970 to 1987, we find the following information at the end of 1987:

V = the market value of Brazil's economy = \$45.85 billion

σ = the standard deviation of $\ln(V_{T+1}/V_T) = 0.3775$

To apply the Black-Scholes option pricing formula to Brazil's financial situation at the end of 1987, we need to know the amount of debt outstanding (E), its duration (t), and the riskless rate of interest (r). We proceed by estimating each of these parameters one by one.

Estimating E, the Amount of debt outstanding

Brazil's debt is not composed of single maturity, zero coupon securities as in the foregoing examples. On the contrary, it is composed of a wide range of securities with differing maturities, interest rates, and amortization schedules. As we saw, however, this problem can be overcome by considering the individual dated cash flows as distinct zero coupon bonds. Then E, face value or nominal debt as defined in the option pricing model, is the sum of all the contractual cash flows coming due in the future, including interest and principal.

In the World Debt Tables published by the World Bank, Brazil had outstanding long-term debt of $106.06 billion at the end of 1987. This is the

Table 6.3 The present value of Brazil's projected debt service at the end of 1987 (billions of US dollars)

Year	Interest	Principal	Total $1+2$	Discount factor (8.05%)	Present value 3×4
	1	*2*	*3*	*4*	*5*
short term	1.30	17.84	19.14	0.96	18.39
1988	8.13	15.87	24.00	0.92	22.15
1989	7.14	12.91	20.05	0.85	17.06
1990	6.58	12.73	19.31	0.79	15.16
1991	5.49	12.76	18.25	0.72	13.23
1992	4.28	14.80	19.08	0.67	12.73
1993	3.03	11.79	14.82	0.62	9.14
1994	2.13	7.70	9.83	0.57	5.59
1995	1.67	3.93	5.60	0.53	2.94
1996	1.37	3.15	4.52	0.48	2.19
1997	1.11	2.91	4.02	0.45	1.80
1998	0.60	3.77	4.37	0.41	1.80
1999	0.30	3.77	4.07	0.38	1.55
Totals	43.13	123.93	167.06		123.75

face value of the outstanding principal. Thus, E is equal to $106.06 billion plus all projected interest payments. Column 1 of Table 6.3 shows the year-by-year estimates of interest payments, including interest on short-term debt. Estimates of interest payments on long and short-term debt are based on projections of the World Bank published in the World Debt Tables and personal calculations. Column 2 shows the schedule for principal repayments including the $106.06 billion of long-term debt and $17.84 billion of short-term debt based on World Bank projections and personal estimates. Column 3 is the sum of columns 1 and 2. Thus, Brazil's total debt outstanding at the end of 1987 is the sum of column 3, $167.06 billion.

Estimating duration (t) and the riskless rate(r)

Since Brazil's debt is not the single maturity, zero coupon liabilities assumed by option pricing theory, we have to estimate the duration of all the projected cash flows to get an estimate of t. This requires knowledge of the discount factor for each cash flow as well as the riskless rate. If the yield curve is not flat, each cash flow should be discounted at the **spot rate** corresponding to its maturity. Spot rates are interest rates on riskless zero coupon bonds. Since the dollar is our base currency, the riskless rates must be associated with a US government security. Unfortunately, US government instruments of this type are only available for a limited number of maturities. Ideally, the term structure of interest rates would be constructed and applied to the corresponding cash flows.[10] However, these procedures are complicated, time-consuming and have several practical shortcomings. Where construction of the term structure is impractical, a simplifying assumption can be made to determine the riskless rate.

The most common practice is to assume that the yield curve is flat. Most estimations of duration make this assumption. In this case, we could use the rate on US treasury bills to represent the riskless rate. Under the flat yield curve assumption, one estimate of the riskless rate would be the bond equivalent of the treasury bill rate, line 60cs in the International Monetary Fund's *International Financial Statistics*. This refers to the simple arithmetic average of daily yields on a coupon equivalent basis on three-month bills.

The problem with this method is that the yield curve is usually not flat and the treasury bill bond equivalent rate is likely to change over the multi-year life of the debt. Thus, a more appropriate estimate of the riskless rate would be the yield to maturity on a government bond whose cash flow profile approximates that of the country's debt service (i.e. the percent of total payments period by period is the same for both). In this case the value t for the country's debt would be the same as the government bond's duration, a convenient outcome for problems associated with the unrealistic assumption of a constant interest rate over the life of the option. Robert Merton has shown that the problems associated with this assumption can be overcome by using the zero coupon bond yield corresponding to the maturity of the option.[11] With perfectly matched cash flow profiles, this condition would be met.

As a practical matter, we have found that the annual average yield to maturity on a US government 10-year constant maturity published in line 61 of *International Financial Statistics* is a reliable proxy. Although the cash flow profile of this security generally differs from that of individual country debt, it is still composed of a series of cash flows distributed over the life of the security and its yield to maturity reflects the term structure over its life. The average yield to maturity on the long-term government bond for 1987 was 8.38%. The appropriate rate for the options pricing formula is the continuously compounded rate, calculated as:

$$\ln(1.0838) = 0.0805 = 8.05\%.$$

Assuming that the yield to maturity on long-term US government bonds is the appropriate riskless rate, the discount factors in column 4 were calculated at the continuous compound rate of 8.05%.

Column 5 is the present value of each year's cash flow $(CF_T e^{-r(T-1987)})$, calculated by multiplying column 3 by column 4. At the end of 1987, the present value of the projected cash flows of Brazil's debt service was \$123.75 billion $(\sum_{T=1987.5}^{1999} CF_T e^{-r(T-1987)})$. The nominal value (E) was \$167.06 billion. The average maturity or duration of Brazil's foreign debt obligations can be calculated by remembering that in the Black-Scholes pricing formula Ee^{-rt} represents the present value of the exercise price or, in the case of country debt analysis, the present value of outstanding debt obligations including interest payments:

$$Ee^{-rt} = \sum_{T=1987.5}^{1999} CF_T e^{-r(T-1987)} \tag{6.5}$$

and solving for t:

$$t = \ln(\$167.06/\$123.75)/0.0805 = 3.73 \text{ years.}$$

Estimating the financial risk premium

We now have all the necessary information for the options pricing formula, which we show here as an explanatory aid. In practice, these tedious calculations are unnecessary. Calculators and computer programmes containing the Black-Scholes algorithm that are fast, cheap, and easy to use, abound. They can be made to do all the work.

$$d_1 = \frac{\ln(\$45.85/\$167.06) + (0.0805 + 0.1425/2)3.73}{0.3775\sqrt{3.73}} = -0.9971$$

$$d_2 = \frac{\ln(\$45.85/\$167.06) + (0.0805 - 0.1425/2)3.73}{0.3775\sqrt{3.73}} = -1.7262$$

$$N(d_1) = 0.1594$$
$$N(d_2) = 0.0422$$

$$C_0 = \$45.85(0.1594) - \$167.06e^{-(0.0805)3.73}(0.0422) = 2.087$$

We can interpret this result as: the value of Brazilian residents' equity in the total value of the economy at the end of 1987 was \$2.087 billion. Proceeding as we did in the example at the beginning of the chapter, the market value of Brazilian debt is equal to the difference between the total value of the economy and the value of Brazilian resident equity:

Market value of Brazilian debt = \$45.85 − \$2.087 = \$43.76 billion.

The risk-adjusted rate of interest on Brazilian debt is equal to the log of the nominal value of outstanding obligations divided by the average maturity:

Risk-adjusted cost of debt = ln(\$167.06/\$43.76)/3.73 = 0.359 = 35.9%

and the financial risk premium is equal to the difference between the risk-adjusted cost of debt and the riskless rate:

Financial risk premium for Brazil at the end of 1987 = 35.9% − 8.05%
= 27.85%.

The zero rate solvency test

The financial risk premium is sensitive to the riskless rate employed in the options pricing formula. As we mentioned above, assuming that the riskless rate remains constant over the life of the option is unrealistic and can be a source of error in the pricing exercise. Although the problem can theoretically be overcome by using the riskless rate appropriate to the maturity of the option, in practice this solution is often unworkable. Where multiple cash flow country debt is concerned, it is virtually always unworkable. Thus, the chosen riskless rate will always be off the mark to a certain extent. One way to partially compensate for this bias is to estimate the risk premium with the riskless rate set at zero. Then, the risk premium will depend only on the economy's volatility (σ), the reciprocal of the leverage ratio (V/E), and the debt's duration (t). We say that the compensation will only be partial because, as we have seen, in most cases the debt's duration itself depends on the riskless rate that has been chosen.

Using the zero rate solvency test to distinguish between liquidity problems and solvency crises

In cross-border risk analysis the distinction must be drawn between liquidity and solvency. As we have seen, measures of liquidity tend to dominate financial risk analysis. This, of course, reflects the lender's primary concern that a country will be able to meet its debt service payments in the near term. In the long term, however, the lender wants to be assured that the country is 'solvent' and that principal will be repaid in full, in spite of short-term liquidity problems. It is an accepted fact that solvency ultimately depends on how productively the economy employs its resources. A country is insolvent when its long-term net cash flows of foreign currency are inadequate to cover foreign debt servicing obligations. This is the case if the amount of debt is excessive. It is also the case if the rate of return on the country's assets is lower than the cost of borrowing.

The simple solvency test of traditional country risk analysis says that the rate of growth of exports must exceed the nominal rate of interest on debt. Otherwise, the debt/exports ratio will grow without limit. While helpful, this test is not reliable. As we mentioned in Chapter 5, the debt/exports ratio presents only one side of the coin, the export side. The ability to meet foreign obligations depends on net exports, that is, exports minus imports. The same goes for solvency. It is the rate of growth of net exports, not the rate of growth of exports that determine solvency. In Chapter 5 we proposed several ratios based on net exports for assessing a country's financial position. The zero rate solvency test complements these ratios by combining macroeconomic volatility and leverage with the payment profile of outstanding obligations to measure the financial risk in terms of interest rate basis points.

In 1987, the average interest rate on new debt commitments to Brazil was 8.3%. Between 1970 and 1987 the average rate was well above 10%. Over the same period exports had a geometric growth rate of over 14%, which means that Brazil was passing the simple solvency test. Other ratios such as interest/exports also looked pretty good, although the total debt/exports ratio was above 400%. In any case, since interest rates were relatively high in 1987, it might be argued that Brazil's problem, including the high risk premium estimated above, was only one of liquidity and that a more reasonable riskless rate would bring the risk-adjusted borrowing rate into line with the economy's rate of return (12%). We can test this proposition by estimating the risk premium with the riskless rate equal to zero. If the risk premium is unreasonable (above 3 or 4%), we conclude that the country is insolvent. If the risk premium is reasonable, we then compare the risk premium with the economy's rate of return. If the rate of return is higher than the risk premium, we might conclude that the problem is only one of liquidity. If, however, the risk premium is close to or greater than the economy's rate of return, we can conclude that there is a solvability crisis.

We applied this 'zero rate' solvency test to Brazil at the end of 1987 and found the financial risk premium to be 35.2%. This is clearly far too high, confirming Brazil's situation of bankruptcy. This outcome was pretty obvious, given the extreme nature of Brazil's financial predicament. Nevertheless, the zero rate solvency test can be very helpful when interest rates are high and the financial situation of the borrowing country is more reasonable. Combined with further analysis, it can be an important element in determining a country's creditworthiness, as we show in a later section of this chapter.

The role of political risk analysis

Political risk analysis has an important role to play in the option pricing approach to macroeconomic financial risk analysis. Although similar in many ways, countries are not companies. We have made this clear in the chapters dealing with political risk. Countries have considerably more autonomy than a private firm. In the most drastic cases, they can declare debt moratoriums or issue decrees that external obligations will be honoured only up to a certain point, a given percentage of exports, for example. This has the effect of subordinating foreign claims to the claims of domestic residents. They can act in more subtle ways as well. For instance, they can finance capital flight with foreign loans, which is equivalent to increasing the debt/equity ratio as in a debt-financed stock buyback, or they can use economic and monetary policy to influence economic activity and resource allocation with consequences on the economy's volatility. All of these things will impact on the economy's financial situation.[12] Their impact can be measured in the option pricing approach. If and when they occur, however, and with what probability and magnitude, pertains to the domain of political risk analysis. Thus, the option pricing approach is a powerful tool for exploiting the insights and analysis of the political risk analyst.

Political risk and subordination

Remember that the application of the options pricing formula to the assessment of country-specific financial risk assumes that the assets are 'sold' to the creditors, who retain ownership in the case of default. This device makes it possible to value the debt and estimate the risk premium. However, the assumption must be handled carefully if the seizure of foreign assets is considered as a practical possibility in the case of default. Most countries have strict controls on foreign ownership of domestic resources. Through legislation and decrees, governments also have the ability to take unilateral decisions against their foreign creditors. Consequently, it cannot be realistically assumed that the full value of the economy could effectively become the property of foreign creditors. The actual figure is probably much lower and must be determined on a country-by-country basis in relation to each country's legal, political, economic, social and cultural conditions. The effect of this unilateral action factor, when it is exercised, is to subordinate foreign claims to those of nationals. The ultimate degree of subordination depends on the extent of the economy's vulnerability to foreign retaliatory actions. For example, even if no assets could be seized directly by foreign creditors in the aftermath of a unilateral government decision to default on interest or principal payments, a shut-down of credit lines and trade financing might cost the economy 10 to 20% of its output. The degree of subordination would thus be limited by this fact. In any case, as we have seen, the principle of subordination has a drastic impact on financial risk premiums and permissible debt levels.

One way of looking at the degree of subordination attached to foreign debt is to establish **collateralization** levels. Collateralization is the flip-side of subordination and refers to the proportion of the economy's total value that is realistically vulnerable to actions undertaken by foreign creditors in the case of default. Thus, collateralization represents the upper limit on a government's capacity to subordinate. Recent experience has shown that although foreign takeovers of domestic resources are severely limited in scope and difficult and costly to implement, other actions can be undertaken by creditors that set limits on the abilities of government to unilaterally modify or repudiate their bona fide international obligations. One promising avenue for exploiting political risk analysis lies in expressing its conclusions in terms of a collateralization level for individual countries. An example will make this clear.

Suppose that instead of the Brazilian economy's total value of $45.85 billion, in-depth analysis of the country's legal, political, social, cultural, and economic conditions concludes that only 20% or $9.17 billion is vulnerable to foreign creditor influence in the case of default. Substituting this figure for V in the options pricing formula and proceeding as we did above yields a risk-adjusted interest rate of 77.8% and a financial risk premium of 69.8%, a figure 2.5 times higher than with 100% collateralization.

Collateralization has this effect because it raises the leverage ratio (lowers the market value/debt (V/E) ratio). Most countries have restrictions on foreign ownership of domestic assets, or the ability to make them off limits to foreigners. Furthermore, these restrictions often concern state-owned sectors that are the heaviest foreign borrowers, or the very sectors, such as natural resources, transport and communications, that would be of interest to foreign investors. Where restrictions on foreign ownership exist, they have the effect of subordinating foreign claims, thereby making them more risky. The collateralization analysis means determining to what extent outstanding debt is subordinate. Once this is done, pricing the subordinated debt through the options pricing formula is straightforward.[13]

Maximum debt levels
The financial risk premium is especially valuable in determining the creditworthiness of a national economy. The absolute level of the premium indicates the economy's overall financial health *vis-à-vis* the rest of the world. The higher the risk premium, the higher the chances of a debt service problem. The zero rate risk premium can also be compared to the economy's rate of return to aid in distinguishing between a simple liquidity crisis and a more serious solvency crisis. Remember that a solvency crisis is implied when the zero rate risk premium is absolutely too high or relatively too high compared to the economy's rate of return. When the zero rate risk premium is low enough and payments problems arise, illiquidity is implied. However, as the debt/assets ratio increases and the zero rate risk premium rises, the economy passes from illiquidity to insolvency. This suggests a theoretical maximum debt level. One definition of the maximum debt level is the point where the marginal cost of debt is just equal to the economy's rate of return. Another could be the point that yields a given zero rate risk

premium. Others, of course, are possible but it is these two that we feel are the most pertinent.

In determining maximum debt levels, three steps are involved:

1. determine which criteria will be used to define the maximum debt level (the country's rate of return or a given risk premium);
2. determine a collateralization level;
3. Substitute the information in the options pricing formula and proceed by trial and error to the level of debt that yields the required criteria (the country's rate of return or the given risk premium).

Suppose, for example, that the maximum level criterion is the country's rate of return. The expected rate of return for the Brazilian economy between 1970 and 1987 was 12%. Supposing 100% collateralization, we can see in Table 6.4 that Brazil's risk-adjusted interest rate approaches 12% at a debt level just over $38 billion (including interest and principal obligations). Thus, in the conditions prevailing at the end of 1987, Brazil's maximum debt level was about $38 billion, far lower than the $167.06 billion that was actually outstanding. A lower collateralization level will, of course, lower the maximum debt level. If astute political analysis had determined that a more reasonable collateralization level was $9.17 billion, the maximum debt level would have fallen to about $7.6 billion.

Using the zero rate risk premium as the maximum level criterion, the maximum debt level would have been even lower. Based on a zero rate risk premium of 3% and a collateralization rate of 100%, the maximum debt level was $25 billion. At a collateralization rate of 20%, it was only $5 billion.

Table 6.4 Maximum debt levels for Brazil under different criteria at the end of 1987

	Criteria: zero rate risk premium = 3%	*Criteria: risk adjusted cost of borrowing = the country's rate of return (12%)*
100% collateralization	$25 billion	$38 billion
20% collateralization	$5 billion	$7.6 billion

Volatility analysis

Political risk and volatility estimates

As we have seen, volatility or operational risk, defined as the standard deviation of the economy's rate of return, plays an important role in determining the macroeconomic financial risk premium. The accuracy of the estimate of the macroeconomic financial risk premium depends on the accuracy of the estimate of the economy's volatility. Up to now, we have used historical volatility. We believe that the use of historical volatility is justified insofar as most factors that determine macroeconomic volatility evolve relatively slowly. Outside of a chance discovery of gold or oil, a country's geography and dotation in natural resources are pretty much given over the medium term. So are its neighbours and the relations it enjoys with them. The evolution of a nation's cultural fabric represented by its social and political organization has also shown itself to be a relatively slow process, no matter what name is given to the dominant regime of the moment. Since all of these factors, whatever they are called – geo-strategic, politico-economic, socio-cultural, etc. – are reflected in a country's past economic performance, and since they seem to evolve relatively slowly, in most cases the fairly recent past should be a good estimator of the not too distant future.

Nevertheless, exceptional situations crop up more or less regularly. Eastern Europe's current transition comes immediately to mind. Time will tell how much has actually changed, but the fact of the matter is that uncertainty has increased. The Philippines is another case, where social and political transition from Marcos to democracy increased uncertainty. Other less obvious situations also exist, and once the analyst has identified them, he should be able to apply his expertise in a systematic fashion.

The nice thing about historical volatility is that it gives a reliable starting point, so that when the analyst says that a country's situation is more risky it will be clear what the new risk level will be and what effect it will have on the country's financial risk. If, for example, an in-depth analysis of Brazil's political, social, strategic and economic conditions suggests that the situation is 50% more risky now than in the past, this conclusion can be translated into a volatility estimate of 56.625% – the historical volatility of 37.75% multiplied by 1.5. This figure can, in turn, be applied in the options pricing formula to determine exactly what effect it will have on the economy's financial health.

Using market information to determine volality

Since operating risk may be changing over time, individual volatility estimates can be checked against the volatility implied by the overall market. Up to now we have been using the options pricing formula to determine the value of the country's call option on the assets 'sold' to the foreign creditors. Since we know the total value of the assets, we can derive the value of the foreign claims by subtracting the value of the call from the value of the total assets. However, if we know the value of the call we can leave the volatility as the unknown and solve the options pricing formula for this variable.

A secondary market for cross-border debt has developed and bid-ask prices for claims on many of the crisis countries are quoted regularly. This information makes it possible to determine the value of the call option and, subsequently, the volatility that this value implies.

Suppose, for example, that Salomon Brothers' bid price for Brazilian debt was 30 at the end of 1987, meaning that it was selling for 30% of its face value. From the World Debt Tables we know that the face value of outstanding Brazilian debt at the end of 1987 was $123.865 billion. The market value of the debt was thus 30% of $123.865 billion = $37.16 billion. It is important to note that here we have to use the face value of outstanding debt and not the total amount of foreign obligations that includes anticipated interest payments. This is because the market value of the debt quoted as a percentage of the face value already represents the present value of all future cash flows. When we apply the option pricing formula, however, E must still include interest payments.

Assuming 100% collateralization the value of the call was equal to the difference between the economy's market value and the market value of the foreign debt:

$$\$45.85 - \$37.16 = \$8.69 \text{ billion.}$$

Substituting this value for C in the options pricing formula and solving for volatility gives:

$$\sigma = 60.35\%.$$

In these conditions the volatility implied by the market is considerably higher than the historical volatility of 37.75%.

THE PERFORMANCE OF THE OPTIONS PRICING APPROACH: RESULTS OF A 60-COUNTRY STUDY

Although the methodology outlined above has strong theoretical foundations and a wide range of potent practical applications, the ultimate test of its eventual usefulness is whether or not it works. In fact, we can show some strong evidence that it does.

In 1988, the options pricing approach to assessing international creditworthiness was applied to 60 countries in a study undertaken for a major financial institution. The general results were published in an article by Ephraim Clark in the 1988 issue of *Euromoney* and in a book, entitled *Cross Border Investment Risk: Applications of Modern Portfolio Theory*, by the same author.[14] We can compare the results forecast by the study back in 1988 with the actual outcomes for the 60 countries in the succeeding four years, 1989-92.

The research was focused on 10 of the major developing countries selected from around the world: four from Latin America – Argentina, Brazil, Mexico, and Venezuela; four from East Asia – Indonesia, Korea, Philippines, and Thailand; and two from Africa – Nigeria and Zimbabwe. They cover a wide spectrum of the developing world and include oil

Table 6.5 Relevant data for 10 selected countries at the end of 1987

	V	σ	E	t	$E(R)$	Risk-adjusted rate[*]	Zero rate risk premium
Argentina	$12.84	0.546	$100.97	7.43	26.2%	31.20%	29.6%
Brazil	$45.85	0.378	$167.06	3.73	12.0%	35.90%	35.2%
Indonesia	$90.65	0.226	$72.71	4.42	21.6%	8.83%	2.6%
Korea	$186.60	0.148	$52.95	3.44	17.0%	8.05%	0.0%
Mexico	$27.48	0.235	$184.51	6.34	9.6%	30.10%	30.0%
Nigeria	$21.47	0.249	$37.25	3.82	7.0%	17.40%	15.5%
Philippines	$33.91	0.155	$41.13	4.08	6.2%	9.91%	6.2%
Thailand	$74.00	0.050	$28.99	4.71	8.6%	8.05%	0.0%
Venezuela	$47.40	0.176	$55.57	5.05	7.1%	9.52%	5.2%
Zimbabwe	$5.69	0.118	$3.33	4.12	8.3%	8.05%	0.0%

[*] where the riskless rate, $r = 8.05\%$

(Source: Clark, E. (1991) *Cross-Border Investment Risk: Applications of Modern Portfolio Theory*, Euromoney Publications, London, p.97.)

importers such as Brazil, the Philippines, Korea, Thailand and Zimbabwe, as well as oil exporters such as Indonesia, Mexico, Nigeria, and Venezuela. Table 6.5 shows the relevant data for the 10 countries at the end of 1987. Looking at this data the conclusion was:

> Based on the raw data, six of the ten countries have expected rates of return lower than the risk adjusted interest rate. This means that they have surpassed their theoretical maximum debt levels. In fact, the extreme financial (zero rate) risk premiums for Argentina, Brazil, Mexico, and Nigeria coupled with their inability to service their debt indicate that these countries are essentially bankrupt. Insofar as Argentina, Brazil, and Mexico are concerned, it is disquieting to see that even after 5 years of intensive discussion about the debt crisis, they are worse off than they were at the end of 1981. Although Venezuela and the Philippines may be relatively better off than Argentina, Brazil, Mexico and Nigeria, bankruptcy is not an inappropriate term for them.[15]

Table 6.6 shows the year-by-year performance from 1989 to 1992 of the six countries judged as bankrupt at the end of 1988. They all underwent major debt restructurings over the period. Argentina, Mexico, Nigeria, and the Philippines rescheduled every year. Brazil rescheduled every year except 1991. Venezuela rescheduled only in 1990, but for a huge sum totaling more than $17.5 billion. Thus, the foregoing conclusion that these countries were bankrupt and would not be able to meet their foreign debt obligations is unambiguously confirmed across the board.

Table 6.6 Annual amounts of debt restructurings for Argentina, Brazil, Mexico, Nigeria, Philippines and Venezuela, from 1987 to 1993

	Debt restructuring (millions of US dollars)				
	1989	1990	1991	1992	Total
Argentina	559	932	856	540	2 887
Brazil	2 496	685	0	12 250	15 431
Mexico	519	36 950	1 337	327	39 133
Nigeria	9 871	1 480	2 615	2 497	16 463
Philippines	1 762	1 126	1 106	1 086	5 080
Venezuela	0	17 659	0	0	17 659
Total	15 207	58 832	5 914	16 700	96 653

(Source: World Bank (1993–4) *World Bank Debt Tables*, vol. II.)

Now let's take a look at what was said about the other four countries:

> Indonesia, Thailand, South Korea, and Zimbabwe seem to be financially sound since their financial risk premiums are small or null. Based on this, new loans could be justified.[16]

The facts bear this conclusion out. Between 1989 and 1992 none of these countries rescheduled at all.

Thus, for the 10 countries in question, the forecast was perfect. Now let's compare the forecast with the outcome for the other 50 countries in the study. Table 6.7 reproduces the rankings of the 60 countries published in the September 1988 issue of *Euromoney*. The ranking process involved three steps:

> First, the countries were ranked by the financial risk premium and grouped in categories of 0%–1%, 1%–2%, etc. Second, countries with the expected rates of return lower than their corresponding risk adjusted interest rate were removed, grouped together in a lower bracket, and re-ranked according to their financial risk premiums. This was necessary to reflect the inherent financial risk of an economy whose marginal cost of foreign funds is higher than the marginal rate of return that can be earned by employing these funds. Finally, countries within each risk category were ranked according to their economic risk premiums and expected rates of return.[17]

The conclusion of the analysis was as follows:

> Rank alone does not tell the whole story: countries 1 to 11 represent little or no financial risk and they are far from a level of external debt which would compromise this situation; countries 12 to 19 represent little or no financial risk but their debt is at a level where increases will begin to affect the financial risk premium; countries 20–25 are in the same position but closer to what financial prudence would dictate as maximum external debt levels; countries 26 to 33 have reached or slightly surpassed their maximum external debt levels and countries 34 to 60 are far past the point where loans could be justified on economic and financial criteria.[18]

Before we compare the forecast with the actual results, it might be a good idea to put the exercise in perspective by reporting what *Euromoney* had to say about the ranking system in the preface to the article:

> This may be the strangest list ever printed in EUROMONEY. How could Taiwan be higher than the United States in a country risk rating? How, for that matter, could El Salvador be a better risk than Australia, Sweden, and Denmark?

Table 6.7 Country rank at the end of 1988 and actual amounts rescheduled, 1989–92

Rank	Country	Total amount re-scheduled 1989–1992 (millions of US dollars)	% of total re-schedul-ings	Rank	Country	Total amount re-scheduled 1989–1992 (millions of US dollars)	% of total re-schedul-ings
1	Taiwan	0		31	Zimbabwe	0	
2	Singapore	0		32	Panama	202	0.16
3	Japan	0		33	Colombia	0	
4	Italy	0		34	Honduras	634	0.47
5	Switzerland	0		35	Sri Lanka	0	
6	US	0		36	Kenya	0	
7	Spain	0		37	Pakistan	0	
8	Netherlands	0		38	Venezuela	17 659	13.56
9	Austria	0		39	Paraguay	436	0.33
10	Germany	0		40	Dom. Rep.	727	0.56
11	France	0		41	Guatemala	68	0.05
12	Norway	0		42	Philippines	5 080	3.90
13	Canada	0		43	Portugal	0	
14	Finland	0		44	Morocco	6 350	3.87
15	Thailand	0		45	Greece	0	
16	South Africa	0		46	Jordan	1 291	1.00
17	India	0		47	Nigeria	16 463	12.78
18	UK	0		48	Costa Rica	1 101	0.85
19	Belgium	0		49	Turkey	0	
20	Korea	0		50	Egypt	8 445	6.48
21	Malaysia	0		51	Bolivia	512	0.39
22	El Salvador	152	0.12	52	Ecuador	1 337	1.03
23	Australia	0		53	Chile	4 329	3.32
24	Sweden	0		54	Zambia	1 398	1.07
25	Denmark	0		55	Israel	0	
26	Indonesia	0		56	Mexico	39 133	30.04
27	Tunisia	0		57	Peru	5 838	4.48
28	Ireland	0		58	Brazil	15 431	11.85
29	New Zealand	0		59	Argentina	2 887	2.22
30	Iceland	0		60	Uruguay	785	0.60
	Total	152	0.12		Total	130 258	100

(Source: Clark, E. (1988) An Alternative Ranking, *Euromoney*, September, 234; World Bank (1993–4) *World Bank Debt Tables*, vol. II.)

In fact, *Euromoney* was right about El Salvador, which rescheduled $152 million between 1989 and 1992. But that is as far as it goes. Of the 33 countries that were deemed creditworthy, one other country, Panama, rescheduled to the tune of $202 million. Together, the sum of their reschedulings amounted to 0.27% of the total $130 258 million rescheduled by the 60 countries over the period. This is almost a perfect score that can be compared with *Euromoney*'s own country ranking that appeared in the same issue on the page preceding the Clark ranking.

Euromoney's ranking system, which was described in some detail in Chapter 3, contained 117 countries at the time of the article. In order to compare the two forecasts, we eliminated the countries not included in the Clark ranking so that both systems would include the same 60 countries and have the same total amount of rescheduled debt between 1989 and 1992 ($130.258 billion). Table 6.8 compares the results for the two rankings. It shows the cumulative amount of rescheduled debt for each system at each rank starting with rank 33, the cut-off point for solvency in the Clark ranking. Less debt rescheduled at the higher rankings indicates more accuracy in the rankings. When two or more countries had the same rank in the *Euromoney* system, we placed them in ascending order beginning with the smallest amount of rescheduled debt. Hence, the *Euromoney* ranking is presented in the most favourable way possible.

The results are striking. The Clark system is clearly superior, by a wide margin. The *Euromoney* system has more cumulative rescheduled debt at every step of the process until rank 58. In fact, by rank 40 the *Euromoney*

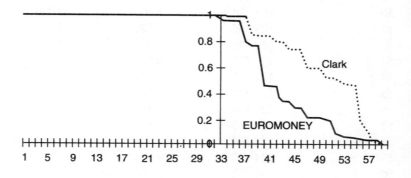

Figure 6.1 Percentage of unrescheduled debt at each rank.

Table 6.8 Comparison of the 1988 *Euromoney* and Clark country rankings: cumulative rescheduled debt at each rank over the period 1989–92

| | Cumulative rescheduled debt (millions of US dollars) | | |
	Euromoney's ranking system	Clark's ranking system	Difference
Ranks 1 to 33	4 329	354	3 975
34	4 329	988	3 341
35	4 329	988	3 341
36	5 620	988	4 632
37	23 279	988	22 291
38	29 629	18 647	10 982
39	29 629	19 083	10 546
40	68 762	19 810	48 952
41	68 762	19 878	48 884
42	68 762	24 958	43 804
43	84 193	24 958	59 235
44	84 978	31 308	53 670
45	90 058	31 308	58 750
46	90 494	32 599	57 895
47	98 939	49 062	49 877
48	98 939	50 163	48 776
49	99 141	50 163	48 978
50	102 028	58 608	43 420
51	103 365	59 120	44 425
52	119 828	60 457	59 371
53	120 929	64 786	56 143
54	120 997	66 184	54 813
55	121 724	66 184	55 540
56	122 358	105 317	17 041
57	122 870	111 155	11 715
58	124 268	126 586	-2 318
59	124 420	129 473	-5 053
60	130 258	130 258	0

(Source: World Bank (1993–4) *World Bank Debt Tables*, vol. II.)

ranking has already reached cumulative rescheduled debt of over $68 billion, whereas at rank 55, the Clark ranking is still only at slightly over $66 billion. Figure 6.1 underlines the superior performance of the Clark ranking by presenting the information in a dominance graph representing the percent of total rescheduled debt outstanding at each rank.

APPENDIX 6.1 DERIVATION OF THE BLACK-SCHOLES FORMULA

H = the value of the portfolio (net investment);
V = the price of the stock;
C = the price of the call;
Q_v = the number of shares owned;
Q_c = the number of calls owned.

The value of the portfolio is:

$$H = Q_v V + Q_c C \qquad (6A.1.1)$$

The change in the value of the portfolio is:

$$dH = Q_v dV + Q_c dC \qquad (6A.1.2)$$

To create the riskless hedge, suppose that one share of stock is purchased so that $Q_v = 1$. Then $Q_c = \frac{-1}{\partial C/\partial V}$. Since this portfolio is riskless, it should earn the riskless rate of return so that $\frac{dH}{H} = rdt$.
Substituting all this into 6A.1.2 gives:

$$rHdt = dV + \frac{-1}{\partial C/\partial V}dC \qquad (6A.1.3)$$

Using 6A.1.1 and the values for Q_v and Q_c in 6A.1.3 and rearranging, gives:

$$dC = \frac{\partial C}{\partial V}dV - rV\frac{\partial C}{\partial V}dt + rCdt \qquad (6A.1.4)$$

The stock price, of course, moves randomly over time. Assume that it follows a geometric Brownian motion process whose rate of return can be described as:

$$\frac{dV}{V} = \mu dt + \sigma dz$$

where:
μ is the instantaneous expected rate of return that measures the drift in the

random walk through time;
σ is the standard deviation of the rate of return;
dz is a Wiener process.

From Ito's lemma it is known that:

$$dC = \frac{\partial C}{\partial V}dV + \frac{\partial C}{\partial t}dt + \frac{1}{2}\frac{\partial^2 C}{\partial V^2}\sigma^2 V^2 dt \qquad (6A.1.5)$$

Substituting 6A.1.5 into 6A.1.4 and rearranging, yields:

$$\frac{\partial C}{\partial_t} = rC - rV\frac{\partial C}{\partial V} - \frac{1}{2}\frac{\partial^2 C}{\partial V^2}\sigma^2 V^2 \qquad (6A.1.6)$$

On the maturity date the value of the option will either be zero, if the stock price is equal to or less than the exercise price, or $V - E$ if the stock price is greater than the exercise price. Solving 6A.1.6 with this boundary condition yields the Black-Scholes formula presented in the text.

APPENDIX 6.2 MEXICO REVISITED 1994

On December 20, 1994 international investors were blitzed by a sudden 13% devaluation of the Mexican peso from 3.4647 per dollar at the end of trading on December 19 to 3.9750 at the end of trading the next day. As investors scrambled furiously to flee Mexican assets, pressure on the peso intensified to the point that two days later the authorities dropped all pretence of defending the exchange rate and allowed the peso to float. By the end of trading on April 14, the peso had fallen by 45% to 6.25 for one dollar. The resulting turmoil transformed Mexico from the handsome prince of the emerging markets back to the ugly frog of a risky developing country. As government authorities hinted ominously of a potential default on outstanding foreign debt, the stock market plunged, interest rates soared, and international investors were left with staggering losses that even the princess kiss of a $50 billion US organized rescue package was unable to reverse. Shades of August 1982?

Explanations of exactly what went wrong abound. They range from fallout from the Chiapas rebellion in January 1994, to over-dependence on 'hot money' (portfolio investment), to an unsustainable current account deficit, to a fall in domestic savings, to a political bungling of the December 20 devaluation, to all of the above. What most of these explanations have in common is the conclusion that Mexico's underlying economic and financial situation did not warrant the humiliating treatment inflicted on it by the international financial markets. They point out that the government's budget was balanced, the economy had been opened up and deregulated, inflation was low at 7%, economic growth was strong, and the North American Free Trade Agreement was signed and being implemented. In other words, conventional wisdom has it that investors were overreacting to perceived changes in the country's political fragility.

Are the analysts right and the investors wrong? A look at the most important traditional analytical parameters in Table 6.A.1 covering 1990–92, the period of the most intense Mexican capital inflows, seems to confirm this conclusion. The debt/exports ratio was stable, the debt/GNP ratio declined steadily, growth of dollar GNP was impressive, and the exports/interest ratio was strong and improving. Based on this information, the Mexican economy seems to have been in good shape. However, a comparison of the data in Table 6A.1 with the data in Table 5.7 shows that Mexico's situation at the end of 1992 was similar to its situation at the end of 1981, the eve of the debt crisis. The data in Table 6A.2, derived from the techniques developed in Chapter 5, shows that rather than robust financial and economic health, Mexico was in an extremely precarious

Table 6A.1 Selected traditional analytical parameters for Mexico (in US dollars)

	1990	*1991*	*1992*
Debt/exports	2.43	2.54	2.43
Debt/GNP	0.45	0.41	0.35
Growth of GNP (%)	18.3	17.5	14.9
Exports/interest	5.85	5.43	6.13

(Source: IMF (1993) Balance of Payments Statistics, *Yearbook*, vol.44, part 1; International Financial Statistics, several issues; World Bank (1993–4) *World Bank Debt Tables*.)

financial situation throughout the entire period of massive capital inflows.

Although average profits were growing steadily over the period, by the end of 1992 volatility of profits was still almost four times higher than average profits themselves. Furthermore, the financial service coverage ratio, while improving, was below one (two is considered a minimum in corporate finance) and the degree of financial leverage was not applicable due to the fact that average profits were lower than the amount of interest due. The picture that emerges from Table 6A.2 is one of a highly volatile economy, borrowed to the hilt, and, thus, extremely vulnerable to the slightest negative development. Shortening the estimation period by half paints an even more dire picture, as we can see in Table 6A.3.

Table 6A.2 Selected analytical parameters for Mexico (in US dollars)

	1970–90	*1971–91*	*1972–92*
Average profits (US$ billions)	5.61	6.87	8.3
σ (Average profits)	29.84	30.34	30.9
Financial service coverage (%)	53	69	87
Degree of financial leverage	N/A	N/A	N/A

(Source: IMF (1993) Balance of Payments Statistics, *Yearbook*, vol.44, part 1; International Financial Statistics, several issues; World Bank (1993–4) *World Bank Debt Tables*.)

Table 6A.3 Selected analytical parameters for Mexico

	1980–90	1981–91	1982–92
Average profits (US$ billions)	4.77	3.97	4.02
σ (Average profits)	40.01	39.44	39.48
Financial service coverage (%)	45	40	42
Degree of financial leverage	N/A	N/A	N/A

(Source: IMF (1993) Balance of Payments Statistics, *Yearbook*, vol.44, part 1; International Financial Statistics, several issues; World Bank (1993–4) *World Bank Debt Tables*.)

What, then, can we conclude? Was (is) Mexico bankrupt and living on borrowed money and time, or was (is) the problem one of liquidity that could be solved by the $50 billion rescue package? The zero rate solvency test can help to answer this question.

The zero rate solvency test

As we mentioned earlier in Chapter 6, the zero rate solvency test combines macroeconomic volatility and leverage with the payment profile of outstanding financial obligations to measure the financial risk in terms of interest rate basis points. The procedure involves estimating the relevant parameters as outlined in Chapters 5 and 6, and applying them in the options pricing model with the riskless rate set at zero. The resulting option value is then used to calculate the risk premium on the country's outstanding debt. If it is higher than a given benchmark, the country is considered insolvent.

At the end of 1992, the relevant information concerning Mexico was as follows.

V_T	$211.29 billion
Outstanding financial obligations	$175.32 billion
Duration of outstanding financial obligations	3.5 years
Standard deviation of the economy's rate of return	34%

With this information we find that the option value is $68.2 billion and the zero rate risk premium is 5.8%. A risk premium of 5.8% is higher than any reasonable level of financial risk. We ourselves use 2% as the maximum financial risk premium. Thus the zero rate solvency test confirms the foregoing ratio analysis. At the end of 1992 Mexico, for all practical purposes, was bankrupt.

Political risk as an agency conflict

It is interesting to note that Mexico appears as insolvent even before political risk is considered. When political risk is considered, the conclusion is even more obvious. As we have shown, political risk can be treated as an agency conflict between foreign creditors and the national authorities, who have the power to make unilateral decisions that can alter the quality of their country's outstanding foreign debt. There is also an agency conflict between local residents in general and foreign creditors. The consequences of these agency conflicts can appear in the form of *de facto* subordination of the foreign creditors' claims on the economy or in the form of increased volatility of the economy's performance.

Unilateral subordination

One effect of the unilateral action factor is to subordinate foreign claims to those of foreign nationals. Collateralization levels, based on a country's legal, political, economic, social and cultural conditions, can be estimated to capture the vulnerability of foreign creditors to unilateral subordinating actions. Remember that collaterization levels reflect the economy's vulnerability to retaliatory actions taken by foreign creditors and represent the limits on a government's ability to subordinate. They are expressed as a percentage of the economy's market value. Table 6A.4 shows Mexico's zero rate risk premium for different levels of collateralization as of the end of 1992.

It is clear from Table 6A.4 that incorporating political risk confirms our conclusion regarding Mexico's insolvency. In fact, for Mexico, we estimate that realistic collateralization levels range between 10% and 25%, which would put Mexico so far from financial solvency that voluntary lending of any sort would be out of the question.

Table 6A.4 Mexico's zero rate risk premium for selected levels of
collateralization at the end of 1992

Collateralization level (%)	Zero rate risk premium (%)
75	9.72
50	17.36
25	34.64
10	60.46

Political risk measured as increased volatility

Besides unilateral actions with subordination consequences, political risk
can also take the form of increased volatility. Insofar as a country's
geography, dotation in natural resources, neighbourly relations, and socio-
political fabric tend to evolve slowly over time, historical volatility is
probably a pretty good estimator of medium-term future volatility.
However, in the case of Mexico at the end of 1992, the country's political
make-up was in full mutation, with a presidential election due at the end of
1994. Consequently, it was likely that decisions would be made and events
would occur that would increase the volatility of the country's economic
performance. In Table 6A.5 we show the effect that increases in volatility
would have on the zero rate risk premium at the 100% collateralization
level.

Table 6A.5 Mexico's zero rate risk premium for selected levels of volatility at
the end of 1992 (collateralization = 100%)

Volatility (% above historical level of 34%)	Zero rate risk premium (%)
+10	6.70
+20	7.63
+30	8.58
+40	9.55

The combined effects of political risk: subordination and volatility

The foregoing analysis is unambiguous. Ratio analysis shows that as far back as 1990, when foreign capital started to pour in, Mexico was financially insolvent. Nevertheless, the situation seemed to be improving somewhat by the end of 1992. In spite of the apparent improvement, the zero rate solvency test shows that Mexico was still far from solvent, even then. Just how far can be estimated by combining subordination and volatility in the zero rate solvency test to reflect the full impact of the economic and political situation facing the country.

A generous but realistic estimate of Mexico's collateralization level is 25%. At the end of 1992 our most conservative estimate of increased volatility was 20%. Using these two figures in the zero rate solvency test gives a risk premium of 35.22% – a rate that is far above anything that could be considered reasonable.

NOTES

1   This methodology was first presented by Ephraim Clark, in: *Cross Border Investment Risk* (1991) Euromoney Books, London, pp. 85–110; Briefing (1991) *Euromoney*, February, pp. 73–6; Briefing (1991) *Euromoney*, April, pp. 79–82.

2   See: Dixit, A.K. and Pindyck, R.S. (1994) *Investment Under Uncertainty*, Princeton University Press, Princeton, N.J.

3   Black, F. and Scholes, M.˙ (1973) The Pricing of Options and Corporate Liabilities, *Journal of Political Economy*, **81** (3).

4   Similar examples were developed by Merton, R. (1974) On the Pricing of Corporate Debt, *Journal of Finance*, **29**, 449–70 and J.C. Cox and M. Rubenstein (1985) Options Markets, Prentice Hall, Englewood Cliffs, pp. 375–84 and Clark (1991), *op. cit.* n.1 above, pp. 86–8.

5   The market value of the bond could be calculated directly by remembering that *B*, the market value of the bonds, is equal to $V_0 - C_0$ and substituting this into equation 6.1 so that:

$$B_0 = V_0 N(-d_1) + Ee^{-rt}N(d_2)$$

where $N(-d_1) = 1 - N(d_1)$ because of the symmetry of the normal distribution.

6   This type of example, presented by Cox and Rubenstein (1985), *op. cit.*, pp. 384–7, was first developed by Fischer Black and John Cox in (1976) Valuing Corporate Securities: Some Effects of Bond Indenture Provisions, *Journal of Finance*, **31** (May), 351–68.

7   Black, F. (1989) How to Use the Holes in Black-Schole, *Journal of Applied Corporate Finance*, **1** (winter); Cox and Rubenstein (1985), *op. cit.*, pp. 274–85, 375–415.

8   See, for example: Cox, J.C. and Ross, S.A. (1976) The Valuation of Options for Alternative Stochastic Processes, *Journal of Financial Economics*, **3** (January-March), 145–66.

9   Some of the best information comes from the international organizations such as: the World Bank, *World Debt Tables*; the International Monetary Fund, *International Financial Statistics*; the Bank for International Settlements, *Annual Report, Evolution de l'Activité Bancaire et Financière Internationale, Ventilation par Echéance et par Secteur des Prêts Bancaires Internationaux, Statistiques sur l'Endettement Extérieur* (with the OECD); OECD, *Financial Market Trends*; among others. See the publication lists of these organizations for a complete list of what is available.

10   Several methods for estimating the term structure of interest rates have been discussed in the literature. See: Carelton, W.T. and Cooper, I.A. (1976) Estimation and Uses of the Term Structure of Interest Rates, *Journal of Finance*, **31** (September), 1067–83; McCulloch, J.H. (1975) An Estimate of the Liquidity Premium, *Journal of Political Economy*, **83** (February), 95–119; Schaefer, S.M. (1981) Measuring a Tax Specific Term Structure of Interest Rates in the Market for British Government Securities, *Economic Journal*, **91** (June), 415–38.

[11] See Merton, R. (1973) Theory of Rational Option Pricing, *Bell Journal of Economics and Management Science*, **4** (Spring), 141–83.

[12] As we showed above, an increase in volatility increases the value of the call option. A *ceteris paribus* increase in the debt/assets ratio improves the shareholders' position at the expense of the bondholders. Subordination weakens the position of bondholders.

[13] It should be remembered that we are referring to macroeconomic financial risk, or the risk that is associated with the overall economy. For individual loans to individual borrowers, their creditworthiness would also have to be evaluated.

[14] Clark, E. (1988) An Alternative Ranking, *Euromoney*, September, 234; Cross Border Investment Risk, *op. cit.* n.1 above, pp. 96–7.

[15] Clark (1991) *Cross Border Investment Risk*, *op. cit.* n.1 above, pp. 96–7.

[16] Clark (1991) *Cross Border Investment Risk*, *op. cit.* n.1 above, p. 97.

[17] Clark (1988) An Alternative Ranking, *op. cit.* n. 14 above.

[18] *Ibid*

PART THREE

Managing the Risk

7 MANAGING POLITICAL RISK

An organization can operate internationally through three different channels:

1. it can choose to export to various foreign countries;
2. it can make a permanent direct investment in these countries via manufacturing units and distribution networks;
3. it can lend money or resources to foreign borrowers.

Each channel has its own dangers, hazards and risks. The exporter, for example, may be paid late or not at all; the foreign investor may have his assets confiscated; the lender may not be reimbursed. Each situation must be examined in order to save the firm from possible loss due to a change in the political environment of the foreign country.

This chapter deals with the political risks associated with each channel. The first section focuses on the 'commercial' exposure to political risk, whereas the second section deals with the risk specific to a foreign direct investment. In the third section, the credit risk related to a bank loan is analysed in detail.

COVERING COMMERCIAL EXPOSURE TO POLITICAL RISK

Many companies exporting to developing countries have to finance their customers in order to enter the market. Exports can either be consumer goods with short terms of payment of a year or less, or capital goods and turnkey factories with terms of payment that can extend to 10 or 15 years. Most large transactions, such as the sale of a power station, automotive factory or oil drilling equipment, are financed through buyer credits, which means that banks will bear the potential default risk. To avoid this, banks often get protection through public insurance contracts, as we will see later in the chapter, and transform their loans into public guaranteed credits. The final risk is then taken by state agencies, such as Hermes in Germany or the ECGD in the UK. Small exports, on the other hand, are often financed directly by the exporter through supplier credits. The exporter's risk is that he will not be paid. This can arise from his client's inability or unwillingness to pay, or from some general cause related to the country's evolution such as a foreign exchange squeeze, a war or a revolution. To hedge this risk, the exporter can either resort to some kind of 'internal' coverage that he sets up himself, or he can take out an insurance policy against political risk.

Internal hedging techniques

Internal hedging techniques aim at reducing political risk by limiting exposure to the risk or by increasing operating earnings.

Reducing exposure
The best and most common means of reducing exposure involves doing business with only the safest countries. Unfortunately, this type of strategy has the unpleasant side-effect of completely eliminating many countries with good trade potential. Another more complicated strategy involves determining individual country exposure limits in the context of a global trade portfolio. In this strategy, exposure limits are determined through the risk-return trade-off in a traditional Markowitz mean-variance optimization. The exercise requires estimating probabilities for non-payment as well as the correlations across customers. Intellectually appealing as this strategy is, besides the obvious problems related to estimating the required probabilities and correlations, it is difficult to implement and monitor on a regular basis for basic commercial reasons: individual orders vary in size and frequency, clients change, etc.

Enhancing operating earnings
The strategy of enhancing operating earnings involves rating the country where the customer is located and then adding a cash premium to the sales price based on the perceived political risk. In effect, the exporter seeks to offset his risk by increasing his return by an appropriate amount. For example, a middle risk country might warrant a 15% increase in the sales price, whereas a high risk country might warrant an increase of 45% or 50%.

The limits to this type of coverage are obvious: it can only work in situations when there is little or no competition. Otherwise, the higher price will have the effect of eliminating the exporter from the market in question. A unilateral rise in the sales price might be possible, for example, when the client is the seller's subsidiary. Besides hedging the political risk, the inflated 'transfer' price would then have the added attraction of accelerating profit repatriation and reducing the risk on the direct investment. Local tax authorities are wise to the transfer price gambit, however, and usually monitor such transactions closely.

External hedging techniques

When the exporter is unable or unwilling to undertake internal hedging techniques, or when such techniques are inadequate, the alternative solution lies in transferring the risk to another entity, usually a bank or an insurance company.

Transferring the risk to a financial institution

The letter of credit
The most common means of transferring the risk to a financial institution is the well-known 'letter of credit', irrevocable and confirmed. The letter of credit offers the exporter a high degree of safety. It is a document addressed to the exporter that is written and signed by a bank on behalf of the importer. In the document, the bank undertakes to guarantee for a certain time span the payment for the specified merchandise, either by paying directly or by accepting drafts, if the exporter conforms to the conditions of the letter of credit by presenting the required documents. The letter of credit is thus a financial contract between the issuing bank and the exporter, separate from the commercial transaction.

Letters of credit can be revocable or irrevocable. Revocable letters of credit can be cancelled at any time by the bank and consequently are rarely used except for transactions between subsidiaries of the same company. An irrevocable letter of credit can be modified or cancelled only with the agreement of both parties. If a bank in the exporter's country adds its guarantee to the letter of credit issued by the importer's bank, it is called a confirmed letter of credit. This means that if the importer's bank does not honour its promise to pay for one reason or another, the exporter's bank will make good on the promise.

A letter of credit is one of the most reliable means of settling foreign accounts receivable. The exporter knows all the requirements for payment because they are spelled out in the letter of credit. The institution guaranteeing payment is a bank. Procedures are standardized and well known to the banking community. Furthermore, it facilitates financing since the banker's acceptance can easily be discounted. It also has the advantage of guaranteeing against order cancellation during the manufacturing stage. The disadvantage is that it is costly and cumbersome to set up. Furthermore, it does not guarantee against all possible risks. Technical errors in the documents can lead to non-payment. Worse again, in many third world countries, importers can sometimes gain access to goods before paying for them. Complaints by the importer about the quality of supposedly protected merchandise are often received at the same time that the issuing bank is refusing payment because of errors in one or more documents. Unconfirmed letters of credit are also subject to government-inspired measures that forbid, reduce or delay payment. In all this, exporters should always deal directly with a trusted bank and resist pressure by the importer to name the receiving bank in the exporter's country. He will thus at least be assured that in the case of a problem his interests will be protected.

Factoring
When selling on open account, political and commercial risk can be transferred to a financial institution through what is known as factoring. In a factoring transaction, the factor purchases a company's receivables. Factors usually belong to cross-border associations, consisting of offices in almost every country. Factoring can be done on a recourse or non-recourse basis. Recourse means that the exporter accepts all credit and cross-border risks. Non-recourse means that the factor accepts all credit and cross-border risk except those involving disputes between exporter and importer. Most factoring is done on a non-recourse basis.

In a typical factoring transaction, the exporter submits new orders directly to the factor. The factor evaluates the creditworthiness of the potential client and makes a recourse/non-recourse decision as quickly as possible – sometimes as quickly as several days, sometimes as long as several weeks, depending on the availability of information. When the decision is made, the exporter sells its claim to the factor and receives payment.

Factoring is expensive, costing around 2% of sales plus interest. Smaller claims are more expensive, due to the fixed costs associated with information-gathering. Nevertheless, it can be worthwhile to many firms, such as the occasional exporter, or the exporter with a geographically diverse portfolio of clients, for whom it would be organizationally complicated and expensive to internalize the collection process of accounts receivable.

Forfaiting
Besides transferring risk to a financial institution, forfaiting is also a means of providing medium-term financing for international trade. It involves the

purchase by a financial institution, usually a bank, of a series of promissary notes signed by an importer in favour of an exporter. The notes usually fall due at regular three-month or six-month intervals and cover a period of three to five years. The language of these notes must be in accordance with legal requirements which are spelled out in the Geneva convention of 1930 and the notes themselves are frequently guaranteed or availed by the importer's bank.

In a forfaiting transaction, the exporter sells the notes at a discount to the purchasing financial institution, called the forfaiter. The forfaiter holds the notes for collection as they come due, without recourse to the exporter. This absence of recourse distinguishes the forfaiting of promissary notes from the discounting of trade drafts for which the exporter is liable to recourse in the case of non-payment. In fact, the absence of recourse explains the origin of the term 'forfaiting': the purchaser of the notes 'forfaits' his right to recourse. The forfaiting operation is summarized in Figure 7.1. Part A shows the exchanges occurring when the transaction is undertaken; Part B shows the subsequent settlements.

The cost of forfaiting, which is effectively a combined hedging-financing technique, is the rate of interest pro rata temporis that is determined by the maturity and currency of denomination plus a risk premium that depends on the country. Table 7.1 gives an idea of how forfaiting rates looked for different countries and maturities as of January 1995.

The main advantage of factoring and forfaiting is that they eliminate most of the risks related to future payment, i.e. insolvency or unwillingness of the importer to pay, country risk or foreign exchange controls. The main disadvantage is that the cost is high. Possible coverage is also limited, since countries with too high a risk are excluded from the list of eligible countries.

Transferring the risk to an insurance company

Two avenues are open to the exporter who wants to transfer his risk to an insurance company. He can either take advantage of a public guarantee scheme that covers political risk, or take out an insurance policy with a private company.

Public insurance schemes
Almost all industrial countries have set up export credit insurance agencies that cover credit risk due to commercial as well as political factors. Such schemes typically cover up to 95% or 100% of the invoice amount. When the export is financed by supplier credits, then the seller must cover the

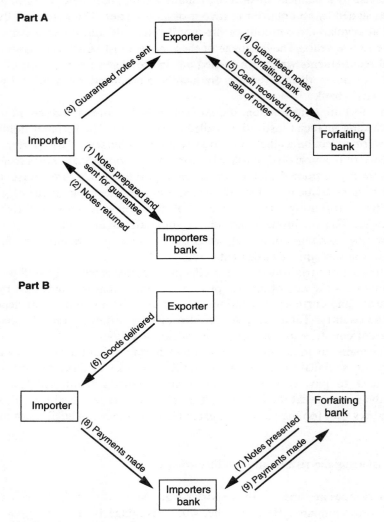

Figure 7.1 Summary of forfaiting activity.

credit he has granted the importer. In the case of a buyer credit, it is the bank lending to the importer who must be insured against credit risks. Since a major part of these risks stem from the political situation of the importing country, a substantial part of the premium goes to cover political risk.

Most export credit insurance agencies have developed insurance contracts

Table 7.1 Discount rates for forfaiting (January 1995)

Country	Max. Maturity	FF Discount	FF Yield	US $ Discount	US $ Yield	DM Discount	DM Yield
Abu Dhabi	3	8	9	$8\frac{3}{8}$	$9\frac{3}{8}$	$7\frac{1}{8}$	$7\frac{7}{8}$
Argentina	5	$10\frac{5}{8}$	$13\frac{3}{4}$	$10\frac{5}{8}$	$13\frac{3}{4}$	10	$12\frac{1}{2}$
Australia	5	$7\frac{3}{8}$	$8\frac{3}{4}$	$7\frac{7}{8}$	$8\frac{3}{4}$	$6\frac{1}{2}$	$7\frac{1}{2}$
Austria	7	7	$8\frac{3}{4}$	$6\frac{7}{8}$	$8\frac{5}{8}$	$6\frac{3}{8}$	$7\frac{3}{4}$
Bahrain	3	$8\frac{1}{4}$	$9\frac{1}{4}$	$8\frac{1}{2}$	$9\frac{5}{8}$	$7\frac{3}{8}$	$8\frac{1}{8}$
Belgium	7	7	$8\frac{3}{4}$	$6\frac{7}{8}$	$8\frac{5}{8}$	$6\frac{3}{8}$	$7\frac{3}{4}$
Botswana	2	*	*	*	*	*	*
Brazil	5	$11\frac{1}{4}$	$14\frac{3}{4}$	$11\frac{1}{4}$	$14\frac{3}{4}$	$10\frac{1}{2}$	$13\frac{1}{2}$
Cameroon	1	*	*	*	*	*	*
Canada	7	7	$8\frac{3}{4}$	$6\frac{7}{8}$	$8\frac{5}{8}$	$6\frac{3}{8}$	$7\frac{3}{4}$
Chile	5	$9\frac{3}{4}$	$12\frac{1}{4}$	$9\frac{3}{4}$	$12\frac{1}{4}$	$8\frac{7}{8}$	11
China	5	$8\frac{3}{4}$	$10\frac{3}{4}$	$8\frac{3}{4}$	$10\frac{3}{4}$	$7\frac{7}{8}$	$9\frac{1}{2}$
Colombia	5	10	$12\frac{3}{4}$	10	$12\frac{3}{4}$	$9\frac{1}{4}$	$11\frac{1}{2}$
Cyprus	3	$7\frac{7}{8}$	$8\frac{3}{4}$	$8\frac{1}{8}$	$9\frac{1}{4}$	$6\frac{7}{8}$	$7\frac{5}{8}$
Czech Rep.	5	$9\frac{1}{4}$	$11\frac{1}{2}$	$9\frac{1}{4}$	$11\frac{1}{2}$	$8\frac{3}{8}$	$10\frac{1}{4}$
Denmark	7	$7\frac{1}{8}$	$8\frac{7}{8}$	7	$8\frac{3}{4}$	$6\frac{1}{2}$	$7\frac{7}{8}$
Dubai	3	8	9	$8\frac{3}{8}$	$9\frac{3}{8}$	$7\frac{1}{8}$	$7\frac{7}{8}$
Egypt	3	$10\frac{7}{8}$	$12\frac{3}{4}$	$11\frac{1}{8}$	$13\frac{1}{8}$	10	$11\frac{5}{8}$
Finland	5	$7\frac{5}{8}$	9	$7\frac{5}{8}$	9	$6\frac{5}{8}$	$7\frac{3}{4}$
France	7	7	$8\frac{3}{4}$	$6\frac{7}{8}$	$8\frac{5}{8}$	$6\frac{3}{8}$	$7\frac{3}{4}$
Gabon	1	*	*	*	*	*	*
Germany	7	7	$8\frac{3}{4}$	$6\frac{7}{8}$	$8\frac{5}{8}$	$6\frac{3}{8}$	$7\frac{3}{4}$
Greece	5	$8\frac{1}{4}$	10	$8\frac{1}{4}$	10	$7\frac{3}{8}$	$8\frac{3}{4}$
Hong Kong	5	$7\frac{3}{8}$	$8\frac{3}{4}$	$7\frac{3}{8}$	$8\frac{3}{4}$	$6\frac{1}{2}$	$7\frac{1}{2}$
Hungary	3	$9\frac{3}{8}$	$11\frac{3}{4}$	$9\frac{3}{8}$	$11\frac{3}{4}$	$8\frac{5}{8}$	$10\frac{1}{2}$
India	3	$8\frac{5}{8}$	$9\frac{3}{4}$	$8\frac{7}{8}$	$10\frac{1}{8}$	$7\frac{3}{4}$	$8\frac{5}{8}$
Indonesia	3	$8\frac{3}{4}$	10	$9\frac{1}{8}$	$10\frac{3}{8}$	$7\frac{7}{8}$	$8\frac{7}{8}$
Iceland	5	$7\frac{5}{8}$	9	$7\frac{5}{8}$	9	$6\frac{5}{8}$	$7\frac{3}{4}$
Ireland	7	$7\frac{1}{8}$	$8\frac{7}{8}$	7	$8\frac{3}{4}$	$6\frac{1}{2}$	$7\frac{7}{8}$
Israel	5	$8\frac{3}{8}$	$10\frac{1}{4}$	$8\frac{3}{8}$	$10\frac{1}{4}$	$7\frac{5}{8}$	9
Italy	7	7	$8\frac{3}{4}$	$6\frac{7}{8}$	$8\frac{5}{8}$	$6\frac{3}{8}$	$7\frac{3}{4}$
Japan	7	7	$8\frac{3}{4}$	$6\frac{7}{8}$	$8\frac{5}{8}$	$6\frac{3}{8}$	$7\frac{3}{4}$
Kuwait	3	$8\frac{3}{8}$	$9\frac{1}{2}$	$8\frac{3}{8}$	$9\frac{7}{8}$	$7\frac{1}{2}$	$8\frac{3}{8}$
Lebanon	1	$8\frac{3}{8}$	$8\frac{7}{8}$	$8\frac{7}{8}$	$9\frac{3}{8}$	$7\frac{3}{8}$	$7\frac{3}{4}$

Table 7.1 Discount rates for forfaiting (January 1995) (*continued*)

Country	Max. Maturity	FF Discount	FF Yield	US $ Discount	US $ Yield	DM Discount	DM Yield
Luxembourg	7	7	$8\frac{3}{4}$	$6\frac{7}{8}$	$8\frac{5}{8}$	$6\frac{3}{8}$	$7\frac{3}{4}$
Malaysia	5	$7\frac{1}{2}$	$8\frac{7}{8}$	$7\frac{1}{2}$	$8\frac{7}{8}$	$6\frac{5}{8}$	$7\frac{5}{8}$
Mauritius	2	$8\frac{1}{8}$	$8\frac{7}{8}$	$8\frac{1}{2}$	$9\frac{3}{8}$	$7\frac{1}{8}$	$7\frac{5}{8}$
Mexico	5	10	$12\frac{3}{4}$	10	$12\frac{3}{4}$	$9\frac{1}{4}$	$11\frac{1}{2}$
Morocco	5	$10\frac{5}{8}$	$13\frac{3}{4}$	$10\frac{5}{8}$	$13\frac{3}{4}$	10	$12\frac{1}{2}$
Netherlands	7	7	$8\frac{3}{4}$	$6\frac{7}{8}$	$8\frac{5}{8}$	$6\frac{3}{8}$	$7\frac{3}{4}$
New Zealand	5	$7\frac{1}{2}$	$8\frac{7}{8}$	$7\frac{1}{2}$	$8\frac{7}{8}$	$6\frac{5}{8}$	$7\frac{5}{8}$
Norway	5	$7\frac{3}{8}$	$8\frac{3}{4}$	$7\frac{3}{8}$	$8\frac{3}{4}$	$6\frac{1}{2}$	$7\frac{1}{2}$
Oman	3	$8\frac{1}{4}$	$9\frac{1}{4}$	$8\frac{1}{2}$	$9\frac{5}{8}$	$7\frac{3}{8}$	$8\frac{1}{8}$
Pakistan	1	$9\frac{1}{4}$	$9\frac{7}{8}$	$9\frac{3}{4}$	$10\frac{3}{8}$	$8\frac{1}{4}$	$8\frac{3}{4}$
Peru	2	$11\frac{3}{4}$	$13\frac{3}{8}$	$12\frac{1}{8}$	$13\frac{7}{8}$	$10\frac{1}{4}$	$12\frac{1}{8}$
Philippines	3	$9\frac{3}{8}$	$10\frac{3}{4}$	$9\frac{5}{8}$	$11\frac{1}{8}$	$8\frac{1}{2}$	$9\frac{5}{8}$
Portugal	5	$7\frac{3}{8}$	$8\frac{3}{4}$	$7\frac{3}{8}$	$8\frac{3}{4}$	$6\frac{1}{2}$	$7\frac{1}{2}$
Saudi Arabia	3	8	9	$8\frac{3}{8}$	$9\frac{3}{8}$	$7\frac{1}{8}$	$7\frac{7}{8}$
Singapore	7	7	$8\frac{3}{4}$	$6\frac{7}{8}$	$8\frac{5}{8}$	$6\frac{3}{8}$	$7\frac{3}{4}$
South Africa	3	$9\frac{3}{8}$	$10\frac{3}{4}$	$9\frac{5}{8}$	$11\frac{5}{8}$	$8\frac{1}{2}$	$9\frac{5}{8}$
South Korea	5	$7\frac{3}{4}$	$9\frac{1}{4}$	$7\frac{3}{4}$	$9\frac{1}{4}$	$6\frac{7}{8}$	8
Spain	7	7	$8\frac{3}{4}$	$6\frac{7}{8}$	$8\frac{5}{8}$	$6\frac{3}{8}$	$7\frac{3}{4}$
Sweden	5	$7\frac{3}{8}$	$8\frac{3}{4}$	$7\frac{3}{8}$	$8\frac{3}{4}$	$6\frac{1}{2}$	$7\frac{1}{2}$
Switzerland	7	7	$8\frac{3}{4}$	$6\frac{7}{8}$	$8\frac{5}{8}$	$6\frac{3}{8}$	$7\frac{3}{4}$
Taiwan	7	$7\frac{1}{8}$	$8\frac{7}{8}$	7	$8\frac{3}{4}$	$6\frac{1}{2}$	$7\frac{7}{8}$
Thailand	5	$7\frac{7}{8}$	$9\frac{1}{2}$	$7\frac{7}{8}$	$9\frac{1}{2}$	7	$8\frac{1}{4}$
Tunisia	3	$9\frac{3}{4}$	$11\frac{1}{4}$	10	$11\frac{5}{8}$	$8\frac{7}{8}$	$10\frac{1}{8}$
Turkey	1	11	$11\frac{7}{8}$	$11\frac{3}{4}$	$12\frac{3}{8}$	10	$10\frac{3}{4}$
United Kingdom	7	7	$8\frac{3}{4}$	$6\frac{7}{8}$	$8\frac{5}{8}$	$6\frac{3}{8}$	$7\frac{3}{4}$
United States	7	7	$8\frac{3}{4}$	$6\frac{7}{8}$	$8\frac{5}{8}$	$6\frac{3}{8}$	$7\frac{3}{4}$
Uruguay	1	$9\frac{1}{4}$	$9\frac{7}{8}$	$9\frac{3}{4}$	$10\frac{3}{8}$	$8\frac{1}{4}$	$8\frac{3}{4}$
Venezuela	*	*	*	*	*	*	*
Vietnam	3	11	13	$11\frac{1}{4}$	$13\frac{3}{8}$	$10\frac{1}{4}$	$11\frac{7}{8}$
Zimbabwe	1	$9\frac{3}{4}$	$10\frac{3}{8}$	$10\frac{1}{8}$	$10\frac{7}{8}$	$8\frac{3}{4}$	$9\frac{1}{4}$

(Source: *Banque des Echanges Internationaux, Paris*).

that deal with risks occurring either during the manufacturing period or after delivery for both private and public foreign customers. The contracts are different, depending on whether the importer is publicly or privately owned. Where publicly owned institutions are concerned, a default is considered a 'political' risk, no matter what the reason actually is. If the buyer is a non-state firm, the insurance contract contains various covenants, dealing with purely commercial matters on the one hand, or real political risks on the other. Table 7.2 shows the various types of coverage depending on the nature of the client.

Table 7.2 Various types of insurance contracts arranged by export credit agencies

State-owned importer		Privately-owned importer	
Nature of the risk	*Events covered*	*Nature of the risk*	*Events covered*
Credit risk	Political risk: war, revolution. uprising, governmental measure	Credit risk	Political risk
	Catastrophic risk: hurricane, earth-quake, etc.		Catastrophic risk
	Non-transfer risk: foreign exchange control		Non-transfer risk
			Insolvency of the buyer
	Default		Default
Risk of manufacturing	Risk of contract cancellation during the manufacturing period	Risk of manufacturing	Risk of contract cancellation during the manufacturing period

Both the credit risk and the manufacturing risk are part of the export credit. The interest rates of this form of financing are regulated by the 'OECD concensus' to avoid unfair competition among industrial countries, which defines minimum rates for all the developing countries.

Most of these export credit insurance agencies run a permanent deficit, which tends to show that premiums are not high enough to compensate the real country risk. For instance, the French COFACE (Compagnie Française d'Assurance pour le Commerce Extérieur) suffered a loss of 11 billion francs in 1990, 6.5 billion in 1992, and 5.3 billion in 1993. The trend here, however, is to diminished losses and is due to the reorientation of French exports towards the more solvent countries. In 1983 only 21 countries were ineligible for coverage, whereas the list included 80 countries in 1993. Consequently, the percentage of exports going to the less solvent countries fell from 48% in 1985 to 28% in 1992.

COFACE is typical of most official export credit insurance agencies. Set up in 1946, its task is twofold. It directly covers all commercial and political risks in OECD countries as well as risks related to short-term export financing. It also acts as a state agency to protect French companies against commercial risk on long-term export financing and the political risk on non-OECD countries. Its main shareholders are French private and state-owned insurance companies and various commercial banks. In 1993, 468 billion francs of trade receivables were guaranteed by the state through COFACE. This amounted to 6.7% of French GNP, or five months of exports.

Each country's agency has its own rules concerning the level of the premium associated with political risk. Thus, the Swedish EKN has set up a system of country risk categories where the premiums on the high-risk countries can reach 14%. As for the American Eximbank, it used to have five risk categories, with three risk classes for each category. For instance, premiums ranged from 0.5% to 1.63% for a class 1 borrower in category A to 5.06% to 10.13% for a class 3 borrower in category E. In October 1992, Eximbank abandoned this system in favour of one where the premium for each insurance policy is defined specifically according to the sovereign and commercial risk of each transaction. Similarly, ECGD, the British agency, treats each transaction separately, basing its premiums on the total expected loss resulting from commercial and operating factors plus losses due to the sovereign risk.

Private insurance contracts
When public insurance is unavailable, the exporter can get in touch with a private insurance company, such as Lloyd's in London, that is willing to cover risk arising from political events. These private contracts include all

the usual credit risks, both commercial (insolvency, default, etc.) and political (wars, uprisings, destruction, etc.). Each transaction is rated and priced individually.

Generally speaking, private insurance is more expensive. It is, however, also more flexible due to tailor made contracts and is more widely available, due to the wider range of countries that are covered.

Managing risky accounts receivable

The foregoing discussion deals with reducing or hedging exposure to cross-border risk. What happens, however, if the risk has not been hedged and the firm faces a payment default on some of its receivables? It is too late to transfer the jeopardized receivables to a bank, a factor, or an insurance company. Other solutions must be found.

Making a deal with the client
When the cause of the default lies with the client's domestic political situation, such as a lack of foreign currency, the exporter can try to make another kind of arrangement. One possibility is for the invoice to be paid in local currency. The problem then is for the exporter to find some use for it, either buying local goods or investing in the country. Local goods, for example, might be purchased with local currency and then sold abroad. If the exporter has no direct use for the goods, a buyer has to be found for them, which is probably more feasible for a large multinational than for a small or medium-sized company. The ideal solution is for the exporter to source some inputs in the client country. In both cases, the arrangement can be viewed as countertrade and will raise the questions of what is worth purchasing, is the price right, and how can the goods be transferred outside the country. Investing in the country only delays the problem of repatriating the proceeds. It also exposes the exporter to new risks and raises the questions of how to identify profitable opportunities, how to monitor the investment and, ultimately, how to recoup the investment.

Selling the receivable
Selling the receivable to a third party is also a possible solution to the problem of non-payment. Two avenues are open. The first avenue is feasible when the client acts in good faith but, because of some series of events outside his control, a foreign exchange squeeze, for example, he is unable to fulfil his obligations. Selling the receivable involves finding a buyer who has need of local currency. This might be a company which wants to invest in

the country or which has current or future liabilities denominated in the country's currency. The problem, of course, is finding the buyer. The second avenue is appropriate when the client acts in bad faith and for some reason refuses to pay up. It involves selling the receivable to a collection agency. Both avenues imply accepting a discount on the face value of the receivables. When the client is in good faith the discount is likely to be reasonable and the transaction resembles the negotiated transaction. When the client is in bad faith and the receivable is sold to a collection agency, the discount is likely to be steep and often amounts to 80% to 90% of the face value.

Legal action
When all else fails, legal action is the only solution. It is usually the worst solution as well, since it often involves hefty outlays for legal expenses with small chance of a favourable outcome in the local court. In some countries it is possible to avoid the hefty outlays for legal expenses by engaging legal representation on a contingency basis. This solution is also costly because the contingency fee is likely to represent a sizeable portion of the amount recovered.

MANAGING EXPOSURE OF FOREIGN DIRECT INVESTMENT TO POLITICAL RISK

As with commercial exposure, hedging exposure of foreign direct investment to political risk has two basic techniques. The exporter can resort to some kind of 'internal' coverage that he sets up himself, or he can take out an insurance policy against political risk.

Internal hedging techniques

Limiting investment to countries offering a good legal environment
The most obvious way to hedge the exposure of direct investment to political risk is to limit investments to countries with a respectable legal environment. Most industrial countries have signed various bilateral agreements on protection of foreign investment. These agreements, normally covering a span of 10 to 15 years with a rollover option, stipulate that no expropriation is valid unless compensation is 'fair'. 'Fair' is defined as the market value of the expropriated assets. An international organization, the International Center for Settlement of Investment

Disputes (ICSID), can be called in as arbitrator if any dispute occurs.

Founded in 1965, ICSID belongs to the World Bank Group. So far 123 countries have signed the Convention of Settlement of Investment Disputes, which the ICSID is supposed to enforce. The ICSID can provide binding arbitration for foreign investors if a dispute arises between them and the host country. In this case, a conciliation commission or an arbitration tribunal is set up to judge the issue. Besides this, ICSID adopted five directives in September 1992:

- to define the scope of intervention by ICSID;
- to give the guidelines for host countries in their dealings with foreign investors;
- to define the investment norms with regard to investment remittances;
- to identify 'legitimate' cases of expropriation;
- to explain the conciliation process.

As a result, ICSID is becoming recognized as an arbitration tribunal. Twenty-seven countries recognize it in their national legislation and 286 bilateral treaties as well as NAFTA identify it as the appropriate body for arbitration purposes.

Limiting the transfer of funds to the subsidiary
Limiting the transfer of funds to the subsidiary is another obvious way to minimize the potential loss on a direct investment due to political risk. Various schemes can be devised to achieve this aim. First of all, the investor can rely more heavily on leasing than on purchased assets. This involves paying rents in local currency for company premises, manufacturing equipment, computers, and vehicles. The scope for leasing will be constrained by the availability of local leasing opportunities, which are often limited. Secondly, when it is feasible, the investor can employ amortized or second-hand equipment, rather than risk the full cost of new equipment. This avenue can have surprising tax consequences, however, and should be studied carefully. Thirdly, the investor can reduce his equity stake by financing the local subsidiary with debt from third parties. To limit transfer risk, preference can also be given to loans in local currency. Higher debt, of course, means higher financial risk. Local authorities often resent financing structures that are too obviously designed to reduce exposure, since reduced exposure means that their control is reduced as well.

Introducing 'sleeping partners'
Several international or regional organizations such as the International Finance Corporation (part of the World Bank Group), the Inter American

Development Bank, or the Asian Development Bank, stand ready to take minority stakes in the equity of foreign subsidiaries. These institutions are supposed to help developing countries on the way to industrialization by bringing in new investors. They typically take 10% to 15% of the equity but without exercising their voting rights. In this way the investor's exposure is reduced and he can take some comfort in the knowledge that his association with an important international institution may shield his investment from the worst abuses of the local authorities.

Setting up joint ventures is another way to reduce exposure since it diminishes the funds to be transferred from the parent company. There is a risk, however, that the sleeping partner will wake up and demand a say in the management of the subsidiary. Thus, it is wise for parent company management to keep as much control as possible over intellectual property such as patents, licences, and marketing and manufacturing know-how.

Organizing an international division of production

The international division of production is a system in which each subsidiary is linked to other subsidiaries of the same multinational in various countries, buying from them and selling to them components and parts of the final products. A similar method would consist of making foreign subsidiaries dependent on the parent company's technology. As we said earlier, a complex, interdependent system reduces exposure. Any measures taken by the local authorities against the subsidiary would result in its destruction. In fact, firms that integrate their production at a world or region-wide level make any form of nationalization useless. It is important to remember, however, that effective exposure reduction depends on the host country understanding to what extent the local investment is dependent on parent technology or integrated production. Otherwise, blinded by ignorance, the host country might undertake measures that are revealed as self-damaging only after it is too late. The automotive industry, computers, electronics and the aircraft industry are some of the sectors particularly adapted to an international division of production.

Adopting a 'good citizen' policy

Table 7.3 outlines the advantages and disadvantages of a foreign direct investment for the host country. In a good citizen policy, the foreign investor will try to accentuate the positive side of the investment by creating new jobs, favouring transfers of technology, and bringing in hard currency. The negative side will be reduced by favouring locally produced inputs over imports, and limiting remittances. The foreign investor should also keep an eye on the image that its subsidiary is conveying locally, by informing public authorities on its development projects and making sure that its record as a 'good citizen' is well known. Again, establishing a joint venture with a local investor can be a plus by increasing the local aspect and bringing in new supporters ready to lobby in favour of the foreign investor.

Table 7.3 Benefits and drawbacks of foreign direct investment

Advantages (+)	Drawbacks (-)

Hard currencies brought in:
  investment
  export of goods and services
	Hard currencies brought out:
	  remittances
	  import of components or raw
	  materials

Employment (new jobs)	Competition to local producers of goods and services (1)
Transfers of technology	Cultural transfers (1)
Industrialization process	Attraction of local resources (1) (workforce, financial flows)
Local development	Pollution
Subcontracting	

(1) Although these features are not negative in absolute terms (competition, for instance, can benefit to consumers by bringing prices down), they can be perceived as potential threat to local business or local cultural traditions.

Practical applications

In practice, most firms will use a combination of the techniques outlined above to control their political risk exposure. The eventual combinations depend on the host country in question and the particular situation of the firm itself. The experience of Remy Cointreau in China and ABB in Poland are good examples of how companies actually proceed to manage their exposure to political risk (see following boxes).

Remy Cointreau in China

At the end of the 1970s, Remy Pacifique (formerly Remy Martin Far East), a subsidiary of Remy Cointreau the well-known French cognac producer, was listed on the Hong Kong stock exchange with 25% of equity held by the public and 75% held by the parent company. In 1979 it set up a joint venture located in Tianjin, which is near Beijing. The local partner, Tianjin Vineyard, a collective farming enterprise, agreed to bring in soil, an infrastructure network, premises, and vineyards. Remy Pacifique's contribution was in the form of equipment with a value of HK$ 1.3 million and paid for by the joint venture with shares amounting to 38% of the total equity, the remaining 62% of equity being held by Tianjin Vineyard. The agreement stated that the joint venture, called The Sino-French Winery, would last 11 years with the possibility of rolling it over for another 11 years. In the case of a rollover, Remy Pacifique's equity share would rise to 44%.

The purpose of the winery was the production of white wine, destined to be sold primarily in Hong Kong, Australia, Singapore, and Malaysia. Only 10% of output was planned for the Chinese market. At the outset, bottles would be imported from Australia with the provision that when the required expertise was acquired, they would eventually be produced by the joint venture. The wine was called 'Dynasty' and production started in 1982 when 100 000 bottles were sold. By 1992, production had reached 10 million bottles.

In this investment, Remy Pacifique concentrated on minimizing its political risk. It limited its stake to the imported equipment and signed a cooperative agreement with Tianjin Vineyard for an initial period of 11 years. It also took advantage of the new Foreign Investment Code established in June 1979 by the Chinese authorities. During the negotiations, Remy Pacifique was aided by the China International Trust and Investment Corporation (CITIC). Finally, in order to guarantee the remittance of profits made by the subsidiary, a formal agreement was signed with the Chinese Foreign Investment Commission.

The success of the Sino French Winery deal has led Remy Pacific to expand its presence in China. In 1991 it set up another joint venture with two Chinese partners, Shanghai Malu Xian and Shanghai Food Import-Export, to produce sparkling wine. Operations started in 1993

Remy Cointreau in China (continued)

with the sale of 150 000 bottles of 'Imperial Court' on the local market.

An important side effect of Remy's direct investment in China comes from its sales of cognac imported from France. Being a local producer makes it easier to import the cognac, to the extent that China is now Remy Cointreau's number one cognac market, ahead of France and Japan.

ABB in Poland

ABB is a major manufacturer for power generation, transmission and distribution for industry and transport. As one of the largest foreign investors in Poland it employs 7000 people in 12 companies. In 1993 income amounted to $230 million and was forecast to rise to $1 billion by the year 2000.

To manage exposure to political risk, ABB has issued a number of guidelines, insisting on the following measures:

- get close to the unions;
- minority employee ownership is desirable;
- give priority to companies you know;
- be honest, even on uncomfortable facts such as overstaffing;
- do not over-promise on such things as expected investment and exports;
- be prepared for high inflation and unrealistic exchange rates;
- insist on high quality;
- multiply costs for technology transfer and training by 3;
- start training before signing the contract to show good faith and to get a flying start;
- be highly selective and look for synergies;
- adopt a 'survival strategy' including such things as a crash plan for exports, emergency raw material supply, alternative transport and telecommunications networks, etc.

Finally, ABB requires its Polish companies to be integrated as quickly as possible into the overall ABB culture.

External hedging techniques

The first and most effective type of external hedging technique involves reducing the probability of a dispute occurring. This can be done by signing a special agreement with the host country government or the appropriate authority such as thè Foreign Investment Committee. When the country is a member of ICSID and a signatory of the Convention of Settlement of Investment Disputes, the agreement can make explicit reference to the Convention and detail how it will be interpreted. If the country is not a member and signatory, the special agreement can be used as a substitute and ICSID can be designated as the arbitration body.

The second type of technique is a straightforward insurance policy that protects the foreign subsidiary against political risk. Insurers for this type of risk will belong to one of the following categories:

- multilateral institutions such as the Multilateral Investment Guarantee Agency (MIGA), a branch of the World Bank;
- national institutions such as Overseas Private Investment Company (OPIC) in the United States, ECGD in the UK, COFACE in France, Treuarbeit in Germany and MITI in Japan;
- private institutions such as Lloyd's of London, American Insurers Guarantee (AIG), UNISTRAAT in France, etc.

The multilateral investment guarantee agency
MIGA was established in 1988 by 42 World Bank members. It currently includes 118 members and 26 others are scheduled for membership in the near future. Its objective is to complement national programmes such as ECGD and COFACE, but not to compete with them. MIGA offers the following types of coverage:

Currency transfers
MIGA policies protect against losses arising from the investor's inability to convert local currency returns from the guaranteed investment into foreign exchange and to transfer it abroad.

Expropriation
MIGA policies protect against losses due to actions depriving an investor of ownership or control of a local subsidiary. The actions include direct nationalization as well as creeping expropriation.

War and civil disturbance

MIGA offers protection against losses from damage to tangible assets caused by politically motivated acts of war or civil disturbance in the host country. Besides that, MIGA can insure any new investment originating in a member country and destined for a member developing country. A wide range of investment vehicles such as equity, shareholder loans, management agreements, etc., are likely to be covered. However, the maximum amount of coverage is set at $50 million and the standard term is 15 years. MIGA cannot unilaterally cancel the contract, whereas the investor has the right to cancel after three years.

Table 7.4 indicates the basic premium rates for MIGA contracts according to the industry class (manufacturing, natural resources, oil and

Table 7.4 Premium rates of MIGA

BASE RATES
All rates are annual rates per US$100 of coverage.

I **Manufacturing and services**

Type of guarantee	Current	Standby
a. Currency transfer	0.50%	0.25%
b. Expropriation	0.60%	0.30%
c. War and civil disturbance	0.55%	0.25%

II **Natural resources***

Type of guarantee	Current	Standby
a. Currency transfer	0.50%	0.25%
b. Expropriation	0.90%	0.45%
c. War and civil disturbance	0.55%	0.25%

III **Oil and gas**

Type of guarantee	Current	Standby
a. Currency transfer	0.50%	0.25%
b. Expropriation	1.25%	0.50%
c. War and civil disturbance	0.70%	0.30%

*Includes agribusiness projects involving land ownership or concessions, or other types of projects where large landholdings are involved.

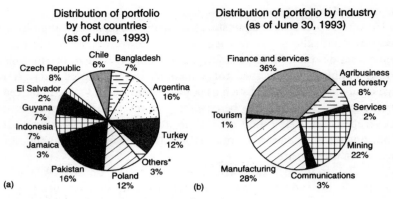

Distribution of portfolio
by host countries
(as of June, 1993)

Chile Bangladesh
6%   7%
Czech Republic
8%
El Salvador   Argentina
2%   16%
Guyana
7%
Indonesia
7%   Turkey
Jamaica   12%
3%
Pakistan   Poland   Others*
16%   12%   3%

(a)

Distribution of portfolio by industry
(as of June 30, 1993)

Finance and services
36%
                      Agribusiness
                      and forestry
                       8%
Tourism   Services
1%   2%
                       Mining
                       22%
Manufacturing   Communications
28%   3%

(b)

*China, Uganda, Russia, Tanzania, Madagascar, Ghana

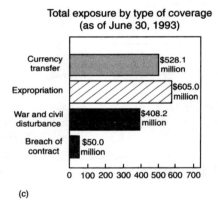

Total exposure by type of coverage
(as of June 30, 1993)

Currency transfer	$528.1 million
Expropriation	$605.0 million
War and civil disturbance	$408.2 million
Breach of contract	$50.0 million

0   100 200 300 400 500 600 700

(c)

Figure 7.2 Distribution of MIGA portfolio of insurance policies.

gas) and the type of guarantee (currency transfer, expropriation, war and
civil disturbance). For each risk category, MIGA can insure equity
investment for up to 90% of the original contribution, plus an additional
180% on earnings. Contracts can be written in Japanese yen, French francs,
US dollars, German marks, or British pounds. The risk assessment itself is
appraised by project and not by country.

Fiscal 1993 was a highly successful year for MIGA with $374 million in
coverage and $5.8 million earned from premiums and commitment fees.

Figure 7.2a shows how MIGA's portfolio was distributed according to host country. Argentina and Pakistan each represent 16%, Poland represents 12%, the Czech republic 8%, Indonesia, Guyana and Bangladesh 7% each and Chile 6%. Figure 7.2b shows the breakdown by industry with finance and services leading at 36%, followed by manufacturing at 28% and mining at 22%. Figure 7.2c sums up total exposure by type of coverage: expropriation $605 million, currency transfer $528 million, war and civil disturbance $408 million and breach of contract $50 million.

An illustration of a government insurance scheme: COFACE insurance against political risk

COFACE manages the French public insurance scheme. In 1993, 49 new foreign investment projects were reviewed and accepted for a total of 7 billion francs. Some 67% of this total pertained to investments in Europe or Asia. Since the beginning of 1994, COFACE is no longer a state-owned company (its two main shareholders, UAP and SCOR, are privately owned) but the agreement between COFACE and the French Ministry of Finance is still in effect.

The main requirements for access to COFACE coverage are:

1.   the foreign investment must be new and at least five years long;
2.   the host country must be either a state belonging to the French franc monetary zone (basically, French-speaking African countries) or a state having signed a bilateral treaty with France protecting foreign investments. Other countries are subject to a pre-review by the French 'Commission des Garanties', a committee consisting of representatives of various ministries. Countries considered too risky are rejected.

The insurance policy itself covers three specific risks:

1.   the risk of nationalization, either direct or indirect, resulting in the loss of the subsidiary;
2.   the risk of non-payment of an indemnity;
3.   the risk of non-transfer of the indemnity.

To obtain the guarantee, COFACE requires the submission of a dossier that includes the following items:

1.   pertinent information on the investor (name, location, financial statements, foreign subsidiaries, etc.);
2.   reasons for investing (market potential, choice of local partners,

perspectives with regard to profits);

3. main features of the investment (type of investment: creation or acquisition, financing sources, local incentives, if any, attitude of local authorities);
4. impact on the French economy (directly, through an increase of exports or indirectly, through subcontracting);
5. scope of the guarantee applied for (initial investment, dividend remittances, retained earnings);
6. other government incentives received by the firm, if any.

The guarantee can include the amount invested as well as profits up to a level of 100% of the sums invested and 50% of repatriated profits. However, the maximum reimbursement covers only 90 to 95% of the amount guaranteed. The duration of the guarantee ranges from 5 to 15 years. The cost of the insurance is around 0.7% to 1.1% per year, depending on the riskiness of the country covered (there are three risk categories).

Table 7.5 shows a cost comparison between COFACE and MIGA, for equivalent coverage of an initial investment of $1 000 000 the first year, $200 000 the second year, $300 000 in year 3, nothing in year 4 and $300 000 in year 5.[1] The MIGA coverage would cost a total of $106 680: $18 700 in year 1, $20 440 in year 2, $22 175 in year 3, $22 175 in year 4, and $23 190 in year 5 – while the COFACE premium would only be $77 000.

Private insurance

Private insurers usually cover the following items:

- investments consisting of net asset value, loans from parent company, bank loans guaranteed by parent and dividends when not convertible into foreign currency;
- equipment and inventories.

Premiums, of course, depend on country ratings and project specifics. Both multi-country and 'first loss' policies are available.

Private insurance schemes have several advantages over government-sponsored ones:

- Greater flexibility in terms of the adequacy and scope of the risks covered – leased assets, for example, can be included in the coverage;
- the guarantee can cover 100% of the amount invested;
- existing projects can also be covered;
- in the event of nationalization, the market value of the assets expropriated can be reimbursed;
- confidentiality.

Table 7.5 Cost comparison between MIGA and COFACE

MIGA (maximum amount covered: 180% of the initial investment)					
Year	*1*	*2*	*3*	*4*	*5*
Amount invested (cumulative)	$1 000 000	$1 200 000	$1 500 000	$1 500 000	$1 800 000
Components of premium •Transfer[a]	$	$	$	$	$
current	100 000	400 000	500 000	500 000	600 000
standby	1 700 000	1 400 000	1 300 000	1 300 000	1 200 000
•Expropria-tion[b]					
current	900 000	1 080 000	1 350 000	1 350 000	1 620 000
standby	900 000	720 000	450 000	450 000	180 000
•Conflict (wars)[c]					
current	900 000	1 080 000	1 350 000	1 350 000	1 620 000
standby	900 000	720 000	450 000	450 000	180 000
Premium	$18 700	$20 440	$22 175	$22 175	$23 190
Rate of premium (%)	1.87	1.70	1.47	1.47	1.28

[a] The first year, only 10% will be insured and 90% on a stand-by basis (lower rate).
[b] The first year: 90% of the investment must be insured.
[c] As above, 90% must be insured on a current basis.

COFACE					
Year	*1*	*2*	*3*	*4*	*5*
Amount invested (cumulative)	$1 000 000	$1 200 000	$1 500 000	$1 500 000	$1 800 000
Premium rate (%)	1.1	1.1	1.1	1.1	1.1
Premium	$11 000	$13 200	$16 500	$16 500	$19 800

The drawbacks are:

● destruction caused by wars cannot be covered for more than 12 months;
● the duration of the coverage usually does not exceed three years;
● the amount of the premium can be increased if the country's risk increases.

Private insurance is not necessarily more costly than government-backed schemes. Usually, industrial firms looking for political risk guarantees approach specialized brokers like Marsh McLennan, Gras & Savoy, or CAURI. These intermediaries help their clients with writing the insurance contracts and negotiating with insurers. Sometimes the private insurers pass on part of their risk to reinsurers such as Skandia, Lloyd's or SCOR.

HEDGING BANK LOANS AGAINST POLITICAL RISK

Besides reducing the amount of lending to the riskier countries, banks have also developed various techniques for hedging their exposure to the political risk embedded in their loans to LDC's. They can transfer risk to government agencies through insurance policies, or reduce their exposure through swap transactions, debt buy-backs and fiscal allowances. When all else has failed, debt must be rescheduled or forgiven (see box overleaf).

Restraining loans to risky countries

The easiest way of hedging political risk is to reduce the rate of lending to risky countries and this, in general, is what the banks have done. Thus, as we can see in Table 7.6, bank credits to LDC countries have decreased from 46.1% of the inflows to developing countries in 1981 to only 13.6% in 1991. At the same time foreign direct investment doubled from 8.3% to 16.7% and the share of bonds was multiplied by almost 8.

Although the rate of lending has slowed considerably, the total amount of debt outstanding has continued to grow. In Table 7.7 we can see that total debt outstanding to the developing countries increased from $658.15 billion at the end of 1980 to a projected $1770.07 billion in 1993, an increase of about 8% per year.

Rescheduling country debt

Many countries find themselves obliged to renegotiate the terms of their external debt. Public debt and public guaranteed debt are rescheduled through the Paris Club. It is called the Paris Club because the first public debt rescheduling, that of Argentina in 1956, took place in Paris. This club includes the various lending countries, represented by their treasury departments, and the borrowers. Rescheduling negotiations usually take place in Paris.

Private non-guaranteed external debt is rescheduled through another format, the London Club. In this format, the lending banks attend a meeting with representatives of the borrower to negotiate a new schedule. As is often the case, the banks are too numerous – 400 or more – so they elect a 'steering committee', which conducts the negotiations on behalf of all the banks. This committee chooses one bank as 'chairman'. The chairman will usually be an American bank if the borrower comes from Latin-America; it will usually be a French bank if the borrower comes from Africa; and it will usually be German for East European borrowers. The Chairman is often the bank that loaned the largest amount of money. The London Club, for example, has recently reached agreements for restructuring debts from Poland, Bulgaria, and Russia. In the Russian case, 600 banks, with Deutsche Bank as chairman of the steering committee, agreed to postpone principal repayments on private Russian debt for five years, with amortization occurring over the succeeding 10 years. In Poland's case, the banks agreed to forgive $14 billion dollars worth of debt.

Table 7.6 Inflows to developing countries.

	1981 %	1991 %
Bank credits	46.1	13.6
Official loans	26.0	26.6
Foreign direct investments	8.3	16.7
Export credits	11.0	14.9
Bonds	1.2	9.4
Portfolio investments	0.1	5.7
Subsidies	7.3	13.1

Table 7.7 Total debt stocks of all developing countries, 1980–93

	1980	1986	1987	1988	1989	1990	1991	1992	1993
Total Debt Stock	658.15	1 217.62	1 381.18	1 373.22	1 411.35	1 518.45	1 605.93	1 662.17	1 770.07

(Source: World Bank (1993–94) *World Bank Debt Tables*, vol. I, p.170.)

Transferring the risk to government agencies

Just as for export financing and direct investments, banks can take advantage of state-sponsored insurance (Hermes in Germany, ECGD in the UK, COFACE in France, etc.). Under these schemes banks pay premiums pegged to the borrowing country's level of risk in return for coverage that includes political risk as well as solvency risk on buyer credits as discussed above. Typically, about 95% of the loan can be covered, leaving the bank's exposure at 5%.

Debt-equity swaps

Debt-equity swaps involve purchasing some of a country's outstanding foreign debt on the secondary market and trading it to the central bank for the domestic currency that will be used to make an investment in the country. The central bank usually takes a cut in the transaction. Debt-equity swaps allow banks to reduce their outstanding claims to risky borrowers. They are attractive to corporations wishing to invest in a debt crisis country because the outstanding foreign debt often sells at a sharp discount to face value. The discount depends on the country's perceived risk. Table 7.8 shows the secondary market prices of various country debt as of December 31, 1993, April 30, 1994, and May 31, 1994. For certain countries such as Argentina, Mexico, or Venezuela, there are various prices depending on the different types of loans. Countries such as Chile and Romania have reduced their debt to the point where it is no longer quoted.

Because of government restrictions and regulations, debt-equity swaps

Table 7.8 Secondary market for international loans to LDC countries

Countries	December 31, 1993		April 30, 1994		May 31, 1994	
	Bid	*Offer*	*Bid*	*Offer*	*Bid*	*Offer*
	(average price)		*(average price)*		*(average price)*	
VERY ACTIVE MARKET						
1. Latin America						
Argentina (PARs)	67.75	68.25	52.25	52.875	55.75	56.125
Argentina (FRBs W/I)	87.50	88.00	72.25	72.875	79.00	79.375
Argentina (DISC.)	85.25	85.75	70.25	70.875	76.625	77.00
Brazil (IDU)	82.75	83.25	72.375	72.75	74.00	74.375
Mexico (par bonds)	82.50	83.00	63.50	63.875	67.875	68.25
Mexico (discount bonds)	95.50	96.00	83.50	84.00	87.25	87.625
Venezuela (par bonds)	73.50	74.00	49.50	49.875	55.00	55.375
Venezuela (discount bonds)	71.25	71.25	48.125	48.50	55.00	55.375
2. Others						
Philippines (PARs)	82.00	83.00	63.625	64.00	66.75	67.50
Poland (DDRA)	49.50	50.00	32.00	32.00	37.375	37.875
Poland (trade)	57.50	58.50	-	-	-	-
SMALL MARKET						
1. Latin America						
Cuba	28.50	29.50	19.00	22.00	18.00	20.00
Ecuador (MYRA)	51.00	52.00	35.50	36.25	39.75	41.50
Panama	61.00	62.00	42.00	44.00	54.75	55.75
Peru (Citi)	68.50	69.50	38.50	40.50	50.50	52.00
2. Others						
Bulgaria (US$) (Dis.)	40.00	42.00	48.00	52.00	43.00	46.00
Morocco	80.75	81.25	67.75	68.00	75.125	75.50
Nigeria (loans)	59.25	59.75	42.375	42.875	43.375	45.75
Nigeria (bills of órder)	43.50	44.50	29.00	31.00	31.25	32.50
VEB (Russia)	49.50	50.00	28.125	29.00	30.25	31.00
VERY SMALL MARKET						
Cameroon	19.50	21.50	23.00	28.00	17.00	23.00
Ivory Coast ($)	22.00	24.00	18.00	21.00	20.50	22.00
Egypt	-	-	46.00	47.50	46.00	47.50
Gabon	-	-	44.00	50.00	44.00	50.00
Jordan (disc.)	52.00	55.00	68.00	70.00	70.00	74.00
Madagascar	45.00	48.00	45.00	48.00	45.00	48.00
Mozambique	10.00	20.00	-	-	10.00	-
Senegal	34.00	36.00	34.00	38.00	31.625	32.50
Togo	10.00	12.00	10.00	12.00	10.00	12.00
Zaire	-	-	12.00	-	12.00	-
Zambia	14.00	16.00	13.00	14.00	12.00	13.50

(Source: Arbitrages Financieres Internationaux, Paris.)

The secondary debt market

The secondary debt market makes restructuring easier for both borrowers and lenders, with a degree of liquidity, depending on the volume of the operations actually completed. In 1990, for instance, Venezuela converted $18 billion in bank loans into fixed and floating rate Brady bonds. Some of these bonds were collateralized by zero-coupon US Treasury bonds. The 'par' and 'discount' bonds included warrants in the form of oil certificates giving their owners the right to receive cash payments if the future price of oil should rise above a given strike price.

New financing instruments are contributing to the secondary market's development. Barings, for example, issued one million American style call warrants on Venezuela par bonds in September 1994. They have a nominal value of $100 million, one year maturity and two classes:

Class A: strike price = $50
Class B: strike price = $55

These warrants are listed on the Luxembourg Stock Exchange.

The prices of LDC debt on the secondary market are available at the main international banks. They are given as bid-ask-prices with a spread of around 1%. The 'Shearson LDC Index', which integrates the price of second-hand loans for 11 developing countries is often used as a benchmark for the secondary market.

can be complex. However, the mechanics of the transaction itself are straightforward.

1. A foreign corporation, usually a multinational that wants to invest in a less developed country with a debt problem, goes to that country's Ministry of Finance and presents its investment project and the proposed financing via the debt-equity swap.

2. The Finance Ministry coordinates the government review of the investment proposal. If it is approved, the Finance Ministry issues the official approval where the percentage of the debt's face value that will be paid to the corporation in local currency is clearly specified. If the Ministry decides to take a 10% commission, for example, the corporation will receive 90% of the debt's face value in local currency.

3. Once the project has been approved, the corporation purchases the required amount of the country's external bank debt at a discount on the secondary market.
4. When the debt has been purchased, the corporation presents the loan to the Finance Ministry. The Finance Ministry cancels the debt by paying the equivalent amount in local currency. The payment can be made in cash or in government debt instruments denominated in local currency. If the payment is made in debt instruments, they will have to be sold on the local secondary market in order to obtain the local currency.
5. The corporation then uses the local currency to purchase the capital stock of either a new or existing entity.
6. The purchased entity then uses the local currency it receives from the corporation to make the desired investment.

Figure 7.3 summarizes the transactions that take place after the project has been approved. The corporation purchases $1 million dollars of the country's external debt through its bank at a discount of 40% on the secondary market. It pays $600 000 and receives the debt paper, which it presents to the appropriate authority (Ministry of Finance or central bank, etc.). The authority takes a 10% commission and gives the corporation 18 million pesos, based on the current exchange rate of 20 pesos for $1. The corporation uses the 18 million pesos to purchase the local entity and receives the equivalent stock in return. Thus, the corporation has made its investment at a saving of $300 000, the country has received an inflow of foreign capital, and the bank has reduced its exposure by $1 million.

It is clear that debt-equity swaps are an attractive financing vehicle for corporations wishing to invest in certain financially vulnerable countries. In practice, however, completing a transaction can be difficult and tedious. Many investment projects are unacceptable to the host country, and access to a swap programme involves negotiating many layers of government red tape (see Appendix 7.2 for the pros and cons of a debt-equity swap for the host country). Nevertheless, as we can see in Figure 7.4, this type of transaction has been popular since 1987, accounting for a sizeable proportion of debt reduction between 1985 and 1992.

Variations of the debt-equity swap

Debt-equity conversion funds
In a debt-equity conversion fund, a bank holding LDC debt sells it to a fund and receives equity in the fund equivalent to something over the market price for that debt. The fund in turn uses the debt to invest in the debtor

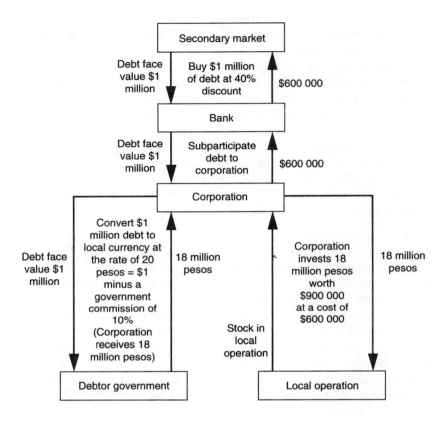

Figure 7.3 The mechanics of a debt–equity swap.

nation by means of a debt-equity swap. These funds can either be 'stockmarket funds', where the money is invested in the equity of existing companies, or 'new venture funds', where the pool of converted debt will be used to finance several individual projects. The fund manages the various investments and pays a return to its shareholders.

Debt-equity conversion funds can be very attractive for small banks with low international exposure and lacking project management experience and country specific knowledge, since these funds provide shared risk and professional management.

Debt-equity syndication
In this type of scheme, a lead bank identifies an equity investment to be funded through debt–equity conversions and apportions it to several

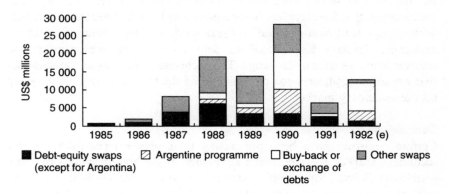

Figure 7.4 Evolution of debt-equity swaps programmes.
(Source: World Bank.)

investors holding debt to be converted. For this it receives a fee in return.

Debt for nature and debt for education swaps
The debt for nature swap is another variant of the debt for equity swap. In this case, a specific investor such as the World Wide Fund for Nature purchases outstanding debt at a discount and exchanges it for local currency that it uses to finance an environmental project, such as a national park or a game reserve. The debt for education swap uses the same technique to finance local investments in education.

Debt for debt swaps
In a debt for debt swap, a bank credit is transformed into a bond that can be traded more easily on the international bond market. The borrowing country has an incentive to accept the transformation since it is usually achieved at a discount to nominal value. For the lender the advantage lies in the tradability of the bonds compared to a defaulted bank loan.

Mexico was the initiator of these swaps in 1988, when Morgan transformed bank loans into 'exit bonds' guaranteed by zero coupon US treasury bonds that had been purchased by the Mexican government. Chile also used the debt for debt swap technique to reduce its outstanding foreign liabilities by about $10 million.

Debt for asset swaps

Debt for asset swaps are used by banks to restructure their loan portfolios. In this scenario, banks will swap one country's debt for another. Suppose, for example, that Barclays feels over-exposed to Brazilian debt and National Westminster feels over-exposed to Mexican debt. They decide to make an exchange. Barclays gives Brazilian debt to National Westminster and receives Mexican debt in exchange. The exchange ratio, that is, the amounts that are exchanged, depends on the ratio of the two countries' debt values on the secondary market.

Debt buy-backs

Certain countries have been purchasing their own external debt on the secondary market, thereby taking advantage of the high discounts on their own loans. Bolivia, for example, bought back approximately 40% of its own debt at a time when the discount exceeded 90%. Lenders, of course, look askance at this type of trick and often refuse to authorize it since it lets the country off the hook at a bargain price. It was accepted for Bolivia because the absolute amounts involved were small and the chances of reimbursement were slim at best.

Fiscal allowances

Many countries allow banks to write off loans to LDC countries through tax deductible allowances, thereby transferring part of the financial cost to the taxpayer. Most international banks have taken advantage of this policy when possible. European banks have been the most active in the field since their national regulators have been more favourable to tax deductible write-offs than have Japanese and American regulators. French banks, for example, have been particularly active. As we can see in Table 7.9, they wrote off more than 615 billion francs worth of debt between 1989 and 1992.

Table 7.9 Write-offs of French banks with respect to LDC loans.

Year	Amount (in billion francs)	Percentage (%)
1989	180.3	53
1990	154.8	54.7
1991	137.6	55.4
1992	143.4	53.5

APPENDIX 7.1 ORGANIZING POLITICAL RISK MANAGEMENT IN INDUSTRIAL FIRMS

Basically, there are two different ways of managing political risk in industrial firms, on a day-to-day basis for business as usual and on an emergency basis in the case of a specific issue such as a sudden expropriation or the kidnapping of an expatriate employee.

Day-to-day organization

Over time, firms face many circumstances which involve risk-taking: signing a large export contract, entering a joint venture abroad, acquiring a foreign company, monitoring accounts receivable, etc. Each time, the political risk must be assessed using the various techniques deemed appropriate, according to a regular process. The techniques adopted and the process employed depends on the particular risks that a company is likely to face on a regular basis. Thus, the person in charge of political risk management has to define:

- the nature of the risk (exporting, investing, lending, etc.);
- the implications in terms of information sources (which data, which format, at what cost?);
- the frequency of the analysis;
- confidentiality (who should be informed?).

The appropriate organization varies according to the size of the firm and its degree of internationalization. A general distinction can be made between the big multinationals and the medium and small-sized companies.

Multinationals

Most large multinationals will have one or several experts in charge of political risk analysis. Oil companies, which endured a host of nationalizations in the 1960s and 1970s, are currently well equipped to deal with political risk. Their system involves parent company people who are responsible for various geographical areas. These experts include political risk in their current analyses of market prospects. Much of their information comes from foreign subsidiaries and licensees.

Besides the oil company system of 'area experts', there are other sources of political risk expertise in big multinationals. There is often a Department of Economic Studies in charge of forecasting macroeconomic data and sectoral trends. One of its tasks can be political forecasting. In this case, the political risk expert operates as part of an in-house team.

A recent survey of 23 French multinational firms showed that nine of them gave responsibility for political risk assessment to line departments that include top management, financial management, and product divisions, whereas six give responsibility to staff departments such as a research (economics) department or an area specialist. Eight involved both line and staff departments acting jointly in managing political risk.

Sometimes part of the risk-management job is subcontracted to external consultants such as BERI and Frost & Sullivan. In this case the external consultants supply data and facts that the in-house people use in the decision-making process.

Medium and small-sized firms

Because of the cost, it is usually not possible for medium and small-sized firms to employ a full-time political analyst. Therefore, day-to-day risk is managed by using the internal and external hedging techniques discussed in the chapter. When the need for a political risk assessment does arise, these firms typically rely on outside consultants to supply the expertise that serves as an input in the decision-making process. In this case, there is no special organization to deal specifically with political risk, and the outside consultant interacts with the line departments.

Emergency situations

There are some events, such as kidnapping, expropriation, blackmail, civil war, etc., that are practically impossible to forecast. When they do occur, they bring a company under particular stress. In these circumstances, the firm typically creates an 'emergency cell' consisting of in-house people and outsiders. This cell then deals with the crisis. The process involves several steps:

1. identifying the people to be included in the cell. The outsiders to be included depend on the type of crisis. In the case of a kidnapping, for example, the outsiders are likely to include military men and diplomats. In the case of an environmental accident, they will include lawyers;
2. planning the different steps to follow in order to make an appropriate answer to the threat;
3. defining the communication policy toward newspapers, employees, shareholders, etc.
4. identifying the most probable scenarios and, if necessary, simulating negotiations and possible outcomes;
5. managing the crisis and settling it.

APPENDIX 7.2 MOST OFTEN CITED ADVANTAGES AND DISADVANTAGES FOR THE HOST COUNTRY OF DEBT-EQUITY SWAPS

Advantages

1. A programme for debt-equity swaps can encourage corporate investors to increase their stake in a country by buying local currency at a good rate.
2. They can serve as a vehicle to repatriate capital which was taken abroad (capital flight).
3. They substitute debt in local currency for debt in foreign currency.
4. They improve the investment climate in the host country.

Disadvantages

1. In some cases the investment financed through debt-equity swaps might have been made anyway. Such a replacement effect harms the local economy because the local government has made a subsidy without getting any additional value.
2. The use of a debt-equity programme may result in a misallocation of resources. By giving the discount to certain foreigners, the government is subsidizing those investors at the expense of others whose activities may be more economically beneficial.
3. Debt-equity swaps can lead to higher inflation if the central bank does not neutralize the purchase of the foreign claim by a reduction in its credit to other sectors of the economy.
4. Too many debt-equity swaps in a single economy can lead to an excess of foreign influence.
5. A type of 'black market' arbitrage can be achieved by purchasing foreign exchange at the official (overvalued) rate, using it to acquire foreign-exchange denominated debt, and then swapping the debt at the subsidized debt-equity swap rate.

NOTE

[1]   Rossignol, Y. (1994) *COFACE-MIGA-Assurances Privés: Les Garanties d'Investissement contre les Risques Politiques*, Etude n° 16, Club Finance International, HEC School of Management, Jouy-en-Josas.

8 MANAGING EXPOSURE TO CURRENCY RISK

In this chapter we will deal with the main issues involved in managing exposure to currency risk. We start with a discussion of how exposure to currency risk can be defined and measured. We then discuss how firms can organize themselves to manage their exposure to currency risk and take advantage of the opportunities that expertise in this field creates. Finally, we review the major hedging instruments and techniques, including forwards, futures and options.

EVALUATING FOREIGN CURRENCY EXPOSURE

A firm is said to have an open foreign exchange position when the variation of the exchange rate of one or more currencies will affect the level of its income or expenditure in domestic currency. An open foreign exchange position implies foreign exchange risk. Thus, an export billed in foreign currency exposes the firm to a loss of income in domestic currency if the value of the foreign currency depreciates and to a gain if it appreciates. When a firm owns an uncovered claim in foreign currency it is said to be 'long'. An import billed in foreign currency exposes the firm to increased expenditure in domestic currency if the foreign currency appreciates, and to a decrease if it depreciates. When a firm has an uncovered liability in foreign currency, it is said to be 'short'.

There are several ways of measuring the foreign currency exposure of a firm. One measure limits the analysis to commercial transactions and financial flows. Other measures look at the overall balance sheet, including foreign investments and liabilities. Here, we will consider the foreign exchange exposure resulting from commercial transactions and financial flows.

The departure point for evaluating the financial consequences of exchange rate variations on the firm's domestic currency cash flows is the information in the company's accounts. Accounts receivable and short-term financial claims grouped by currency indicate the firm's long position. Accounts payable and short-term financial liabilities grouped by currency indicate the firm's short position. The accounting information must be complemented by expected cash flows resulting from decisions that have already been made or that are likely to be made. The effects of outstanding orders by foreign clients and suppliers will affect the firm's foreign exchange position. Bids on potential export projects will also affect it if they are accepted. Even domestic orders and bids can affect the firm's foreign exchange position, insofar as the production process requires foreign inputs. These effects should be taken into consideration.

Cash flows resulting from non-commercial transactions must also be considered. Expected dividends from foreign subsidiaries will increase the firm's long position. Interest and principal payments on the firm's long-term foreign currency debt will increase the short position. In fact, judicious assessment of the firm's foreign exchange position requires mastery of all the firm's decision-making circuits. The treasurer has to be aware of purchasing policy, sales policy, investment policy, and financing policy in order to project future cash flows. From this perspective, the foreign exchange position is more than just an accounting exercise. It reflects the firm's economic position in foreign exchange.

INTERNAL METHODS AND PROCEDURES FOR MANAGING FOREIGN CURRENCY EXPOSURE

Payment Terms in International Trade

Controlling foreign exchange exposure begins when the terms of the agreement specifying the price of the merchandise and how and when it will be paid for are negotiated. In international transactions prices can be set in any number of currencies. Determining the precise method that will be used to make the payment is also more complicated because traditional methods like cheques and drafts pose legal and technical problems in processing, clearing, and enforcement. As a result, the financing terms of an international transaction are often restricted.

Currency choice in invoicing

One of the most important elements in an international commercial transaction is the currency used for invoicing. In many types of transactions no choice exists, such as when convention has it that all deals are done in a certain currency. Crude oil trading, for example, is done exclusively in US dollars. It can also be the case when a firm refuses trade in any currency other than its own home currency. Many small or medium-sized firms lacking international experience have such a policy. The reasons are often related to fear of the unknown in general, or of foreign exchange risk in particular. Often, however, they fear neither but cannot afford to work out new price lists and manage the resulting exchange risk. However, for firms willing and able to make the effort, currency flexibility in invoicing can be commercially advantageous and financially profitable.

Choosing an invoicing currency involves comparing the amount of the invoice billed directly in domestic currency with the domestic currency equivalent of the amount of the invoice if billed in foreign currency. Making the comparison is not a straightforward operation. Since payment will be made at some time in the future, the spot rate cannot be used in making the comparison because the spot rate can, and probably will, change in the mean time. The forward rate is the obvious solution. In practice, however, the forward rate is not always directly applicable. Take the case where deliveries and invoices will occur several times over the year. Applying the appropriate forward rate to each separate invoice implies a different price for each delivery. In this case, an average forward price would probably be better.

The problem is the same for both buyer and seller. If the buyer agrees to be billed in foreign currency, the amount he owes will be exposed to foreign exchange risk. If the seller agrees to bill in foreign currency, the amount he receives will be exposed to foreign exchange risk. One or the other is going to have to cover his foreign exchange risk and they will both have recourse to the same financial intermediaries offering the same products. If markets were completely efficient, it seems, then, that the choice of the invoicing currency would be completely neutral. In fact, it is not neutral at all. In the first place, not all companies have access to the same financial products at the same prices. Smaller companies are limited in the products they can use and often pay higher prices for the ones that are available to them. Furthermore, rules and regulations imposed by the monetary and tax authorities can create barriers and supplementary costs. Finally, not all companies are equally endowed with the knowledge and expertise to deal with problems associated with foreign exchange transactions. Thus, companies with the required know-how can offer the financial service of billing in their clients' domestic currency along with the merchandise they are selling, and make a profit on both ends.

There can also be a speculative element involved in pricing and billing in foreign currency. A professional who follows the foreign exchange market closely is going to form opinions on how different currencies will do. He may feel that some currencies are strong and likely to appreciate. Others, he may feel, are weak and likely to depreciate. If he has any confidence in his opinions, he will try to take advantage of them by selling in strong currencies and purchasing in weak ones. A word of caution is in order. Most corporate treasurers agree that multi-currency invoicing should exclude exotic currencies with narrow markets, where financial services are costly or non-existent.

Methods of making payments

For international payments, the traditional means of settling debts in a domestic economy, such as cash, credit cards and traveller's cheques, are only relevant for tourism. Bank transfers are probably the fastest and most efficient means of settling international debts. In a bank transfer, the importer instructs his bank to debit his account and credit the exporter's account at the exporter's bank. The transfer is made by telex or SWIFT, which guarantees its speedy execution. The disadvantage of a bank transfer is that it is generated at the initiative of the importer and the exporter has no guarantee in the case of non-payment. Consequently, except for cash payments in advance, bank transfers are appropriate only for the most trustworthy relationships.

Cheques are another instrument generated at the initiative of the importer. Unlike the bank transfer, however, they are not rapid. First of all, they have to be sent, which takes time, and they can get lost in the mail. Furthermore, banks credit foreign cheques only after a long delay, due to difficulties in processing and clearing them.

A promissory note is a written promise by the importer to pay a given sum on a given date in the future. They play a small role in international trade but are often used as a support to financing operations, as in bridging loans, for example.

A **draft** or **bill of exchange** is the most common means of payment in international trade. A draft is an unconditional order in writing, initiated and signed by the exporter, ordering the importer to pay on demand or at a given future date a given sum of money. A draft is usually addressed to the importer or the importer's agent. It can be payable to a particular beneficiary or to bearer. Bearer drafts are negotiable. When it is payable on demand it is called a **sight draft**. When it is payable at a future date it is called a **time draft**. One of the most reliable means of payment is a draft accepted by a bank, known as a **banker's acceptance**.

Documentary methods of payment

Documentary draft

Documentary payment is the most common method for settling international commercial transactions. The simplest method of documentary payment, called a documentary draft, is a draft accompanied by certain documents. In this scenario, the exporter, after having shipped the merchandise, forwards the draft along with the required documents to his bank. The required documents include a commercial invoice and sometimes a consular invoice as well, an insurance certificate, a certificate of origin, and a **bill of lading** in negotiable form. The bill of lading is a contract between the shipper (exporter) and a transportation company in which the latter agrees to transport the goods under specified conditions which limit its liability. It is the shipper's receipt for the goods as well as proof that the goods have been or will be shipped. An **order bill of lading** consigns the goods to the order of a named party (usually the exporter) and is negotiable. Ownership can be transferred by endorsing the bill on the reverse side. Therefore, it can serve as collateral for loans. When goods are sent by air, the equivalent of the bill of lading is called an **air waybill**.

The negotiable bill of lading is the most important document for a documentary draft because it gives its holder title to the merchandise in question. Having received the required documents, the bank notifies the importer, who then accepts the draft and receives the bill of lading in return. In this way, the exporter is sure that the importer will not get title to the goods until he has accepted the draft.

Documentary drafts are not foolproof, because drafts are not always accepted and paid. If the draft is refused by the importer, the exporter still has the problem of either repatriating the goods or selling them somewhere else, probably at a loss. If the draft is not paid, the exporter is left with a bad debt. As we explained in Chapter 7, a letter of credit can be used to overcome this type of problem.

Other payment terms

1. *Cash in advance* Cash in advance is the safest way for the exporter to sell, because he receives payment for the goods before they are shipped. For made-to-order goods, cash in advance is the rule. For other types of merchandise, it is less widespread than before, except in particularly unstable countries or for importers with doubtful credit. Cash against

documents, however, is still a popular way to do business.

2. *Open account*   Selling goods on open account enables the importer to avoid the cost of opening a letter of credit and provides him with financing. It is the way much business is done domestically. It involves shipping the goods to the importer, invoicing him and trusting him to pay within the prescribed limits. Payment may be made by draft, by cheque, or by bank transfer. Selling on open account should only be considered for the most trustworthy clients. As we explained in Chapter 7, selling on open account can be combined with factoring or forfaiting as a means of managing accounts receivable and providing short-term financing.

3. *Consignment*   Selling on consignment involves shipping goods to the importer but maintaining title to them until they have been sold to a third party. In this kind of arrangement payment is not made by the importer until after he has sold them. If they remain unsold, the exporter is left holding the proverbial bag. He either has to take them back or find another purchaser.

INTERNATIONAL CASH MANAGEMENT

The basic requirements for effective international cash management

To be able to manage exchange rate risk, the treasurer has to know what these risks are for the company. This involves setting up a computerized system fulfilling at least five requirements.

1. A currency by currency forecast of income and expenditure for each day is set up. The necessary information can be found in the budget, orders outstanding, accounts receivable, and accounts payable.

2. Once the day-by-day forecast of income and expenditure for each currency has been established, the second requirement is to measure the exchange exposure in each currency generated by the company's operations.

3. All foreign exchange transactions, both spot and forward, then have to be accounted for. This is probably the most difficult task because, as we shall see, hedging instruments have become increasingly complex. They include forwards, futures, swaps, options, borrowing and lending. Positions can be closed out and rolled over. Only by recording and measuring their impact can the company's true foreign exchange position be accounted for.

4. All the foregoing information must then be translated into a value date forecast of all the company's bank accounts in foreign exchange. This must be done day by day, account by account, currency by currency. Any sizeable international company will have numerous foreign currency accounts with a number of banks, so the task is complicated. Many types of transaction, such as spot trades, forward trades, and options premiums, pose no problem since the transaction date and both sides of the operation in domestic and foreign currency are known in advance. Commercial transactions are another story, however. Exact dates are often not known in advance. Sometimes, even the amounts are uncertain, depending on whether or not the client takes advantage of a discount. The forecast must be updated regularly to account for transactions that have actually taken place.

The reason for laying out all the foreign currency cash flows on a day-by-day, value date basis is the same as for domestic cash management – that is, to minimize financial charges and maximize financial income by reducing non-interest-paying balances to zero on a value date basis. This involves transferring funds from surplus accounts to deficit accounts and lending anything that is left over. Borrowing and lending decisions should take into consideration the company's policy on its foreign exchange position.

5. The final requirement corresponds to the needs of internal control. Where foreign exchange is concerned these needs are quite elaborate. The treasurer must verify that the bank's conditions regarding value dates, commissions, interest rates, day count factors, etc., have been assiduously respected. The same goes for the sophisticated hedging instruments, which require a high-quality 'back office'. Furthermore, discrepancies between forecast and realized figures must be available for commercial as well as for financial transactions.

In-house hedging

Hedging exchange risk operation by operation can prove extremely costly because of the large number of transactions and the commissions, fees, and spreads they imply. Many operations could be avoided if a company's successive claims and debts in a given currency are brought together. Suppose that a Finnish company has made the following forecast:

November 15: collect £60 000
December 3: pay out £40 000
December 20: pay out £50 000
December 30: collect £40 000

Taken separately, each flow would generate a forward transaction with all the costs and fees they entail. Taken together, there is only a difference of £10 000 that would have to be covered. Ignoring interest, this could be achieved by lending £40 000 from November 15 to December 3, and £20 000 from November 15 to December 20. On December 3, the proceeds from the first loan go to make the payout. On December 20 the proceeds from the second loan go towards the £50 000 payout, and £30 000 is borrowed until December 30 to make up the difference. On December 30, the proceeds from the collection go to pay off the loan, and £10 000 is left over.

Globalized accounts

This technique is appropriate for a company with small amounts of income and/or expenditure on a frequent and regular basis in a given currency. Administratively and transactionally, it would be too costly to cover each transaction. To avoid the cost, the company sets up a central or global account through which all transactions in the foreign currency will be handled. Periodically, every month, for example, the company converts the balance. If it is positive, the company purchases domestic currency. If it is negative, the company purchases foreign currency to make up the difference. Over the course of the month the company monitors the account. As it becomes positive, the company invests the balance and earns interest. If it is negative, interest is paid.

The exchange risk can be managed on the basis of the periodic balances. Suppose, for example, that the treasurer forecasts income of £10 000 000 over the period in question and no expenditure. His foreign exchange exposure is thus £10 000 000, since it is at the end of the period that he will convert into domestic currency. As we will see later in the chapter, he can cover his position by making a forward sale of foreign exchange or by purchasing an option.

Netting

Many multinational corporations have their production organized on a worldwide basis, where raw materials, spare parts, sub-assemblies and finished products are exchanged among the subsidiaries of the group. These physical flows of goods and services generate financial flows and cross-border fund transfers. Foreign exchange transactions are costly in terms of the bid–ask spread. There are also bank charges for transferring funds, and opportunity costs of lost interest while the funds are being transferred (value dates applied by the banks).

The netting procedure seeks to reduce the cost of foreign exchange management within groups, where many currencies and many transactions are involved. A multinational, for example, may have subsidiaries in Paris, London, Dusseldorf and Madrid, each one dealing regularly with each other in pounds, francs, marks and pesetas. The relationships are too complex to be handled by a system of globalized accounts. A more sophisticated system is necessary. Netting is a system of intra-group compensation. It involves setting up a control point called the **netting centre** that handles all the financial transactions. Very often, a subsidiary created especially for this purpose is set up in a location where there is a minimum of foreign exchange controls.

In order to set up a netting system, the company has to establish the periodic basis on which it will operate – the day, the week or the month. It then has to identify the characteristic payment flows between the group's subsidiaries for the period in question. This involves setting up a clearing matrix. An example will illustrate the major issues.

PHI Inc. is composed of four subsidiaries:

Achtung – the German subsidiary;
Tally Ho – the UK subsidiary;
MOI – the French subsidiary;
Cuidado – the Spanish subsidiary.

PHI has decided that the US dollar will serve as its base currency. The following intra-group payment flows have been established:

- Achtung owes DM2 000 000 to Tally Ho and FF6 000 000 to MOI;
- Tally Ho owes £500 000 to MOI and £750 000 to Cuidado;
- MOI owes Pta80 000 000 to Cuidado;
- Cuidado owes Pta150 000 000 to Achtung.

The reference exchange rates are as follows:

£1 = $1.50
FF1 = $0.20
Pta100 = $0.75
DM1 = $0.65.

Converting the debts between the different subsidiaries at the reference exchange rates gives the following matrix where columns represent claims and lines represent liabilities.

Table 8.1 Intra-group claims and liabilities for PHI Inc. (millions of US dollars)

Liability	Achtung	Tally Ho	MOI	Cuidado	Total
Achtung		$1.300	$1.200		$2.500
Tally Ho			$0.750	$1.125	$1.875
MOI				$0.600	$0.600
Cuidado	$1.125				$1.125
Total	$1.125	$1.300	$1.950	$1.725	$6.100

Thus, for example, MOI has a $1 200 000 claim on Achtung and a $750 000 claim on Tally Ho. Its total claims are $1 950 000. On the other hand MOI has a liability of $600 000 to Cuidado. Before compensation, bilateral payments between group members amount to $6 100 000.

Using the information from Table 8.1, it is possible to determine the net position of each subsidiary, as presented in Table 8.2.

Instead of making all the bilateral payments implied in Table 8.1, each subsidiary will be credited or debited for its net position in its domestic currency. Hence, Achtung is debited for DM2 115 000 and Tally Ho for £383 000. On the other hand, MOI is credited for FF6 750 000 and Cuidado

Table 8.2 Net positions of subsidiaries of PHI Inc. in local currency

	Claims	Liabilities	Net position in millions of dollars	Compensation in local currency (millions)
Achtung	$1.125	$2.500	-$1.375	-DM2.115
Tally Ho	$1.300	$1.875	-$0.575	-£0.383
MOI	$1.950	$0.600	+$1.350	+FF6.750
Cuidado	$1.725	$1.125	+$0.600	+Pta80.000
Total	$6.100	$6.100	0	

for Pta80 000 000. These transfers are effected on a given date, such as the last business day of the month. By netting, total fund transfers fall from $6 100 000 before compensation to $3 900 000 after compensation.

There are many advantages to the netting procedure. First of all, commissions on foreign exchange transactions and fund transfers are drastically reduced. Secondly, by reducing the size and number of transfers, thereby reducing the number of days lost in transferring funds and the amounts, the opportunity cost of float is reduced. Furthermore, the individual subsidiaries have reduced foreign exchange risk, since payments are made in their domestic currency.

An effective netting system requires a solid administrative organization, good bankers and advantageous banking terms concerning values dates, spreads, commissions and fees. When these are present, profits can be substantial. It should not be forgotten, however, that some countries impose restrictions on netting operations. Thus, it is also necessary to have a thorough knowledge of the exchange controls in the countries where operations take place.

Reinvoicing centres

Netting is a solution to intra-group currency flows. It does not solve the problem of currency flows between subsidiaries and outside institutions. Each subsidiary has its own set of suppliers and clients that generate flows of funds in different currencies. There are two solutions to this problem. One solution is to let each individual subsidiary manage its own foreign currency situation. The other solution is to set up a centralized operation that handles all foreign exchange transactions for the whole group; this is called a reinvoicing centre.

The reinvoicing centre does not get involved with the flow of goods to and from the subsidiaries. Commercial practices and customs formalities remain unchanged. The role of the reinvoicing centre is strictly financial. By concentrating all currency transactions in one place, it should be possible to negotiate better bank terms and reduce opportunity costs, in the same way as a netting centre. It also eliminates the problem of export financing for the individual subsidiaries. In this way it is more than a simple centralized foreign exchange trader. It is a full fledged financial service centre responsible for financing current operations and managing the collection of accounts receivable.

This brings up the question of assigning costs throughout the group for the financial services of the reinvoicing centre. The most typical solution is to have the reinvoicing centre operate as an autonomous profit centre in a low-tax country, with commissions and fees for each type of service rendered. The group's subsidiaries then pay according to the transactions performed on their behalf by the reinvoicing centre.

An example will illustrate the idea. Consider a British multinational with subsidiaries in the United States and France. The British company imports goods billed in German marks. It also exports goods to its French subsidiary billed in French francs. The American subsidiary exports and bills in Japanese yen. Figure 8.1 summarizes these transactions.

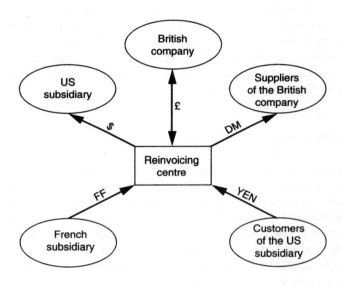

Figure 8.1 Reinvoicing operations.

Reinvoicing operations can be done on a continuous basis, or a weekly, bi-monthly or monthly basis. Invoices in the different currencies are transmitted to the centre and the subsidiaries are credited and debited in their own domestic currency. The exchange rate used is based on the forward rate plus a commission corresponding to the payment date of each invoice. Thus, the British company is debited for the sterling value of its liability in German marks. It is credited for the sterling equivalent of its claim in French francs. Interest will be charged and credited according to when the funds are actually transferred. It has no exchange risk. The exchange risk has been taken on by the reinvoicing centre, which has the responsibility of collecting from the French subsidiary and paying the exporter.

Leads and lags

Leading means accelerating payments; lagging means delaying payments. Before the development of financial products, leading and lagging was a means of speculating on currency movements. Payments were accelerated on debts in currencies that were expected to appreciate and they were delayed on payments in currencies that were expected to depreciate. Needless to say, a wrong guess could be costly. Nowadays, leading and lagging for currency speculation is obsolete because of the wide range of financial products that can do the job more efficiently. Leading and lagging does exist to a certain extent within groups, however, as a means of shifting liquidity between subsidiaries to avoid bid–ask spreads and take advantage of interest rate differentials. The following example will illustrate the point.

Subsidiary Australia Inc. has a six month financing need of £10 million and owes UK Subsidiary Ltd £10 million payable now.

UK Subsidiary Ltd has a cash surplus of £10 million that will last for six months.

The bid rate on six-month sterling is 6% and the credit rating of Subsidiary Australia Inc. enables it to borrow six-month sterling at 6.5%. If Subsidiary Australia borrows to pay off UK Subsidiary Ltd, it will pay:

$$£10\,000\,000 \times 0.065 \times \frac{6}{12} = £325\,000$$

If UK Subsidiary Ltd lends £10 million in the Euromarket it will earn:

$$£10\,000\,000 \times 0.06 \times \frac{6}{12} = £300\,000$$

There is a loss on the interest rate spread of £25 000 that the group could save if UK Ltd allowed Australia Inc. to lag its payment by six months.

Short-term lending in foreign currency

Short-term lending in foreign currency poses the same problems as short-term lending in domestic currency. Selection criteria are the same: the quality of the borrower, the liquidity of the asset, the expected evolution of the interest rate, and tax consequences. To these criteria, certain restrictions must be added. The amounts involved must be large enough to gain access to certain products and to obtain the best terms. Direct management requires constant monitoring and an efficient back office that only the largest firms can afford. In the absence of these requirements, there is always the possibility of sticking with simple term deposits or farming the management out. Farming out the short-term lending function involves investing in professionally managed money market funds.

Bank deposits and foreign currency loans are the simplest kinds of short-term investment. They can be useful for the in-house hedging operations of commercial transactions. They are pretty tame insofar as risk goes. They also have pretty low returns. On the other hand, a treasurer might be tempted to improve the rate of return on his investment by choosing a weak currency with a high interest rate. Consider the German treasurer who has a choice between a three-month deposit in marks yielding 5% and a three-month deposit in Italian lira yielding 10%. If the exchange rate does not change too much over the three-month life of the loan, he can make a considerable gain. However, a 5% devaluation of the lira will make him lose 2.625% on his investment.

The market for short-term negotiable instruments has grown considerably over the last decade. Euro-CD's and **Euro-CP**s can offer attractive opportunities for the knowledgeable treasurer. CDs are negotiable certificates of deposit. CPs, or commercial paper, are negotiable, short-term notes or drafts of a governmental agency, bank or corporation. Using CDs and commercial paper exposes the company to credit risk. Even if the market for these instruments is dominated by the most prestigious names, their fortunes can and have changed overnight. One of the ways to manage this credit risk is to rely on one of the rating agencies. Standard and Poor's and Moody's worldwide, Duff and Phelps in the US, Australian Ratings in Australia, and IBCA Banking Analysis in the UK all supply regular ratings on the paper of the major issuers. Table 8.3 shows some of the major rating agencies' notation for commercial paper, which differs from the notation for longer-term debt.

Corporate treasurers should not hesitate to imitate their banking brothers by fixing lending limits for each borrower in order to control default risk. Finally the company treasurer must have a solid internal organization that

Table 8.3 Notation for rating short-term debt

Euro Ratings	Fitch Investors Service	Moody's Investors Service	Standard & Poor's	Duff & Phelps	Japan Credit Rating Agency
E-1+	F-1+	P-1	A-1+	Duff-1+	A1
E-1	F-1		A-1	Duff-1	
				Duff-1-	
E-2+	F-2+	P-2	A-2	Duff-2	A2
E-2	F-2				
E-3+	F-3+	P-3	A-3	Duff-3	A3+
E-3	F-3				A3
					A3-
E-4	F-4		B		B+,B,B-
			C		C
			D		D

enables him to verify that credit limits are respected and to ensure that the back office follows up on all the decisions that have been made.

Short-term financing in foreign currency

Besides the export credit facilities that were discussed in Chapter 7, medium-sized companies as well as the large multinationals have access to the Eurocurrency market. Maturities are standardized:

1 day overnight (funds are credited on the same day);
1 day Tom next (funds are credited d+1);
1 day spot next (funds are credited d+2);
7 days;
1, 2, 3, 6, and 9 months.

Interest is calculated *ex post*, usually on the basis of the actual number of days in a 360-day year (but some countries, including the UK, use a 365-day year). The usual reference rate is LIBOR.

The Eurocurrency markets can be used as a financing instrument as well as a means of covering foreign exchange risk. If a French company has made an export sale for $1 000 000 due in three months, it can do the following:

- borrow $1 000 000/$(1+r)$ dollars;
- sell dollars spot for francs;
- use the francs to finance ongoing operations;
- receive the $1 000 000 and use it to pay off the loan.

$1 million worth of financing was achieved and there was no foreign exchange risk, since the foreign exchange transaction took place at the beginning of the operation.

The financing needs of a firm dealing in many different currencies can vary according to the evolution of its operations as well as in relation to market conditions in the individual currencies. In response to this, the banks developed a product called the **Multi-Option Financing Facility (MOFF)** that was popular in the 1980s but has since fallen from favour. A MOFF is a syndicated confirmed credit line with attached options. The confirmed credit line gives the firm the right to borrow in different currencies at terms that are fixed when the credit line is granted. For this right the firm pays a commission whether the credit facility is drawn on or not. When the firm requires financing in one currency or another, it solicits bids from banks. If the conditions that the banks are offering are more favourable than the conditions of the MOFF, the firm borrows at the more favourable conditions and does not draw on the MOFF. If the conditions of the MOFF are more favourable, the firm draws on the MOFF.

Euronote facilities and Euro-MTNs are currently two of the most popular forms of international financing. Euronotes are short-term, fully negotiable bearer promissary notes, issued at a discount to face value and typically of one, three, or six-month maturity. Euro–MTNs are medium-term bearer notes of small denomination with maturities ranging from one to five years.

USING THE FOREIGN EXCHANGE MARKET

Retail rates and settlement procedures

The bid–ask spreads on the exchange rates that the banks charge their customers are different from the spreads that are found in the interbank market that we described in Chapter 1. Spreads on the interbank market are based on the breadth and depth of a market for a given currency, as well as on the currency's volatility. Currencies that are more volatile or less widely traded usually have higher spreads. Spreads also tend to widen in general in times of financial or economic turbulence. Because of competition, spreads to bank customers reflect the spreads on the interbank market but include a commission. The commission depends on the size of the transaction. Generally speaking, the larger the transaction the lower the spread. For relatively large transactions of $1 million equivalent or more in the major currencies the spread is usually very small.

Suppose, for example, that the interbank spot rate on French francs for US dollars is 5.0100–5.0120. On a purchase of FF10 million the best retail quote might be 5.0000–5.0220, representing a one centime commission between the interbank bid rate and the rate the bank is charging the money manager. This works out to 0.2%. The commission would probably be higher on an equivalent amount of Portuguese escudos since they are not traded as heavily as French francs.

The principles of hedging with forward contracts

Spot exchange rates are quoted for delivery two business days after a transaction is concluded, but foreign exchange traders in the interbank market also quote exchange rates for delivery further than two days in the future. Deals like this are called forward contracts. The rates and the amounts are agreed on today but settlement occurs some time later than two days in the future. Contracts can be negotiated for just about any maturity but most banks supply regular quotes on maturities of 30, 60, 90, and 180 days.

Regular quotes on forward contracts are limited to a relatively small number of currencies – the German mark, the Japanese yen and the British pound make up a large part of the whole market, although the Swiss franc, the Canadian dollar, the French franc and the Netherlands guilder also do considerable volume. Much of the activity comes from banks offsetting positions that they have taken in other transactions. As we mentioned, banks tend to trade on even multiples of 30 days, such as one month, two months, three months, etc. However, when dealing with customers, banks stand ready to organize forward contracts for anywhere from three days to several years. Using the forward market is the most straightforward method of hedging foreign currency exposure.

Hedging a long position

Take the case of an American producer of machine tools that sells $65 million worth of equipment to a German importer for delivery and payment in six months at an agreed price of DM100 million. The spot exchange rate in New York is:

$$S_0(\$/Dm)\text{bid} = 0.6500.$$

If the exchange rate stays the same, the American exporter will receive $65 million, the dollar value of the goods. If the mark falls in value – to 0.6200, for example – he will receive only $62 million, a loss of $3 million. However, if the mark rises in value – to 0.6800, for example – he will make a windfall profit, of $3 million. In order to avoid the uncertainty surrounding the dollar income on the transaction, the American exporter can enter into a forward transaction with a bank. The bank quotes a six-month forward rate of:

$$F_{\frac{1}{2}}(\$/Dm)\text{bid} = 0.6410,$$

a discount of 2.77% on the mark. The discount exists because German interest rates are higher than US interest rates (see the paragraph on interest rate parity in Chapter 4). If the American exporter locks in his income in dollars by selling his mark income forward, he will only receive $64.1 million, a loss of $900 000 or 1.38%. (Premiums and discounts are quoted in yearly percentages. The yearly discount is 2.77% or 1.38% for six months.) Thus, if the American company intends to hedge, its price should be determined in relation to the forward rate, and not the spot rate.

Figure 8.2 illustrates the change in the company's dollar income resulting from the forward transaction. The solid line represents the company's income in dollars before making the forward transaction. It depends on the level of the exchange rate. At higher values of the dollar, dollar income is lower. At lower dollar values it is higher. The broken line represents the company's income after the forward transaction. Dollar income is insensitive to the level of the exchange rate. No matter what the value of the dollar, dollar income is the same. However, the dollar income that is locked in is lower by *B-A* than it would be at the current spot rate.

The situation is different when the foreign currency to be received is at a premium. If, for example, German interest rates were lower than those in the US, the mark would be at a premium to the dollar. When price is no problem, there is a windfall gain to be made from the forward transaction.

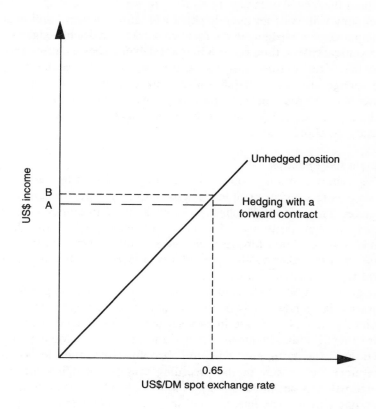

Figure 8.2 Hedging a long position.

When price is a problem and forward hedging is planned, the forward premium will make the mark price more competitive.

Eliminating foreign exchange risk has disadvantages as well as advantages. The advantage is that if the value of the mark falls, the company has no loss of income, which is guaranteed at $64.1 million. The disadvantage is that if the value of the mark goes up, the company will not benefit from the appreciation. Furthermore, hedging the foreign exchange risk exposes the company to another kind of risk. If the exporter is not paid on time, or some of his merchandise is refused, he will not have enough marks to honour forward contract. In order to make up the difference he will have to buy marks at the going spot rate, which might be higher or lower than the 0.6410 exchange rate of the forward contract. If it is higher the company will make an unanticipated loss. If it is lower it will make an unanticipated gain. Hedging in the forward market is a double-edged sword.

As a general rule of thumb, for a long foreign currency position, then, we can say that if the treasurer feels that there is a strong chance that the value of the foreign currency will fall and a weak chance that it will rise, the treasurer should hedge. In the opposite case, where there is a strong chance that the foreign currency will appreciate and a weak chance that it will depreciate, he should not hedge.

Hedging a short position

Hedging a short position involves buying foreign exchange forward in order to avoid paying a higher price in domestic currency if the foreign currency appreciates. The forward purchase locks in the price in domestic currency. In the case of short positions, a discount is favourable to the hedger because it enables him to obtain foreign exchange at a rate lower than the current spot rate. On the other hand, a premium is unfavourable because it makes forward foreign currency more costly.

Here again, eliminating foreign exchange risk has disadvantages as well as advantages. The advantage is that if the value of the foreign currency rises, the company has no increase in expenditure, which is guaranteed at the forward rate. The disadvantage is that if the value of the foreign currency goes down, the company will not benefit from the depreciation. Furthermore, as we saw in the preceding example, hedging the foreign exchange risk exposes the company to another kind of risk. Suppose that delivery dates are not respected, or that some of the merchandise is not up to standards and must be refused. Expenditure for the merchandise will be lower than expected, which will leave the company with foreign currency balances once the forward contract is consummated. When the foreign currency balances are converted back into domestic currency, the spot exchange rate might be higher or lower than the rate of the forward contract. If it is higher the company will make an unanticipated gain. If it is lower it will make an unanticipated loss. This kind of risk would not be present in the absence of the forward contract.

Hedging by banks

The counterparties to the foregoing hedging operations are banks or institutions with access to the interbank market. When a bank enters into a forward contract, it exposes itself to foreign exchange risk, just like any other enterprise. This risk can also be hedged. In fact, the forward rate charged by the bank will be calculated in relation to its hedging costs.

Suppose that a bank makes an agreement with an Italian oil importer to sell $10 million three months forward and the interbank exchange rate on Italian lira for dollars and Eurocurrency interest rates are:

1126–1128
3 month dollars: 4–$4\frac{1}{8}$
3 month lira: $11\frac{5}{8}$–$11\frac{3}{4}$

The bank calculates the forward rate it will charge the Italian importer based on its cost of hedging the transaction. In order to hedge its position with the Italian exporter, the bank will buy dollars spot at 1128 per dollar and lend the dollars for three months at 4% per year. The bank needs to deliver $10 million to the Italian importer in three months. Thus, it will buy

$$\frac{\$10\,000\,000}{1 + (0.04)\frac{3}{12}} = \$9\,900\,990.1$$

and pay

$$\$9\,900\,990.1 \times 1128 \text{ lira}/\$1 = 11\,168\,000\,000 \text{ lira.}$$

It can finance the dollar purchase by borrowing 11.168 billion lira at 11.75% for three months. At the end of three months it will pay

$$11\,168\,000\,000 \text{ lira} \times \left(1 + \frac{0.1175}{4}\right) = 11\,496\,060\,000 \text{ lira.}$$

Thus, the bank would be fully hedged if it charged a forward rate of 1149.61 (11.49606 billion lira/$10 million). This represents the lowest forward ask rate it could charge. Anything above it represents the bank's gain. At a rate of 1151, for instance, the bank's profit will be the difference between the 11.51 billion lira it will receive from the forward transaction and the 11.49606 billion lira to pay off the loan.

Hedging positions longer than one year
The transactions undertaken by the bank in the foregoing example are known as one-way arbitrage. It is called one-way arbitrage because it begins in one currency and ends in another. The covered interest arbitrage that we described in Chapter 4 began and ended in the same currency. In the face of

bid–ask spreads, covered interest arbitrage is more expensive than one-way arbitrage and in practice one-way arbitrage determines the forward spread. Equation 8.1 relates the spot and forward bid rates to the bid–ask interest rates in dollars for marks based on one-way arbitrage.[1]

$$F(\$/Dm)\text{bid} = S(\$/Dm)\text{bid}\frac{(1 + r_{\$,\text{bid}})}{(1 + r_{\text{Dm,ask}})} \tag{8.1}$$

We can generalize these arbitrage relations for periods longer than one year. Suppose, for example, that the period to be covered is n years. Equation 8.1 becomes

$$F_n(\$/Dm)\text{bid} = S(\$/Dm)\text{bid}\frac{(1 + r_{\$,\text{bid}})^n}{(1 + r_{\text{Dm,ask}})^n} \tag{8.2}$$

where $r_\$$ and r_{Dm} represent the interest rates on n year zero coupon dollar and mark loans.

Consider the following information:

- spot $/mark exchange rate $= 0.6005$–0.6015;
- interest rate on two-year zero coupon dollar loans $= 4\frac{1}{2} - 4\frac{3}{4}$;
- interest rate on two-year zero coupon mark loans $= 9\frac{3}{4} - 10$.

According to equation 8.2 the bank could hedge a two-year forward contract to sell dollars by borrowing marks for two years, selling the marks spot for dollars and lending the dollars for two years. The forward rate that the bank would have to charge its customer would be somewhere below

$$F_2(\$/Dm)\text{bid} = 0.6005\frac{(1.045)^2}{(1.10)^2} = 0.5420.$$

In practice there are not many zero coupon loans available. Consequently, an exact hedge calculation must take into consideration the cash flows resulting from interest payments at the end of the year. In Appendix 1 we show how this is done.

Rolling over and closing out forward contracts

As we mentioned above, expected inflows or outflows of foreign currency are not always realized. When this happens, the company can ask its bank to roll over the forward contract or to make a partial settlement and roll over the difference. The procedure is straightforward and is equivalent to closing out the old forward contract and making a new one.

Take the case of a French company that bought $1 million three months forward at the end of June at 5.5000. At the end of September, the merchandise that it ordered still has not been shipped, so the treasurer calls his bank and asks to roll the forward contract over for two months. On the day he calls, the spot ask rate is 5.6500 and the two-month forward rate is 5.7265. However, the company has made a profit on the difference between the current spot rate and the old forward rate equal to:

$$5.6500 - 5.5000 = 0.15.$$

The effective rate that the company will pay for the dollars after the forward contract is rolled over is equal to the new forward rate less the profit on the old forward contract:

$$5.7265 - 0.15 = 5.5765.$$

It is higher than the 5.5000 that it would have paid had the merchandise been shipped on time but it is lower than the 5.7265 that it would have had to pay if there had been no forward cover at all.

A company can also terminate a forward contract before maturity. Suppose that for some reason foreign currency that was expected in three months is actually paid at the end of two months. The company can terminate the forward contract by buying foreign currency one month forward to offset the ongoing forward three month contract. It then sells the currency it has received on the spot market. Consider the following information:

- an ongoing forward contract matures in one month to sell $1 million at 5.0100 francs per dollar;
- spot exchange rate = 4.9950 – 5.0050;
- one-month forward rate = 5.0100 – 5.0231.

The company can terminate the ongoing forward contract by buying $1 million one month forward at the ask rate of 5.0231. It loses the difference between what it receives for the dollars it sells in the ongoing contract and what it pays for the dollars in the new one-month forward contract:

$$(5.0100 - 5.0231) \times \$1\,000\,000 = -13\,100 \text{ francs.}$$

It then sells its dollars at the spot bid rate and receives

$$4.9950 \times \$1\,000\,000 = 4\,995\,000 \text{ francs.}$$

Thus, ignoring discounting on the 13 100 francs it loses on the difference between the two forward contracts, it nets only 4 981 900, or 4.9819 francs per dollar. Part of the difference is that the dollar is selling at a premium and part is due to the bid-ask spreads on the supplementary forward and spot transactions. If the dollar were at a discount, there would be a gain if the ongoing forward contract were terminated prematurely. However, part of the gain on the offsetting forward transaction would be neutralized by the cost implicit in the bid–ask spreads.

OTHER HEDGING METHODS

Hedging with foreign currency loans

Besides the foreign exchange risk, a company that has accounts receivable in foreign currency also has to worry about financing its claim. As we have seen, using forward contracts solves the problem of foreign exchange risk but it does not solve the financing problem. Financing in foreign currency solves both problems simultaneously. Furthermore, the technique is simple, easy to set up, and is accessible to medium-sized companies. It involves borrowing in foreign currency and then using the spot market. Going back to the American exporter, for example, he could have eliminated his foreign exchange risk by borrowing marks, converting them into dollars and then using the mark income from the sale of the merchandise to pay off the loan. This type of operation is especially attractive to professionals when interest rates in foreign currency are low. Nevertheless, it should not be forgotten that the premium on the forward dollar offsets the interest rate advantage. Still, borrowing in foreign currency can be advantageous insofar as it reduces the number of transactions (the forward transaction is eliminated) and the Eurocurrency market is generally more competitive than domestic financial markets and spreads are lower.

For companies with a foreign exchange liability, the Eurocurrency markets can also be used to cover. In this case, the company buys foreign currency on the spot market and then sets up a foreign currency loan to coincide with the future foreign currency payment. This type of transaction has the disadvantage of tying up the company's money for the duration of the loan. Only companies with excess liquidity would find it advantageous, and then only if the conditions in foreign currency are better than those available in the national market. Consequently, the company with the liability would let the bank do the work and use the forward market. One-way arbitrage ensures that both routes to the same end are equivalent.

Hedging with swaps

In Chapter 7, we looked at the swap transactions available for managing loan exposure to risky countries. A swap is an exchange of streams of payments between two counterparties, either directly or through an intermediary. They are useful for cash management in a multi-currency environment.

Foreign exchange swap
Foreign exchange swaps involve a spot buy (sale) of foreign exchange and a simultaneous offsetting forward sale (buy). They are useful when a treasurer is confronted with a temporary excess in one currency and shortage in another.

Suppose, for example, that a treasurer of a multinational company has £100 000 that he won't need for 30 days and a current shortage of marks. Rather than lending the pounds and borrowing the marks, he can make a swap with his banker. He sells the £100 000 for marks at the spot rate. At the same time he makes a 30-day forward contract to sell the marks and buy back the pounds.

Fixed rate currency swaps
In the case of a fixed rate currency swap a company seeks to exchange a loan in one currency for a loan in another. Three stages are involved. First, the principal is exchanged at the spot rate. Second, on each coupon date, interest payments are exchanged. Finally, at the swap's maturity, the principal is re-exchanged, usually at the original exchange rate.

Suppose, for example, that a German company wants to invest in Spain. If it finances its investment by borrowing marks, it will be exposed to exchange risk. The problem is that it is not known by Spanish banks and cannot borrow pesetas directly on favourable terms. It decides to borrow 1 000 000 marks at 6% for five years, with the principal to be repaid at maturity. To eliminate the foreign exchange risk, it wants to exchange its mark debt for debt in pesetas and use the peseta cash flows generated by the investment to service the peseta debt. It goes to its bank and arranges a swap with the following terms:

- 6% on the mark loan;
- 12% on the peseta loan;
- spot exchange rate = 84 ptas/Dm.

The outcome of the operation is summarized in Figure 8.3. On day 1 the company gives the bank 1 000 000 marks and receives 84 000 000 pesetas. Each year on the coupon date the bank gives the company 60 000 marks and receives 10 080 000 pesetas from the company. On the maturity date the bank gives the company 1 000 000 marks and the company gives the bank 84 000 000 pesetas.

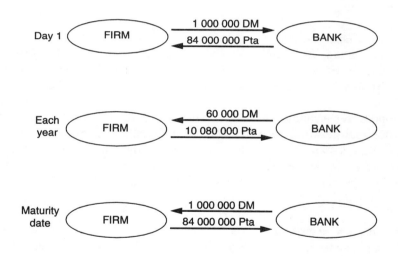

Figure 8.3 Fixed rate currency swaps.

The swap permits the company access to credit in pesetas. By exchanging its mark loan, it is able to use 84 000 000 pesetas for five years. There is no exchange risk on the principal because it is exchanged at the same, fixed rate. There is no exchange risk on the interest payments because the 60 000 marks paid by the bank cover the 60 000 marks that the company is obliged to pay on its loan. A currency swap, then, is like a series of forward foreign exchange contracts. The forward rate for each year that only involves interest payments is the ratio of the two cash flows:

$$10\,080\,000 \text{ pesetas}/60\,000 \text{ marks} = 168.00.$$

On the last year of the swap, both interest and principal are exchanged. The cash flow in pesetas is:

$$84\,000\,000 + 10\,080\,000 = 94\,080\,000.$$

The cash flow in marks is:

$$1\,000\,000 + 60\,000 = 1\,060\,000.$$

The forward rate for this year is the ratio of these two cash flows:

$$94\,080\,000/1\,060\,000 = 88.7547.$$

Hedging with futures contracts on organized markets

Mechanics of the futures markets
The organized futures markets have four important features:

1. the contracts are standardized;
2. trading takes place in one location (the trading pit);
3. contracts are settled through the exchange's clearing house;
4. contracts are **marked to market** each day, which means that they are revalued according to their market value.

The Chicago Mercantile Exchange (CME) is one of the world's largest commercial exchanges. It began as a commodities market and for many years only commodities were traded on it. In 1972 it opened the International Monetary Market to trade foreign exchange futures on the pound sterling, the Canadian dollar, the German mark, the yen, the Mexican peso, the Swiss franc and the Italian lira. Since then futures contracts in foreign currency have spread around the world. Table 8.4 gives an idea of some of the currency futures contracts that were available in 1992.

CME currency futures contracts were patterned after the futures contracts for the commodities that it had been trading for over a hundred years.

Table 8.4 Selected currency futures contracts

Currency	Exchange
Australian dollar	Sydney Futures Exchange (SFE)
Australian dollar	CME
Australian dollar	Philadelphia Board of Trade (PBOT)
British pound	Singapore Monetary Exchange (SIMEX)
British pound	CME
British pound	MidAmerica Commodity Exchange
British pound	PBOT
Canadian dollar	CME
Canadian dollar	MidAmerica CE
Canadian dollar	PBOT
Deutschmark	Mercantile and Futures Exchange
Deutschmark	SIMEX
Deutschmark	CME
Deutschmark	MidAmerica CE
Deutschmark	PBOT
Ecu	PBOT
Ecu	New York Cotton Exchange
French franc	CME
French franc	PBOT
Japanese yen	Mercantile and Futures Exchange
Japanese yen	SIMEX
Japanese yen	CME
Japanese yen	MidAmerica CE
Japanese yen	PBOT
Japanese yen	Tokyo International Financial Futures Exchange (TIFFE)
New Zealand dollar	NZ Futures and Options Exchange
Swedish krona	Stockholm Options Market
Swiss franc	CME
Swiss franc	MidAmerica CE
Swiss franc	PBOT
Euro-DM	MATIF
US dollar	Mercantile and Futures Exchange
US dollar	NZ F&O Exchange

(Source: The 1992 Dictionary of Directives, supplement to *Euromoney* (June 1992).)

Hence, contrary to the workings of the interbank market, trading conforms strictly to the exchange's internal rules. The currencies that are traded are strictly limited. Maturities are based on a quarterly cycle of March, June, September and December, and each contract has a precise delivery date. Each contract also corresponds to a given amount of foreign exchange. For example, the yen contract is for 12 500 000 yen and the mark contract for 125 000 marks. Consequently, hedgers cannot usually get the exact maturities and amounts that they need and have to settle for the nearest date and the closest amount. The maturity date is probably more of a problem than the amounts because maturity dates are relatively rare, whereas the size of the contracts is small enough that most users' needs can be approximated quite well. Furthermore, the small size of the contract makes the futures market accessible to smaller investors. Finally, when contracts mature, the delivery procedure is effected according to the rules established by the exchange.

Contrast this with the interbank over-the-counter market. On the interbank market there is no unique trading area and transactions are carried out by phone between traders and brokers. On the organized futures markets only those owning or renting a seat on the exchange are allowed to trade. Thus, if an outsider such as a company or a bank wants to buy or sell on the exchange, it must do so through the intermediary of an authorized broker. The order is communicated to the broker, who transmits it to the pit where it is executed in a system of open outcry by a trader employed by the broker. Once the order has been executed, the client is notified. This system of continuous open outcry is transparent and competitive and ensures that the buy price is the same as the sell price. There is no bid-ask spread as there is in the interbank market. The broker makes his money by charging the client a commission; in practice this is quite small. **A round trip**, meaning one buy and one sell, can be effected for as little as 0.05% of the value of the contract.

Once a transaction has been concluded in the trading pit, each counterparty must notify the clearing house. The role of the clearing house is threefold. It records the existence of the contract; it manages settlement of day-to-day operations; and it guarantees delivery at the contract's maturity. Thus there is no individual counterparty risk because all clients have the clearing house as the ultimate counterparty.

Although the clearing house is the ultimate counterparty between all buyers and sellers, it does not accept excessive risk. It requires guarantees from the brokers in the form of deposits based on their individual positions. The deposits represent a small proportion of the total contract and are virtually costless, since interest-bearing treasury bonds can be used. This is important because contracts are marked to market each day.

Marking to market means that profits and losses are paid every day at the end of trading, equivalent to closing out a contract each day, paying off losses or receiving gains, and writing a new contract.

Hedging with futures

The futures markets are easy to use. To cover a short position in foreign currency, a futures contract can be bought with a maturity closest to that of the short position. To cover a long position in foreign currency, a futures contract with the maturity closest to that of the long position can be sold. Because the contracts are standardized and guaranteed by the Clearing House, they are liquid and positions can be closed out easily. A short position in futures can be closed out by a purchase of the same contract. A long position in futures can be closed out by a sale of the same contract.

The facility of opening and closing out positions makes it possible to manage relatively small levels of foreign exchange exposure on a continuous basis. This is especially attractive to commercial customers who have a fairly regular stream of payments and receipts. Furthermore, pricing advantages between futures and forward markets should also be negligible. Arbitrage between the futures and forward markets ensures that prices between the two will stay in line. It is true, though, that because of marking to market, forward and futures prices can theoretically differ, with the difference between the futures price minus the forward price depending negatively on the correlation of the riskless bond price with the futures price.[2] However, comparisons of futures and forward prices in the foreign exchange market have consistently revealed the absence of a significant difference between the two.[3]

While futures and forward prices generally tend to be equal, the same cannot be said for the futures price and the spot price. Because of the interest rate differential the two will usually be different. As the delivery date gets closer and closer, however, the interest rate differential has less and less effect and the futures price approaches the spot price. At maturity, the futures price and the spot price should be equal. Before maturity the difference between the futures price and the spot price is called the **basis**:

$$\text{Futures price} - \text{spot price} = \text{basis}.$$

Since the interest rate differential determines the basis in currency markets, and since this differential can vary over the life of a contract, the basis can also vary over the life of a contract. Unexpected variations in the basis, as opposed to expected variations, constitute **basis risk**. Expected variations in the basis are associated with the passage of time and the convergence of the futures and spot prices. Unexpected variations are associated with unexpected changes in the interest rate differential. With this in mind, a perfect hedge using futures contracts can only be achieved if the hedge date corresponds perfectly with the futures maturity date. Investors should be aware of this risk and should realize that the basis increases with a contract's time to maturity. In practice, because of basis risk, investors with imperfect hedges tend to use contracts closer to maturity, in spite of the cost of rolling them over.

HEDGING WITH CURRENCY OPTIONS

Setting up a fixed hedge enables the company treasurer to avoid a loss when the exchange rate moves against him. On the other hand, it eliminates the possibility of making a gain if it moves in his favour. A fixed hedge strategy is right when the treasurer attaches a strong probability to a move against him and a weak probability for a move in his favour. Another way to look at foreign exchange hedging, however, is to consider the case where the treasurer feels that there is an equally strong chance for favourable and unfavourable moves. Then, the argument for a fixed hedge is less obvious. The advantage of avoiding the loss is offset by the disadvantage of missing out on the gain. This does not mean that the fixed hedge loses its usefulness. It only means that its usefulness is diminished. In this case another type of coverage might be preferable: the currency option. Proper use of currency options requires a clear understanding of what exactly an option is and how it is priced.

Characteristics of currency options

In Chapter 6, we spelled out the basics of option pricing theory. In this section we will study how options pricing theory applies to currencies and exchange rates.

A currency option gives its owner the right for a given period of time to buy or sell a given amount of one currency for another currency at a fixed price, called the exercise price or the strike price. If the right can be exercised at any time during the life of the option it is called an American option. If the right can be exercised only at the option's expiration date, it is called a European option. The right to buy is called a call. The right to sell is called a put. The buyer of the option pays the seller, or the writer, a certain sum, called the premium, for the right to buy or sell at the prescribed price. In summary, the characteristic elements of an option contract are:

- the nature of the transaction: call or put;
- the underlying currency;
- the quotation currency;
- the amount of the underlying currency;
- the strike price;
- the expiration date;
- the premium.

Consider a European call option on $500 000 for French francs with a maturity of three months and a strike price of 5.19. This gives the buyer the right to buy $500 000 for French francs at the rate of 5.19 francs per dollar in three months. The underlying currency is the dollar and the quotation currency is the French franc. If the premium is 2.83%, this means that the buyer has to pay the writer $14 150 ($500 000 × 2.83%) at the outset. The premium can also be expressed in francs. In this case the spot exchange rate is used to make the conversion. If, for example, the spot bid rate is 5.2000, the premium is 73 580 francs ($14 150 × 5.2 000).

A European put option on £1 000 000, a strike price of 2.95 marks, and a maturity of six months gives the buyer the right to sell £1 000 000 at the rate of 2.95 marks per pound in six months. If the premium is 3.58%, the buyer has to pay the writer £35 800 (£1 000 000 × 3.58%) at the outset. The premium can also be expressed in marks by using the spot exchange rate. If, for example, the spot bid rate is 2.9400, the premium will be 105 252 marks (£35 800 × 2.9400).

Option contracts are listed according to the underlying currency, the expiration date and the strike price. The two types of option are calls and puts. All options of the same type in the same currencies constitute an option **class**. All options in the same class with the same expiration date and the same strike price constitute an option **series**.

In the over-the-counter bank market, maturities are variable. Although maturities of three or six months are customary, it is possible to find options with maturities of a day or a week, up to a year or more. On the organized exchanges such as the Philadelphia Stock Exchange, expiration dates are standardized; for example, the Saturday that precedes the third Wednesday in the months of March, June, September, and December.

Strike prices are standardized in both the over-the-counter market, where two decimal places is the norm, and the organized exchanges, where the norm varies from exchange to exchange.

On the organized exchanges a clearing house records the transactions concluded by each one of its members. Each member also has an obligation to keep records of its clients' accounts. Just as in the futures markets, the role of the clearing house is essential. It guarantees the execution of all contracts negotiated on the exchange and effectively becomes the counter-party to both sides of the transaction. The role of the clearing house and contract standardization facilitate trading and make the market more liquid, with the exchanges continually writing new options as well as closing out ongoing positions. An investor who has written an option can close out his position by buying an equivalent option while an investor who has bought an option can close out his position by selling an equivalent option. Since the contracts are standardized and the clearing house is the counterparty to both sides of the contract, all options in the same series are equivalent, no matter who the end buyers and sellers are.

In the over-the-counter market, transactions are done on a person-to-person, deal-to-deal basis. There is no standard contract and no unique counterparty. Consequently, there is no real secondary market that would enable an investor to make low-cost, rapid or frequent changes in position.

The scope for currency options extends into the futures markets. Some exchanges, such as the Chicago Mercantile Exchange, offer options on futures contracts. In this case, the buyer of a call has the right to buy a given futures contract on the Exchange at a price equal to the option's strike price. The buyer of the put has the right to sell a given futures contract at a price equal to the option's strike price. In practice, these options are used in a manner similar to options linked directly to the spot rate. Thus, their usefulness is relatively marginal.

Pricing currency options

In the early 1970s, Black and Scholes were the first to propose a complete option pricing model.[4] Today this model is a standard tool for professionals and amateurs playing the options markets. In 1983, just when currency options were becoming popular, Garman and Kohlhagen succeeded in adapting the Black-Scholes model to the foreign exchange markets.[5] Since they adopted most of Black and Scholes' original hypotheses, their results are very close to the original model. The Garman-Kohlhagen formula for the price of a foreign currency call is given as:[6]

$$C(S, t) = S(t)e^{-r(T-t)}N(d_1) - Ee^{-r_d(T-t)}N(d_2) \qquad (8.3)$$

where

T is the expiration date

S is the spot exchange rate, defined as the number of units of domestic currency for each unit of foreign currency

E is the strike price

r is the riskless rate on the foreign currency

r_d is the riskless rate on domestic currency

$N(d)$ = the value of the cumulative normal distribution evaluated at d

and

$$d_1 = \frac{\ln\left[\frac{S(t)}{E}\right] + \left(r_d - r + \frac{\sigma^2}{2}\right)(T - t)}{\sigma\sqrt{T - t}}$$

$$d_2 = d_1 - \sigma\sqrt{T - t}$$

The main difference between this formula and the original Black-Scholes formula stems from the fact that the opportunity-cost to the investor is not the domestic riskless rate, as it would be for an ordinary asset. In fact, the opportunity cost is the difference between the domestic and foreign riskless rates. The principle behind this is that when setting up the riskless hedge domestic currency is borrowed, exchanged for foreign currency, and then invested. The cost of the hedge is the difference between the cost of borrowing at the domestic rate less the return on the investment at the foreign rate.[7]

HEDGING WITH OPTIONS

Positions to be hedged can come from many sources – commercial transactions, foreign investments or from loans raised in other currencies. The positions can be long or short, and the options to hedge them can be traded on either the domestic market or a foreign market. Finally, the hedge can be constructed by buying an option, by selling an option or by a combination of both. In this section we will consider only the basic strategies. In Appendix 8.2 we outline some of the more sophisticated strategies.

Hedging with an option purchase

The position to be covered can be short if, for example, it is used to finance imports. It can be long if the exposure comes from a future receipt from the sale of exports. The appropriate hedging strategies should therefore be symmetrical. In the first case, when the exchange rate is quoted as the number of units of domestic currency to buy one unit of foreign currency [$S(d/f)$], calls should be bought. In the second case from the same perspective, puts should be bought. It is important to remember how the exchange rate is quoted, because if it were quoted the other way [$S(f/d)$] the operations would be reversed.

Hedging a short position on an organized exchange

Suppose that an American importer has to pay a bill for 25 million yen in two months' time. The spot rate in New York, $S(\$/yen)$ is $0.9800 per 100 yen. The importer fears that the rate will rise (the yen will appreciate) but he is not too sure that this, in fact, will actually happen. The markets are volatile and a fall in the exchange rate (the yen depreciates) cannot be excluded. If the yen does fall, the other importers will pay fewer dollars for their imports and thus be able to lower their prices. Competition is tough and the importer cannot afford to be wrong either way.

The key to the importer's problem is the number of dollars that he will have to pay for the 25 million yen. The purchase of a call will allow him to hedge against a rise in the value of the yen without eliminating the gains that he can realize if the value of the yen falls. A call to his broker confirms that the Philadelphia Stock Exchange has a call contract for 6 250 000 yen with a strike price of 99 and expiration time of two months selling at 1.18. In other words, the importer can buy the right to buy 6.25 million yen in two months for $0.99 per 100 yen for 1.18 cents per 100 yen. To cover the 25 million yen that he owes, he will have to buy four contracts. If in two months the exchange rate is higher than $0.99, the calls will be exercised and he will pay $247 500 for the 25 million yen. The total cost of the operation will be $250 450 ($247 500 for the yen plus $2950 for the premium) and the effective exchange rate will be $1.0018 [$250 450/(25 000 000/100)]. If the exchange rate is lower than $0.99, the calls will expire worthless.

Suppose that the exchange rate falls to $0.96. He will pay $240 000 for the yen and his total cost will be $242 950 ($240 000 for the yen and $2950 for the premium). The effective exchange rate would be $0.9718. Although he would pay more for the yen than the current exchange rate because of the premium, he still would benefit considerably from the yen's fall.

Besides the obvious advantages of hedging with a call option, there are also disadvantages. One of the main disadvantages cited by professional investors is the cost. When the maximum cost of foreign currency hedged with a call option (the strike price plus the premium) is compared with the cost of a forward contract, option hedging is always more costly because of the premium. The question, then, is when should a call be used to hedge foreign exchange risk? To answer this question we must distinguish between three situations:

1. when a rise in the exchange rate is expected and the probability of this outcome is very high;
2. when a fall in the exchange rate is expected and the probability of this outcome is very high;
3. when there is an expected movement one way or the other but there is also a strong possibility of a move in the opposite direction.

Figure 8.4 compares the three cases. In the first case, when a rise in the exchange rate is very probable, a classic forward hedge is the best strategy because it is the least costly. In the second case, when a fall in the exchange rate is very probable, the best strategy is not to cover and avoid all costs while benefiting fully from the lower rate. In the third case of considerable uncertainty, the option might be the best strategy. If there is a sharp rise in the exchange rate, total costs are limited. If there is a sharp fall, some of the benefits are captured. Only in the zone of relative stability, between *A* and *B* in Figure 8.4 is an option hedge clearly the inferior strategy. This is because it is the costliest strategy and no benefits accrue to the option-holder if the exchange rate does not move outside the range *AB*. In conclusion, we can say that hedging with options is the most advantageous when uncertainty is the greatest and big moves in both directions are a strong possibility.

Purchasing a currency call does not always constitute an appropriate hedge. It should not be forgotten that the American exchanges offer written contracts on exchange rates in terms of US dollars. From the point of view of a non-US importer, however, the problem is in reverse. He wants to protect himself against an appreciation of the dollar in his domestic currency or, put another way, against a depreciation of his domestic currency against the dollar. Consequently, when hedging on an American exchange, it is a put that he must purchase and not a call.

Hedging a long position in the over-the-counter market
Suppose that a French company has just signed a contract for $1 million worth of exports that will be paid for in three months. The spot rate in Paris is 5.50. The company treasurer fears that the dollar might depreciate and reduce his income in French francs. On the other hand, there is also a strong chance that the dollar will appreciate and, if this happens, he does not want to miss out on the increase in income that this will bring. His banker offers to sell him a dollar put with a strike price of 5.50 and an expiration date that

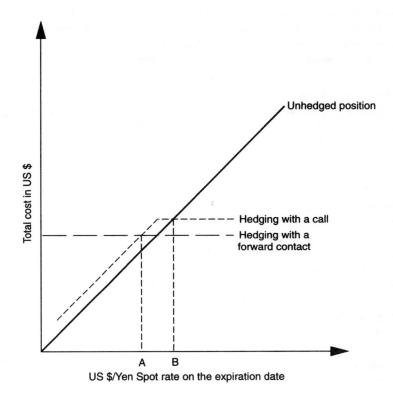

Figure 8.4 Three exchange rate situations.

coincides with his expected dollar income in three months. The premium is 2% which is to be paid on the expiration date. This put on $1 million will cover him if the dollar falls sharply. If, for example, it falls to 5.10, the treasurer will exercise the put and receive an effective rate of 5.39 (5.50 − 0.02 × 5.50). If the dollar rises above 5.50, the put will expire worthless and the treasurer will sell his dollars at the spot rate. His effective rate will be equal to the spot rate less the premium of 0.11.

Note that here again an option hedge is only advantageous if the exchange rate has a good chance of making a wide swing in either direction. We should also point out that the option hedge has another advantage when the commercial cash flow is not entirely certain. The order could be cancelled, for example. With a classic hedge of dollars sold forward, the exporter would find himself in a purely speculative position. On the maturity date he would have to come up with the dollars. If the value of the dollar had fallen he would make money but if it had risen he would lose money. The potential loss is theoretically unlimited. As we saw above, it is always possible to close out the position but that generates another transaction cost and the treasurer would still have to pay the difference in the two forward prices if the rate had moved against him. In the case of a put, he is still in a speculative position but his exposure is limited to the amount of the premium. In a case like this of a potential unwanted speculative position generated by foreign currency hedging, the option hedge is clearly preferable.

Hedging by selling options

The main criticism by company treasurers of using options to hedge foreign exchange risk is the cost, that is, the premium that they must pay. As we have seen, an option purchase is only advantageous if wide swings of the exchange rate in either direction are probable (high volatility). If the forecast is for relative stability (low volatility), it might be better to sell options. In this section we will consider two examples: covering imports by selling puts and covering exports by selling calls.

Covering imports by selling puts

An importer billed in foreign exchange is exposed to the risk that the foreign exchange will become more costly before the bill is due. To reduce or eliminate this risk he can buy calls on the foreign currency if he uses his domestic market, or buy puts on the domestic currency if he uses a foreign market. Another way of generating the same effect is to sell a put on the foreign currency.

Imagine the case of an Italian importer of petroleum products who has a bill of $10 million to pay in three months' time. The current spot exchange rate in Milan is 1129/$ and the three-month forward rate is 1151. A three-month dollar put with a strike price of 1129 is selling over the counter at 3.4%, or about 38 lire per dollar. If the dollar appreciates to 1160 lire in three months, the put will expire worthless and the importer will keep the premium. The cost of his dollars will then be 1160 lira paid spot less the 38 lire received for the premium, for a total of 1122 lira per dollar. This rate is far better than the spot rate of 1160, or the 1151 he could have paid to cover himself with a forward contract. If the value of the dollar falls to 1110, the put will be exercised and the importer will pay 1129 for the dollars. His all-in cost will be the 1129 paid less the 38 received for the premium for a total of

1091, a much better price than the market rate of 1110 or the forward rate of 1151.

The situation looks almost too good to be true. In fact, it is. If the dollar falls to 1000, for example, the put will be exercised and the cost to the importer will still be 1091, far higher than the spot rate. By the same token, if the dollar rises to 1300, the put will expire and the cost of the dollars will be 1262, the spot rate less the premium. This rate is higher than the 1151 that could have been obtained with a forward contract and, thus, the hedge was inadequate.

Hedging by selling puts is the best strategy as long as the exchange rate stays between 1091 (1129 – 38) and 1189 (1151 + 38). One of the reasons that the band is so wide is that the forward dollar is at a premium. If it had been at a discount the band would have been narrower. In any case, selling puts can be a profitable hedging strategy if the exchange rate is expected to remain relatively stable.

Covering exports by selling calls

An exporter who bills in foreign currency fears a fall in the value of that currency before he is paid. To reduce or eliminate this risk he can buy puts on the foreign currency if he uses his domestic market, or buy calls on the domestic currency if he uses a foreign market. Another way of generating the same effect is to sell a call on the foreign currency.

Imagine a Spanish exporter selling in Africa and billing his clients in French francs. He wants to protect himself against a fall in the value of the franc. In Madrid the franc spot exchange rate is 18.9215 and 19.1350 three months forward. He sells a three-month call on French francs with a strike price of 19 to his bank for 2.7%, or 0.51 pesetas for each franc. If the value of the French franc falls below 19, to 18.70, for example, the call will not be exercised. He will sell his francs for the spot rate of 18.70 and pocket the premium of 0.51 on the call. His effective exchange rate will be 19.21, better than the spot rate or the forward rate of 19.135 he could have contracted for.

Suppose that the French franc appreciates to 19.40. The call will be exercised and he will receive 19 pesetas for each franc. His effective rate will be the 19 peseta strike price plus the 0.51 peseta premium for a total of 19.51, a rate that is better than the spot rate of 19.40 and the forward rate of 19.135.

The risk from selling the call comes if the franc falls sharply in value, to 18, for example. The call is not exercised and the exporter receives the spot rate plus the premium for each franc, a rate of 18.51, far lower than the forward rate.

Hedging by selling calls is the best strategy as long as the exchange rate stays in the band between 18.625 (19.135 − 0.51) and 19.51 (19 + 0.51). Selling calls can be a profitable hedging strategy if the exchange rate is expected to remain relatively stable.

APPENDIX 8.1 HEDGING LONG-TERM FOREIGN EXCHANGE RISK WITH NON-ZERO COUPON LOANS

Going back to the example in the text, we have:

- spot $/mark exchange rate = 0.6005–0.6015
- interest rate on two-year zero coupon dollar loans = $4\frac{1}{2}$–$4\frac{3}{4}$
- interest rate on two-year zero coupon mark loans = $9\frac{3}{4}$–10

If the bank borrows 0.826446 marks $\left[\left(\frac{1}{1.1}\right)^2\right]$, changes them for 0.496281 dollars at the spot rate (0.6005), and invests them at 4.5% for two years, according to equation 8.2, it would be completely hedged and end up with $0.5420. The situation is different, however, if the loans are not zero coupon. If interest payments are made annually, for example, it would pay 0.082645 marks and receive $0.0223333 at the end of the first year. Since the rate at which the dollar income could be converted into marks to pay the interest liability is unknown, it would be exposed to foreign exchange risk.

In order to avoid this exposure, the hedging operations are more complicated. Rather than borrowing in one currency and lending in the other, both borrowing and lending operations will have to be undertaken in each of the currencies. In marks, more will have to be borrowed for two years, some of which will be re-lent for one year to meet the interest payment at the end of the first year.

In the forward contract the bank buys one mark, which it will use to pay off the loan. Hence the amount owed at the end of year 2 including interest and principal must be equal to one. Since interest is paid yearly, the outstanding principal at the beginning of year 2 will be the same as the amount borrowed at the beginning of year 1. At an interest rate of 10% that amount will be:

$$\frac{1}{1.10} = 0.909091 \text{ marks.}$$

Suppose that the bid rate on one year marks is 9.75%. Then the amount that must be lent for one year to meet the interest payment is:

$$\frac{0.1(0.909091)}{1.0975} = 0.082833 \text{ marks.}$$

The amount of the two-year loan available to buy dollars spot will be equal to the proceeds from the two-year borrowing less the amount loaned for one year:

$$0.909091 - 0.082833 = 0.826258.$$

At the spot rate of 0.6005 this will yield $0.496168 (calculated as 0.826258×0.6005).

Now we have to find the amount of dollars that must be borrowed for one year that will be paid off with the interest received at the end of the first year from the two-year loan. Suppose that the ask rate on one year dollars is 4.75%. Some dollars will have to be borrowed for one year and reinvested for two years, along with the $0.496168 obtained in the spot transaction. Let X represent the amount to be borrowed. Then:

$$\frac{0.045(X + \$0.496168)}{1.0475} = X$$

and solving for X:

$$X = \$0.022272.$$

The amount to be lent for two years is $0.51844, the proceeds from the spot transaction ($0.496168) plus the amount borrowed for one year ($0.022272). At the end of year 1 the bank will owe $0.02333 for interest and principal on its one-year borrowing and will receive $0.02333 in interest on its two-year loan. It uses the one to pay the other. At the end of year 2, the bank will receive:

$$\$0.51844 \times 1.045 = \$0.5418$$

in interest and principal on its two-year loan.

All the cash flows for interest and principal are perfectly matched and the bank ends up owning $0.5418 and owing 1 mark. Thus, the bank can offer a two-year forward $/Dm bid rate of 0.5418 and be fully covered. This is lower than the 0.5420 obtained from equation 8.2, due to the difference between the one and two-year interest rates and the increased amounts that are borrowed. It is interesting to note, then, that when interest payments occur during the life of the forward contract, the forward rate cannot be determined by the interest rate differential alone. Differences in the term structure of interest rates are also explicitly involved.

APPENDIX 8.2 ADVANCED HEDGING STRATEGIES USING OPTIONS

Tunnels: an introduction to hedging with sales and purchases of options

Hedging by purchasing options is costly because of the premium and effective only in times of high volatility. Hedging by selling options can be advantageous in times of low volatility. The two strategies are complementary, leading professionals to devise strategies combining both of them.

The tunnel for imports

Covering exchange risk on an import transaction can be achieved on the domestic market by buying calls or by selling puts. To reduce the cost of an option hedge, the treasurer may want to combine both of them. Selling the put enables him to choose an out-of-the-money call that is less expensive. The cost reduction is complete if the premium on the sale of the put covers the premium on the call purchase.

Take the case of the German importer who has a bill in dollars to pay in three months. The spot exchange rate is 1.54 marks/$ and the three-month forward rate is 1.559. He can buy a three-month out-of-the-money call with a strike price of 1.64 for 0.4%. The call is not expensive because the strike price is high. He can also sell a three-month put with a strike price of 1.49 for 0.4%. The two premiums offset each other and the cost is zero.

If the dollar appreciates sharply, the importer will exercise his call at 1.64 and pay 1.64 marks per dollar. On the other hand, if the dollar depreciates sharply, the put will be exercised and he will pay 1.49 marks per dollar. The band between these two limit rates is called the **tunnel**. Inside the tunnel the importer will receive whatever the spot rate happens to be, but he can never pay more than 1.64 and never less than 1.49. The cost of this position resides in the fact that if the rate goes below 1.49 he will not benefit from the lower rate. Treasurers like this kind of position because their risk is limited, they can benefit from favourable moves in the exchange rate, and costs are low.

The tunnel for exports

The export tunnel is symmetrical to the import tunnel. The treasurer simultaneously buys a put and sells a call. Both instruments are chosen out-of-the-money. Thus, if the value of the foreign currency falls sharply, the put guarantees a minimum price. If it rises sharply, the call will be exercised but will have benefited from the rise up to the strike price. Costs are reduced because the premium he receives from the sale of the call goes to offset the purchase of the put. The two premiums might not be equal, so the final result must include the difference between the two.

Combinations of simple options

Calls and puts offer investors the possibility of adjusting their risk exposure to desired levels. New opportunities can be created by combining one or more simple options. The tunnel is one example. The operations often seem complex. In any case, the language that describes them is colourful. We can distinguish between two types of combinations. The first type, called **spreads**, combines options of different series but of the same class, where some are bought and others are written. The second type, like **straddles** and **strangles**, combines different types (calls and puts) of options.

Strategies based on call and put combinations
The simplest strategies combine the purchase and sale of calls or puts with the same expiration date but with different strike prices or with the same strike price but different expiration dates. When the expiration date is the same and the strike price is different, they are called **vertical spreads**. When the expiration date is different and the strike price is the same, they are called **horizontal spreads**.

Straddles and strangles
When the purchase of a call is combined with the purchase of a put, the result is either a **straddle** or a **strangle**. A straddle is when the two options have the same strike price and expiration date. In the other cases a strangle results.

An investor buys a straddle when he expects a sudden large rise or fall in the underlying exchange rate. When a sharp rise occurs, the call generates a profit, while the put becomes worthless. When a sharp fall occurs, the put generates a profit while the call becomes worthless. The rise or fall must be sharp enough to offset the cost of buying the options. If the rise is not sharp enough, the straddle will generate a loss. The loss is maximum when the exchange rate ends up at the strike price on the expiration date. To summarize, then, we can say that a straddle strategy will end in a loss if the exchange rate stays stable or moves only moderately.

Second-generation options

The over-the-counter options markets have outgrown their development stage and become mature markets, at least for products involving exchange rates and interest rates. Consequently, the margins that banks can charge for these products have fallen sharply. Furthermore, as investors have learned to use options, they have also become aware of their limits and disadvantages – high initial costs and the necessity of constant monitoring. Based on this, the banks have sought innovative products as a means of developing new markets. The fruits of their effort are what are called second-generation options. Some of these have proved to be highly complex and are lacking any real market. Others have been more successful. Without going into an exhaustive survey of the second-generation options, whose details can vary from bank to bank, we will present several examples that underline the features of the most characteristic contracts.

Look-back options
A look-back option gives its holder the right to purchase or sell foreign exchange at the most favourable exchange rate realized over the life of the option. The buyer of a look-back call, for example, has the right to purchase a certain amount of foreign exchange at the lowest exchange rate realized between the creation of the call and its expiration date. The buyer of a look-back put has the right to sell foreign exchange at the highest exchange rate realized between its creation and its expiration date. In other words, the strike price of a look-back option is not known until the expiration date. This is the fundamental difference between a traditional option and a look-back. Since the new twist is favourable to the owner, the premium of a look-back is higher than the premium on a traditional option. Historically, the premium has been approximately twice as high.

Average rate options
An average rate option gives its owner the right to the nominal amount of the difference between the strike price and the arithmetic average of the daily spot exchange rates realized over the life of the option. This type of option makes it possible to hedge a series of daily cash inflows over a given period in one single contract.

In practice, it operates like this. The company treasurer changes his foreign currency income day by day at the exchange rate of the moment. On the expiration date of his average rate option, if the average rate is lower than the strike price, he gets the difference between the two. A lower average rate means that over the life of the option he has been changing his foreign currency income at a relatively unfavourable rate. The pay-off from the option enables him to make up the difference so that he effectively has changed all his foreign income at the strike price, less the value of the premium. If the average rate is higher than the strike price, the option expires worthless. A higher average rate means that over the life of the option he has been changing his foreign currency income at a favourable rate. His effective exchange rate is the average rate diminished by the value of the premium.

It is important to note that an average rate option is not the same thing as the purchase of a series of options with the same strike price, each one expiring on a different day over the period to be covered. In this case some options would be exercised while others would expire worthless. Consequently, the average effective rate would be higher than the strike price. Since the outcome for this strategy is higher than the outcome for the average rate option, its premium should be higher.

We can look at this in another way. The underlying support for a normal option is the spot exchange rate. The underlying support for an average rate option is the average rate. An average is less volatile than the rate itself and thus lowers the premium relative to the premium of a normal option.

The advantages of an average rate option for a company with regular daily foreign currency cash flows is obvious. If the flows are not regular, the average rate is not an accurate reference for hedging them. However, it might be a pretty good approximation. Furthermore, it would be difficult and costly to set up a series of options designed to expire on a daily basis. Just trying to manage such a system would be complicated and costly. Hence, an average rate option might be an imperfect substitute that gives adequate coverage, is relatively inexpensive and is easy to monitor and manage.

Basket options

Some companies are confronted by foreign exchange exposure in a number of currencies. In this case there might be an advantage to grouping its exposure and negotiating a basket option with its bank. A basket option does not have one single underlying currency – it has several. For example, a basket option might be used to cover a long position of $30 million worth of yen and German marks respectively, $15 million of pounds and francs respectively and $10 million worth of Italian lira. The premium will be based on a contract for $100. Suppose the strike price is $98 million. If the weighted average exchange rate yields less than $98 million, the option is exercised. If it yields more, the option expires.

Instead of the basket put, the company could have purchased five different puts for the different amounts in question in each separate currency at a strike price 2% below the exchange rate being covered. Neither the results nor the costs, however, would be the same. The puts do not have to be exercised or abandoned *en masse*. Some can be exercised while others can be abandoned. Thus, the strategy of individual puts has a good chance of getting a better outcome than the basket option, which only guarantees the average rate. The average of the exchange rates has less volatility than each individual currency. Thus its cost should be lower than the cost of the strategy composed of individual puts.

Compound options

A compound option is an option on an option. This kind of instrument is useful for managing risks associated with conditional cash flows. The classic example is that of a company preparing to tender a bid for a contract. The deadline for the bid is three months in the future and the results will be known six months after that, a total of nine months in the future. The currency risk takes effect only when the bid has been submitted, that is, in three months' time. Once the bids are submitted the company is sure to want to hedge its exposure with the purchase of an option. However, it might want to know right now how much that coverage will cost. A three-month compound option on the cost of the six-month option that it might want to buy if it wins the contract would do the trick.

Shared currency option under tender (SCOUT)

As with the compound option, a scout is designed to help companies in the context of tendering a bid for a contract. The procedure is straightforward. The bank that is offering the scout persuades its client to purchase an option and to share its cost with the other companies that are bidding on the contract. When the outcome of the bidding is announced, the company that has won becomes the owner of the option and its bid is covered for a fraction of the cost. The losing bidders, however, lose the part of the premium they have paid, but they would have lost the premium anyway had they elected to take out individual coverage. This technique reduces the cost of the hedge considerably for all the participating companies in all circumstances. The problem is getting the competing companies to collaborate in the collective coverage.

Hybrids

Hybrid contracts, such as participating forwards, employ a mixed formula with one element of fixed forward cover and one element of option coverage. They can also belong to the category of zero premium coverage.

Zero premium, of course, does not mean zero cost. The contracts that are proposed revolve around import and export coverage and can generally be classed as export participating forwards and import participating forwards.

In the case of an export participating forward, the bank guarantees its client a minimum exchange rate for a given amount of foreign currency, plus the possibility of a higher rate if the exchange rate appreciates. An example will make this clear.

Assume the following market conditions:

$$S(FF/\$)bid = 5.0000$$
$$F_{\frac{1}{4}}(FF/\$)bid = 5.0700$$

The bank offers to guarantee an exchange rate of 5.00 plus 50% of anything over 5.00. Thus, if the dollar is quoted at 4.80 on the maturity date, the company receives 5.00 francs per dollar. If the dollar goes to 5.50, the company will receive 5.25 francs per dollar – the five franc minimum rate plus 50% of the 0.50 francs above 5.00. Figure 8A.2.1 compares the pay-off profiles of the participating forward with a classic forward contract, a simple call, and no coverage at all.

If the exchange rate falls or appreciates slightly, forward coverage is the optimal strategy. If the exchange rate appreciates sharply, a simple option is the best hedging strategy, but the participating forward is better than the classic forward coverage. The export participating forward is a mixture of forward coverage and option coverage. Its premium will be lower than simple option coverage because the percentage of gains is only 50% and because the guaranteed exchange rate is lower than the forward rate. The guaranteed rate and the percentage of gains can be calculated so that the company has no premium to pay.

Import participating forwards are symmetrical to export participating forwards. In this case the bank guarantees a maximum exchange rate and the possibility of sharing the gains if the exchange rate falls below the guaranteed rate. Thus, it is a mixture of a forward contract and a simple call option. If it is to be zero premium, the guaranteed rate will be higher than the current forward rate to offset the cost of the call.

Hybrid contracts like these are relatively costly. They can be interesting to small and medium-sized companies, however, because they make it possible for them to take advantage of some of the opportunities offered by options without having to pay a premium and without having to actively manage and monitor them.

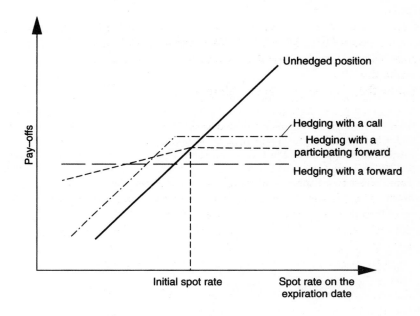

Figure 8A.2.1 An example of an import participating forward.

NOTES

1   The equivalent equation for the ask rates is:

$$F_{\frac{1}{4}}(\$/\text{Dm})\text{ask} = S(\$/\text{Dm})\text{ask}\frac{(1 + r_{\$,\text{ask}})}{(1 + r_{\text{Dm,bid}})}.$$

2   See: Cox, J., Ingersoll, Jr J. and Ross, S. (1981) The Relation between Forward Prices and Futures Prices, *Journal of Financial Economics*, **9**, 321–46.

3   See: Cornell B. and Reinganum, M. (1981) Forward and Futures Prices: Evidence from the Foreign Exchange Markets, *Journal of Finance*, **36**, 1035–45; Park, H.Y. and Chen, A.H. (1985) Difference between Futures and Forward Prices: A Further Investigation of Marking to Market Effects, *Journal of Futures Markets*, **5**, 77–88; Chang C.W. and Chang, J.S.K. Forward and Futures Prices: Evidence from the Foreign Exchange Markets, *Journal of Finance*, **45**.

4   Black, F. and Scholes, M. (1973) The Pricing of Options and Corporate Liabilities, *Journal of Political Economy*, **81** (May-June), 637–59.

5   Garman, M. and Kohlhagen, S. (1983) Foreign Currency Option Values, *Journal of International Money and Finance*, December, 231–7.

6   The equivalent formula for the price of a European put is:

$$P(t) = S(t)e^{-r(T-t)}(N(d_1) - 1) - Ee^{r_d(T-t)}(N(d_2) - 1).$$

7   For a detailed development of currency options pricing, see: Clark, E. Levasseur, M. and Rousseau, P. (1993) *International Finance*, Chapman & Hall, London, Chapter 11.

9 ADVANCED TECHNIQUES FOR MANAGING POLITICAL, ECONOMIC AND FINANCIAL RISK

In Chapters 7 and 8 we dealt with the management of political and currency risk. In this chapter we concentrate on managing exposure to country-specific economic and financial risk in the context of foreign direct investment. We start with the conventional techniques of net present value and go on to show how the required rate of return can be adjusted so that only the non-diversifiable, systematic risk will be priced. We then present the option approach to investment under uncertainty and how it modifies the net present value rule. Finally, we go beyond the mean-variance framework and consider political risk that is dependent on particular investment outcomes.

THE ORTHODOX THEORY OF INVESTMENT

Net present value

In Chapter 3 we pointed out that the orthodox theory of investment under uncertainty taught in most business schools and economics departments revolves around the net present value (NPV) rule. According to this rule, expected flows of income and expenditure are estimated for each period. These flows are then discounted at the appropriate discount rate. The NPV is found by subtracting the present value of the expenditure stream from the present value of the income stream. If the NPV is positive, the project is accepted. If it is negative, the project is rejected. If it is zero, we are indifferent.

Consider, for example, a project that involves an initial outlay of $2250. The income for year zero is $250. There is a 50% probability that in one year's time annual income will rise to $350 and remain there for ever. There is also a 50% probability that in one year's time annual income will fall to

$150 and remain there for ever. The expected annual income in one year's time is equal to:

$$(0.5 \times \$350) + (0.5 \times \$150) = \$250.$$

If we suppose that the appropriate discount rate is 10%, the NPV is equal to:

$$NPV = -\$2250 + \sum_{t=0}^{\infty} \$250(1.1)^{-t} = \$500$$

Where foreign direct investment is concerned, the two main questions for the NPV rule revolve around just how the expected cash flows should be estimated and what discount rate should be used for calculating present values.

Identifying the cash flows
In the international context, determining the cash flows to be incorporated in the capital budgeting process and estimating their expected values is more complicated than in the traditional domestic capital budgeting problem. First of all, a distinction must be made between the cash flows accruing to the project and the cash flows accruing to the parent company. The nature of cross-border investing is such that a substantial difference can exist between the two. Exchange controls, for example, can reduce the flows to the parent relative to the project, whereas fees and royalties can increase them. Judicious project evaluation requires that the analysis include all the pertinent incremental cash flows to the parent arising from the project.

Joint projects
The proposed project might have a direct effect on the company's existing operations. A company contemplating an investment in a country to which it is already exporting must consider whether or not export sales will be lost as a result of the investment. On the other hand, incremental sales from other units of the company might be generated if those units are suppliers of inputs to the project's production process. When determining the cash flows, lost exports should be deducted and incremental sales should be added.

The subject of incremental sales brings up the sensitive problem of transfer pricing. Market prices do not always exist for some of the intermediate products moving through a vertically integrated firm. The question then is how much to charge for them. Theoretically, the price should be equal to the firm's marginal cost of production. In practice, however, many intermediate goods moving between different divisions of the same firm are sold at monopolistic prices, thereby distorting the relative price system and the true incremental cash flows that should be generated by the project. Furthermore, transfer pricing is often used as a means of skirting foreign exchange controls and other types of government interference. For example, the parent company might charge excessively high prices for project inputs in order to get around limits on profit and principal repatriation. It can achieve the same effect by paying excessively low prices for the project's outputs.

Fees and royalties
Supervisory fees and royalties are a source of flows to the parent company. They should be included in the assessment of the project. As with intermediate inputs, fees and royalties are often used as a means of remitting funds to the parent.

Scale economies
Certain production processes feature important economies of scale. Thus, individual small projects should be charged for the incremental costs or diseconomies associated with decentralization.

Taxes and subsidies
Non-economic considerations such as taxes and subsidies can have important consequences for parent cash flows. Although tax laws and treaties vary from country to country and change over time, most countries acknowledge that dual taxation is unjust and give full credit for taxes paid in another country. However, for individual investments, even where tax treaties and special incentive programmes exist, tax consequences on cash flows should be carefully analysed. For example, withholding taxes on dividends remitted to the parent should be charged to the project.

Tax laws are notoriously complex and subject to the vagaries of individual interpretation. In fact, the complexity of calculating after-tax cash flows often makes it necessary to make simplifying assumptions. For example, assuming the least favourable tax scenario in the first stage of a project evaluation might be justified under the argument that if the project is acceptable under these conditions, it will certainly be acceptable under more favourable ones. While this is a good way to avoid bad investments, many good investments will also be eliminated. Later on in this chapter we will present an approach to investment decision-making under uncertainty that makes it possible to overcome this drawback.

Currency fluctuations
The preceding chapters have emphasized the importance of the exchange rate on base currency cash flows. Where direct investments are concerned, however, it is important to remember the relationships developed in Chapter 4. Currency fluctuations can affect the demand for a product as well as its price. However, because of varying time lags and demand elasticities, the prices of different products will react in different ways to currency fluctuations. If, for example, the project is producing for a clientele that gains as a result of the devaluation, cash flows to the project in host country currency might increase enough to more than offset the effects of the depreciation in the exchange rate and thereby increase parent company cash flows. On the other hand, the cost of inputs will also vary and could offset the gains. Parent cash flows could also be affected if project output varies as a result of the devaluation and changes the quantities of transferred inputs or the amount of royalties and fees that are due. Hence, besides the direct effect of a lower exchange ratio, devaluation scenarios should also include estimates of the consequences on the cash flows of the project itself.

Estimating the expected values
Once the various cash flows arising from the project have been identified, expected values for these cash flows must be estimated. This is a well-known problem in capital budgeting and there are no easy solutions. The accuracy of the estimations depends on the quality of the analysis. The process requires input from all sectors of the company, including sales, marketing, production, finance, etc. and usually involves the probabilization of different possible outcomes. Just how the probabilities are calculated depends on the sophistication of the budgeting process, and methods range from subjective 'gut feelings' to complex Monte Carlo simulations.

Where foreign direct investment is concerned, the process is complicated by the existence of political risk and the possibility of currency fluctuations. In Chapter 3 we showed how political risk could be integrated into the analysis by either including a probability of loss factor when estimating the cash flows or adding a risk premium to the discount factor when calculating the NPV. As we pointed out, however, there is some serious doubt about the theoretical justification for incorporating political risk in this way. First of all, a probability of loss factor applied to the overall expected cash flow implicitly assumes that the consequences of political risk affect all components of the overall cash flow in exactly the same way. This is a highly dubious proposition. Different types of flows are likely to be affected in different ways, depending on how the political risk manifests itself. Furthermore, if the cash flow analysis is done thoroughly, the consequences of political risk will be directly accounted for. Adding a probability of loss factor to account for political risk amounts to double-counting. Secondly, as we mentioned in Chapter 3, accounting for political risk in a premium added to the discount factor treats all political risk as non-diversifiable and, thus, does not distinguish between systematic risk, which, according to portfolio theory, should be priced, and unsystematic risk, which should not.

Estimating systematic economic risk

Without getting into the theoretical complications concerning optimal capital structure and the cost of capital, we can say that it is generally accepted that a project be discounted at the rate that reflects its systematic riskiness. In cross-border projects, systematic riskiness should include economic, financial, currency and political risk. One possibility is to use a multi-index model to account for the systematic risk of each risk source taken individually. The drawback to this method is that it is practically impossible to estimate the individual betas. New projects, by definition, have no historical data to regress on. Given the intricate relationships among the different risk sources, subjective estimation of the individual betas also looks like a dead end street. Another more promising method involves a three-step procedure using the CAPM and the international index developed in Chapter 5.

The method proceeds as follows. In step 1, the project's required rate of return is presented in terms of its systematic risk relative to the performance of the overall economy. This is information that the investor either already knows from experience or can estimate with little difficulty. In step 2, systematic country risk is estimated according to the procedures outlined in Chapter 5. In step 3, systematic project risk us combined with systematic country risk to determine the project's required rate of return.

Step 1

Start with the following definitions.

r_f = riskless rate of interest on the dollar
$\overline{R}_i$ = expected return on an unlevered project in dollars
$\overline{R}_c$ = country's expected return in dollars (see Chapter 5 for estimation procedure)
$\overline{R}_w$ = expected return on the world index
β_i = measures the systematic variation of the unlevered project's returns with respect to the performance of a national economy
β_c = measures the systematic variation of the performance of the national economy with respect to the performance of the world economy

The required rate of return on an unlevered project can be expressed in the CAPM as follows:

$$\overline{R}_i = r_f + \beta_i(\overline{R}_c - r_f) \tag{9.1}$$

where β_i measures the systematic variation of the unlevered project's returns with respect to the performance of a national economy. We use the unlevered rate of return in order to establish a common standard of comparison among the different projects that will be used in the estimation of beta. The assumption here is that similar projects will have similar reactions to macroeconomic performance in all countries. A company in the tool and dye industry, for example, should have a good idea of how cash flows from tool and dye projects react to macroeconomic performance, just as a car manufacturer or textile producer should for its products. Thus, past data from similar projects in other countries can be used to get an estimate of the project's systematic correlation with macroeconomic performance. From a practical standpoint, this assumption will be all the more robust if the project being considered is similar to others that have already been undertaken elsewhere in similar conditions. Least squares regressions and other more sophisticated statistical techniques can be used to get a precise estimate of the beta.

Step 2
Step 1 captures the systematic relationship between the project and the performance of a national economy. We know, however, that because of their dotation in human and natural resources, their institutional and social organization, their economic management, etc., individual national economies have their own particular risk characteristics that must be taken into consideration. Again, only systematic risk should be considered. We can capture the systematic relationship between an individual national economy and the overall world economy in the expression:

$$\overline{R}_c = r_f + \beta_c(\overline{R}_w - r_f) \tag{9.2}$$

In Chapter 5 we showed how to estimate individual country betas using $\overline{R}_c$, the country's ROI, and $\overline{R}_w$, the return on the international market index. It is important to remember that the resulting β_c captures the systematic, country-specific economic, currency and political risk. It does not, however, include the country's financial risk. This is because we use ROI, the return on total investment, rather than the return on investment financed by local residents. In this sense the resulting β_c is an 'unlevered' beta. The country's financial risk must be considered separately. We will show how this can be done later on.

Step 3
Total systematic economic and operating risk associated with the project is a combination of the systematic risk of the project relative to the country's economy and the systematic risk of the country's economy relative to the world economy. This can be found by substituting equation 9.2 into 9.1 and simplifying:

$$\overline{R}_i = r_f + \beta_i\beta_c(\overline{R}_w - r_f) \tag{9.3}$$

Thus, $\beta_i\beta_c$ measures the project's total systematic economic and operating risk.

An example: a retail investment project in India
In 1993, PHI Consultants was asked to estimate the economic and operating risk premium in US dollars for an investment project in India. After explaining the methodology outlined above to its client, a well-known retail manufacturer, PHI worked with them to determine the beta that would capture the systematic relationship between the proposed project and the performance of the Indian economy. This was done by looking at the performance of other similar investment projects that the company had undertaken in the past. It was found that 1.2 was an accurate estimate. Using the international market index and 20 years of historical data on the Indian economy, PHI then estimated that the Indian economy's beta was 1.5. The average return on the market index over the same period was 10% and the riskless rate at the time of the analysis was given as 6%. PHI thus had the following information:

$r_f = 6\%$
$\overline{R}_w = 10\%$
$\beta_i = 1.2$
$\beta_c = 1.5$

This information was applied to equation 9.3:

$$\overline{R}_i = 6\% + (1.2)(1.5)[10\% - 6\%] = 13.2\%$$

and the project's required rate of return necessary to compensate for systematic, country-specific economic, currency and political risk as well as project specific operating risk was calculated as equal to 13.2%. PHI was careful to point out to its client that besides the project-specific operating risk and the country-specific economic, currency and political risk, the proper discount rate for the project should also include the risk arising from the Indian economy's foreign debt.

Estimating systematic country financial risk

The relationship in equation 9.3 gives the project's required rate of return in terms of systematic economic risk relative to the world economy. Country financial risk is not included. Most countries, however, have outstanding foreign debt. Servicing this debt can jeopardize project flows to the parent company to the extent that debt payments eat up available foreign exchange. Consequently, country financial risk should be included in the project's required rate of return.

As with economic and operating risk, only systematic financial risk should be considered. The most obvious way to estimate systematic financial risk is with the CAPM. Extending the CAPM to debt instruments poses no serious theoretical problems. Furthermore, as we show in Appendix 9.1 at the end of this chapter, the relationship between the CAPM and the Black-Scholes options pricing model is such that the Black-Scholes formula can be used to estimate the risk premium associated with systematic financial risk. You will remember that this is exactly what we did in Chapter 6. Thus, the country financial risk premium estimated in Chapter 6 measures systematic risk and is appropriate for investment decision-making.

Estimating the appropriate discount rate

Without bankruptcy costs

The orthodox theory of project evaluation says that the appropriate discount rate must account for systematic financial risk as well as economic and operating risk. Remember that for purposes of comparison, we are considering an unlevered project. If, however, the country has outstanding foreign debt that can affect cash flows to the parent, this leverage must be considered in the project's cost of capital. Equation 9.3 measures systematic economic and operating risk. It gives the required rate of return on a project in a country with no outstanding foreign debt. We can get from equation 9.3 to r_s, the required rate of return when systematic financial risk is included, by using Modigliani-Miller proposition 2.[1] This expresses the required rate of return on levered equity as the required rate of return on unlevered equity plus a risk premium weighted by the debt/equity ratio:[2]

$$r_s = r_u + (r_u - r_b)\frac{B}{S} \tag{9.4}$$

where
r = weighted cost of capital
r_u = required rate of return on the project in a country with no foreign debt
r_s = required rate of return on the project in a country with outstanding foreign debt
r_b = component cost of foreign debt
S = market value of the portion of the country's economy owned by residents
B = market value of the country's outstanding foreign debt
$V = S + B$ = market value of the country's economy.

r_u corresponds to $\overline{R}_i$ in equation 9.3. r_b corresponds to the riskless rate plus the financial risk premium as calculated in Chapter 6. We recognize S as the value of the call option in Chapter 6 and B as the difference between V and S. We showed how to estimate V in Chapter 5. Thus, we have all the necessary information to estimate the appropriate required rate of return.

Example
Going back to the investment project in India, remember that the discount rate adjusted for systematic country specific economic, currency and political risk as well as project-specific operating risk was 13.2%. Suppose that at the same time India's cost of foreign borrowing was 9% and that the procedures outlined in Chapter 6 gave the total value of the Indian economy as $1000 with a resident equity value of $750. We would then have the following information:

$r_u = \overline{R}_i = 13.2\%$
$r_b = 9\%$
$V = 1000$
$B = 250$
$S = 750$.

To find r_s we use equation 9.4:

$$r_s = 13.2\% + (13.2\% - 9\%)\frac{250}{750}$$
$$r_s = 14.6\%$$

Thus, r_b would be the appropriate discount rate for the investment project in India completely financed with equity. This rate includes, however, a 1.4% financial risk premium caused by the country's foreign indebtedness.

Adjusted net present value

Adjusted net present value (APV) is an interesting offshoot of the orthodox NPV rule. Instead of one average discount rate applied to the overall net cash flows, APV breaks the cash flows down into their component parts and discounts each one at the appropriate risk adjusted discount rate. This makes it possible to analyse the interactions between investment and financing decisions. For cross-border projects, the APV approach is particularly useful since these projects often include complicated financial arrangements that would be difficult, if not impossible, to account for in a single discount rate. Three steps are involved:

1. discount the project's operating cash flows at the all equity required rate of return;
2. analyse the financing side effects of the project and discount them at the appropriate rate adjusted for the systematic risk they represent;
3. add the net present values of the operating cash flows and the financial side effects to obtain APV.

Consider, for example, a $10 million investment in Thailand lasting for five years financed with 50% equity and 50% debt. Normally, the cost of debt would be 12% for a project of this type in Thailand.[3] The World Bank, however, is willing to lend the $5 million at a subsidized rate of 10%. The project is expected to generate $3 million in operating cash flows before interest expenses every year for five years and the marginal tax rate is 40%. Thus, there are three cash flow streams to consider: the operating cash flows, the tax saving on interest payments, and the interest rate subsidy on the loan.

Suppose that the all equity discount rate for the project is 14.6%, as calculated in equation 9.4. The present value of the operating cash flows is then equal to:

$$\$3 \sum_{t=1}^{5}(1.146)^{-t} = \$10.152 \text{ million.}$$

Annual interest payments are equal to 10% × $5 million = $0.5 million and the tax saving is 40% × $0.5 million = $0.2 million. The tax saving is only as risky as the debt that generates it. In the absence of the interest rate subsidy, the debt would cost 12%, so 12% is the appropriate discount rate for calculating the present value of tax savings on interest payments:

$$(40\% \times \$0.5) \sum_{t=1}^{5}(1.12)^{-t} = \$0.721 \text{million.}$$

Without the interest rate subsidy from the World Bank, interest on the $5 million debt would be 12% × $5 million = 0.6 million and the subsidy is worth $0.6 million − $0.5 million = $0.1 million. As with the tax saving, the interest rate subsidy is only as risky as the debt that generates it, i.e. 12%. The present value is:

$$\$0.1 \sum_{t=1}^{5}(1.12)^{-t} = \$0.360 \text{ million.}$$

Thus:

$$APV = -\$10.000 + \$10.152 + \$0.721 + \$0.360 = \$1.233 \text{ million.}$$

With bankruptcy costs
It is conceivable that the debt/equity ratio becomes so large that it threatens the viability of the firm or, in the case that interests us, of the country. This situation engenders incremental costs associated with bankruptcy and reorganization. Where a country is concerned, bankruptcy costs include the

money, time, and effort spent negotiating with creditors and the international organizations such as the IMF and the World Bank. Reorganization can be even more costly since it implies political changes and social upheaval. Long before these difficulties come to pass, however, other costs, such as capital flight, reduced import credits, emigration, etc., will manifest themselves. At this point, Modigliani-Miller proposition 2 (equation 9.4) no longer holds and the costs of bankruptcy and reorganization begin to raise the average cost of capital and reduce the value of the firm or the country. The appropriate discount rate will then be equal to the riskless rate plus a premium for systematic economic and operating risk plus a premium for systematic financial risk:

$$r_s = r_f + \lambda_u + \lambda_b \tag{9.5}$$

where
λ_u = the premium for systematic economic and operating risk
λ_b = the premium for systemtic financial risk.

From equation 9.3, λ_u is equal to $\beta_i \beta_c (\overline{R}_w - r_f)$ and λ_b can be estimated in the Black-Scholes formula using the procedures outlined in Chapter 6.

Example
Suppose we have the following information:
$r_f = 6\%$
$\overline{R}_w = 10\%$
$\beta_i = 1.2$
$\beta_c = 1.5$
$r_b = 18\%$.

From equation 9.3 we get the economic and operating risk premium:

$$\lambda_u = (1.2)(1.5)[10\% - 6\%] = 7.2\%$$

and, subtracting the risk-free rate from the required rate of return on foreign debt, we have the financial risk premium:

$$\lambda_b = 18\% - 6\% = 12\%.$$

Thus, from equation 9.5, the appropriate discount rate (required rate of return) is:

$$r_s = 6\% + 7.2\% + 12\% = 25.2\%.$$

THE OPTION APPROACH TO INVESTMENT UNDER UNCERTAINTY

As useful as it is, the NPV rule has a weakness in that it is based on the unrealistic implicit assumptions that the investment is either a now or never proposition that will be unavailable in the future, or that it is reversible and that the expenditures can somehow be recovered in the event that things do not turn out as expected. Most investments do not meet these conditions. In fact, in practice, irreversibility and the possibility of delay are important characteristics of most investments. The option approach to investment under uncertainty complements the NPV rule by directly incorporating these characteristics into the decision-making process. An example will make this clear.[4]

Going back to the example at the beginning of the chapter, we had a project that involved an initial outlay of $2250. The income for year zero was $250 and there was a 50% probability that in one year's time annual income would rise to $350 and remain there for ever. There was also a 50% probability that in one year's time annual income would fall to $150 and remain there forever. The expected annual income in one year's time was equal to:

$$(0.5 \times \$350) + (0.5 \times \$150) = \$250,$$

and, supposing that the appropriate discount rate was 10%, the NPV was:

$$NPV = -\$2250 + \sum_{t=0}^{\infty} \$250(1.10^{-t} = \$500.$$

Since the NPV is positive, according to the NPV rule, the investment should be undertaken. Suppose, however, that we decide to wait and see what happens. If income falls to $150, the NPV will be equal to the project's net value at the beginning of period 1 discounted back one period (remember that there is no income or expenditure in year 0):

$$NPV = \left[-\$2250 + \sum_{t=0}^{\infty} \$150(1.1)^{-t} \right] \frac{1}{1.1} = [-\$600]\frac{1}{1.1} = -\$545.45.$$

Since the NPV is negative, the project will not be undertaken. If income rises to \$350, the NPV will be:

$$NPV = \left[-\$2250 + \sum_{t=0}^{\infty} \$350(1.1)^{-t} \right] \frac{1}{1.1} = [\$1600]\frac{1}{1.1} = \$1454.54$$

and the project will be undertaken. Thus, since no income or expenditure occurs if the project is not undertaken, the NPV of the project is equal to the NPV of the project if it is undertaken times the probability (50%) that it will effectively be undertaken:

$$NPV = 0.5[\$0.00] + 0.5[\$1454.54] = \$727.27.$$

By waiting a year, the value of the project is \$727.27, whereas it is only worth \$500 if we invest today. It is clearly preferable to wait and the value of the option to wait is the difference between the two NPVs:

$$\$727.27 - \$500 = \$227.27.$$

Simple applications: a shoe factory in Russia

Buster Black Inc., an American footwear company, is negotiating to build a shoe factory in Russia near Moscow. The initial investment will amount to \$12.5 million and will generate expected net cash flows of \$5.5 million per year for 10 years, at which point the personnel and local investors will inherit the plant. Given the ongoing economic, social and political turmoil in the country, Buster Black has estimated its required rate of return at a relatively high 15% but, even with this, the project still looks worthwhile with an NPV of \$15.1 million:

$$NPV = -\$12.5 + \sum_{t=1}^{10} \$5.5(1.15)^{-t} = \$15.1.$$

Buster Black is hesitating however. Although cash flow repatriation has been negotiated with the government and guaranteed, Buster Black's directors are worried that the national elections due in two years' time will bring in a new government that will throw out the agreement, making the project unprofitable. The company's political analyst is asked to assess the situation. His conclusion is that there is a 40% possibility that such a government will come to power in two years' time. In this case, cash flows will fall to zero. Thus, he estimates that expected cash flows will be:

$$(0.6 \times \$5.5) + (0.4 \times \$0) = \$3.3$$

and that NPV will fall to:

$$NPV = -\$12.5 + \sum_{t=1}^{10} \$3.3(1.15)^{-t} = \$4.06.$$

The NPV is still positive, however, and it seems that it should be undertaken. By waiting two years, however, the analyst points out that the NPV is:

$$NPV = 0.6 \left[-\$12.5 + \sum_{t=1}^{10} \$5.5(1.15)^{-t} \right] \frac{1}{(1.15)^2} = \$6.85.$$

This is $2.79 million higher than if the investment were undertaken immediately, so it would be better to wait.

With this in mind, the Marketing Department feels that waiting two years is feasible but in the mean time at least, some presence is absolutely necessary as a means of maintaining contacts and keeping a finger in the market. The Economics Department brings up the objection that the cost of the project could vary considerably in the course of two years. To this the analyst points out that $2.79 million, the value of the option to wait, could be spent to get the project underway and keep involved in the country. He also calculates how high the cost of the project would have to go to make waiting undesirable by equating the NPV of investing now and the NPV of waiting and leaving cost as the unknown:

$$\$4.06 = 0.6 \left[-Cost + \sum_{t=1}^{10} \$5.5(1.15)^{-t} \right] \frac{1}{(1.15)^2}$$

Cost = \$18.65.

The cost of the project would have to rise by almost 50%, to \$18.65 million, to make immediate investment preferable to waiting for the outcome of the elections in two years' time. The Economics Department calculates that cost could rise by a maximum of 10%, and could even fall by that much. Thus, it is decided that the investment will be put off for two years but that in the meantime \$2 million will be invested in office space and recruitment and training of management personnel.

More complicated applications: investments in natural resources

Assumptions and methodology

Projects involving exploitation of natural resources with an active spot market lend themselves particularly well tö the options approach to investment evaluation. Natural resources on the whole are homogeneous, and with an active spot market furnish a perfect **spanning** asset, that is, an asset whose risk tracks the risk of the investment. Brennan and Schwartz showed that the purchase and exploitation of a gold mine is equivalent to a series of options on the gold contained in the mine.[5] Paddock, Siegel and Smith used the same approach to evaluate investments in oilfields.[6] Many other applications have followed.[7]

In its simplest form, the procedure involves associating the income from the investment with the market price of the natural resource that is being produced. The life of the investment is divided into periods (years, quarters, months, etc.) and the decision to produce or not to produce at the beginning of each period is considered as an option that can be valued using traditional option pricing techniques. The information required to value the options is either directly observable or can be calculated from observable data. Using the notation from Chapter 6, it includes:

- V_0 = the market price of the spanning asset at time 0, which can be directly observed;
- t_i = the length of time (i = 0, 1, 2 ... n) between time 0 and the beginning of each future period (t_1, t_2, ... t_n);
- E_0 = the after tax production costs at time 0 which make it possible to estimate after tax production costs (E_1, E_2 ... E_n) for the following periods. It is assumed that production costs evolve slowly and predictably;
- σ = the standard deviation of the spanning asset's continuously

compounded annual rate of return, calculated from historical data on the market price;

- r_i = the continuously compounded riskless rate of interest corresponding to each period ($i = 0, 1, 2, ... n$), which can be observed directly or calculated from current data (see Chapter 6).

Thus, C_0^i, the value of the call option for period i, is given by the traditional Black-Scholes formula:

$$C_0^i = V_0 N(d_1) - E_i e^{-rt_i} N(d_2) \qquad (9.6)$$

where $N(d)$ is the value of the standardized normal cumulative distribution evaluated at d.

The project's NPV is equal to the sum of the option values less the amount of the investment:

$$NPV = -Cost + \sum_{i=0}^{n} C_0^i \qquad (9.7)$$

This procedure has several advantages over the traditional NPV approach. First of all, the well-known, tried and tested Black-Scholes option pricing formula can be used. Secondly, it overcomes the difficulty of forecasting long-term commodity prices, well known for their unpredictability. Third, since all discounting is done at the riskless rate, it eliminates the necessity of estimating the risk-adjusted discount factor. It does, however, make some unrealistic assumptions above and beyond those that we pointed out in Chapter 6. The central assumption is that the exploitation activity can be stopped or started at will with little or no cost. (In many countries, where exploitation of natural resources is concerned, this assumption may not be far from the truth, however.) It is also assumed that overhead and maintenance costs during shutdowns are negligible and that there is no middle ground between full production and full stop. Stocking is impossible as well and all output is sold at the going market price. In fact, all income and expenditure is realized at the beginning of the period, with deliveries taking place during the period.

In many situations, these assumptions will not be too far from the truth and, consequently, will not distort the analysis. When this is not the case, the analysis must be adapted to the specific situation. Using some sophisticated modelling techniques adopted from financial economics, we give an example of how this can be done in Appendix 9.2 at the end of the chapter.

Exploiting an oilfield: Petroleum Capital L.C. in South America

Consider the classic case of a South American government that has decided to concede the exploitation of a fully equipped oilfield and invites bids on an international tender for an initial period of 10 years. The installed capacity of the oilfield is 1 000 000 barrels per year.

Petroleum Capital L.C., a small oil company operating out of Dallas, Texas, was considering bidding on the project. To get an estimate of how much they could bid, they used the options approach and decided to reason on a yearly basis. They realized that more frequent evaluations based on a shorter time unit, the month or the quarter, for example, would give a more precise estimate, but they knew that the difference is relatively small. They also knew that more frequent evaluations would give the project a higher value. Since they wanted to avoid overbidding at all cost, the undervaluation resulting from the lower frequency of evaluation guaranteed them a safety margin.

They continued their estimate by making several assumptions.

1. The wells would either function at full capacity or not at all and the cost of turning them on and off as well as maintenance costs during shutdowns were null. In fact, the wells could operate at less than full capacity and the start-up/shut-down and maintenance costs were not zero but they were very low. After analysis, Petroleum Capital L.C. concluded that the gain from flexible output just about offset the costs and justified the assumption.

2. Production costs, including royalties and taxes, were equal to $12 per barrel and would remain constant over the life of the contract. They represent the exercise price, E, in the options pricing model.

3. The decision of whether or not to produce would be made at the beginning of each year. If the spot price of oil was higher than the after-tax cost of production, the decision to produce would be made. On that day, expenditure for the total year's production costs would be made and the total year's output would be sold at that day's spot price. If the spot price of oil was less than the cost of production, the field would be shut down for the year. Thus, income would either be equal to the difference between the spot price and and the cost of production or zero, whichever was larger.

4. The standard deviation of the percentage change in the spot price of oil would be constant and equal to the historical standard deviation, which was estimated as 0.25.

5. The riskless rate of interest for each option would be constant over the life of the option and equal to the current riskless rate. The current term

structure, estimated by a well-known investment bank, was given as follows:

Riskless rate on one-year a loan	8.00%
Riskless rate on a two-year loan	8.20%
Riskless rate on a three-year loan	8.35%
Riskless rate on a four-year loan	8.45%
Riskless rate on a 5 to 10-year loan	8.50%

At the time of the analysis, the current spot price of a barrel of crude oil was $15. All the information necessary for the estimation exercise can be summarized as follows:

$$V_0 = \$15$$
$$\sigma = 0.25$$
$$E_0 = E_1 = \ldots = E_{10} = \$12$$
$$t_i, (i = 0, 1, 2, \ldots, 10) = 1, 2, 3, 4, 5, 6, 7, 8, 9, 10$$
$$r_{f1} = 8.00\%$$
$$r_{f2} = 8.20\%$$
$$r_{f3} = 8.35\%$$
$$r_{f4} = 8.45\%$$
$$r_{f5\ldots10} = 8.50\%$$

Using equation 9.6, Petroleum Capital L.C. estimated the maximum price that they could bid for the oil concession by calculating the value of each option to produce one barrel of oil and multiplying by the number of barrels of output. This information is summarized in Table 9.1. This shows that the maximum they could bid was $75 464 190.

On the merits of the project itself, Jim Renfro, the Managing Director of Petroleum Capital L.C., had no problem with a bid in the $70 million range. He did, however, fear that once the contract was signed and the payment had been made, politics in the host country might disrupt his operations. The danger was not so much for the immediate future, but a populist, nationalistic, anti-American movement was starting to spread from some of the less populous regions of the country to the cities. He feared that if it

Table 9.1 Values of the option to produce and present values of expected cash flows for oilfield exploitation

1	2	3
Option value for year i	No. of barrels per year	PV of expected cash flow (column 1 × column 2)
$C_0^1 = \$4.09785$	1 000 000	$4 097 850
$C_0^2 = \$5.11485$	1 000 000	$5 114 850
$C_0^3 = \$6.00967$	1 000 000	$6 009 670
$C_0^4 = \$6.80599$	1 000 000	$6 805 990
$C_0^5 = \$7.51478$	1 000 000	$7 514 780
$C_0^6 = \$8.14213$	1 000 000	$8 142 130
$C_0^7 = \$8.71136$	1 000 000	$8 711 360
$C_0^8 = \$9.22965$	1 000 000	$9 229 650
$C_0^9 = \$9.70271$	1 000 000	$7 702 710
$C_0^{10} = \$10.13520$	1 000 000	$10 135 200
Total = $75.46419		Total = $75 464 190

gained too much force, operations such as his would be jeopardized. Consequently, he hired a consulting firm to estimate the probabilities for each year of the contract that some unforeseen political event would not upset his oilfield operations. The results of the analysis are summarized in Table 9.2.

Table 9.2 Probability of no disruptions due to unforeseen political events

Year	1	2	3	4	5	6	7	8	9	10
Prob.	0.95	0.95	0.93	0.90	0.90	0.85	0.85	0.80	0.75	0.75

Using the probabilities supplied by the consulting firm, Renfro then recalculated the price he was willing to pay for the oilfield concession by multiplying each year's expected cash flow by the corresponding probability, as shown in Table 9.3. He thus concluded that he could make a top bid of $64 million.[8]

Table 9.3 Expected cash flows adjusted for political risk

1	2	3
PV of expected cash flow	*Probability*	*PV of expected cash flow adjusted for political risk*
$4 097 850	0.95	$3 892 957.50
$5 114 850	0.95	$4 859 107.50
$6 009 670	0.93	$5 588 993.10
$6 805 990	0.90	$6 125 391.00
$7 514 780	0.90	$6 763 302.00
$8 142 130	0.85	$6 920 810.50
$8 711 360	0.85	$7 404 656.00
$9 229 650	0.80	$7 383 720.00
$9 702 710	0.75	$7 277 032.50
$10 135 200	0.75	$7 601 400.00
Total = $75 464 190		Total = $63 817 370.00

Concluding remarks on the option approach to investment

In this section we have outlined the principles behind the option approach to investment under uncertainty and shown some of its simplest applications to problems associated with foreign direct investment. In fact, insofar as the option approach itself is concerned, we have done little more than scratch the surface. There is a rich and growing literature on the subject, employing relatively complicated techniques, that has opened the science of investment decision-making to vast new horizons.[9] The techniques involved are generally beyond the scope of this book, although we have used some of them in the appendices at the end of several chapters. It is important to remember, however, that these new techniques are not substitutes for judicious, country-specific risk assessment in the decision-making process. If anything, they increase its importance, insofar as they make it possible to exploit country-specific risk analyses more effectively and creatively. This said, they do require more focus and precision than traditional country-specific risk analysis has been able to supply. It is no longer sufficient, for example, to signal the existence of a general political risk or the probability of an unfavourable outcome. The analyst must be able to distinguish between political risk that is diversifiable and that which is not. He must also be clear as to how unfavourable outcomes will affect the investment in question. Consequently, it is important for the analyst to understand the requirements of the option approach, as well as its strengths and weaknesses. It is also important to understand how the country-specific element can be integrated into the analysis. The background to this exercise was developed in Chapters 5 and 6.

BEYOND MEAN-VARIANCE

Political risk and the shortcomings of mean-variance analysis

The thrust of our analysis up to now has relied on the mean-variance criterion and the Markowitz paradigm. As useful and powerful as it is, however, this analytical framework does have some shortcomings. The main shortcoming is that it is not always consistent with expected utility maximization. In fact, it is certain to be consistent with expected utility maximization only in the cases of a quadratic utility function or normally distributed outcomes.

To see how the mean-variance criterion can differ from the criterion of expected utility maximization consider, for example, two investments with the following characteristics:

Investment 1			
Outcome	Probability	Mean	Variance
1	0.8	20.8	1468
100	0.2		

Investment 2			
Outcome	Probability	Mean	Variance
10	0.99	19.9	9703
1000	0.01		

In mean-variance space any rational individual would prefer investment 1 to investment 2 because investment 1 has the higher mean and the lower variance. Now consider an individual with a logarithmic utility function $u(R) = \ln(R)$. He will choose the investment that will give him the highest expected utility:

$$E[u(\tilde{R}_1)] = 0.8u(1) + 0.2u(100) = 0.8\ln + 0.2\ln100 = 0.4$$
$$E[u(\tilde{R}_2)] = 0.99u(10) + 0.01u(1000) = 0.99\ln(10) + 0.01\ln(1000) = 1.02$$

Investment 2 gives the higher expected utility and is preferred to investment 1 even though its variance is higher and its mean lower. In this case, mean-variance is not a good decision-making criterion.

The foregoing is important for political risk analysis because political risk often manifests itself in ways that make the assumption of normally distributed outcomes and the validity of the mean-variance criterion inappropriate. In fact, the precise nature of political risk often depends on the performance of a firm or the state of the economy. For example, some governments have a tendency to act mainly in bad times when the firm or the economy is in trouble. Others may act mainly in good times. Their actions can take many forms. They may reduce employers' social charges or increase them, grant investment tax credits or impose price controls, expand credit or cut red tape, raise or lower the minimum wage, etc. The options are virtually limitless. The point is that the action they take is generated by the outcome or the state of nature. In this sense, the risk associated with their actions is said to be dependent. When this is the case, the criterion of expected utility maximization rather than the mean-variance criterion should be used in the analysis.

Clark and Jokung have shown that where the dependent risk occurs is important when discriminating among investments.[10] In fact, as we show in Appendix 9.3, *ceteris paribus*, projects where the political risk is associated with good outcomes are preferred to projects where the political risk is associated with less favourable outcomes. Thus, besides estimating what the risks are, it is also important to establish in what conditions the different risks are likely to occur. With this in mind, the criterion of expected utility maximization can be combined with the mean variance criterion to discriminate between mutually exclusive investments. The procedure involves five steps.

1. Pinpoint the dependent political risk and then estimate the magnitude of its effects and the probabilities of its occurrence.
2. Assume that the dependent political risk is completely diversifiable and then estimate expected cash flows and the required rate of return according to the methods presented in the foregoing chapters.
3. Choose a well behaved utility function, that is, one that is strictly concave so that

$$u'(w) > 0, u''(w) < 0, u'''(w) > 0$$

where w represents wealth and the primes indicate the first, second, and third derivatives. Any function with these characteristics will do since we are not interested in precisely how much expected utility is involved in each investment but rather in the ranking by which investment has more expected utility. We find that the logarithmic function is the easiest to work with.
4. Apply the information generated in step 1 in the chosen utility function to calculate the estimated utilities of the individual investments.
5. Compare the expected utilities and choose the investment with the highest.

Pinpointing the political risk: an investment in the United States

In 1992, Little Snay, a British producer of wood furniture, had been considering building a factory in the southern United States for over three years. All the preliminary studies had been completed and, because of capacity constraints in its other factories, the decision could no longer be put off. It was decided to locate in the area of the lowlands of South Carolina at a cost of $100 million. The decision was based on three equiprobable scenarios drawn up by the Economics Department. Using traditional techniques, the required rate of return on the project had been estimated at 10%. Figure 9.1 shows the NPV for the three scenarios as well as the expected NPV, estimated at $600 million.

The only decision left to be made was the actual site of the factory. The choice had been narrowed down to two cities: Charleston, South Carolina and Savannah, Georgia. There was little to differentiate the two cities. Both had good port facilities, road and rail links to potential markets as well as a well-developed economic infrastructure and a supply of relatively cheap, well-qualified labour. The only significant difference was in city government. Joe Riley, Charleston's long-standing mayor, had a well-earned reputation for high-quality management and long-term planning. His strategy was to act in economic good times using tax breaks and subsidies to attract companies and property taxes and targeted assessments to fund development projects and improve city services. This smoothed the ride through the

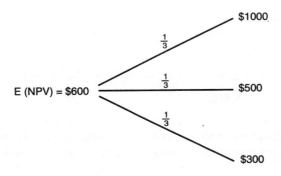

Figure 9.1 The project's NPV under different scenarios and the expected NPV.

bad times and made it possible to avoid costly or unpopular emergency measures. Savannah, on the other hand, had a history of not acting until the last minute and under duress. When the decisions were finally undertaken, they were generally sound, however, which is why Little Snay was seriously considering Savannah as the home for its factory. The Little Snay personnel who had visited both cities were indifferent between Savannah and Charleston as a place to live.

When Little Snay's Economics Department was asked to assess the effects of local government on the investment project, it came to the conclusion that the effects would basically be the same for both cities. For Charleston there was a 50–50 probability of plus or minus $100 million on the rosy scenario, while for Savannah there was a 50–50 probability of plus or minus $100 million on the rainy scenario. Thus, there was still nothing to separate the two cities. The project's expected NPV and standard deviation was the same for both. This information is summarized in Figure 9.2.

Finally, following the advice of an external consultant, the Economics Department decided to class the investments on the basis of expected utility using the logarithmic function with the following result.

Charleston

$$Eu(NPV_c) = \frac{1}{6}\ln(\$1100) + \frac{1}{6}\ln(\$900) + \frac{1}{3}\ln(\$500) + \frac{1}{3}\ln(\$300)$$
$$= 6.273.$$

Savannah

$$Eu(NPV_s) = \frac{1}{3}\ln(\$1000) + \frac{1}{3}\ln(\$500) + \frac{1}{6}\ln(\$400) + \frac{1}{6}\ln(\$200)$$
$$= 6.256.$$

On the criteria of expected utility, Charleston was clearly superior to Savannah and, consequently, the decision was made to build the factory in Charleston.

Charleston :

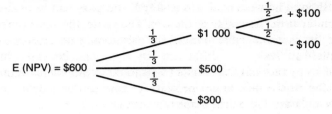

$$\sigma^2 = \frac{1}{6}\ (1\ 100 - 600)^2 + \frac{1}{6}\ (900 - 600)^2 + \frac{1}{3}\ (500 - 600)^2 + \frac{1}{3}\ (300 - 600)^2 = 90\ 000$$

$$\sigma = \sqrt{90\ 000} = 300$$

Savannah :

E (NPV) = $600 —— $\frac{1}{3}$ —— $1 000

—— $\frac{1}{3}$ —— $500

—— $\frac{1}{3}$ —— $300 —— $\frac{1}{2}$ —— + $100

—— $\frac{1}{2}$ —— - $100

$$\sigma^2 = \frac{1}{3}\ (1\ 000 - 600)^2 + \frac{1}{3}\ (500 - 600)^2 + \frac{1}{6}\ (400 - 600)^2 + \frac{1}{6}\ (200 - 600)^2 = 90\ 000$$

$$\sigma = \sqrt{90\ 000} = 300$$

Figure 9.2 The project's expected NPV and standard deviation – Charleston and Savannah.

APPENDIX 9.1 THE RELATION BETWEEN THE CAPM AND THE BLACK-SCHOLES OPTION PRICING FORMULA

In Chapter 6 we showed how the equity in a levered company can be valued as a call option on the firm's assets. If, at the debt's due date, the value of the firm's assets is higher than the the amount of the debt to be paid, the debt is paid and shareholders keep the difference. In the opposite case, the shareholders walk away and leave the firm's assets to the debtholders. In this scenario, where the firm issues only one class of zero coupon debt, the Black-Scholes formula gives the firm's equity value as:

$$C_0 = V_0 N(d_1) - E_e^{-r_f t} N(d_2) \qquad (9A.1.1)$$

where:
C_0 = the present value of the firm's equity;
V_0 is the present value of the firm's assets;
E is the debt's face value;
$N(d)$ is the value of the standardized normal cumulative distribution evaluated at d;
r_f = the continuously compounded riskless rate of interest;
t = the debt's time to maturity.

d_1 and d_2 are given by:

$$d_1 = \frac{\ln\left(\frac{V_0}{E}\right) + \left(r_f + \frac{\sigma^2}{2}\right)t}{\sigma\sqrt{t}} \qquad (9A.1.2)$$

$$d_2 = \frac{\ln\left(\frac{V_0}{E}\right) + \left(r_f - \frac{\sigma^2}{2}\right)t}{\sigma\sqrt{t}} \qquad (9A.1.3)$$

where:
σ the standard deviation of the continuously compounded annual rate of return on the firm's assets.

In note 5 of Chapter 6 we showed that the market value of the bond could be calculated directly by remembering that B, the market value of the bonds, is equal to $V_0 - C_0$. Substituting this into equation 9A.1.1 gives the value of the bond:

$$B_0 = V_0 N(-d_1) + E e^{-r_f t} N(d_2) \qquad (9A.1.4)$$

Finally, so that the assumptions of the Black-Scholes formula and the CAPM are consistent, we can express the required rate of return on risky bonds in the continuous time version of the CAPM derived by Merton (1973):[11]

$$\overline{R}_b = r_f + \beta_b(\overline{R}_m - r_f) \qquad (9A.1.5)$$

where:

$\overline{R}_b$ = required rate of return on a risky bond;

$\overline{R}_m$ = expected return on the market portfolio;

$\beta_b = \frac{Cov(R_b, R_m)}{Var(R_m)}$;

$\overline{R}_b - r_f$ = the financial risk premium expressed in the CAPM.

In order to link the Black-Scholes formula, equation 9A.1.4, to the CAPM, equation 9A.1.5, we can use Ito's lemma to write:[12]

$$dB = \frac{\partial B}{\partial V}dV + \frac{\partial B}{\partial t} + \frac{1}{2}\frac{\partial^2 B}{\partial V^2}\sigma^2 V^2 dt. \qquad (9A.1.6)$$

Taking the limit of 9A.1.6 as dt goes to zero and dividing by B, gives:

$$\lim_{dt \to 0} \frac{dB}{B} = \frac{\partial B}{\partial V}\frac{dV}{B} = \frac{\partial B}{\partial V}\frac{dV}{V}\frac{V}{B}. \qquad (9A.1.7)$$

$\frac{dB}{B}$ is the bond's rate of return, R_b, and dV/V is the rate of return on the firm's assets, R_v. Therefore:

$$R_b = \frac{\partial B}{\partial V}\frac{V}{B}R_v. \qquad (9A.1.8)$$

Using equation 9A.1.8 and the definition of Beta, we can write the instantaneous covariance as:

$$\beta_b = \frac{\partial B}{\partial V}\frac{V}{B}\beta_v \qquad (9A.1.9)$$

Taking the first partial derivative of 9A.1.4 with respect to V gives:

$$\frac{\partial B}{\partial V} = N(-d_1) \tag{9A.1.10}$$

so that 9A.1.9 becomes:

$$\beta_b = N(-d_1)\frac{V}{B}\beta_v. \tag{9A.1.11}$$

Substituting 9A.1.11 into 9A.1.5 gives:

$$\overline{R}_b = r_f + \beta_v N(-d_1)\frac{V}{B}(\overline{R}_m - r_f) \tag{9A.1.12}$$

From the CAPM, we know that $\overline{R}_v - r_f = \beta_v(\overline{R}_m - r_f)$. Substituting this into 9A.1.12 and rearranging gives the risk premium in terms of the options pricing formula:

$$\overline{R}_b - r_f = N(-d_1)\frac{V}{B}(\overline{R}_v - r_f). \tag{9A.1.13}$$

APPENDIX 9.2 VALUING A DEVELOPED OIL RESERVE

Many governments lease offshore tracts of land for oil exploration and development. To determine bids for these leases that can involve hundreds of millions of dollars, companies perform valuations. Because of the sums involved, it is important that the valuations be done as accurately as possible. A bid that is too low means that the company will lose out on the lease, whereas a bid that is too high means that the company will lose money.

The valuation and exploitation of an offshore oil tract can be broken down into three stages: the exploration stage, the development stage and the extraction stage. The decision to proceed from the exploration stage to the development stage depends on how much oil is present and how much it would cost to extract it. If the results of the exploration stage are unfavourable, the project will be dropped. If they are favourable, the company may proceed to the development stage. Since the development stage requires a sizeable capital investment in platforms, wells and the like, the question of when to make the investment is critical. Hence, it is at this stage that the option of whether or not to invest is the most pertinent and has the most value. Once the investment has been made and the reserve has been developed, extraction almost always proceeds at a relatively regular rate.

The value of an undeveloped reserve depends on the value of a developed reserve, which, in turn, depends on the price of oil. The relationship can be compared to an American call option on a dividend-paying stock. In the case of an undeveloped reserve, the call option is whether or not to develop the reserve. The underlying asset is the value of a developed reserve and the dividend is the after-tax, after-depletion profit to be made from extracting and selling the oil once the reserve has been developed. The exercise price is the development cost and the expiration date is the relinquishment requirement that limits the time that the company can hold the tract before developing it. Thus, deciding whether and when to develop the reserve depends on the value of the developed reserve.

The value of a developed oil reserve to the owner is composed of two components, the flow of profits from production and the capital gain on the remaining oil.[13] Let:

G_t = the number of barrels in the reserve;
V_t = the per barrel value of the developed reserve;
R_t = the instantaneous return to the owner of the reserve;
ω = the fraction of oil produced each year;

π_t = the after-tax profit from producing and selling a barrel of oil.

It is assumed that the per barrel value of the developed reserve follows the price of oil on the spot market.

Production from a developed reserve can be expressed as an exponential decline where a fraction of the oil, ω, is produced each year:

$$dG_t = -\omega G_t dt \qquad (9A.2.1)$$

With this in mind, the return on the reserve can be written as:

$$R_t dt = \omega G_t \pi_t dt + d(G_t V_t) = \omega G_t \pi_t dt + G_t dV_t - \omega V_t G_t dt \qquad (9A.2.2)$$

The rate of return on the developed reserve is equal to $\frac{R_t dt}{G_t V_t}$. Assuming that the rate of return on the developed reserve follows a Brownian motion, we can write:

$$\frac{R_t dt}{G_t V_t} = \mu_v dt + \sigma_v dz \qquad (9A.2.3)$$

where μ_v is the risk-adjusted expected rate of return required by a competitive capital market. Let:

$$\delta_t = \frac{\omega(\pi_t - V_t)}{V_t}$$

represent the payout rate (profit from extracting and selling the oil less the cost of depletion) from a unit of producing developed reserve. Combining equations 9A.2.2 and 9A.2.3 gives the dynamics for the value of a barrel of developed reserve:

$$dV = (\mu_v - \delta_t)V dt + \sigma_v V dz \qquad (9A.2.4)$$

Determining the value of the undeveloped reserve involves using equation 9A.2.4 and Ito's lemma to get a partial differential equation, establishing the boundary conditions and then solving the partial differential equation subject to the boundary conditions.

APPENDIX 9.3 INVESTMENT CHOICE WITH DEPENDENT POLITICAL RISK

Consider a company with initial wealth, w_0, considering two investments, both with outcomes x_1, x_2, x_3 where $x_1 > x_2 > x_3$ and $\Pr(x_1) = \Pr(x_2) = \Pr(x_3) = \frac{1}{3}$. Investment 1 has an equiprobable additive political risk, ε, associated with outcome 1 while investment 2 has the same equiprobable additive political risk associated with outcome 2. Figure 9A.3.1. shows the firm's position depending on which investment it makes.

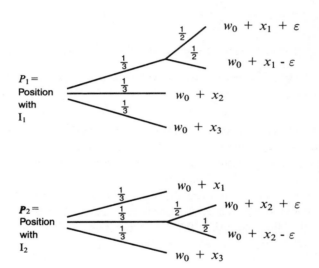

Figure 9A.3.1 Investment choice.

Assume a strictly concave utility function, $u(w)$, where $u'(w) > 0, u''(w) < 0, u'''(w) > 0$ and the primes denote first, second, and third derivatives. $u'(w) > 0$ implies that investors prefer more to less. $u''(w) < 0$ implies that investors are risk averse and $u'''(w) > 0$ implies that the risk aversion decreases as wealth increases. Then in mean variance space, the two investments are equivalent:

$$E(P_1) = E(P_2) = w_0 + E(x) \tag{9A.3.1}$$

$$\sigma_{P_1} = \sigma_{P_2} = \sigma_x + \frac{1}{3}\varepsilon^2 \tag{9A.3.2}$$

Taking the expected utility, however, shows that the expected utility of P_1 is greater than the expected utility of P_2:

$$Eu(P_1) - Eu(P_2) =$$

$$\left[\frac{1}{6}u(w_0 + x_1 + \varepsilon) + \frac{1}{6}u(w_0 + x_1 - \varepsilon) + \frac{1}{3}u(w_0 + x_2) + \frac{1}{3}u(w_0 + x_3) \right]$$

$$- \left[\frac{1}{3}u(w_0 + x_1) + \frac{1}{6}u(w_0 + x_2 + \varepsilon) + \frac{1}{6}u(w_0 + x_2 - \varepsilon) + \frac{1}{3}u(w_0 + x_3) \right]$$

$$= \frac{1}{6}(\{[u(w_0 + x_1 + \varepsilon) - u(w_0 + x_1)] - [u(w_0 + x_1) - u(w_0 + x_1 - \varepsilon)]\}$$

$$- \{[u(w_0 + x_2 + \varepsilon) - u(w_0 + x_2)] - [u(w_0 + x_2) - u(w_0 + x_2 - \varepsilon)]\})$$

$$\tag{9A.3.3}$$

The four terms in parentheses represent marginal utility and are positive because the utility function is well behaved and $u' > 0$. The two terms in braces are negative because the differences between the two parentheses in each brace represent the differences between the successive slopes of the utility function. The slopes are decreasing because $u'' < 0$. The difference between the two terms in braces is positive because marginal utility is convex and $u''' > 0$. Thus, equation 9A.3.3 is positive, which signifies that the expected utility of P_1 is greater than the expected utility of P_2:

$$Eu(P_1) > Eu(P_2).$$

NOTES

[1] See Modigliani, F. and Miller, M.H. (1963) Corporate income taxes and the cost of capital: A correction, *American Economic Review*, June, 433–43.

[2] The debt equity ratio is just another way of expressing the debt total assets ratio used in the options pricing formula:

$$\frac{B}{S} = \frac{\frac{B}{V}}{1 - \frac{B}{V}} ; \frac{B}{V} = \frac{\frac{B}{S}}{1 + \frac{B}{S}}$$

[3] The CAPM can be used to estimate this rate. It will be equal to the cost of debt reflecting the country's systematic financial risk plus a premium for the project debt's systematic risk. As explained above, the cost of debt reflecting the country's systematic risk can be estimated through option pricing techniques. The risk premium for the project debt's systematic risk can also be estimated using the same methodology as for the project's systematic operating and economic risk. First, the required rate of return on debt is presented in terms of its systematic risk relative to the performance of the overall economy:

$$\overline{R}_{ib} = r_f + \beta_{ib}\left(\overline{R}_c - r_f\right)$$

where
$\overline{R}_{ib}$ represents the required rate of return on the projects debt and β_{ib} represents the measure of the debt's systematic risk relative to the economy's performance.

Second, systematic risk on the project's debt is combined with systematic country risk:

$$\overline{R}_{ib} = r_f + \beta_{ib}\beta_c(\overline{R}_w - r_f)$$

Thus, $\beta_{ib}\beta_c(\overline{R}_w - r_f)$ represents the risk premium for the debt's systematic risk.

[4] Most of this section follows, Dixit, A.K. and Pindyck, R.S. (1994) *Investment Under Uncertainty*, Princeton University Press, Princeton, N.J.

[5] Brennan, M. and Eduardo Schwartz, E. (1985) Evaluating Natural

Resource Investments, *Journal of Business,* **58** (January), 135–57.

[6] Paddock, J. Siegel, D. and Smith, J. (1988) Option Valuation of Claims on Real Assets: The Case of Offshore Petroleum Leases, *Quarterly Journal of Economics,* **103** (August), 479–508.

[7] See, for example, Morck, R. Schwartz, E. and Strangeland, D. (1989) The Valuation of Forestry Resources under Stochastic Prices and Inventories, *Journal of Financial and Quantitative Analysis,* **24** (December), 473–87; Gibson, R. and Schwartz, E. (1990) Stochastic Convenience Yield and the Pricing of Oil Contingent Claims, *Journal of Finance,* **45** (July), 959–76.

[8] The project's systematic operating risk was effectively priced in the Black-Scholes formula (see Appendix 9.1). The country-specific risk, however, was not. Given the nature of an oilfield exploitation concession where costs are generally determined by international prices or fixed by contract and output is sold abroad for dollars, there is little in the way of country specific economic, financial or currency risk. Country-specific political risk is another question, however, and Renfro, acting as he did, was treating the political risk as totally non-diversifiable.

[9] In their excellent book, *Investment Under Uncertainty,* ((1994) Princeton University Press, Princeton), Avinash K. Dixit and Robert S. Pindyck give a clear and thorough presentation of the approach and its applications, as well as an exhaustive bibliography.

[10] Clark, E. and Jokung, O. (1994) Wealth, Prudence, and Political Risk: A Theory of Cross Border Capital Flows, Association Française de Finance International Conference, Tunis.

[11] Merton, R.C. (1973) An Intertemporal Capital Asset Pricing Model, *Econometrica,* September, 867–87.

[12] See Hsia, C.C. (1981) Coherence of the Modern Theories of Finance, *Financial Review,* Winter, 27–42.

[13] This example follows Dixit, A. and Pindyck, R. (1994), *op. cit.* n. 9 above Paddock, J., Siegel, D. and Smith, J. (1988) *op. cit* n. 6 above.

BIBLIOGRAPHY

BOOKS

Antl, B. (ed.) (1986) *Swap Finance*, Euromoney Publications, London.

Brealey, R.A. and Myers, S.C. (1988) *Principles of Corporate Finance*, McGraw-Hill Book Co., Singapore.

Brewer, T. (1995) *Political Risk in International Business: New Directions for Research, Management, and Public Policy*, Praeger, New York.

Brigham, E.F. and Weston, J.F. (1981) *Managerial Finance*, The Dryden Press, Hinsdale, Ill.

Clark, E. (1991) *Cross Border Investment Risk: Applications of Modern Portfolio Theory*, Euromoney Publications, London.

Clark, E., Levasseur, M. and Rousseau, P. (1993) *International Finance*, Chapman & Hall, London.

Cobbaut, R. (1987) *Théorie Financière*, Economica, Paris.

Copeland, T.E. and Weston, J.F. (1988) *Financial Theory and Corporate Policy*, Addison-Wesley Publishing Company, Reading, Mass., pp. 17–76.

Cox, J.C. and Rubenstein, M. (1985) *Options Markets*, Prentice-Hall, Englewood Cliffs, N.J.

Diaz Alejandro, C.F. (1970) *Essays on the Economic History of the Argentine Republic*, Yale University Press, New Haven and London.

Dixit, A.K and Pindyck, R.S. (1994) *Investment Under Uncertainty*, Princeton University Press.

Earl, P. and Fisher, III, F.G. (1986) *International Mergers and Acquisitions*, Euromoney Publications, London.

Elton, E.J. and Gruber, M.J. (1984) *Modern Portfolio Theory and Investment Analysis*, 2nd edn, John Wiley & Sons, New York.

Ergueta, A.J. and Shrieve, R. (1982) Assessing the debt servicing capacity of Peru, in *International Finance: Text and Cases*, (eds Feiger, G. and Jacquillat, B.) Allyn and Bacon, Boston.

Feiger, G. and Jacquillat, B. (1982) *International Finance: Text and Cases*,

Allyn and Bacon, Boston.

Fisher, I. (1930) *The Theory of Interest*, Macmillan, New York.

Friedman, M. (ed.) (1956) *Studies in the Quantity Theory of Money*, The University of Chicago Press.

Hayek, F. (1933) *Monetary Theory and the Trade Cycle*, trans. Kaldor, N. and Croome, H.M. Jonathan Cape, London.

Hayek, F. (1941) *The Pure Theory of Capital*, Routledge and Kegan Paul, London.

Hayek, F. (1975) *Prix et Production*, trans. Tradecom, Calmann-Levy, Vienna.

Hicks, J. (1950) *A Contribution to the Theory of the Trade Cycle*, Clarendon Press, Oxford.

Hicks, J. (1987) *Capital and Time: A Neo-Austrian Theory*, Clarendon Press, Oxford.

International Monetary Fund, *International Financial Statistics*, published monthly.

International Monetary Fund, (1977) *Balance of Payments Manual*, 4th ed. Washington, DC.

International Monetary Fund, (1977) *The Monetary Approach to the Balance of Payments*, IMF, Washington DC.

Klein, J. and Marois, B. (1993) *Gestion et Stratégie Financière Internationale*, 2nd edn, Dunod, Paris.

Levi, M.D. (1990) *International Finance*, McGraw-Hill, New York.

Little, I. and Mirrlees, J. (1969) Manuel d'analyse des projets industriels dans les pays en voie de développement, in *L'analyse Coûts-avantages du Point de Vue de la Collectivité*, Vol. 2, OECD, Paris.

Markowitz, H. (1959) *Portfolio Selection: Efficient Diversification of Investments*, John Wiley & Sons, New York.

Marois, B. (1990) *Le Risque Pays*, Presses Universitaires de France, Collection 'Que Sais-Je', Paris.

Merton, R.C. (1990) *Continuous Time Finance*, Basil Blackwell Cambridge, Mass.

Nagy, P. (1984) *Country Risk*, Euromoney Publications, London.

Polk, J. *et al.*, *U.S. Production Abroad and the Balance of Payments*, National Industrial Conference Board, New York.

Robock, S. and Simmonds, K. (1973) *International Business and Multinational Enterprise*, R. Irwin, Homewood, N.J.

Roddock, D. (1986) *Assessing Corporate Political Risk*, Rowman and Littlefield Publishers, Totowa, N.Y.

Rogriguez, R.M. and Carter, E.E. (1984) *International Financial Management*, 3rd edn, Prentice-Hall, Englewood Cliffs, N.J.

Root, F. (1973) Analysing Political Risks in International Business, in Multinational Enterprise in Transition, (eds Kapoor and Grub), Darwin Press, Princeton.

Root, F. (1990) *International Trade and Investments*, 6th edn, South-Western Publishing Co., Cincinnati, Ohio.

Rousseau, P. (1990) *Théorie Financière et Décision d'Investissement*, Economica, Paris.

Shapiro, A.C. (1989) *Multinational Financial Management*, 3rd edn, Allyn and Bacon, Boston, Mass.

Sharpe, W.F. (1985) *Investments*, Prentice-Hall, Englewood Cliffs, N.J.

Solberg, R. (1992) *Country Risk Analysis*, Routledge, London and New York.

Solnik, B. (1988) *International Investments*, Addison-Wesley Publishing Co. Reading, Mass.

Tapley, M. (ed) (1986) *International Portfolio Management*, Euromoney Publications, London.

Triffin, R. (1960) *Gold and the Dollar Crisis*, Yale University Press., New Haven.

UNIDO, (1973) *Directives pour l'Evaluation des Projets*, (United Nations, New York).

United Nations (1968) *A System of National Accounts, Studies in Methods*, Series no. 2, Rev. 3, UN, New York.

Vernon, R. and Wells, L.T. (1976) *Manager in the International Economy*, 4th edn, Prentice Hall, Englewood Cliffs, N.J.

The World Bank, *World Debt Tables 1989–1900, vol. 2*, The World Bank, Washington DC pp. xii–xvi.

Zinc, D.W. (1973) *The Political Risks for Multinational Enterprise in Developing Countries*, Praeger., New York.

ARTICLES

Abuaf, N. and Jorion, P. (1990) Purchasing power parity in the long run. *Journal of Finance,* **45**, March, 157–74.

Adler, M. and Dumas, B. (1983) International portfolio choice and corporation finance: a synthesis. *Journal of Finance,* **38**, June, 925–84.

Agmon, T. and Lessard, D. R. (1977) Investor recognition of corporate international diversification. *Journal of Finance,* **32**, September, 1049–56.

Alesina, A. and Tabellini, G. (1989) External debt, capital flight and political risk. *Journal of International Economics*, **27**, 199–220.

Alexander, S.S. (1952) Effects of a devaluation on a trade balance. *Staff*

Papers, **II**: (2), April, 263–78.

Aliber, R. (1973) The interest rate parity theorem: a reinterpretation. *Journal of Political Economy,* **81,** 1451–59.

Aliber, R.A. and Stickney, C. P. (1975) Accounting measures of foreign exchange exposure: the long and the short of it. *The Accounting Review,* January, 44–57.

Bahamani Oskooee, M. and Das, S.P. (1985) Transactions costs and the interest parity theorem. *Journal of Political Economy,* **93,** August, 793–99.

Baldwin, R. and Krugman, P. (1987) The persistence of the U.S. trade deficit. *Brookings Papers on Economic Activity,* no.1, 1–43

Bank for International Settlements, (1991) *Evolution de l'Activité Bancaire et Financière Internationale,* November.

Barnett, W. A. (1983) New indices of money supply and the flexible Laurent demand system. *Journal of Business and Economic Statistics,* **1,** January, 7–23.

Barro, R. and Sala i Martin, X. World Real Interest Rates, *NBER Working Paper 3317.*

Bates, P. S. and Saini, K. G. (1984) A survey of the quantitative approaches to country risk analysis. *Journal of Banking and Finance,* **8,** 341–56.

Belongia, M. T. and Chalfant, J. A. (1989) The changing empirical definition of money: some estimates from a model for money substitutes. *Journal of Political Economy,* **97,** (2), 387–97.

Bennett, P. (1984) Applying portfolio theory to global bank lending. *Journal of Banking and Finance,* **8,** 153–169.

Black, F. and Cox, J. (1976) Valuing corporate securities: some effects of bond indenture provisions. *Journal of Finance,* **31,** May, 351–68.

Black, F. and Scholes, M. (1973) The pricing of options and corporate liabilities. *Journal of Political Economy,* **81,** June, 637–59.

Brennan, M. and Schwartz, E. (1985) Evaluating natural resource investments. *Journal of Business,* **58,** January, 135–57.

Brewer, T. and Rivoli, P. (1990) Politics and perceived country creditworthiness in international banking. *Journal of Money, Credit and Banking,* **22** (3), 357–69.

Callier, P. (1981) One way arbitrage, foreign exchange, and securities markets: a note. *Journal of Finance,* **36,** December, 1177–86.

Carelton, W.T. and Cooper, I.A. (1976) Estimation and uses of the term structure of interest rates. *Journal of Finance,* **31,** September, 1067–83.

Cassel, G. (1916) The present situation in the foreign exchanges. *Economic Journal,* 62–5.

Cassel, G. (1918) Abnormal deviations in international exchanges. *Economic Journal,* 413–15.

Chang, C.W. and Chang, J.S.K. (1990) Forward and futures prices: evidence from the foreign exchange markets. *Journal of Finance*, **45**.

Clark, E. (1987) Country risk analysis in globalized financial markets. *The Business Economist*, **19** (1), Winter, 40–6.

Clark, E. (1987) L'analyse du risque-pays des années 70 à la période actuelle. *Revue Banque*, no. 477, November, 1006–10.

Clark, E. (1988) An alternative ranking. *Euromoney*,.September, 234.

Clark, E. (1991) Briefing. *Euromoney*, February, 73–76.

Clark, E. (1995) A general international market index. *International Journal of Finance*, **3**, No. 7, 1288–1312.

Clark, E. and Jokung, O. (1976) Wealth, prudence, and political risk: a theory of cross border capital flows. Association Française de Finance International Conference, Tunis, Tunisia.

Clinton, K. (1988) Transactions costs and covered interest arbitrage: theory and evidence. *Journal of Political Economy*, **96**, April, 358–70.

Cohen, D. (1993) A valuation formula for LDC debt. *Journal of International Economics*, **34**, 167–80.

Cornell, B. and Reinganum, M. (1981) Forward and futures prices: evidence from the foreign exchange markets. *Journal of Finance*, **36**, 1035–45.

Cosset, J.C. and Roy, J. (1991) The determinants of country risk rankings. *Journal of International Business Studies*, **22** (1), 135–42.

Cox, J. Ingersoll, J. Jr. and Ross, S. (1981) The relation between forward prices and futures prices. *Journal of Financial Economics*, **9**, 321–46.

Cox, J.C. and Ross, S.A. (1976) The valuation of options for alternative stochastic processes. *Journal of Financial Economics*, **3**, January–March, 145–66.

Cumby, R. and Obstfeld, M. (1981) A note on exchange rate expectations and nominal interest differentials: a test of the Fisher hypothesis. *Journal of Finance*, **36**, 697–703.

Deardorff, A.V. (1979) One way arbitrage and its implications for the foreign exchange markets. *Journal of Political Economy*, **87**, April, 351–64.

Deppler, M. C. and Ripley, D. (1978) The world trade model: merchandise trade flows. **25**, *Staff Papers*, IMF March, 147–206.

Dornbusch, R. (1976) Expectations and exchange rate dynamics. *Journal of Political Economy*, **84**, December.

Dornbusch, R. and Krugman, P. (1976) Flexible exchange rates in the short term. *Brookings Papers on Economic Activity*, no. 3, 537–75.

Eaton, J. Gersovitz, M. and Stiglitz, J. (1986) The pure theory of country risk. *European Economic Review*, 481–513.

Edison, H.J. (1987) Purchasing power parity in the long run: a test of the dollar/pound exchange rate (1890–1978). *Journal of Money, Credit , and Banking, 19,* August, 376–87.

Elton, E.J. Gruber, M.J. and Padberg, M.F. (1976) Simple criteria for optimal portfolio selection. *Journal of Finance,* **11** (5), December, 1341–57.

Elton, E.J. Gruber, M.J. and Padberg, M.F. (1977) Simple rules for optimal portfolio selection: the multi-group case. *Journal of Financial and Quantitative Analysis,* **12** (3), September, 329–45.

Elton, E.J. Gruber, M.J. and Padberg, M.F. (1978) Simple criteria for optimal portfolio selection: tracing out the efficient frontier. *Journal of Finance,* **13** (1), March, 296–302.

Elton, E.J. Gruber, M.J. and Padberg, M.F. (1978) Optimal portfolios from simple ranking devices. *Journal of Portfolio Management,* **4** (3), Spring, 15–19.

Eshag, E. and Thorp, R. (1965) Economic and social consequences of orthodox economic policies in Argentina in the post war years. *Bulletin of the Oxford University Institute of Economics and Statistics,* **27** (1), February, p. 1 and 3–44.

Euromoney, (1984, August; 1986, August) 198–201; (1987, August) 121–4; (1988, August) 99–104; (1993, September) 363–8.

Euromoney (1987) An A to Z guide of the services. *Euromoney,* August, 127–30.

Fama, E. (1970) Efficient capital markets: a review of theory and empirical work. *Journal of Finance,* **25,** May, 383–417.

Fama, E.F. and French, K.R. (1992) The cross section of expected stock returns. *Journal of Finance,* **XLVII** (2), June, 427–65.

Feder, G. and Just, R. E. (1977) A study of debt servicing capacity applying logit analysis. *Journal of Development Economics,* **4,** 25–39.

Folks, W.R. Jr and Stansell, S. R. (1975) The use of discriminant analysis in forecasting exchange rate movements. *Journal of International Business Studies,* **6,** Spring, 71–81.

Frank, C. R. and Cline, W. R. (1971) Measurement of debt servicing capacity: an application of discriminant analysis. *Journal of International Economics,* **1,** 237–44.

Frenkel, J.A. (1980) Test of rational expectations in the forward exchange market. *Southern Journal of Economics,* 1083–101.

Frenkel, J. and Levich, R. (1977) Transactions costs and interest arbitrage: tranquil versus turbulent periods. *Journal of Political Economy,* **85,** 1209–26.

Friedman, M. (1956) The quantity theory of money, a restatement. in *Studies in the Quantity Theory of Money,* (ed. M. Friedman), The

University of Chicago Press.

Galliot, H.J. (1971) Purchasing power parity as an explanation of long term changes in exchange rates. *Journal of Money, Credit and Banking,* 3, August, 348–57.

Garman, M. and Kohlhagen, S. (1983) Foreign currency options values. *Journal of International Money and Finance,* 2, December, 231–7.

Gelach, S. (1989) Intertemporal speculation, devaluation and the J-curve. *Journal of International Economics,* 27, 335–45.

Gerakis, A.S. (1964) Recession in the initial phase of a stabilisation program: the experience of Finland. *Staff Papers,* XI: (1), November, 434–45.

Geweke, J. and Feige, E. (1979) Some joint tests of the efficiency of markets for forward exchange. *Review of Economics and Statistics,* 61, 334–41.

Gibson, R. and Schwartz, E. (1990) Stochastic convenience yield and the pricing of oil contingent claims. *Journal of Finance,* 45, July, 959–76.

Giddy, I.H. and Dufey, G. (1975) The random behaviour of flexible exchange rates. *Journal of International Business Studies,* 6, Spring, 1–32.

Goldberg, L. and Spiegel, M.M. (1992) Debt writedowns and debt equity swaps in a two sector model. *Journal of International Economics,* 33, 267–83.

Hansen, L. P. and Hodrick, R.J. (1983) Risk averse speculation in the forward exchange market: an econometric analysis of linear models, in (ed. J.A. Frenkel) *Exchange Rates and International Macroeconomics,* University of Chicago Press, Chicago.

Hayn, R. (1962) Inflacion, formacion de capital, y balance de pagos de la Argentina 1940–1958. *Revista de Economica y Estadistica,* VI (2), 21–49.

Hertz, D.B. (1976) Uncertainty and investment selection, in *The Treasurer's Handbook,* (eds J.F. Weston and M.B. Goudzwaard), Dow Jones-Irwin, Homewood, Ill. pp. 376–420.

Hodgson, J. and Phelps, P. (1975) The distributed impact of price level variation on floating exchange rates. *Review of Economics and Statistics,* 57, February, 58–64.

Hsia, C.C. (1981) Coherence of the modern theories of finance. *Financial Review,* Winter, 27–42.

Isard, P. (1977) How far can we push the law of one price? *American Economic Review,* 67, December, 942–48.

Jacquillat, B. and Solnik, B. (1978) Multinationals are poor tools for diversification. *Journal of Portfolio Management,* Winter, 8–12.

Johnson, R. A. Srinivasan, V. and Bolster, P. J. (1990) Sovereign debt ratings: a judgemental model based on the analytic hierarchy process. *Journal of International Business Studies,* 21, 95–117.

Jorion, P. and Schwartz, E. (1986) Integration versus segmentation in the Canadian stock market. *Journal of Finance,* **41**, July, 603–16.

Kaminsky, G. and Peruga, R. (1990) Can a time varying risk premium explain excess returns in the forward market for foreign exchange? *Journal of International Economics,* **28**.

Kane, E. and Rosenthal, L. (1982) International interest rates and inflationary expectations. *Journal of International Money and Finance, 1,* April.

Kelly, R. (1965) Foreign trade of Argentina and Australia 1930–1960. *Economic Bulletin for Latin America,* **X** (2), October, 188–203.

Kobrin, S. (1979) Political risk: a review and reconsideration. *Journal of International Business Studies,* **X** (1), Autumn.

Kouri, P.J.K. and Porter, M.G. (1974) International capital flows and portfolio equilibrium. *Journal of Political Economy,* **82**, May–June.

Kravis, I.B. and Lipsey, R.E. (1978) Price behaviour in the light of balance of payments theory. *Journal of International Economics,* **8**, May, 193–246.

Kritzman, M. (1989) A simple solution for optimal currency hedging. *Financial Analysts Journal,* November/December, 47–50.

Krugman, P. (1985) Internal debt strategies in an uncertain world, in *International Debt and the Developing World,* (eds G. Smith and J. Cuddington), World Bank, Washington.

Leisserson, A. (1966) Notes on the process of industrialization in Argentina, Chile and Peru. Institute of International Studies, University of California, Berkeley.

Marois, B. (1982) French firms and political risk abroad. Working Paper no. 197, Groupe HEC.

Marston, R.C. (1976) Interest arbitrage in the Eurocurrency markets. *European Economic Review,* **20**.

McCulloch, J.H. (1975) An estimate of the liquidity premium. *Journal of Political Economy,* **83**, February, 95–119.

Merton, R. (1973) Theory of rational option pricing. *Bell Journal of Economics and Management Science,* **4**, Spring, 141–83.

Merton, R.C. (1973) An intertemporal capital asset pricing model. *Econometrica,* **41**, September, 867–87.

Merton, R. (1974) On the pricing of corporate debt. *Journal of Finance,* **29**, May, 449–70.

Miller, M. H. (1990) Index arbitrage and volatility. *Financial Analysts Journal,* July-August, 6–7.

Mishkin, F.S. (1984) Are real interest rates equal across countries? – an empirical investigation of international parity relations. *Journal of Finance,* **39**, December.

Modigliani, F. and Miller, M.H. (1963) Corporate income taxes and the cost of capital: a correction. *American Economic Review*, **53**, June, 433–43.

Morck, R. Schwartz, E. and Strangeland, D. (1989) The valuation of forestry resources under stochastic prices and inventories. *Journal of Financial and Quantitative Analysis*, **24**, December, 473–87.

Otani, I. and Tiwari, S. (1981) Capital controls and interest rate parity: the Japanese experience 1978–1981. *IMF. Staff Papers*, **28**, 793–815.

Paddock, J. Siegel, D. and Smith, J. (1988) Option valuation of claims on real assets: the case of offshore petroleum leases. *Quarterly Journal of Economics*, **103**, August, 479–508.

Park, H.Y. and Chen, A.H. (1985) Difference between futures and forward prices: a further investigation of marking to market effects. *Journal of Futures Markets*, **5**, 77–88.

Pearce, I.F. (1961) The problem of the balance of payments. *International Economic Review*, **II**: (1), January, 1–28.

Polak, J.J. and Argy, V. (1977) Credit policy and the balance of payments, in *The Monetary Approach to the Balance of Payments*, IMF, Washington D.C.

Poynter, J. (1980) Government intervention in less developed countries: the experience of multinational companies. Working paper no. 238, University of Ontario, March.

Raff, H. (1992) A model of expropriation with assymetric information. *Journal of International Economics*, **33**, 245–65.

Richardson, J.D. (1978) Some empirical evidence on commodity arbitrage and the law of one price. *Journal of International Economics*, **8**, May, 342–51.

Robock, S. (1971) Political risk: identification and assessment. *Colombia Journal of World Business*, **6** (4), July, 6–20.

Rogalski, R. J. and Vinso, J.D. (1977) Price variations as predictors of exchange rates. *Journal of International Business Studies*, **8**, Spring-Summer, 71–83.

Roll, R. (1977) A critique of the asset pricing theory's test: on past and potential testability of the theory. *Journal of Financial Economics*, **4**, March.

Roll, R. (1979) Violations of purchasing power parity and their implications for efficient commodity markets. in (eds M. Sarnat and G. Szego) International Finance and Trade, Ballinger, Cambridge, Mass.

Roll, R. and Ross, S.A. (1992) On the cross sectional relation between expected returns and betas, paper presented at the French Finance Association's International Conference in Finance, Paris, June 29.

Roll, R. and Solnik, B. (1977) A pure foreign exchange asset pricing model. *Journal of International Economics*, **7**.

Rossignol, Y. (1994) COFACE-MIGA-Assurances Privés: les garanties d'investissement contre les risques politiques. Etude no. 16, Club Finance International, HEC School of Management, Jouy-en Josas.

Schaefer, S.M. (1981) Measuring a tax specific term structure of interest rates in the market for British Government securities. *Economic Journal*, **91**, June, 415–38.

Schwartz, E.S. and Zurita, S. (1992) Sovereign debt: optimal contract, underinvestment, and forgiveness. *Journal of Finance*, **XLVII** (3), July, 981–1004.

Shapiro, A. C. (1983) What does purchasing power parity mean? *Journal of International Money and Finance*, **2**, 295–318.

Smithies, A. (1965) Argentina and Australia 1930–1960. *American Economic Review*, **55** (2), May, 17–31.

Solnik, B. (1974) Why not diversify internationally rather than domestically? *Financial Analysts Journal*, July/August, 48–54.

Solnik, B. (1974) An equilibrium model of the international capital market. *Journal of Economic Theory*, **8**, August.

Stockman, A.C. (1978) Risk, information, and forward exchange rates, in (eds J.A. Frenkel and H.G. Johnson) *The Economics of Exchange Rates*, Addison-Wesley, Reading, MA.

Triffin, R. (1964) The myth and realities of the so-called gold standard. *The Evolution of the International Monetary System: Historical Reappraisal and Future Perspective*, Princeton University Press, Princeton, N.J.

Wheeler, D. and Mody, A. (1992) International investment location decisions. *Journal of International Economics*, **33**, 57–76.

GLOSSARY

Adjusted present value The net present value of an asset if financed solely by equity plus the present value of side effects associated with financing.

APV Adjusted present value (q.v.).

Arbitrage The purchase of goods or securities in one market for immediate resale in another market in order to exploit price discrepancies between the two markets.

Asset for asset swap Creditors exchange the debt of one defaulting borrower for the debt of another.

Balance of payments The record of the economic and financial flows that take place over a specified time period between residents and non-residents of a given country.

Bank for International Settlements Originally set up in 1930 to enable the various national central banks to coordinate their receipts and payments arising from German war reparations. Since then, it has acted as a bank for central banks by accepting deposits and making short-term loans.

Basis The difference between the futures price and the spot price.

Beta The measure of systematic risk in the CAPM. Beta is calculated as the covariance between returns on the asset and returns on the market portfolio divided by the variance of returns on the market portfolio.

Bill of exchange See draft.

Bill of lading A contract between the shipper (exporter) and a transportation company in which the latter agrees to transport the goods under specified conditions which limit its liability. It is the shipper's receipt for the goods as well as proof that the goods have been or will be shipped.

Branch An operation in a foreign country incorporated in the home country.

Capital account In the balance of payments is the net result of private and public borrowing, lending, and investing between residents and non-residents.

Capital asset pricing model (CAPM) The first well-known and widely used model of market equilibrium. It assumes that the investor must be compensated for the time value of money plus systematic risk, that is, risk that cannot be eliminated through diversification. Systematic risk is measured by beta.

CAPM Capital asset pricing model (q.v.).

Certificates of deposit (CD) Certificates of deposit are negotiable instruments that can be traded on the secondary market.

CHAPS (Clearing house automated payments system) A computerized clearing system for sterling funds that began operations on February 9, 1984. It includes 14 member banks, nearly 450 participating banks, and is one of the clearing companies within the structure of the Association for Payment Clearing Services (APACS).

CHIPS (Clearing house interbank payments system) A computerized network for international transfers of dollar funds that links close to 150 depository institutions with offices in New York. The system is owned and operated by the New York Clearing House Association whose members are 12 New York money centre banks including three foreign-owned–Marine Midland, NatWest USA and European American Bank.

Clearing House Interbank Payments System See CHIPS.

Collateralization The upper limit on a government's ability to subordinate foreign claims to those of domestic residents.

Correspondent bank A bank located in another city, state or country that provides a service for another bank.

Country beta Covariance of a national economy's rate of return and the rate of return of the world economy divided by the variance of the world economy.

Country economic risk Developments in the national economy that can affect the outcome of an international financial transaction.

Country financial risk The ability of the national economy to generate enough foreign exchange to meet payments of interest and principal on its foreign debt.

Country risk See Country-specific risk.

Country-specific economic risk See Country economic risk.

Country-specific financial risk See Country financial risk.

Country-specific risk The volatility of returns on international business transactions caused by events associated with a particular country as opposed to events associated solely with a particular economic or financial agent. It can be broken down into economic risk, financial risk, currency risk and political risk.

Covered interest arbitrage Exploits interest rate differentials by borrowing in one currency, selling the borrowed currency on the spot market, investing the proceeds of the sale, and simultaneously buying back the borrowed currency on the forward market.

Crawling peg An automatic system for revising the exchange rate. It involves establishing a par value around which the rate can vary within a given margin. The par value is revised regularly according to a formula determined by the authorities.

Cross hedge A hedge using a futures contract on an asset that is different from the asset being hedged.

Cross rate The exchange rate between two currencies calculated from the dollar rate for each currency.

Currency option A contract that gives its owner the right for a given period of time to buy or sell a given amount of one currency for another currency at a fixed price, called the exercise price or the strike price.

Currency risk The variability of the value of financial stocks and flows due to uncertainty about changes in the exchange rate.

Current account In the balance of payments is the net flow of goods, services, and unrequited transfers between residents and non-residents.

Devaluation A decrease in the spot value of a currency.

Debt-equity swap Debt is purchased at a discount by an investor and traded to the central bank (which takes a percentage) for the domestic currency necessary to make the investment.

Draft or bill of exchange An unconditional order in writing, initiated and signed by the exporter, ordering the importer to pay on demand or at a given future date a given sum of money.

Dynamic segmentation approach Divides society into various behaviour-homogeneous groups, or segments. A segment can be socio-economic or ethnic. Power in the society is based on the coalition of a number of these segments while segments outside the coalition form the opposition.

Efficient market hypothesis All relevant information is fully and immediately reflected in a security's market price.

Eurocurrency (sometimes referred to as offshore currency) Any freely convertible currency, such as a dollar or a mark, deposited in a bank outside its country of origin.

European Currency Unit (ECU) The accounting unit of the European Monetary System. It is a weighted average of each of the EMS currencies.

European Monetary System (EMS) Created in 1979 by the major countries in the EC. The EMS is a fixed exchange rate system with an accounting unit called the European Currency Unit (ECU) (q.v.).

European Union (EU) Formerly the European Community (EC) and once called the European Economic Community. Founded by the Treaty of Rome on March 25, 1957 by Belgium, France, Italy, Luxembourg, the Netherlands, and West Germany. It started as a customs union but now resembles full economic union under the Single European Act of 1987 and includes, besides the original six members, the United Kingdom, Denmark, Ireland, Greece, Spain, Portugal, Austria, Sweden and Finland.

Expert systems approach Replicates the thinking of an expert through the chains of causality. Thus, it enables potential users to ponder the real consequences of a political event on a series of different factors.

Factoring The sale of company receivables to a specialized buyer at a discount.

Fixed exchange rate The price of the home currency in terms of another currency or commodity is fixed by the government. The gold standard and the gold exchange standard are two fixed rate systems that have been adopted in the recent past.

Flexible or floating exchange rate The exchange rate is allowed to adjust freely to the supply and demand of one currency for another.

Floating rate loan A loan where the interest rate is adjusted periodically according to an index.

Floating rate notes (FRNs) Generally medium-term CDs (q.v.) where the interest rate is fixed at a percentage above LIBOR (q.v.), usually 15 to 30 basis points. Adjustments are made at regular intervals of every three or six months according to the prevailing LIBOR.

Foreign exchange in the balance of payments includes monetary authorities' claims on non-residents in the form of bank deposits, treasury bills, short-term and long-term government securities, European currency units (ECUs), and other claims usable in the event of balance of payments need, including non-marketable claims arising from inter-central bank and intergovernmental arrangements, without regard as to whether the claim is denominated in the currency of the debtors or the creditors.

Forfaiting This involves the purchase by a financial institution, usually a bank, of a series of promissory notes signed by an importer in favour of an exporter. The forfaiter holds the notes for collection as they come due without recourse to the exporter. Thus, forfaiting is also a means of providing medium-term financing for international trade.

Forward exchange rate The current price of one currency for another for delivery at a specified date in the future.

Forward market Where goods, securities, and currencies are traded for future delivery.

Forward rate parity hypothesis The forward exchange rate quoted at time 0 for delivery at time 1 is equal to what the spot rate is expected to be at time 1.

Fundamental analysis This involves examining the macroeconomic variables and policies that are likely to influence a currency's performance.

Futures contract A contract for future delivery of goods, securities, or currencies. A futures contract is similar to a forward contract, except that futures contracts are standardized, traded on an organized exchange and marked to market each day.

Global political risk The overall political risk associated with an international firm's foreign activities.

Gold exchange standard A system of fixing exchange rates adopted in the Bretton Woods agreement. It involved the United States pegging the dollar to gold and the other countries pegging their currencies to the dollar.

Gold standard A system whereby governments of participating countries fix the prices of their home currencies in terms of a specified amount of gold.

Good citizen policy In such a policy a foreign investor will try to accentuate the positive side of its investment by creating new jobs, favouring transfers of technology to the host country, bringing in hard currency, and limiting remittances.

Gross domestic product (GDP) An economy's output defined as the total flow of goods and services produced by an economy over a specified time period. It is obtained by valuing the outputs of both final and investment goods and services at the market prices of the country in question and then aggregating.

Gross national product (GNP) An economy's total income. It is equal to GDP plus the income from abroad accruing to domestic residents minus income generated in the domestic market accruing to non-residents.

Hard political risk The macro risk associated with events or measures that are very damaging to foreign investors such as expropriation, nationalization or destruction of local assets.

Hedging Refers to the technique of making offsetting commitments in order to minimize the impact of unfavourable potential outcomes.

Interest rate parity relation On perfect money markets the forward discount or premium on the foreign exchange market is equal to the relative difference between the two interest rates.

International Bank for Reconstruction and Development (IBRD), also World Bank Established at Bretton Woods along with the International Monetary Fund, the purpose of the bank is to encourage capital investment for the reconstruction and development of its member countries either by channelling the necessary funds or by making loans from its own resources.

International division of production   A system whereby each subsidiary is linked to other subsidiaries of the same multinational in various countries, buying from them and selling to them components and parts of the final product.

International Fisher relation or the Fisher open condition   The ratio of nominal investment values in terms of relative real rates of interest and expected rates of inflation. It should not be forgotten that this relation is not a market arbitrage condition like PPP and interest rate parity. It is a general equilibrium condition derived from first-order optimality conditions from individuals' utility optimization.

International Monetary Fund   An international organization created at Bretton Woods in 1944 to administer a code of fair exchange practices and provide compensatory financial assistance to member countries with balance of payments difficulties.

Law of one price   Identical commodities or goods must have the same price in all markets.

Letter of credit   A document addressed to the exporter that is written and signed by a bank on behalf of the importer. In the document, the bank undertakes to guarantee for a certain time span the payment for the specified merchandise, either by paying directly or by accepting drafts, if the exporter conforms to the conditions of the letter of credit by presenting the required documents.

LIBOR (London interbank offer rate)   The deposit rate on interbank transactions in the Eurocurrency market quoted in London.

M1   Demand deposits plus the currency and coins outside the banking system.

M2   M1 plus quasi-money.

Macroeconomic accounting discipline   An economy's consumption and investment of resources cannot be greater than the resources that it produces plus the resources that it borrows.

Macroeconomic balance sheet   Assets = the sum of net investment from time 0 to the end of time T measured in foreign currency units. Liabilities = net short, medium, and long-term foreign liabilities outstanding at the end of period T plus net portfolio and direct investment outstanding at the end of period T plus the sum of reinvested macroeconomic profits from time 0 to the end of time T, all measured in foreign currency units.

Macroeconomic financial risk premium   The difference between the risk-adjusted cost of foreign borrowing and the riskless rate.

Macroeconomic market value The present value of expected net exports from time T to time n measured in foreign currency units.

Macroeconomic profits Net exports for period T measured in foreign currency units plus the net capital gain (or loss) over the period measured in foreign currency units.

Macroeconomic return on investment (ROI) Macroeconomic profits for period T divided by macroeconomic assets outstanding at the end of period T-1.

Macro political risk, sometimes called country risk Includes all events and measures likely to affect all foreign investments in a given country.

Managed float, sometimes called a 'dirty float' A system of flexible exchange rates whereby the authorities occasionally intervene by buying or selling domestic currency to smooth the transition from one rate to another.

Mapping systems Similar to the 'rating system' insofar as they use a common set of relevant parameters to compare a country's riskiness. However, rather than determining an ordinal ranking of country riskiness, the analytical results are mapped on a two dimensional graph divided into four quadrants.

Market maker Stands ready to buy and sell on a more or less continuous basis.

Market risk Variations in the returns on an investment in host country currency.

Mean deviation The average of the absolute value of the difference between each observation and the mean, the mode or the median.

Micro political risk The political risk of a particular firm in a given country.

MIGA Multinational Investment Guarantee Agency (q.v.)

Monetary gold Gold held by the authorities as a financial asset.

Money base (Mo) Composed of currency and coins outside the banking system plus liabilities to the deposit money banks.

Multi-currency loans These give the borrower the possibility of drawing a loan in several different currencies.

Multinational Investment Guarantee Agency Subsidiary of the World Bank, MIGA was established in 1988. It currently includes 118 members and offers the following types of insurance on cross-border transactions: currency transfers. expropriation, war and civil disturbance.

Nationalization A government takeover of a private company.

Netting Reducing transfers of funds between subsidiaries to a net amount.

Nominal interest rates or exchange rates Actual market rates that do not compensate for inflation.

Non-tradables Goods and services produced and consumed domestically that are not close substitutes of exportables and importables.

OECD concensus In order to avoid unfair competition among industrial countries, OECD countries define minimum interest rates on export credits for all the developing countries.

OPEC A cartel of oil-producing countries.

PIBOR (Paris interbank offer rate) The deposit rate on interbank transactions in the Eurocurrency market quoted in Paris.

Political risk The probability of politically motivated change that affects the outcome of foreign-based transactions.

Price elasticities The percentage change in the quantity divided by the percentage change in price.

Price-specie flow Balance of payments disequilibrium will be adjusted through adjustments in the country's money supply.

Probabilistic approach This uses the decision tree process. It involves computing the various alternative outcomes of a specific political event and the probability of each outcome.

Promissory note A written promise by the importer to pay a given sum on a given date in the future.

Public insurance scheme Almost all industrial countries have set up export credit insurance agencies that cover credit risk due to commercial as well as political factors. They typically cover up to 95% to 100% of the invoice amount.

Purchasing power parity (PPP) The theory linking inflation and exchange rate movements.

Range The difference between the largest and smallest values of a distribution.

Rating systems Grade countries based on selected criteria designed to reflect different aspects of risk and weighted to reflect the relative importance of each. The grade determines the country's rank for riskiness.

Real interest rate or exchange rate The rate after compensating for inflation.

Reinvoicing centre A centralized operation that handles all foreign exchange transactions between group subsidiaries and third party clients. It takes title to all goods sold, pays the seller and collects from the buyer.

Reserve position in the Fund Basically the difference between the member's IMF quota plus other claims on the Fund less the Fund's holdings of that member's currency.

Reserves Include monetary gold, special drawing rights, the reserve position in the Fund, and foreign exchange.

Risk See Standard deviation.

SDRs Reserves created by the International Monetary Fund (IMF) as bookkeeping entries and credited to the accounts of IMF member countries according to their established IMF quotas. A decision to create SDRs requires the approval of a majority of the member countries holding 85% of the weighted voting power of the IMF. Once created they may be used in the settlement of balance of payments imbalances among countries participating in the Special Drawing Account administered by the IMF.

Semi-interquartile range One half of the difference between the value of the outcome greater than 75% of the observations and the value of the outcome greater than 25% of the observations.

Separation theorem The ability to determine the optimum portfolio without having to know anything about the investor except that he is risk averse.

Sociological approach Seeks to identify a set of variables that can be specific to each country as a means of apprehending the country's degree of stability.

Soft political risk The macro risk associated with less visible and violent measures, such as price controls, regulations, strikes, etc.

Sovereign risk The possibility that a government will not be able to meet its external obligations because of a lack of foreign exchange.

Spanning asset An asset whose risk tracks the risk of the investment.

Special report approach Involves one or several 'experts' that examine the key variables that they feel describe a given country's main characteristics. The findings are communicated in the form of a 'report'.

Specific political risk The political risk stemming from one particular investment in a given country.

Spot exchange rate The exchange rate for the closest delivery date (usually two working days).

Spreads The difference between bid and ask prices.

Standard deviation The simplest statistical measure of how much a variable is likely to diverge from its expected value. It is sometimes referred to as volatility and in finance it is often used to indicate the riskiness of an asset, a portfolio of assets or a market. The standard deviation is the square root of the variance.

Subordination Ranking one type of claim below another for payment in the case of default.

Subsidiary An operation in a foreign country that is incorporated under the law of the foreign country.

Swap   An exchange of streams of payments between two counterparties, either directly or through an intermediary.

Swap rate   The forward rate as a discount or premium on the spot rate.

SWIFT (Society for Worldwide International Financial Telecommunications)   A special satellite communications network based in Belgium that connects over 1800 banks, brokerage firms and non-banking financial institutions worldwide.

Technical analysis   Makes no use of the economic and financial fundamentals deemed relevant to exchange rate determination. It focuses on prices and seeks to detect repetitions of past price patterns.

Term deposit   Conventional term deposits are non-negotiable bank deposits with a fixed term where the interest rate is fixed for the duration of the deposit.

Terms of trade   The number of units of imports that one unit of exports will buy (or vice versa); can be calculated by dividing the price of exports by the price of imports.

The international macroeconomic market index   The sum of the macroeconomic market values outstanding of all national economies measured in foreign currency units.

Transfer risk   The risk that a government might impose restrictions on debt service payments abroad.

Variance   See Standard deviation.

Velocity of money   The rate at which the stock of money circulates through the economy in order to finance transactions.

Volatility   See Standard deviation.

World Bank   See International Bank for Reconstruction and Development.

INDEX